SCULPTORS OF
THE WEST PORTALS OF
CHARTRES CATHEDRAL

SCULPTORS OF

THE WEST PORTALS OF

CHARTRES CATHEDRAL

*Their Origins in Romanesque
and Their Role in Chartrain Sculpture*

Including the West Portals of Saint-Denis and Chartres,
Harvard, 1952

WHITNEY S. STODDARD

W·W· NORTON & COMPANY
New York   London

Published simultaneously in Canada by Penguin Books Canada Ltd., 2801 John Street,
Markham, Ontario L3R 1B4.
Printed in the United States of America.

Library of Congress Cataloging-in-Publication Data

Stoddard, Whitney S.
    The sculptors of the early Gothic west portals of
Chartres Cathedral.

    1. Sculpture, Gothic—France—Chartres.
2. Sculpture, French—France—Chartres. 3. Doorways—
France—Chartres. 4. Cathédrale de Chartres.
I. Stoddard, Whitney S.   West portals of Saint-Denis
and Chartres.   1986.   II. Title.
NB551.C45S76   1986   730'.944'51   85-21702

ISBN 0-393-02365-6
ISBN 0-393-30043-9 pbk

W. W. Norton & Company, Inc., 500 Fifth Avenue, New York, N.Y. 100110
W. W. Norton & Company Ltd., 37 Great Russell Street, London WC1B 3NU

1 2 3 4 5 6 7 8 9 0

CONTENTS

INTRODUCTION

This publication contains two books, an old one and a new one: *The West Portals of Saint-Denis and Chartres* (Harvard University Press, 1952) and *The Sculptors of the West Portals of Chartres Cathedral*. The former, which is reprinted unchanged but in a slightly smaller format, evolved out of a doctoral dissertation concentrating on the ornament of Saint-Denis and Chartres and was submitted in 1941, following research in France in the summer of 1939. In the rewriting of the dissertation for publication, discussion of ornament was reduced and analysis of figure style increased. The new book attempts to discover the individual, artistic personalities of the four major Chartres sculptors as well as those of their five identifiable assistants. These nine sculptors carved the Royal Portals in one campaign of approximately five years in the middle of the 1140s, after the dedication of Saint-Denis in 1140 and the completion of Étampes in the early 1140s. Since sculptural programs for portals were determined by the clergy, not the sculptors, discussion of iconography is included only as it affected the artists.

In the Renaissance, documents often specifically identify the works of major architects, sculptors, and painters, while in twelfth-century France, fires are the main events that help establish different building campaigns with their attendant sculpture and stained glass. Since consecrations and even dedications usually do not reveal how far construction had progressed at the time of those events, they are often of little help in dating specific parts of monuments. In the case of the Abbey of Saint-Denis, Abbot Suger recorded in detail the dedication of the new narthex and façade on June 9, 1140. At Chartres, the fire of September 5, 1134 destroyed a great deal of the town and the west end of the early eleventh-century cathedral. In 1145, the Abbot of Mont-Saint-Michel visited Chartres and mentioned two towers under construction. The entire cathedral, with the exception of the relatively new west towers, Royal Portals, and the famous three stained glass windows, were consumed by a huge conflagration on June 10 and 11, 1194. These three dates establish only the *terminus post quem* of 1134, the *terminus ante quem* of 1194, and the fact that two towers were under construction in 1145. No documents refer to sculpture or stained glass, with the result that the only evidence is the monument itself: masonry of portals

and towers (their interconnection or lack of same), nineteen preserved over life-size jamb statues, forty-eight small figures on doorjambs, twenty-two capitals, three tympana, five lintels, and sixty-four archivolt blocks.

With this paucity of documentation, one is forced to rely on measured drawings of masonry and carved blocks and hundreds of photographs, including many details, in order to attribute this large amount of sculpture to individual artists, whose names must be fabricated. Only after much study and photography of the Royal Portals, together with seminars devoted specifically to the study of Chartres West, is it possible to attribute all the sculpture to individual artists. Further, by assigning a period of time for the carving of each block, depending on size and complexity, it is feasible to estimate that the six splays of the three portals, including jamb statues, doorjamb reliefs, capitals, tympanum, and lintel of the central portal, and two lintels of the right portal, all were completed by three sculptors and their four assistants in approximately three years. The fourth sculptor and his assistant took longer to finish the superstructure. With all figural sculpture attributed to individual masters (see foldout elevation), the collaborative effort and workshop procedures, which produced the Royal Portals, are recreated. Finally, by discovering three of the Chartres sculptors in earlier and later monuments, the dating of Chartres to the middle years of the 1140s is, one hopes, firmly established.

Following discussion of the individual sculptors of Chartres West, the archaeology of the Early Gothic campaigns at Chartres, and a new section on the south portal of Étampes, Part IV concentrates on a search for the earlier work of the sculptors of Chartres and Étampes in Burgundian Romanesque monuments. In the process of tracing the careers of individual sculptors over time, some of the accepted dating of monuments has been questioned and, it is hoped, corrected. Much more research is obviously necessary. Part V includes an updated discussion of a selection of Post-Chartres portals, while the portals of Notre-Dame of Corbeil and Sainte-Anne of Paris, in which specific Chartres sculptors participated, have been added. The career of one sculptor appears to span over thirty years in his involvement in the sculpture of five monuments.

An attempt has been made to incorporate the research

in relevant articles and books published since 1952. Mistakes in the first book have been admitted and corrected, but that does not mean that I accept all criticism that has been offered by subsequent scholars. No new conclusions on the west portals of Saint-Denis have been reached, nor has there been any attempt to determine the complicated origins of their sculpture.

Research for this new book was carried out in numerous visits, often with students, to the major monuments on the way to and from the Williams College excavation of the Benedictine monastery of Psalmodi, near Aigues-Mortes. In the Williams College Graduate Program in The History of Art, offered in cooperation with the Clark Art Institute, students in seminars integrated with undergraduate courses in Romanesque and in Gothic art have contributed to my research. Adrian Hoch, Franklin Kelly, and Paula Koromilas made many important observations. In 1982, five students became involved in every detail of the portals of Chartres West. Three of them collaborated with me on sections of the book: John Wetenhall, on the sculpture of the west portals of Saint-Denis; John Pultz, on the capital-frieze of Chartres; and Ruth Pasquine, on Saint-Bénigne de Dijon. Two students each wrote entire sections: Nancy Sojka, the inner door jamb figures of Chartres, and Minott Kerr, the tympanum, lintels, and archivolts of Chartres. Conclusions of each section were essentially agreed on by the entire class. I wish to express my deepest appreciation to all of these students.

As an undergraduate, I was greatly influenced by two professors: Karl E. Weston and Andy Keck. At Harvard, Fred Deknatel, Wilhelm Koehler, Arthur Pope, Chandler Post, Benjamin Rowland, Paul Sachs, and Langdon Warner introduced me to a broad range of cultures in varying degrees of specialization. At Williams, I have benefited greatly from many colleagues, especially Lane Faison, Bill Pierson, and E. J. Johnson. I have shown the illustrations of this book to Professors Pamela Blum, William Clark, and Clark Maines and have profited by their constructive criticism.

Conversations with John James, Malcolm Miller, and Jean Villette in front of Chartres and inside the narthex were most helpful. Ernie and John LeClaire have struggled with my negatives of varying degrees of quality. Susan Eder made careful and handsome drawings of the Royal Portals of Chartres and also made the map. With utmost patience, Sybil Sherman deciphered my handwriting and produced drafts and the final manuscript. Starting in 1939, Jean, my wife of fifty years now, was always present to assist measuring portals, cataloguing negatives, criticizing drafts of manuscripts, and to help support my efforts in every way. I wish to express my appreciation to all these people.

I wish to dedicate this book to the memory of Karl E. Weston, Williams '96, whose enthusiasm of and dedication to the arts inspired many students to pursue careers in museums or in art history.

W.S.S.
Williamstown, Mass.
March 1985

THE WEST PORTALS OF

SAINT-DENIS AND

CHARTRES

Sculpture in the Île de France from 1140 to 1190

Theory of origins

HARVARD UNIVERSITY PRESS

Cambridge, Massachusetts

1952

Distributed in Great Britain by
GEOFFREY CUMBERLEGE
OXFORD UNIVERSITY PRESS
LONDON

LIBRARY OF CONGRESS CATALOG CARD NUMBER 52–5043

PRINTED IN THE UNITED STATES OF AMERICA

For Jean, Brooks, Beth, and Larry

PREFACE

THIS STUDY is a development of my doctoral dissertation, presented at Harvard University in 1941, on portal sculpture in the Île-de-France from 1140 to 1190. It originated as a discussion of ornamental sculpture of the twelfth century in the royal domain. Evidence gained from the study of ornament alone, however, appeared to shed new light on the larger problem of the evolution of monumental sculpture in the fifty years following Suger's portals at Saint-Denis.

Mid-twelfth-century ornament had never been photographed in detail. Types of motifs had not been classified, nor had the style of the ornament been examined. As the character of the development of ornament became evident, the question naturally arose whether the monumental sculpture, the relation of ornament to jamb statues, and the portal design as a monumental ensemble had undergone the same sort of evolution. The identification of fragments of sculpture from Saint-Denis — two heads in the Walters Art Gallery, Baltimore; one head in the Fogg Museum of Art, Cambridge; and the relief excavated by Professor Sumner Crosby at Saint-Denis — have provided new material for comparison with earlier and later works. When the portals were studied as a whole, including their construction and the relation of ornament and jamb statues to the architecture, their general development began to emerge with greater clarity than heretofore.

Previous analyses of the origins of Île-de-France sculpture have always been limited to studies of monumental sculpture. No attempt has been made to explore the possible origins of the Saint-Denis–Chartres ornament or to ascertain whether there is a relationship between the sources of ornament and figured sculpture.

The first part of this study deals with the sculpture of Saint-Denis, the ornament on the façade, the columns now in the Musée de Cluny in Paris, and the heads now in collections in the United States. Part II contains a comparative study of Saint-Denis and the Royal Portal of the cathedral of Chartres and a detailed analysis of the Royal Portal. Part III is a discussion of the portal of Notre-Dame at Étampes as a possible source for Chartres. The evolution of sculpture in the Île-de-France and its environs in the second half of the twelfth century is described in Part IV. Part V offers a tentative theory of origins for the Saint-Denis–Chartres sculpture. Parts I through IV remain substantially as written in 1940–1941. Reference to subsequent literature appears in footnotes, but in some instances the text has been altered to take into account important articles published during the war and years following.

In carrying out this project I have benefited greatly from the friendly advice and encouragement of Professor Wilhelm Koehler. It is impossible to express in words my appreciation of his untiring help. My wife rendered invaluable service in the cataloguing of photographs and assisted in the measuring of portals and in correcting the text.

I am greatly indebted to Professor S. Lane Faison, Jr., and to Professor Karl E. Weston for their valuable criticism of the manuscript. Professor Sumner Crosby very kindly put at my disposal his notes on the restorations and alterations of the façade of Saint-Denis and allowed me to publish Professor Kenneth Conant's drawing of Saint-Denis (Plate A) which is based on Mr. Crosby's research. Mr. Crosby also permitted me to include a brief analysis and reproductions of the bas-relief which he excavated at Saint-Denis in 1947.

The problem of procuring photographs from Europe during the past few years has been greatly facilitated by the kindness of colleagues and friends. John Savacool studied the Cistercian manuscripts at Dijon and as a result of the splendid coöperation of the authorities of the Bibliothèque de Dijon had them photographed. Effingham Humphrey, Jr., James J. Rorimer, Margaret B. Freeman, and Louis Grodecki unearthed the remaining photographs necessary to complete the plates. Also I wish to thank Professor William H. Pierson for his technical help in photographic problems. Mrs. Arthur Kingsley Porter was most helpful in allowing me to study the extensive collection of photographs taken and procured by her husband.

I wish to express my gratitude to the authorities of Harvard Universty who granted me a Sachs Fellowship for the summer of 1939, enabling me to carry out the necessary research in France. I also wish to thank President James P. Baxter 3rd and the Trustees of Williams College for a grant from the 1900 Fund which helped defray photographic costs.

Two additional grants from the same fund helped in the preparation of the plates. Finally, I wish to state my deepest appreciation of the generous grants, which made possible the publication of this book, from Mrs. Henry K. Babcock and the President and Trustees of Williams College (through the 1900 Fund).

Williamstown, Massachusetts
Fall 1951

CONTENTS

xiii

CONTENTS

PART FIVE

A THEORY OF ORIGINS OF THE ORNAMENTAL AND MONUMENTAL SCULPTURE OF SAINT-DENIS AND CHARTRES

APPENDICES

PLATES

All photographs are by the author unless otherwise indicated. The author wishes to thank the following for permission to reproduce photographs: Mrs. Arthur Kingsley Porter, Professor Kenneth Conant, Professor Sumner Crosby, James J. Rorimer and the Metropolitan Museum of Art, Professor Clarence Ward, Fogg Museum of Art, Walters Art Gallery, Archives Photographiques in Paris, Kunstgeschichtliches Seminar in Marburg.

Parts of portals are designated by letters and numerals. For example, RP.L: right portal, left side; CP.R.4: central portal, right side, fourth jamb from the door.

PLATES

PLATES

THE WEST PORTALS OF SAINT-DENIS AND CHARTRES

PART ONE

THE WEST PORTALS OF
THE ABBEY OF SAINT-DENIS

WHEN ABBOT SUGER dedicated the narthex of Saint-Denis on June 9, 1140,[1] he partially realized his dream of rebuilding the Royal Abbey and unwittingly founded a new tradition. As the most powerful patron of the twelfth century, Suger had at his command the personal prestige, political influence, and financial support to utilize the artistic talents of the best craftsmen in western Europe. With Suger's dedication the whole course of sculpture changed direction. A new portal design enhanced by monumental jamb figures and delicately carved ornament was introduced. Although the effects of this achievement are readily seen in monuments of the Île-de-France such as Chartres, they transcend narrow geographical limits.

The artistic procedure resulting in the creation of the Saint-Denis portals has direct parallels in the experimental character which architecture assumed during the second half of the twelfth century. The High Gothic of Amiens and Reims is a synthesis of earlier imaginative innovations, for it embodies the elegance of the choir of Saint-Denis, the massive boldness of Laon, and consummate engineering skill as demonstrated by the original flying buttresses of the nave of Notre-Dame at Paris. The Saint-Denis portals played an equally important role in the formation of thirteenth-century sculptural ensembles. In spite of their damaged condition the west portals of Saint-Denis, many details of which remain untouched *in situ*, many preserved as fragments in the museums of France and the United States, are a necessary point of departure for any study of mid-twelfth-century French sculpture.

GENERAL CHARACTER OF THE PORTALS: RELATION OF SCULPTURE TO ARCHITECTURE

Before analyzing the portal design of Saint-Denis as it exists today (Plate I, 1, 2), it is necessary to delete the unfortunate applications of nineteenth-century restorers and replace the monumental sculpture destroyed during the eighteenth century (see Plate A for original condition of portals). If jamb figures similar to those at Chartres replace the ugly nineteenth-century columns and if the central trumeau and all three lintels are restored, some idea of the

original character of the portals can be grasped. The disastrous alterations which took place in 1771 have greatly changed the proportions and appearance of the ensemble.[2] To clarify the relationship between portals and façade, the pavement in front of the abbey must be lowered 1.60 meters.[3] The present raised level accounts for the squatness which is so incompatible with the rest of the façade. The destruction of the lintels tends partially to correct this loss of verticality.

When we restore the façade to its primary condition, the portals take on a visual and structural unity not to be found in High Romanesque sculpture. In contrast to the portals of Autun or Moissac, Saint-Denis presents a more integrated character. At Moissac the sculpture is divided between the tympanum, archivolts, jambs, trumeau, and capitals. By contrast the Saint-Denis portals have a more harmoniously architectural character than previous Romanesque entrances. Here the observer's eye is led up the jambs and around the archivolts and down again to the pavement without any serious interruption. The decorated plinths crown the walls supporting the jambs and emphasize the bases for the columnar figures which were directly above (Plate I, 3). These plinths tend to retard the vertical action, but also prepare the way for the standing statues. Above the figures, which echo the verticality of the façade, the capitals give a horizontal interlude which slows down the upward motion. The capitals uphold abaci which act as imposts for the archivolts. The sculptured jambs flanking the doors together with the small spiral columns help support the lintels which, in their turn, uphold the tympana. Each part of the portals has a specific function.

Figured sculpture is located on jambs, archivolts, tympana, and lintels. These positions have structural overtones. The ornamental sculpture gives the appearance of an overlay across the portals; but on close study this is not the case, for in every place where ornament is found, it bears a definite relationship to the figured sculpture as well as to the architectural ensemble. The horizontal plinths with their low reliefs can only be thought of in relation to the foundations and the bases of the statues above them. The narrow vertical bands of ornament which flank the Wise and Foolish

---

[1] Panofsky, *Abbot Suger on the Abbey Church of St.-Denis and its Art Treasures*, pp. 43–45.

[2] Crosby, *The Abbey of St.-Denis*, I, 6. Also F. Debret, *Monuments historiques*, Docs. 41–76, p. 19.

[3] Sumner Crosby informed me of this fact.

Virgins on the central portal (Plate III, 2), the Signs of the Zodiac on the left portal, and the Occupations of the Months on the right portal (Plate II, 4) act as a decorative border for these flat jambs which support the lintels and tympana. In each instance the ornament does not jump out from the portals, but takes its place as a decorative and mural adjunct to the more monumental sculpture. The relationships are always kept clear; column statues are subservient to the architecture, while ornament enhances the figures. The triple portal as a whole emphasizes the structure of the façade.

On the basis of the dimensions of the three preserved heads from Saint-Denis, discussed later, it is possible to establish the relationship between the ex-jamb figures and the spaces now occupied by the modern, ornate columns. All three heads are approximately .35 meter in height. The drawings made for Montfaucon in the eighteenth century when the statues were *in situ* and the engravings made from them show figures which are roughly five heads high.[4] This suggests a total height of 2.72 meters for each figure, which corresponds exactly to the dimensions of the modern columns. It can thus be concluded that the jamb statues originally extended up to the capitals. Further proof is found in Montfaucon, plate xviii (Plate X, 2), which shows one destroyed figure. Only a section of drapery is left attached to the plain shaft, while the top of the column is capped by a molding at the same height as the top of the heads of the flanking statues.

CONDITION OF THE PORTALS: RESTORATIONS

How is the observer to distinguish between the twelfth-century carving and nineteenth-century imitations? In general, the latter lack the vitality of the badly worn original parts, although in most instances the restorers preserved the old motifs. First, a study of the existing façade without any regard to documentary evidence (discussed later) points to the possibility that the upper part of all three portals has been cut back. Along the whole façade at the distance of .93 meter above the present pavement, the jambs flanking each portal begin to slant inward (Plates I, 3, and II, 1). After continuing on the diagonal for approximately .21 meters, the jambs resume their perpendicular direction. The difference between the front plane of the plinth crowning the foundations and the sculpture above is .04 to .05 meter.

Taking the first jamb to the left of the right portal (RP.L.1)[5] as a typical example of this phenomenon, unique in medieval art, the front plane is represented by the horizontal panel of rinceau directly above the modern block decorated with a torus molding (Plate II). The slanting section

which contains the beginning of the possible recutting extends up through the lower part of the atlas figure and the lower portion of the first medallion containing the Month of January. The new plane of the portal is established on a line running through the knees of the atlas and through the lower part of the table in the medallion (Plate II, 4). All the area above is the result of the nineteenth-century recutting. The jeweled border on the extreme left exhibits a distinct break in style and condition at a point just above the second ellipse (Plate II, 2, 3). The comparatively plastic rendering of the lower part is transformed into a flat, almost linear pattern. The left edge of this motif shows a definite break above the second ellipse. Marks of the restorer's tools appear above and to the left of this border.

The restorer proceeded somewhat as follows. The masonry was cut back .04 meter from the level of the capitals down to a point 1.14 meters above the present pavement. With the lower part of the ornament as a model, the motif was run up the height of the jamb. This procedure would apply only to the jeweled border where the projection of the sculpture is very slight. With the main decoration, the Occupations of the Months, where the relief is higher, the nineteenth-century restorers cut the whole design back into the façade to the depth just described. The whole motif was not cut away as would be necessitated in the case of the shallow jeweled border.

The other five jambs flanking the doors exhibit this same phenomenon. The undulating vine which runs vertically and borders the Wise Virgins on the first jamb on the left side of the central portal (CP.L.1) shows the same break in style and preservation (Plate III, 1, 2). The lower part, or about .18 meter, is almost completely destroyed. It is possible to discern, however, two bends of the stem and two floral fillers. There is a delicacy and vitality in the five leaves in the lowest unit of the motif, while directly above, the rinceau is uniform in surface and has the same lack of quality found in all sculpture above this point in all three portals. The lower piece of this border is on the front plane of the portal, while the upper part, extending up to the capitals, is set back .04 meter. The striations at the left of the border of this floral motif are further evidence of nineteenth-century work. The figures of the virgin and the atlas have been cut back in the same manner.

In many instances, the floral borders mentioned above change in width, while on the right of the central portal, the floral pattern ends half way up the jamb (Plate I, 1). These miscalculations are the doing of nineteenth-century carvers. The contrast between the bottoms of these jambs flanking the three portals and all the area above in condi-

[4] Montfaucon, *Les Monumens de la monarchie françoise* (1729), I, 195ff., pl. xvi–xviii. Montfaucon drawings.

[5] The following system of designation for the location of jamb figures and ornament will be utilized throughout, for example: CP.R.4 for central portal, right-hand side, the fourth jamb from the door.

tion, in style, and in quality makes it possible to conclude that the portals have been skinned to a point just above the horizontal plinths.

While there is no document which specifically describes the recarving, there are several references to restorations which help substantiate this theory. In his admirable book on Saint-Denis, Crosby has summarized the havoc wreaked upon the abbey during two hundred years.[6] The first half of the nineteenth century witnessed the almost complete denaturing of the entire façade. Legrand, Cellérier, and Debret are more to blame than the passage of time for the complete transformation of the western exterior.[7] Debret, who was named architect in 1813, seems to have done the greatest damage.[8] As a result of these restorations there arose a battle which can be followed in the contemporary literature. Some acclaimed Debret's results,[9] while a greater number expressed their disgust.[10] Baron de Guilhermy, the leader of the opposition, has handed down a fairly complete record of the restorations carried out by Debret.[11] Debret's excuse to carry his mutilations further was afforded him by a bolt of lightning which struck the north spire on June 9, 1837. In the following year, he raised sufficient funds to rebuild the spire, this time in stone instead of light materials. In 1839, Debret, still undaunted, cut the entire surface of the façade back from .05 to .08 meter.[12] This mistake, combined with the overheavy spire, caused large cracks to appear in the masonry.[13] Finally, in 1846 the spire had to be dismantled and the following year the upper part of the north tower was likewise removed. The scandal which resulted from these costly errors brought about the expulsion of Debret in 1846 and the appointment of Viollet-le-Duc in 1847.[14]

It seems quite possible that when Debret supervised the recarving of the façade in 1839, including all the moldings and ornament above the portals, he continued right down over the jambs which flank each entrance. There is no document which specifically describes this, yet the derogatory references to Debret, the notes taken by Guilhermy, and the correspondence in depth between the cutback on the portals and the documented mutilations of the façade — all seem to point to the conclusion that the portals as well as the west façade were shaved back. One reference, written in the heat of the controversy over Debret's restorations, seems to imply that the original surface of the entire façade was scraped off.[15] Even more important than the reasons just cited is the study of the portals in their present condition. Since Debret indicates in the drawings of his restorations, now preserved in the archives of the Commission des Monuments Historiques, that the masonry behind the ex-jamb figures was either replaced by new blocks or recarved at his command and since the striated tool marks beside the ornamental borders of the inside jambs on each portal (see Plates II and III) continue into the masonry which is obviously reworked, it follows that the process of recarving the ornament took place at the same time as the restoration of the remainder of the unadorned masonry. Combining documentary and visual evidence, we are forced to eliminate as twelfth-century work all sculpture of the west façade of Saint-Denis except some of the plinths below the former jamb figures, fragments preserved in museums in France and the United States, and some of the tympanum and archivolts of the central portal.[16]

This conclusion disagrees with all previous studies of the problem.

[6] Crosby, pp. 6–11. Also Vitry and Brière, *L'Église abbatiale de Saint-Denis et ses tombeaux*, pp. 34–43.

[7] *L'Église impériale de Saint-Denis et ses tombeaux par les auteurs de la monographie de Saint-Denis* (1867), p. 6: "Pendant quarante ans, de 1806 à 1846, trois architectes se sont succédés, MM. Legrand, Cellérier, et Debret. Le monument fut réparé et décoré avec un certaine magnificence; mais les études sur l'art du moyen âge étaient alors si peu avancées, que cette longue et laborieuse restauration, accomplie au prix de plus de sept millions, avait eu pour résultat de dénaturer complètement le caractère de l'édifice."

[8] Léon, *Les Monuments historiques, conservation restauration*, p. 120: "C'est à propos des travaux éxecutés par Debret à l'église abbatiale de Saint-Denis que se manifesta la divergence profonde des deux écoles. Nommé architecte du monuments des 1813, Debret s'était livré aux plus désastreuses restaurations: ravalement des murailles, amincissement des contreforts et des arcs-boutants, grattage des ornaments, refouillement des moulures, incrustation de sculptures neuves, de motifs empruntés sans critique à toutes les époques, addition d'une ridicule et imaginaire galerie des Rois. . ."

[9] Flamand-Grétry, *Description complète de la ville de Saint-Denis depuis son origine jusqu'à nos jours* (1840), p. 150: "On en peut juger par les immense changements qui y ont été faits et qui s'y font encore maintenant par les soins de M. Debret, un des plus habiles architectes de Paris. . ."

[10] Guilhermy, *Monographie de l'église royale de Saint-Denis* (1848), p. 10, "L'édifice, après tant de mauvais jours, fut, pour humiliation dernière, condamné à être restauré par les mains de l'école impériale. Ce que les fureurs du vandalisme le plus sauvage n'avaient pas eu le temps de faire, des architectes sont venus l'accomplir avec tout le loisir, tout l'argent

et toute la securité désirable. Ils ont nivelé, régularisé, gratté, embelli, aggrandi, raccommodé, si bien que le monument n'a plus rien de son caractère primitif." Léon, p. 120, writes of the gallery of kings: "La Commission manifesta une indignation violente. Le 14 juin 1841, Vitet dénonce 'cette restauration d'un système déplorable, mélangeant le faux et le vrai.' "

[11] Mss. de Baron de Guilhermy, Bibl. Nat., fol. 1, pp. 51–61.

[12] Didron, "Achèvement des restaurations de Saint-Denis," *Annales Archéologiques*, V (1846), 110: "Il l'a tondu, dans toute la hauteur de la façade, jusqu'à une profondeur de 0, 05 cent., pour retrouver la pierre net; c'est-à-dire qu'il a affaibli tout le parement d'un cinquième."

[13] Viollet-le-Duc, *Monuments Historiques Dos.*, (1841–1876), pp. 109–110, describes the recutting of the façade: "Les anciens paremens extérieurs étaient altérés par le temps, on a fait refaire tout le ravalément de l'édifice à neuf, et tous les paremens ont été recoupés depuis trois jusqu'à huit centimètres de profondeur. La malheureuse Église de Saint-Denis n'a jamais subi une mutilation plus désastreuse que celle-là. Ce singulier moyen de restauration a plusieurs inconveniences serieux. . ."

[14] Crosby, pp. 9–10.

[15] "Saint-Denys: Restauration de l'église royale," *Annales Archéologiques*, I, (1844), 232: "Est-il permis, sous prétexte d'embellissement de modifier l'ornementation et la sculpture d'un édifice ancien, au point de leur donner un aspect tout différent de celui qu'elles avait dans leur état primitif? La réponse à cette question serait certainement la condamnation."

[16] Sumner Crosby showed me several recent photographs of the tympanum and archivolts of the central portal. After the accumulated dirt has been removed, sections of twelfth-century sculpture will undoubtedly be discovered. This study will not discuss that sculpture.

ORIGINAL SCULPTURE IN SITU

Most of the original sculpture at Saint-Denis is found on the plinths which cap the foundations and originally supported the jamb figures (Plate I, 3). There are twenty of these plinths, each presenting two decorated sides.[17] Of these, only three blocks are modern, and their motifs correspond to other original ones. There are six panels of ornament below the sculptured jambs flanking the doors. Only one of these is modern.

The ornament is controlled by the limits of each block. No pattern continues from one plinth to the next (Plates I, 3, and VI, 3). The relief is kept very low with only the slightest undercutting, which catches some light and casts a slight shadow. The shallow relief combined with small units of design in each motif makes this ornament invisible until the observer gets close to the portals. In each instance, the horizontal shape of the block is emphasized by the direction of the design, and at no time is the structural function of the plinth weakened or violated by the carved ornament.

Of the twenty-six panels, including those below the jambs flanking each doorway, five are decorated with inorganic or abstract patterns, sixteen with floral motifs, and five with combinations of the two. Of the floral plinths, seven have undulating vines with simple floral fillers, two exhibit complex fillers, while seven consist of separate units of floral patterns.

Typical of the geometric motifs is the pattern (Plate III, 3) which consists of three tiers of diamonds running horizontally. The design is kept flat; variety is created by the alternation of raised and recessed rows. A similar motif (Plate III, 4) contains a pair of flat, folded ribbons running across the block. The badly damaged block (Plate III, 5) exhibits four rows of small double-axe or pin-wheel motifs. As the pattern is incised on the block, most of its original surface is preserved.

Floral motifs are reproduced in Plates III and IV. From the undulating vine (Plate III, 6) grow floral fillers which alternate in direction across the block. In contrast to the geometric patterns, the stems and leaves of these motifs are relatively more plastic. Very similar is the vine motif in Plate IV, 1. The rolled leaves, acting as fillers, are enclosed in secondary stems and do not grow directly from the main vine. In spite of the ravages of time, it is possible to see the delicate veins which designate the midribs of stems and leaves. Small dependent leaves serve to fill the voids along the sides of the block. Most of the design extends to the front plane of the block, while the modeling is confined to the edges of the vines. A more complicated pattern is seen in Plate IV, 2. The floral fillers, growing from the undulating vine at its point of tangency with the sides of the block, are made up of leaves which fan out from knots which bind the main stem. The leaves with their minutely detailed midribs of small squares and alternation of axis subtly animate the plinth.

A complex floral pattern in which the fillers do not grow from the main stem is exemplified by the plinth of CP.L.1 (Plate III, 2). These units of seven leaves, alternating in upward and downward direction, fill the voids by entwining the main vine. Some of the surface subtleties can still be seen on the left-hand section; the right-hand part is modern.

Plate IV, 3, is typical of the palmette pattern. Balanced floral patterns of leaves encircling buds grow out of an elaborate base. The central, vertical axis of each unit is accentuated by small leaves which alternate in direction, left and right. Another type may be seen in RP.L.2 (Plate I, 3) which consists of a series of rosettes arranged horizontally.

Of the hybrid motifs, which are combinations of abstract and floral patterns, Plate IV, 4, consists of beautifully rhythmic, elongated S-shaped sections leaning into each other, resembling Pieter Brueghel's "The Blind Leading the Blind." Two other hybrid motifs are seen in Plate IV, 5 and 6. The former exhibits two rows of floral leaves, vaguely similar to classic ornament, which are separated by a three-part band of circles and ridges. The latter contains a diagonally folded band running horizontally with trefoil floral fillers. One side of the band is decorated with incised squares or diamond-shaped patterns, while the other is adorned with S-shaped, schematized leaves. The existence on LP.L.2 of a modern and sterile duplicate of this plinth is sufficient evidence to prove that this motif is twelfth century.

The capitals and abaci crowning the jambs and serving as imposts for the archivolts are, for the most part, either modern or resurfaced, although the battered ones to the left of the left portal may have escaped the nineteenth-century recarving. The latter, consisting of acanthus leaves and interlaces and fantastic animals, show a considerable amount of undercutting.

Although the plinths have suffered severely from weathering since 1140, they still give ample evidence of the sensitivity of the twelfth-century carvers and their consciousness of the problem of decorating a structural part of the portals. In each instance, the modeling is very slight with delicately incised details. It is almost draftsmanship with stone as a medium.

COLUMN IN THE MUSÉE DE CLUNY AND
TWO FRAGMENTS IN THE LOUVRE

The best-preserved piece of sculpture from Saint-Denis is the column in the Musée de Cluny, Paris (Plate V).[18] Origi-

---

[17] See Appendix I for location, dimensions, and brief description of all plinths.

[18] Haraucourt and de Montremy, *Musée des Thermes et l'Hôtel de Cluny, Catalogue général I: la pierre, le marbre et l'albâtre*, p. 31, fig. 61: "Fût de colonnette; décor de rinceau perlés, d'enfants nus et d'animaux.

nally it supported one of the three lintels, since destroyed. In 1796 Alexandre Lenoir removed all the sculpture left over from Saint-Denis and formed the Musée des Monuments Français. His catalogue of 1800 published engravings (in reverse) of a spiral column like the Cluny one and another like the three nineteenth-century columns now *in situ* on the right side of each portal.[19] Ten years later Lenoir discussed four columns then in the Musée des Petits-Augustins and referred to the engravings just mentioned.[20] Lenoir's journal describes the objects sent back to Saint-Denis following the decree of December 18, 1816, suppressing the museums. He mentions four columns and links them with those illustrated in his publication of 1800.[21] Evidently, two of them were used to support an altar[22] and finally served as models for the six which were carved under Debret in 1840.[23]

The Cluny column (Plate V, 1–3, 5, 6) measures 1.47 meters in height and .43 meter in circumference at both top and bottom. As can be seen by contrasting figures 1 and 4 of Plate V, the Cluny column, from the point of view of motifs, was followed very closely by the nineteenth-century sculptor. None of the superb crispness and delicacy of carving is in evidence in the three copies now adorning the left jambs of all three portals at Saint-Denis.

The column consists of two spiral bands separated by narrow borders. Both decorated bands and borders make one and three fourths revolutions to the right. The slightly concave surfaces of the borders (Plate V, 5) are adorned with embossed circular designs alternating with pairs of smaller dots.

Of the two wider spiral sections, one is decorated with pure floral ornament and the other with undulating vines and figures. The first (Plate V, 3) has an extremely sensitive pattern of connected heart-shaped units. The undercutting is slight and never exceeds .015 meter. The leaves and vines are kept flat with only slight modeling at their edges. The effect of this pattern (Plate V, 3) almost suggests that a drawing had been pasted on the uncarved column, the voids

cut out to a narrow depth, and then the surface of the vines and leaves animated by raised edges and incised lines. Although the motion is controlled, the whole design has a rhythmic flow up the column (Plate V, 1).

The spiral pattern with vines and figures possesses even more variety. Plate V, 6, shows the lowest corner of this panel beautifully filled by a dragon's head emitting the main vine which undulates up the entire column. The main stem gives off secondary vines and leaves which embrace birds, putti, and animals. The most characteristic detail may be seen in the putto (Plate V, 2) with head in profile, full-front chest, and legs in silhouette. This figure, like the others, is so arranged that the broadest aspect of each part follows the curvature of the column. Like the treatment of vines and leaves, the whole body comes out to the surface plane of the column, with only the extremities rounded off. The triangular voids left between the floral medallions are filled by the head and foot of the figure.

The back of the column, roughly one-eighth of the diameter, has the design merely indicated, while the rest is sufficiently undercut to catch enough light to make the ornament carry. The units of design are small enough not to detract from the sculpture on the jambs flanking each doorway. In general, the whole design is two-dimensional, cut away slightly to a uniform depth. Two planes are apparent, the outer with most of the sculpture remaining close to the original surface of the column and the other behind the shallow relief echoing the curvature of the column. Intermediate planes are merely suggested. Because of its excellence of condition and quality, the column in the Musée de Cluny is the best example for comparative analysis with the ornament of later portals.

The two fragments in the Louvre (Plate VI, 1) served as models for three spiral columns which were carved during Debret's restorations for the first, right-hand jamb of each portal (see Plate I, 1, 2). They were catalogued in the Musée des Petits-Augustins[24] and later in the Louvre.[25] These frag-

Art français, milieu du XIIe siècle. Provient de l'église de Saint-Denis, (portail occidental). Musée des Monuments français. Chantiers de Saint-Denis. Musée du Louvre."

[19] Lenoir, *Musée des Monuments Français* (1800), t. II, pp. 28–29, and pl. 61: "Nous joignons à cette gravure celle de deux colonnes en pierre dure, provenant du principal portail de l'église de Saint-Denis. . ."

[20] Lenoir, *Musée impérial des Monuments Français, histoire des arts en France, et description chronologique* (1810), p. lx, no. 523: "Quatre colonnes en pierre dure, sculptée à jour; ouvrage du dixième siècle. (Voyez la planche 61)."

[21] Courajod, *Alexandre Lenoir, Son journal et le Musée des Monuments François*, I (1878), 182: "On a porté à l'église de Saint-Denis les objets suivants. . . Quatres colonnes sculptées à jour, ornées de figures d'hommes, d'animaux, et de feuillages." Vol. II, first ed., p. 24; second ed., p. 29, the latter containing pl. 61, described in notes 19 and 20, above.

[22] Mss. de Guilhermy, fol. l., p. 130, "Autels du Jubé (1827-30). . . les colonnes, provenant de la façade sont travaillées à jour, avec feuillages, bandeaus, et signes de Zodise. Elles sont peintes et dorées."

[23] Mss. de Guilhermy, p. 61, Porte Centrale: "Deux colonnettes ouvragées, moulées sur celles des autels du jubé, semblent soutenir le linteau." p. 49,

Porte Nord: "Le linteau de la porte semble avoir pour soutiens deux colonnettes ouvragées, perlées avec rosaces et feuillages enveloppant des enfants et des panthères. Ces deux colonnes, en pierre factise, ont été moulées sur des colonnes qui se trouvaient jadis à la même place et qui sont aujourd'hui aux autels de jubé." p. 53, Porte latéral du Sud: "Deux petits colonnes moulées sur pierre factise, portent les linteau, qui parait avoir été entaillé comme aux deux autres portes."

[24] See note 19. Pl. 61 shows a column like one in the Musée de Cluny and one like the three nineteenth-century columns now *in situ* on the right side of each doorway. The latter is like the Louvre fragments.

[25] Courajod, III, 391, illustrates one of the Louvre fragments. "D'autres fragments d'architecture sculptée, provenant de Saint-Denis, de l'abbaye de Saint-Geneviève et d'autres églises de Paris, attendaient encore dans la poussière le retour du goût public et le regard d'amis compatissants. Nous citerons: deux fûts de colonnes déposés en spirales datent du douzième siècle. Ces colonnettes sont en pierre et proviennent de l'église de Saint-Denis. Elles ont appartenu à quelque portail roman, comme la Cathédrale de Chartres nous en montre un si beau spécimen. Lenoir avait classé aux Petits-Augustins deux monuments semblables sous le numero 523 et les a fait graver dans le tome II du *Musée des Monumens Français*,

ments consist of two floral bands in a spiral separated by borders of rosettes. The relatively small amount of undercutting and the crispness and clarity of carving, are analogous to the Musée de Cluny column (Plate V), which they also resemble in having uncarved sections on the back.

The borders contain rosettes between narrow frames of chevron patterns. This motif is related to the plinth RP.L.2 (Plate I, 3). When the undulating vine with floral fillers is compared with the badly worn plinth, LP.L.1 (Plate IV, 2), the similarity of motif, accentuation of midribs, and character of leaves can be observed. The movement of the ornament is controlled. Vines, leaves, and borders hug the outer surface of the block. These pieces and the spiral column in the Musée de Cluny are the finest in quality of all the Saint-Denis ornamental sculpture.

TWO FRAGMENTS OF COLUMNS IN THE MUSÉE DE CLUNY

Two restored fragments of columns (Plate VI, 2) measuring .79 and .80 meter in height and .42 meter in circumference are in the Musée de Cluny in Paris. Perhaps these are all that is left of the many ornamented colonnettes between the jamb figures on the west portals. One fragment is made up of three pairs of birds encircled by or embracing pairs of climbing vines. The second represents paired birds flanking putti with floral fillers in the center. Parts of these fragments are in plaster, but the original sections, if combined, would more than make one complete unit of design. It is thus possible to discuss them as examples of twelfth-century sculpture.

There is some evidence in the catalogues of the Musée de Cluny which may refer to these fragments. The project for the creation of the museum was launched in 1833 by Albert Lenoir, son of Alexandre,[26] but it was not until 1844 that it was inaugurated.[27] In the meantime, objects from Saint-Denis and Paris had begun to pour into this growing institution. In 1839, many sculptural fragments were sent to the Musée de Cluny from Saint-Denis.[28] The chapters on sculpture in plaster in various nineteenth-century catalogues of the museum describe two columns from Saint-Denis.[29] Certainly there is no proof that these notices refer to the fragments just described, yet because so much of their surface

is actually plaster and because they were until recently covered with paint, the possibility remains.

Some evidence exists for the original location of these fragments between the jamb figures. Debret has indicated in his drawings of the central portal that all the masonry behind the columns which he put in the places formerly occupied by the jamb statues is either the result of replacement or resurfacing under his supervision. Thus, a study of the splays in general does not bear on the problem. There are, however, elaborate incised bases directly below the modern, uncarved half-colonnettes. The best examples of these are found on the RP.R between the large recarved bases which once supported the jamb statues (Plate VI, 3). It is difficult to explain the existence of these ornate bases without considering their possible relationship to decorated columns like those in the Musée de Cluny. The fact that only these two fragments are known to exist is not surprising when only three heads of the jamb figures have been identified.

In contrast to the documented Musée de Cluny spiral column, the entire backs of these fragments consist of vines, birds, and putti in plaster. Instead of the slightly uncarved ridge on the back of the former, at least one half of these two is modern. If they were between the jamb statues, there would be no need to carve the backs, but it would be necessary to carve most of the columns supporting the lintels because almost three quarters of their surface can be observed.

There may be objections to the location of these fragments between the jamb figures on the grounds that the size of the units of design is considerably larger than in the Musée de Cluny spiral column. Their place on the façade may answer this objection. If they were between the overlife-sized jamb statues, there would be no problem of encroaching on the neighboring sculpture, as was the case with the spiral column in its original place beside the smaller sculpture: the Wise Virgins, Signs of the Zodiac, and Occupations of the Months. One would expect that designs which contain larger figures and larger floral patterns would be placed between the jamb figures and not beside the much smaller sculpture on the jambs flanking each doorway.

The style of these fragments is somewhat different from

2e édition, Plate LXI." See footnotes 19, 20. The history of these columns as far as can be ascertained by documents may be summarized as follows: (1) Four columns from the façade of Saint-Denis were in the Musée des Petits-Augustins at the beginning of the nineteenth century. (2) Four were returned to Saint-Denis after 1816. (3) Two were used on a *jubé* and served as models for the six which Debret made in 1840. (4) Two fragments like the three columns on the right side of each Saint-Denis portal found their way back to the Louvre. (5) The column now in the Musée de Cluny, according to the catalogue of 1922, was in the Musée des Petits-Augustins, then in the *chantiers* of Saint-Denis, then in the Louvre, and finally went to the Musée de Cluny. There still remains the possibility that a treasure hunt might unearth another or fragments of the other columns with once adorned Suger's façade.

[26] Haraucourt, *L'Histoire de la France expliquée au Musée de Cluny: guide annoté par salles et par series*, p. 14.

[27] Haraucourt, *L'Histoire*, p. 14.

[28] Lenoir, *Le Musée des Thermes et de l'Hôtel de Cluny; Documents sur la création du Musée d'Antiquités Nationales suivant le projet exposé au Louvre en 1833* (1882), p. 7: "Dans le nouveau Musée ont été placés tous les fragments de sculpture et l'architecture recueillis à Paris." *Ibid.*, p. 64, letter of 1839: "Les chantiers de Saint-Denis regorgent d'objets qu'on ne sait où placer."

[29] *Musée des Thermes et de l'Hôtel de Cluny; Catalogue et description des objets d'art* (1859), p. 38: "No. 190 — Colonne de la façade de la basilique de Saint-Denis — Moulage en plâtre. No. 191 — Colonne de même provenance et de même époque." These are described as above in the catalogues de la Musée de Cluny published in 1849, 1855, and 1877. Sommerard, *Musée des Thermes et de l'Hôtel de Cluny; Catalogue et description des objets d'art*, p. 54 of 1881 edition: "No. 661 — Colonnes de la façade de la basilique de Saint-Denis. Moulages en plâtre."

that of the Musée de Cluny spiral column. The treatment is more plastic and the undercutting is slightly deeper. The modeling of the vines and knots suggests relatively greater three-dimensionality. As a whole, the original shape and surface of the columns are respected as in the spiral column. The floral fillers are similar, voids are small and compact, and the bodies of birds and putti remain quite flat with only their extremities rounded. A comparison of the two putti in the second fragment with the one in the middle of the column (Plate V, 2) exhibits more similarities than differences. The same distortion exists so that the broadest aspect is presented. The same squat proportions and birdlike heads are found on both putti. The very slight differences mentioned above may be explained on the basis of their original location on the portals. Like the capitals, which are partly in shadow, they are undercut to a greater extent than the columns supporting the lintels which are in full light. The columns between the jamb statues require a more marked undercutting.

This evidence combined with the fact that columns with the same motifs but with a more advanced style are found between the jamb statues at Chartres makes it feasible, at least, to suggest the possibility that these badly damaged fragments formerly framed the jamb figures of Saint-Denis.

THREE HEADS FROM SAINT-DENIS IN THE UNITED STATES

Before the new attribution of three heads (Plates VIII, IX) in two American museums to Saint-Denis, the monumental sculpture which formerly adorned the west portals was known only from the early eighteenth-century drawings made for Bernard de Montfaucon and the subsequent engravings which appeared in his voluminous publication entitled, *Les Monumens de la monarchie françoise*.[30] The drawings (Plate VII), of which there are two sets, one made in the presence of the statues and the other copied in reverse for the benefit of the engraver, are preserved in the Bibliothèque Nationale in Paris.[31] Although sporadic attempts have been made in the past to utilize these drawings as comparative material, they have been neglected because of the lack of any fragments which would determine their accuracy. It was difficult to isolate the twelfth-century characteristics from the fancy of an eighteenth-century draftsman. As a result of the

discovery by Marvin Ross of the original location of these heads on the portals of Saint-Denis, it is now possible not only to contrast these dated masterpieces with succeeding sculpture but also to employ the Montfaucon drawings in analyzing the development of figure style in the twelfth century.[32] The very fact that the general contour of the heads and the arrangement of hair, beard, and crown closely resembles Montfaucon's illustrations is sufficient proof to accept the position of arms and drapery and the types of costumes. It is necessary to eliminate certain details, such as the rendering of eyes, feet, and hands, and the accents of light and shade, both of which are in the spirit of a later age.

Two of the heads are in the Walters Art Gallery, Baltimore (Plate VIII and Plate IX, 1, 2); and the Fogg Museum of Art, Cambridge, owns the third (Plate IX, 3, 4). In spite of the fact that all three have suffered from weathering and the unfortunate restorations of the nineteenth century, they still exhibit a vigor and vitality which give an insight into the fine quality of the Saint-Denis sculpture. The sensitive modeling of cheeks, lips, and eyes and the striking rendering of hair and beards produce the more monumental counterpart of the subtle spiral column from Saint-Denis in the Musée de Cluny. In their general appearance all three heads have many common characteristics, although at least two different hands were at work.

In his description of the three Saint-Denis portals Montfaucon identifies incorrectly the sixteen prophets of the Old Testament as the kings of France who ruled in Paris from Clovis to the end of his dynasty.[33] Ross identifies one of the heads from the Walters Gallery (Plate VIII) with the "Clothair III" (Plate VII, 2), although he points out the resemblance to "Clovis II" (Plate VII, 1).[34] For the reasons listed below [35] I am inclined to disagree with his conclusions and argue that this head is related to the sketch of the so-called "Clovis II." Much of the front part of the crown, most of the nose, right eye, and cheek have been destroyed, yet the remaining sections portray a decided facility of modeling. The silhouette consists of a rectangular shape rising from the pointed contour of the beard (Plate VIII, 2). The head is long in proportion to its width. Beneath the jeweled crown, decorated with large diamond-shaped sections alternating with pairs of teardrop patterns, the hair

[30] Montfaucon, pages and plates cited.

[31] Bibliothèque Nationale, drawings cited.

[32] Ross, "Monumental Sculptures from Saint-Denis, an Identification of Fragments from the Portal," *Journal of the Walters Art Gallery*, pp. 91–109. Mr. Ross's admirable article contains an interesting account of the removal of the nineteenth-century additions and of the successful treatment by Mr. Rosen which enables them to be exhibited in spite of their damaged condition.

[33] Montfaucon, p. 193.

[34] Ross, p. 99.

[35] The Clovis drawing (Plate VII, 1) has a more pointed beard, terminating in two knobs of hair, which corresponds more closely to the Baltimore head than the Clothaire sketch (Plate VII, 2) with its squared-off

beard of three units. Moreover, the number of curls of the beard and the length of intervals separating them (compare Plate VII, 1, 2, with Plate VIII, 1, 3) gives more evidence for identifying this head with the Clovis drawing. The upper curvature of the crown in spite of its damaged condition is more closely related to Clovis. The main pattern of the crown is similar in both drawings, yet the larger size of units in relation to the design as a whole and the vertical axis of the raised diamond motifs are exactly like the Clovis drawing (see Plate VIII, 1). These reasons combined with the more widely separated and staring eyes and the more prominent and carefully modeled cheeks, free from beard, point to the conclusion that this Baltimore head originally was part of the jamb figure identified as Clovis II by Montfaucon.

falls in a series of waves each terminating in a tight curl. The beard, which joins the flowing hair, ends in two separate points, while two groups of whiskers extend from the lower lip to the edge of the chin. The almond-shaped eyes are kept close to the surface of the block. The eyeballs are separated from the lids by a slightly deeper cutting, and the retina is undercut still further. The expressive and clearly defined lips, the subtle rendering of the cheeks in three separate planes which are unified because of their proximity — all give this head a ruggedness and monumentality resembling the finest archaic Greek sculpture.

The other head in the Walters Gallery (Plate IX, 1, 2) is definitely identified as the "Childebert" (Plate VII, 3).[36] Although its height is the same, it is slightly wider at the level of the crown and narrows gradually, so that the silhouette becomes almost triangular with the sides bulging in contrast to the rectangularity of the other head.[37] The ears project beyond the outer contour line established at the top by the crown. The decoration of the crown consists of a chevron pattern punctuated with diamond-shaped incisions. The arrangement of hair and beard also differs from that of the first head. Instead of falling in a manner interrupted by the staccato notes of small curls, the hair flows sinuously across the forehead, over and around the ears. The latter are given greater prominence than in the other head, and their curved forms echo the general undulating series of lines of each strand of hair. In the relative stiffness of the beard in contrast to the fluent quality of the moustache and hair it differs from the first head where both were treated

alike. In place of the technique of incisions, each unit is carefully modeled. The elongated eyeballs are more delicately rendered, and the separation of the cheeks into three curved planes is less obvious than in the other head. The modeling is softer and smoother. Greater fluidity is thus achieved although some of the angular strength of the first head is lost in the process.

The stylistic differences between these two heads can be explained by assuming that they were carved by two sculptors. The head illustrated in Plate VIII belonged to the central portal, while the other is located on the left portal.[38] By overlooking the drawing of the eyes these differences in the engravings of the central as opposed to the left portal are apparent. The contrast in general figure style is also noticeable in both the engravings and the drawings of the two portals.

The head in the Fogg Museum (Plate IX, 3, 4), correctly identified by Ross with Montfaucon's "Clothair I," has suffered more than the two just discussed.[39] A great deal of the face seems to have been recarved during its restoration with the resulting loss of original surface of cheeks and eyes. The sides (Plate IX, 3) showing accentuated ears which are echoed by the curls of hair, are in a fine state of preservation. The crown is ornamented with staggered rows of scales. The head is the same shape as the Walters Gallery "Childebert," and the ears are treated in a similar manner. This affinity might be expected since both these heads originally decorated the left portal [40] and are possibly the work of the same sculptor.[41]

[36] Ross, pp. 98–99.
[37] Measurements: "Clothaire III" or "Clovis II," .35 meter high, .20 meter wide at top, and .16 meter wide at level of ears; "Childebert," .36 meter high, .21 wide at crown, .22 wide at level of ears; Fogg Museum head, .36 meter high, .21 meter wide at top of crown.
[38] Montfaucon, pl. XVI, bottom left figure.
[39] Ross, pp. 100–102. Fig. 18, depicting the drawing of "Clothair I" made for Montfaucon's pl. xvi, lower left figure, is very similar in contour and all details to the Fogg head.
[40] Montfaucon, pl. xvi (left portal). Upper right figure is Baltimore head "Childebert" and lower left is Fogg head "Clothaire I."
[41] Ross, p. 101, believes that these two heads are by different hands. In a recent article in the *Bulletin monumental*, CIII (1945), 243–248, en-

titled "Tetes de statues-colonnes du portail occidental de Saint-Denis," Marcel Aubert utilized the Baltimore and Fogg heads to reinterpret the date and style of the Saint-Denis jamb figures. He argues that the heads, which agree quite closely with the Montfaucon drawings, prove that the Saint-Denis façade was unfinished in 1140 and that the jamb statues were added toward 1155 and after Suger's death in 1151. Aubert also states that the ornament of the portals was carved in the 1150's. These conclusions are based on the greater freedom in the jamb statues when compared to Chartres, the stylistic connections with the sculpture at Senlis and Mantes, and the fact that Suger does not mention the sculpture of the portals in his memoirs. Further discussion of Aubert's conclusion appears below. See Appendix III for description and analysis of the Saint-Denis bas-relief discovered by Sumner Crosby in 1947.

PART TWO

THE ROYAL PORTAL
OF CHARTRES CATHEDRAL

THE STYLISTIC connection between the west portals of Saint-Denis and the Royal Portal at Chartres points to strong connections in problems of administration. In his admirable articles on the façade of Chartres, Maurice Lanore has analyzed the documents which deal with the contacts between abbey and cathedral.[1] Many letters were exchanged from 1115 to 1148 between Geoffroy de Lèves, Bishop of Chartres, and his personal friend Suger.

More important than these letters were the visits made by Bishop Geoffroy to Saint-Denis in 1130, 1137, and 1140. During the last two trips, the portals of Saint-Denis were being built.[2] Geoffroy assisted Suger during the consecration of the choir on June 11, 1144, and at the same time, dedicated the altar of Saint-Étienne in the crypt. A document which describes the celebration of the anniversary of King Dagobert on January 19, probably in the year 1143, emphasizes the intimate relationship between these two men. Geoffroy was conducting mass at the high altar of the abbey during a very bad storm. Only the ribs of the vaults were in place; the danger of their destruction was imminent. The Bishop of Chartres raised toward the sky the sacred relic of the arm of Saint Simeon. The unfinished choir withstood the wind and rain.[3] It would be hard to believe that the portals, under construction in 1137 and finished by 1140, did not have a profound effect on Geoffroy of Chartres during the rebuilding of the western part of Chartres following the fire of 1134. The Chartres portals and windows seem to be a simplification of Saint-Denis (see Plates A, B).

I

The Relationship Between Saint-Denis and Chartres

METHODS OF CONSTRUCTION

The extent of restoration of the Saint-Denis portals makes it almost impossible to determine how the blocks of masonry were joined. There are, nevertheless, certain structural tendencies, recurring in the twelfth-century parts of the bases, which give some idea of their former arrangement. Today, three courses of masonry remain between the pavement and the ornamented plinths (Plate I, 3). The lowest has been reduced to insignificance (contrast Plates A and I). The middle course is the widest, while the topmost one includes the torus molding. In the next course the blocks contain the recarved bases of the former jamb figures and the original plinths, the latter running perpendicular to the east-west axis of the abbey. The ends of the blocks generally make a ninety-degree turn at the reëntrant angles of the jambs and carry over a few centimeters into the next jamb. This overlapping from one jamb to the next can be seen in even the worst-damaged embrasures.

The left portal right gives the clearest picture of these structural features. The second from the bottom, or largest course, exhibits instances of overlapping. Blocks of the first, second, and third jamb extend into the next jamb. This recurs in the second and third jamb of the tier above, except that the direction of the overlapping is from right to left. Since weathering is more likely to take place in the angles between the jambs, this directional alternation between tiers as well as the overlapping itself has a definite structural reason. Even more important from a structural point of view is the fact that this dovetailing of blocks of masonry knits the jambs together in a solid unit, making a sturdier support for the superstructure of the portals.

It is difficult to ascertain whether this structural system is followed in the other embrasures of Saint-Denis. Certain areas show the system already described. In the left splay of the central portal (Plate I, 1), the patching executed in the nineteenth century has considerably denatured the masonry. In the opposite side of the same portal, however, this same overlapping may be seen. In the second tier the blocks of the first two jambs continue into the second and third jamb; the fourth and fifth jambs exhibit the reverse direction of this overlapping so that the two opposing actions meet in the middle or third jamb. Starting from the third jamb in

---

[1] Lanore, "Reconstruction de la façade de la Cathédrale de Chartres au XIIe siècle," *Revue de l'Art Chrétien* (1899), pp. 328–332, and (1900) pp. 32–39; 137–145.

[2] Lanore, p. 139.

[3] Lanore, p. 140.

the third tier of masonry, the direction of the overlapping goes to the left and to the right, which is the opposite of the row below. The first and second jambs in the third tier have modern patchings which camouflage this system. This logical arrangement is not followed to the letter in the right embrasure of the right portal (Plate VI, 3).

In contrast to the structural treatment at Saint-Denis, the pedestals of the three portals at Chartres are strictly uniform. At Chartres each pedestal of the jamb statues is made up of three courses of masonry (Plates XI, XII, 2, and XIII, 3). The lowest consists of a narrow layer of blocks which becomes wider as the steps descend. Above this level platform is a second course of narrow blocks crowned by a *congé* molding. These blocks are placed on the east-west axis of the cathedral, resulting in an overlapping of jambs in the area of the moldings, from right to left in the right embrasure and from left to right in the left splays. The blocks of the next course, which extend up through the bases of the columns, run north and south. It is difficult to trace the joints in this tier from photographs, but they are located directly to the right of the first oval panel in each jamb (Plate XIII, 3).

In general, the structural dissimilarities of Saint-Denis are not apparent at Chartres. One concludes that at Chartres a system of uniformity was established, following and developing the experiments made at Saint-Denis.

PORTAL DESIGN: RELATION OF SCULPTURE TO ARCHITECTURE

By lowering the pavement level and restoring the lintels and jamb figures of Saint-Denis (Plates A and I), a fair contrast may be made between the general arrangement of the various parts of the two monuments. Chartres possesses a more elaborate organization (Plate XI). Just as Saint-Denis combines something of the exuberance of late "baroque" Romanesque with a new architectural quality, so the west portals at Chartres seem to intensify these characteristics.[4] The tapestrylike overlay of ornament and figured scenes, which at Saint-Denis does not destroy the sense of the wall, begins to encroach upon the masonry at Chartres. This tendency toward a relatively greater undercutting of the structure is counterbalanced by an even more striking articulation of each portal as a unit. A more logical unity, made up of dependent parts, is achieved, although many details lose the architectonic feeling which they contained at Saint-Denis. These two features would seem to be working at cross purposes, yet, strangely enough, the synthesis of these oppo-

site points of view gives a tremendous vitality and grandeur to the Royal Portal at Chartres.

From the purely structural side, the sculpture of both buildings echoes and reëmphasizes the architecture. Although it is true that a new type of unified portal design is created at Saint-Denis when contrasted to High Romanesque, some of the details of each portal show that these ideas are still in a formative stage of development. For example, the lintels at Saint-Denis were originally upheld, visually at least, by the small columns flanking each doorway (Plate I), and they were on the same level as the capitals above the jamb statues and thus competed with them in importance. The Wise and Foolish Virgins at the top of the central portal (Plate I, 1) seem crushed between the lintel and capitals. One gets the impression that the portals have been pieced together; but when the parts are amalgamated, they give a unified appearance. The atlas figures support small columns which in turn sustain the lintels. The flanking panel of decoration together with the lintels supports the tympanum. At Chartres, the rather assembled look of the Saint-Denis portals is altered, and a more harmonious and architectural conception is created (Plate XI). The lintels are now placed directly above the capitals and are supported by the first jambs. The somewhat awkward relationship between the ex-lintels, the flat first jambs, and the capitals is thus eliminated. These changes in design result in a different location of the sculpture. Some of the scenes which decorated the jambs of the doorways at Saint-Denis are found in the archivolts at Chartres. The structural innovations of Saint-Denis are continued. The observer's eye is carried up from the bases, through the jamb statues, around the archivolts and back again to the pavement (Plate XI). Plate XII, 1, illustrates how completely the figures have been carved to conform to the shape of the pedestals and the abaci above the capitals. Greater attention is focused on the tympanum as a result of the suppression of the wide, flat first jambs. The whole superstructure of the portals is sustained by uniform jamb statues.

The stylistic treatment of the pedestals and capitals minimizes the new structural advancement. The rugged and solid quality of the Saint-Denis bases is eliminated in the Chartres pedestals with their elaborate flutings and undercut moldings. Because of the rhythmic sequence of the abaci as well as by the continuous nature of the Passion scenes, the Chartres capitals act as a kind of horizontal frieze (Plate XI). On the contrary, the capitals of Saint-Denis are relatively isolated (Plate I). The extensive undercutting of the Chartres

[4] As employed in this study, the word "baroque" refers to tendencies which appear in late Romanesque sculpture from the middle to the end of the twelfth century. It is not, of course, the baroque of Rubens, Bernini, or Borromini, but rather a transformation of the strictly architectonic Romanesque of the late eleventh and early twelfth century into a more pictorial mode of expression. More dramatic effects of light and shade are

created by deeper undercutting. A greater sense of movement is achieved. It is thus a phenomenon which appears within the context of Romanesque art and is relatively mild in character when compared to the Pergamon altar, the works of Claus Sluter, or other more truly baroque monuments. See Focillon, *L'Art des sculpteurs romans*, pp. 286–288.

capitals casts a band of shadow across the three portals, and creates an interlude between the vertical accents of the jamb statues and the archivolts.

The relative proportions of parts of the portals of the two monuments are quite different. At Saint-Denis the bases originally occupied over one third of the total height between pavement and capitals, but at Chartres the pedestals measure less than one quarter of the total height. This alteration is partly offset by the short colonnettes on which the jamb statues stand.

As in the case of the comparative study of the methods of construction of Saint-Denis and Chartres, the latter monument displays more uniformity and greater over-all unity of pedestals, jamb figures, and archivolts. The clumsy and disorganized relationship between lintel, capitals, and the carved flat jambs of Saint-Denis is eliminated, and a more harmonious integration of sculpture and architecture is thereby achieved.

ORNAMENT

The sculptors at Chartres utilized many of the ornamental motifs of Saint-Denis. When the abstract and floral patterns of the two monuments are compared, one discovers three important differences: the location of the ornament does not follow completely the Saint-Denis precedent, new combinations of Saint-Denis patterns make their appearance, and the treatment of the ornament exhibits a definite stylistic transformation.

In place of the plain bases capped by the low relief of floral and geometric plinths at Saint-Denis, the Chartres pedestals are uniformly decorated with an elaborate system of paneling and indented moldings (Plate XIII, 3). All the geometric motifs, some of them found on the Saint-Denis plinths, are here located on the short columns below the jamb figures, while all the organic patterns, many of them exhibiting a similarity to or development of the Saint-Denis designs, are placed on the small colonnettes framing the large figures. It has already been pointed out that small ornamented columns may have decorated the jambs at Saint-Denis (Plate VI, 2), yet there is no way of ascertaining their total character.

Of the geometric motifs (Plates XII, 2, and XIII, 3, right-hand column), the folded band or ribbon decorating both columns flanking the central portal at Chartres may be compared to Plate III, 4, of Saint-Denis. The pattern is essentially the same in both monuments, but the treatment shows a marked change. Instead of keeping close to the surface of the horizontal plinth, the design at Chartres eats into much of the curved surface of the vertical column. A sort of interrupted waterfall effect is produced. A similar transformation into a more plastic rendering is seen in a comparison of the double-axe motifs of the Saint-Denis plinth (Plate III, 5)

and on the column of CP.L.2 at Chartres (Plate XIII, 3). Unlike the delicately incised pattern at Saint-Denis, the Chartres column exhibits a considerable three-dimensionality. The general curvature of the column is preserved, yet the lobes of the double axes project markedly. Small lines decorate the curved section of the motif in both examples, but raised knobs replace the engraved circles of Saint-Denis. The Chartres ornament, instead of implying the use of the draftsman's tools, proclaims the implements of the sculptor.

The limited number of geometric motifs found on both monuments is dwarfed by the wealth of organic patterns. In the case of floral designs, Chartres possesses an even greater variety of motifs than Saint-Denis. Many new combinations of motifs found at Saint-Denis appear, while many floral patterns with fillers varying in complexity are altogether different. These differences might not have been so striking if Saint-Denis were originally decorated with colonnettes between the jamb statues.

The stylistic development of the floral designs is even clearer than that of the abstract patterns. In comparing the spiral column from Saint-Denis in the Musée de Cluny (Plate V) and several colonnettes at Chartres, we must remember that the problem is identical: the ornamentation of a column. The inverted heartshaped units as they appear on the Saint-Denis example (Plate V, 3) are found in the Chartres CP.R.1 (Plate XIV, 2). Disregarding the putti heads of the latter, we find that in both examples paired vines climb into knots from which grow secondary leaves. The whole concept of decoration has changed from one of flatness and angularity to fluid plasticity. The squareness of the vines has been replaced by a continuous modeling which never allows flat areas to appear on the front plane of the block. On top of the round vines and stems are minute ridges and dots which accent the midribs and, at the same time, augment the three-dimensional feeling. In the column from the Musée de Cluny, the decoration applied to stems and leaves has the effect of flattening the whole motif. Through extensive undercutting at Chartres, most of the original surface of the block is lost. The whole design is more elastic and rhythmic. As the units progress up the colonnette, there is greater variety in the arrangement of the filling leaves. The difference between the two monuments is even greater if the same part of the Saint-Denis column (Plate V, 3) is compared with the lower section of CP.R.2 (Plate XIII, 1, 2). In the latter, the motif is slightly different, yet the plastic treatment of stems and leaves portrays very clearly a decided formal evolution. The suggested three-dimensionality of the Saint-Denis ornament is now strikingly expressed. The whole design at Chartres is attenuated. The new freedom and elasticity serve as an animated foil to the strict verticality of the jamb figures (see Plate XIII, 1).

The main spiral band of vines and figures on the same

column from Saint-Denis (Plate V, 2, 5, 6) is employed several times at Chartres. The upper part of the LP.L.1 colonnette is made up of undulating vines with floral off-shoots which entwine nude figures (Plate XIV, 1, 3). The tightness and compactness of the Saint-Denis pattern becomes much looser. Stems, vines, and leaves are more extensively modeled. Instead of being rigidly coerced into the column, the figures now twist and turn on their axes. The putto in Plate V, 2, when compared with the nude figure at Chartres (Plate XIV, 1), shows a decided stylistic evolution. In the former, the figure follows the curvature of the column and the modeling is confined to the rounded sides of torso and leg. The protruding abdomen and chest and the carefully modeled leg and head illustrate the extent of the transformation at Chartres. Beneath the rhythmic flow of this vine, the shape and surface of the block is submerged. As a result of the deeper cutting, a flicker of high lights interspersed with shadow give the Chartres ornament a vibrant character.

Much of the ornament at Chartres becomes so elaborate that virtually all connection with Saint-Denis is lost. The pairs of climbing vines entwining paired animals combined with floral offshoots (Plate XIV, 4) possess a new forward-and-backward movement which is foreign to any ornament preserved at Saint-Denis. Although the appearance and disappearance of stems and birds nearly annihilate the structural sense of the colonnette, the general outline of the columnar shape remains evident. The very complexity of the motif is new.

Assuming that the two fragments of columns in the Musée de Cluny (Plate VI, 2, left column) originally decorated Saint-Denis, one can observe that the paired birds of Chartres (Plate XV, 1) have more vigor and less regard for the surface of the block. The voids are here comparatively larger and flow into the undulating curves of vines and leaves; the whole motif is attenuated. The accentuated flatness of the other fragment from Saint-Denis (Plate VI, 2) is not apparent in the more fluid treatment of similar details at Chartres (Plates XIV, 1, and XVII, 2, jamb 3).

Basing judgment solely on the relationship of ornamental motifs and sculptural treatment, we may say that Chartres shows both a continuation and an alteration of the Saint-Denis style. The strongly architectonic quality of the Saint-Denis ornament is partially lost, and the designs achieve a new and independent existence. The direction of the evolution is toward the further intensification of the baroque tendencies already present at Saint-Denis. Stemming from sculpture with the draftsman's line as its basis, one observes that the Chartres ornament emerges as sculpture liberated from dependence on masonry and free to play through its expressively delicate shapes an important role in the total effect of the portals.[5]

FIGURE STYLE

Until the unearthing of more fragments of the monumental sculpture of Saint-Denis, one must rely on the Montfaucon drawings, the Baltimore and Fogg heads, and the Saint-Denis bas-relief (Appendix III). A comparison of these Saint-Denis heads (Plates VIII and IX) and the related drawings (Plate VII), demonstrates that the eighteenth-century draftsman followed his models very closely, especially in the rendering of contours and details of beards, hair, and crowns. He imparted an animation to eyes, noses, ears, and lips which is foreign to the medieval point of view; and this articulation of certain features of the faces had its counterpart in a general smoothing out of the disjointed transitions of shoulders and arms in the originals. The hands are given a false importance because of their strongly penciled silhouette and extensive shading. In interpreting these drawings, therefore, great care must be exerted to eliminate eighteenth-century transformations of the twelfth-century originals.

The monumental sculpture at Chartres is clearly the work of several sculptors and their assistants. A detailed discussion of these various hands appears in the next chapter. For a comparison with Saint-Denis only the major divisions of styles need be considered.

The jamb statues most closely resembling those at Saint-Denis appear on the extreme right embrasure (Plate XVI, 2). The figure nearest the doorway exhibits the same organization of drapery and arrangement of hands as the Montfaucon drawing in reverse (Plate VII, 5). The differences of media and of the rendering of the human body in epochs separated by six centuries makes it impossible to arrive at definite conclusions concerning their chronological relationship. On the other hand, in a comparison of this Chartres head (Plate XIX, 2) with one from Saint-Denis (Plate VIII) a stylistic evolution is manifested. The tightness of the treatment of hair and beard in the Saint-Denis head (note Plate VIII, 3) gives way to greater ease and fluidity at Chartres. The graceful curve of upper and lower eyelids of the Chartres head has no counterpart in the three preserved heads from Saint-Denis. Although the head in the Montfaucon drawing (Plate VII, 5) is superficially more similar to the Chartres head than to the three Saint-Denis heads, one must remember that the eighteenth-century draftsman has altered many details in his desire to emulate nature.

The extreme left jambs (Plate XVI, 1) represent another

---

[5] In his recent article on the Saint-Denis heads (*Bulletin monumental*, 1945), Aubert argues that the ornament as well as the jamb figures were carved after Suger's death in 1151 and Saint-Denis was thus later than Chartres. Aubert, p. 246: "Comme les bas-reliefs des piédroits, les statues-colonnes des ébrasements n'ont sans doute été sculptées qu'après sa mort en 1151, peut-être, étant donné les troubles qui ont suivi la mort du grand abbé, vers 1155, mais sans doute sur le programme qu'il avait dicté."

distinct hand at work on the Royal Portal. Although these three statues, two male and one female, are close in style to the sculpture of the south portal of Notre-Dame at Étampes (Plates XXIII, XXIV), there are also certain relationships to Saint-Denis. When compared to similar Saint-Denis statues (Plate VII, 1 and 6) the central figure displays a more elongated silhouette and greater interest in delicately modeled folds of drapery. The actual organization of garments is different, yet the staff and treatment of the left knee of Plate VII, 6, are similar to the Chartres jamb. More important than the relatively slenderer contours of the Chartres figure is the actual contrast of heads, the Saint-Denis head (Plate VIII) and the Chartres head of the statue under discussion (Plate XIX, 1). The archaic ruggedness of the Saint-Denis head is superseded. The modeling of forehead and cheeks is no longer broken into planes forming edges over the eyes. The Chartres head consists of subtle and continuously curving surfaces which model the eyes, nose, and cheeks. Like the body, the head is more attenuated.

These same differences can be seen in comparing a female statue from Saint-Denis (Plate VII, 4) with the Chartres LP.L.1 (Plate XVI, 1). The squatness and lack of harmony between the hands and the central axis of the columnar statue of Saint-Denis is altered radically. The tassels fall in parallel lines and accentuate the verticality of the entire mass. The treatment of drapery is more delicate. As a whole, in spite of the disjointed wrists and hands, the various parts of the Chartres figure are more integrated into an artistic entity.

When compared to the Saint-Denis drawings (Plate VII, 1, 2, 5), the four statues on the right splay of the central portal (Plate XVII, 2), which were carved by the Headmaster, exhibit the differences just described to an even greater degree. In silhouette, the stylistic changes manifest themselves at once. At Saint-Denis (Plate VII), the outlines describe a rectangular shape with the greatest width at the level of the elbows and tapering inward so that the narrowest part is just above the feet. At Chartres, the width of the elongated rectangle is preserved from shoulders to feet. This extreme rigidity, with only the slightest curve to indicate the position of the left elbows, gives them a new architectural character. The original shape of the block is preserved to a greater extent. The statues reflect in their outer contours the columnar shape of the colonnettes behind them, of which they are a part. Looking at the figures from an angle, one sees that the heads of the Saint-Denis jambs bend forward and away from the column, while at Chartres the haloed heads are kept flat against the columns (see Plate XX, 3).

In the arrangement and treatment of parts of the bodies inside their silhouettes, the differences are more apparent. In the Montfaucon drawings and engravings, the hands, holding books, scrolls, or making gestures, are not always placed on the central vertical axis of the figures as they are in the four Chartres figures (Plate XVII, 2). The whole surface treatment changes at Chartres. Instead of flowing drapery with large folds, the rendering of the garments at Chartres resembles the small flutes of a column. Multiple parallel folds fall in straight lines from waist to feet.

Compare single figures of Saint-Denis (Plate VII, 2) and Chartres CP.R.2 (Plates XII, 1, and XVII, 2). The Chartres figure echoes in its entire curved V-shaped mass the angle of the pedestal below and the capital and abacus above. The line of greatest projection passes through the middle of the statue, the hands and edge of the book, and finally through the nose. At Saint-Denis the off-center arrangement of book and hands reduces the emphasis of the architectural members above and below the statue.

The three heads in America (Plates VIII and IX), offer firmer grounds for comparison than do the Montfaucon drawings. These Saint-Denis heads have more pointed silhouettes, with the beards tapering in a wedgelike manner. The heads at Chartres (Plate XXI, 1) have a squareness of contour which respects the rigid shape of their bodies. If one of the Baltimore heads (Plate IX, 1, 2) is compared with the Chartres CP.R.2 (Plate XIX, 3, 4) the relationship of the former to Romanesque sculpture of 1100 to 1130 and the more humanistic character of the latter, prophetic of High Gothic, are clearly exhibited. The directness of the Saint-Denis heads have given way to a maturer and more monumental conception. The staring eyes of the birdlike faces of Saint-Denis and the modeling of the cheeks in three planes are softened by delicately continuous contours. Hair and beard are less stylized. A sense of majestic calm and confidence permeates the Chartres head. As in the comparative study of the ornament of the two monuments, a stylistic evolution has taken place, and there is no doubt that the direction is from Saint-Denis to Chartres. Whereas the Chartres ornament, derived from Saint-Denis, loses its mural character, the jamb figures at Chartres become more structural. The directions of the development of ornament and figures seem to be at variance, but this is not actually the case since the designers, as sensitive artists, created a synthesis of the rigidity of pose of the jambs and the subtle movement of the adjacent ornamental colonnettes. The result is the creation of three portals, in which the architectural lines are reaffirmed by the sculpture to a greater extent than at any other moment in the Middle Ages.

To place Saint-Denis and Chartres in the larger context of the whole twelfth century, the greater freedom of poses and lesser amount of coördination between monumental sculpture and the design of the entire portal at Saint-Denis have many parallels with earlier twelfth-century sculpture such as that of Vézelay, Moissac, and Autun. By contrast Chartres represents the synthesis of experiments begun at Saint-Denis.

Further evidence to substantiate the chronological relationship is the character of the dated portals within or on the periphery of the Île-de-France all of which were inspired by Chartres, not Saint-Denis. Le Mans, finished in 1158, and Saint-Ayoul at Provins of the late 1150's or early 1160's, discussed in Part IV, exemplify the continuation of the Chartres formula. It is only in the 1180's at Senlis that the influence of the Royal Portal of Chartres comes to an end.[6]

II

Twelfth-Century Chartres

HISTORY OF CHARTRES AND RESULTS OF EXCAVATIONS

Doubt concerning the date of execution and the original emplacement of the Royal Portal has caused archaeological duels which still persist. The excavations made in 1901, 1903, 1937, and 1938 have led to a series of articles with varying conclusions.

Before launching into a summary of this debate, it is essential to mention briefly the early history of Chartres, since the eleventh-century church bears a definite relationship to the twelfth-century construction. In 1020, the fire of September 7–8 destroyed the existing structure. Saint Fulbert, then bishop, caused the erection of a new church. This is depicted in the miniature of André de Mici made in 1028 at the time of Fulbert's death.[7] The authors who published this miniature believed that the tower which they reconstructed on the southwest corner of the church belonged to the Carolingian edifice. In 1030 another fire swept the town but did not damage Fulbert's church excessively. The upper part and the roof were rebuilt, and the transepts were added by Bishop Thierry, according to Merlet. The dedication took place on October 17, 1037.[8] The present width of the nave was established at that time.

Toward the middle of the century Canon Raimbaud added porches on the west façade and on the transepts. In 1075 William the Conqueror paid for the construction of a wooden tower somewhere on the roof of the church. In 1092, the substantial financial backing of Dean Abalard made possible the completion of a tower in masonry.[9]

On September 5, 1134, a fire destroyed the town of Chartres. The contemporary reports state that although the church was engulfed in flames, it miraculously escaped damage. However, the west end of the church does seem to have been damaged considerably, for the Hôtel-Dieu, located only a few meters to the southwest, was completely destroyed.[10] Some critics believe that destruction caused by the fire was minimized by pious writers.[11] The fact that a new campaign of building began immediately with tremendous enthusiasm seems to substantiate the latter assumption. Documents exhibit donations for a tower given by Archdeacon Gautier, who died between 1134 and 1138, and by Archdeacon Ansgerius of Blois, who died between 1139 and 1142.[12] In both instances, mention is made of only one tower. It has been proved conclusively by Lanore in a careful study of moldings, capitals, and types of vaults that these documents could only refer to the north tower.[13] He also discovered that the north tower was freestanding because of the existence of a window on the east side of the tower.[14]

In 1145 Robert de Thorigny, Abbot of Mont-Saint-Michel, reported that towers were under construction.[15] At this time, according to Lanore, Fulbert's church was extended one bay to meet the north tower, and the south tower and portals were begun. Lanore argues that the strong influence from Saint-Denis and the powerful renewal of faith which developed in the region around Chartres at this very time brought about this extensive building program.[16]

Thus, before the first real excavations had been made, Lanore had demonstrated that the north tower, originally isolated, was begun soon after the fire of 1134, that the south tower was being erected in 1145, and that the Royal Portal was at least begun by 1145, because of the lack of

---

[6] In the same article, pp. 244–247, Aubert relates the Saint-Denis heads to the heads at Mantes and Senlis and argues that Saint-Denis is later than Chartres: p. 244, "Ces têtes, très proches par bien de points de celles du Portail royal de Chartres, témoignent cependant d'un art plus avancé, d'une certaine énergie de facture qui ne se trouve pas à Chartres"; p. 247, "Le Portail royal de Chartres serait donc le plus ancien, la première expression de la statuaire gothique. Celui de Saint-Denis aurait suivi de peu." Mme. Cécile Goldscheider in a summary of her thesis entitled "Les Origines du portail à statues-colonnes," *Bulletin des Musées de France*, XI (Musée de Louvre, 1946), 22–25, concludes that Saint-Denis is later than Chartres and was carved around 1155. She argues that the tympanum of the central portal can be dated in the late 1130's but that the rest of the sculpture is of the 1150's. The main reasoning behind these conclusions is the fact that Suger makes no mention of the monumental sculpture on the west façade and that the sculpture possesses movement and energy which would date Saint-Denis later than Chartres. It is impossible to agree with Beenken, who dates La Charité-sur-Loire after 1178 and concludes that most of

Chartres can hardly be dated before 1170. See Hermann Beenken, "Die Tympana von La Charité sur Loire," *Art Studies* (Cambridge: Harvard University Press, 1928), VI, 145-159.

[7] Merlet and Clerval, *Un Manuscrit Chartrain du XIe siècle*.

[8] Merlet and Clerval, pp. 74–81.

[9] Merlet and Clerval, pp. 82–4.

[10] Merlet and Clerval, 57 and 84–85.

[11] Lasteyrie, "Études sur la sculpture française au moyen âge," *Fondation Piot*, VIII, 708.

[12] Merlet and Clerval, p. 87.

[13] Lanore (1899), pp. 330-335.

[14] Lanore (1899), p. 333.

[15] Bouquet, *Recueil des historiens des Gaules et de la France*, XIII, p. 290: "Hoc eodem anno coeperunt homines prius apud Carnotum carros lapidibus onustos et lignis, annona et rebus aliis suis humeris trahere ad opus ecclesie cujus turres tunc fiebant."

[16] Lanore (1900), pp. 33-34.

connection in moldings and decoration between the north tower and portals and the correspondence between portals and the south tower.[17]

The findings of Lefèvre-Pontalis as result of the excavations of 1901 bear out and alter only slightly the conclusions reached by Lanore and Merlet.[18] The front wall of Fulbert's church, marked A and B on the plan (Plate XXXVIII, 1), was located running into the third pier of the thirteenth-century nave. The walls discovered at E and F, running perpendicular to this façade, were identified as the foundations of the porch of Raimbaud added about the middle of the eleventh century. Following the fire of 1134, these foundations were changed to support the new façade which was placed 2.20 meters behind the north tower.[19] Lanore, writing before these excavations, had thought that the portals stood between the eastern foundations of the towers, but the diggings in this area did not disclose any walls.[20] While the portals and the connected south tower were being built, a vaulted porch three bays wide was constructed behind the façade. The evidence for this was found in the foundations (marked C and D on Lefèvre-Pontalis' plan, Plate XXXVIII, 1) which were added to Fulbert's façade and the engaged columns X and Y which are still attached to the back of the Royal Portal in its present location. Lefèvre-Pontalis reconstructed the plan of the cathedral prior to the removal of the portals to their present position between the west faces of the towers (Plate XXXVIII, 2).[21] He also excavated at the southeast corner of the north tower and proved that the base (marked R on his plan) is attached to the tower and has nothing to do with the location of the portals. The excavations carried out between the towers unearthed a large wall, marked O, Z, P on the plan (Plate XXXVIII, 1). As a result of a study of the masonry, Lefèvre-Pontalis thought that these foundations were later than those of the north tower. He was uncertain about the original function of these foundations, although he believed that they might have supported a temporary wall perhaps constructed during the process of moving the portals to the west. In conclusion, he attempted to prove that the portals were moved around 1180, on the evidence that cracks found in the original emplacement had necessitated this action. He claimed that the vaulted porch behind the portals was left intact and was supported by the piers (marked M and N). He also argued that the portals were

moved before the fire of 1194 since the stained-glass windows above them still exist.[22]

These conclusions were attacked by Mayeux, who accused Lefèvre-Pontalis of not following the official plan of the excavations.[23] He offered a hypothesis that the portals were never moved at all. According to this theory, the north tower was built first and then a porch, opened to the west and south, was added. Following the construction of the west portals on their present site, the south tower was built. This order of building necessitated the dismantling of the Virgin portal and accounted for its present damaged condition.[24]

In Lefèvre-Pontalis' response, which appeared in the same publication, the hypothesis of Mayeux was strongly attacked. Arguments were strengthened and more evidence, based on the excavations of 1903, was produced.[25] He built up elaborate data to prove more conclusively the existence of a vaulted porch in front of Fulbert's church and behind the three portals. The wide intermediate foundations between the towers (O, Z, P in Plate XXXVIII, 1) were now explained as an abandoned project. Using plans and elevations of the south side of the north tower and the north side of the south tower (Plate XXXVIII, 4, 5), Lefèvre-Pontalis claimed that it would be impossible to build a vaulted porch between the towers. He argued that the squeezed character of the portals, the cutting back of the south corner of the north tower, and the loss of ten centimeters of the lintel of the right portal are ample evidence to prove that the portals were moved.[26] He failed, however, to give further proof of the arbitrary date of 1180 for the moving of the portals.

This only partially resolved state of affairs lasted until Trouvelot conducted new excavations inside the south tower in 1937 and inside the north tower in 1938. He lowered the pavement of both towers and unearthed entrances into the crypt from the east side of both towers. In 1938, Fels excavated in the area between the towers. Unfortunately, the official results with diagrams, plans, and photographs have not been published, but a summary of the findings was published by Aubert.[27] Fels, in a speech given to the Société Nationale des Antiquaires de France on January 29, 1939, proved that the hitherto unexplained foundations (marked O, Z, P on Lefèvre-Pontalis' plan, Plate XXXVIII, 1) originally supported a large central tower which incorporated a

[17] Lanore (1900), p. 37.

[18] Lefèvre-Pontalis, "Les Façades successives de la cathédrale de Chartres au XIe et au XIIe siècle," *Congrès Archéologique de France* (1900), pp. 256–307; same article in *Mémoires de la Société Archéologique d' Eure-et-Loir* (1901–1904), XIII, 1–48.

[19] Lefèvre-Pontalis, "Les Façades successives," pp. 259–266.

[20] Lanore (1900), p. 32.

[21] Lefèvre-Pontalis, pp. 286–287 and plan.

[22] Lefèvre-Pontalis, pp. 270–301.

[23] Mayeux, "Réponse à M. Eugène Lefèvre-Pontalis sur son article,"

Mémoires de la Société Archéologique d'Eure-et-Loir (1904), XIII, 414–433.

[24] Mayeux, pp. 430–433.

[25] Lefèvre-Pontalis, "Nouvelles Études sur les façades et les clochers de la Cathédrale de Chartres; réponse à M. Mayeux," *Mémoires de la Société Archéologique d'Eure-et-Loir* (1904), XIII, 434–483.

[26] Lefèvre-Pontalis, "Nouvelles Études," pp. 441–483.

[27] Aubert, "Le Portail royal et la façade occidentale de la Cathédrale de Chartres, essai sur la date et leur exécution," *Bulletin monumental* (1941), C, 177–218.

porch and gallery above.[28] Fels reasoned further that the tower supported by these foundations, together with those discovered by Lefèvre-Pontalis in the first bay of the nave (marked H, K, I on his plan), replaced the porch of Raimbaud.[29] Aubert suggested that this tower was related to the extensive donations by Dean Abalard in 1092.[30]

On the basis of these new excavations, Aubert reinterpreted the history of the Chartres façade (see the reconstruction, Plate XXXVIII, 3) as follows. After the fire of 1134, work was commenced on the north tower. A comparative study of moldings and capitals substantiated the conclusions of Lanore that the north is the older tower and was originally isolated.[31] The south tower was begun between 1142 and 1145 and, at the same time, the aisles were extended westward to the towers. This campaign of building must have been contemporary with the construction of the south tower because no evidence exists to show its isolation from the rest of the cathedral. Aubert argued that, at the same time as the extension of the aisles, and after the central eleventh-century tower had been demolished, the nave was elongated and the new façade was begun between the eastern piers of the towers.[32] As evidence for this original emplacement of the Royal Portal, he cited a foundation wall discovered on the north side of the northeast pier of the south tower (see Plate XXXVIII, 3).[33] Aubert claimed that the sculptural ensemble planned for this original location (which measured 14.23 meters as opposed to the 16.23 meters of the present position) resembled Vézelay, with a large central portal and two small flanking portals.[34] Some of the sculpture was carved in this period (1145–1150), but was probably never put in place because it was decided around 1150 to move the façade to its present location, to design a new (the present) portal and to enclose as a narthex the porch, which had been planned but never constructed.[35] To increase the circulation between crypt and exterior, a new doorway was cut in the south side of the south tower.[36]

Unfortunately, several questions still remain unanswered by these interpretations of the recent excavations. (1) How could the thin foundation wall discovered by Fels on the north side of the northeast pier of the south tower have supported a Vézelay-type portal? Its dimension, according to Fels, precludes its use as a foundation for portals with jamb statues (see Plate XXXVIII, 3, for location of foundations).[37]

(2) If the unfinished portals were moved around 1150, how was the area between the towers vaulted? The evidence cited by Lefèvre-Pontalis to prove that it would have been impossible to vault this area still stands: the shapes of the bays would have been irregular and the heights of the imposts on the towers would have been a meter different (see Plate XXXVIII, 4, 5).[38]

(3) How is it possible to account for the crowded effect of the Royal Portal if the ensemble as a whole was constructed in its present position towards 1150? The right portal is only 2.22 meters wide as opposed to 2.32 for the north portal. Both lintels of the right portal have lost half of their right-hand figures (Plate XX, 2). The outer figures of the central lintel are pushed against the inner archivolt (Plate XI). The modern decorative border framing the archivolts of all three portals stops awkwardly above their rightful imposts (Plate XI). Aubert argues that after the sculpture had been carved in the *chantier*, it was discovered that the axis of the cathedral was off center to the right; this necessitated the cutting off of the right lintels.[39] Since there is definite evidence of crowding in the central portal as well as the damage to the lintel of the right portal, one would have to assume that the sculptors badly miscalculated the distance between the towers. It is difficult to discount this evidence of overcrowding on the entire Royal Portal and to argue that the portals were not moved as a whole from the foundation in the first bay of the present nave where, according to the reconstruction of Lefèvre-Pontalis (Plate XXXVIII, 2), there was ample room for all three portals.

---

[28] Aubert, "Le Portail royal," p. 180.

[29] Aubert, "Le Portail royal," p. 180. In a letter written to me, M. Étienne Fels stated that these foundations supported a tower like that of Saint-Benoît-sur-Loire and that this tower was built before 1100.

[30] Aubert, "Le Portail royal," p. 180 and n. 2.

[31] Aubert, "Le Portail royal," pp. 181–183.

[32] Aubert, "Le Portail royal," pp. 184–185.

[33] Aubert, "Le Portail royal," p. 185 and n. 2.

[34] Aubert, "Le Portail royal," p. 186.

[35] Aubert, "Le Portail royal," p. 188–190. Mâle, *Notre-Dame de Chartres*, p. 23. Mâle writes in the footnote: "M. Marcel Aubert, dans l'article du *Bulletin monumental*, suppose que les deux portails de droite et de gauche étaient à l'origine plus petits et n'avaient qu'un seul linteau. On y aurait ajouté plus tard, à droite, le linteau de la Présentation au Temple, à gauche les quatres anges s'adressant aux apôtres au moment de l'Ascension. L'hypothèse est ingénieuse, mais ne va pas sans quelques difficultés."

[36] Aubert, "Le Portail royal," p. 191.

[37] In a letter written to me in the fall of 1947, M. Fels stated that the foundation between the east piers of the towers was of insufficient width to sustain portals with jamb statues.

[38] Lefèvre-Pontalis, "Les Façades successives," pp. 298–299. Aubert ("Le Portail royal," p. 214) concedes that the imposts on the towers would have to be adjusted, yet there is no evidence on the towers to prove that this adjustment was carried out. The bases marked R and S (Plate XXXVIII, 1) are part of their respective towers and have nothing to do with any possible vaults (see Lefèvre-Pontalis, "Les Façades successives," p. 268).

[39] Aubert ("Le Portail royal," pp. 192–193) argues as follows: "Le maître d'oeuvre avait prévu, sur son projet, deux portes symétriques, absolument semblables, de chaque côté de la porte centrale, et avait préparé la décoration sculptée en conséquence. Mais l'axe de la cathédrale passe légèrement au sud du centre de la ligne qui réunit les faces occidentales des deux tours; voulant, au moment de monter la construction, faire coincider l'axe de la porte centrale avec celui de la cathédrale — ou du moins rapprocher, le plus possible l'un de l'autre — il dut rétrécir légèrement toute la travée de droite de la façade, et notamment la porte dont la largeur n'est plus que de 2ᵐ 22, tandis que celle qui lui fait pendant à gauche mesure 2ᵐ 32. Cette différence, insensible à l'oeil, entraîna la réduction des linteaux et du tympan, et l'on dut scier en deux un des moutons et un des bergers du premier linteau, du côté droit, un des petits personnages du deuxième, du même côté, et rogner les deux bords de la dalle qui porte la Vierge de majesté au tympan, ce qui supprima l'extrémité des ailes des anges qui l'accostent."

(4) If the sculpture and the three stained-glass windows were never moved, how can one explain the loss of the right-hand border of the right window and the fact that there is less masonry bordering the right-hand window on the right side than borders the left-hand window on the left side?

(5) The present appearance of the total façade (Plate B) with the Royal Portal between the west faces of the towers is open to question. Without the thirteenth-century rose window and high gable, the twelfth-century portals and windows would appear squashed between the huge towers. If the portals were set back east of the towers, this lack of harmony and crowded character would not exist. In addition, such churches as Vendôme and Saint-Nicholas at Caen provide ample evidence for such a treatment.

Further discussion of these problems will appear after the Chartres sculpture has been studied in detail. At this point, however, Lefèvre-Pontalis' argument that the portals were located originally in the nave and then moved later in their entirety seems correct.

TWELFTH-CENTURY CAPITALS AT CHARTRES

The capitals of the north and south towers at Chartres offer considerable evidence of the development of ornament and the changing relation of ornament to architecture in the mid-twelfth century. The dated capitals of Saint-Denis in the narthex and chevet as well as on the portals help to establish the chronology of those at Chartres. The whole problem is complicated by influences from earlier churches in the Île-de-France and outlying regions. An analysis of these capitals helps to establish the approximate date of various parts of the towers.

Possibly the earliest series of capitals is to be found in the north tower of Chartres, begun soon after the fire of 1134 (Plate XXII, 3). Of approximately the same period are the capitals in the Saint-Denis narthex and on the portals, known to have been finished by 1140 (Plate XXII, 1). In each corner of the ground story of the north tower of Chartres, groups of three capitals (Plate XXII, 3) support the ribs and transverse arches of the domical vault. Despite a coat of cream-colored paint, they exhibit distinctive characteristics. Most of the decoration is made up of paired, straplike flat bands culminating in volutes. The shape of the capitals is not disguised by the ornament; the volutes help to emphasize their structural significance. With the exception of the volutes, modeling is kept at a minimum. The left capital in the group at the southeast corner has narrow straps which interweave on the flat side of the capital. In the more elaborate central one, the straps are decorated with a chevron pattern very similar to those found on all the abaci and ribs. The three other groups are variations on those just described. Pairs of abstract leaves capped by small volutes or a large single leaf flanked by big volutes form the majority

of the designs. One of the capitals in the northeast corner has addorsed birds. Except for the modeled knobs at the extremities of the volutes the general flatness is apparent in all. The same breadth of treatment and the same accentuation of the angles are found in the capitals flanking the doors leading into the narthex. Since the masonry from the tower into the cathedral proper is continuous, we may conclude that all the capitals on the pier separating the doors and along the outer sides of each entrance belong to one campaign (see south elevation of north tower, Plate XXXVIII, 4). The same type of flattened, stylized foliage exists. The motives include pure ornament and scenes of combat between grotesque horses and humans. Other features of the north tower which indicate its early date are the archaic vaulting construction and the primitive moldings of the bases. The pavement has recently been lowered to its original level, and the entrance to the crypt has been restored. Directly above this entrance on the east side of the tower a window, now walled up, clearly establishes the fact that the tower was formerly isolated.

The two series of capitals at Saint-Denis, executed in the late 1130's, have some characteristics similar to those found in the north tower capitals at Chartres, although the ornamental motifs are different. The capitals on the Saint-Denis portals, many of which have probably been recarved, have floral designs made up of several rows of acanthus leaves (Plate I, 1, 2). As in the north tower at Chartres, the angle of the block is accentuated either by pairs of leaves or by heads of fantastic monsters. Instead of the flatness and abstraction of the Chartres ornament, the motifs consist of vines and leaves which are modeled to a much greater extent. Those on the left side of the left portal are in the best state of preservation. The narthex capitals at Saint-Denis (Plate XXII, 1) have more affinity with those on the neighboring portals than with those in the north tower at Chartres, yet they seem to be the work of a different workshop. The structural role of the narthex capitals is more formidable; the function of the portal capitals is more decorative. The difference is expressed by less pronounced undercutting in the latter. Most of the motifs consist of pure ornament arranged in two or three horizontal tiers. Some have staggered rows of frontal acanthus leaves that give firm support to the corner of the abaci, while others show paired leaves that curve around and form floral knobs corresponding to the volutes of the Chartres capitals already described.

The capitals in the south tower at Chartres show a great change both in the rendering of the ornament and in the relation of capital to architecture (Plate XXII, 4). The acanthus tiers which hugged the curved surface of the capitals in the Saint-Denis narthex now flare out. The rugged structural quality is gone and the delicate carving of the sculptor is emphasized. The single capitals supporting the ribs are more architectural in character than those adorning the doors into the narthex. The capital in the northeast corner of the vault (Plate XXII, 4, upper right-hand corner) bears a striking resemblance to those in the chevet of Saint-Denis which were finished in 1144 (Plate XXII, 2). Ornamental patterns of leaves, their arrangement in tiers, and the depth of the carving is almost identical. The Corinthian-like capitals on the south side of the pier between the two doors leading into the narthex of Chartres (Plate XXII, 4) illustrate the transformation which has taken place since the carving of those in the north tower (Plate XXII, 3). The whole surface of the blocks is eaten away by the delicately carved groups of leaves. The shape of the capitals is preserved only in the general outline made by the tiers of floral projections. Thus because of the similarity of the south tower capitals at Chartres to those in the chevet at Saint-Denis and because of the many differences which distinguish the former from the series in the older north tower at Chartres, it is possible to conclude that a strong influence came from Suger's abbey in the middle of the 1140's after a local group of carvers had completed their work in the north tower.

The same development is seen in a comparative study of the moldings of the two towers. The profiles of the bases of the south tower are not archaic and the abaci have become more elaborate. The difference in date between the north and south towers is further established by studying the capitals on their respective exterior west sides. Instead of the simple capitals of grotesques or flat leaves and volutes, the patterns on the south tower are complicated, foliated tiers with greater three-dimensionality in all details.

A portal on the south side of the south tower has caused much disagreement among archaeologists (Plate XXII, 5). Lefèvre-Pontalis believed that this doorway was cut into the south tower about 1150 so that direct communication could be established between the Hôtel-Dieu and the crypt via the staircase descending from the south tower.[40] Others have held that it was part of the original construction of the tower. The break in continuity of moldings near the bases of each side of the door as well as the style of the capitals would seem to substantiate the first hypothesis. On the left side of the left base the wall has been shaved off (see Plate XXII, 5), while on the right two blocks have lost their original decoration. The ornamental pedestals correspond to those on the west portals. The capitals are very close in style to those inside the south tower although the acanthus foliage seems even more plastic (Plate XXII, 6).

The Chartres south tower capitals thus exhibit a tendency away from abstract motifs toward more detailed foliage which is modeled to such an extent that some structural

significance is lost. The capitals in the ground story of the north tower were carved in the 1130's following the fire of 1134, while those in the south tower, known to have been in the process of construction in 1145, were probably made between 1145 and 1150. Since the latter series are related to the capitals in the chevet of Saint-Denis, they can be dated slightly later than the dedication of Suger's choir in 1144. Except for the north tower examples, the same differences that were apparent in the ornament on the façades of the two monuments also exist in the capitals.

ORNAMENT ON THE ROYAL PORTAL

Unlike the capitals in the towers at Chartres, the ornament of the Royal Portal does not exhibit any evolution of style.[41] When differences do appear, they are qualitative and may be accounted for by one of two possibilities: either sculptors of varying ability were assigned to decorate specific areas on the portals, or when the sculpture was actually put in place the finest ornamental work was assembled in conspicuous locations and the less successful work relegated to inferior positions.

Plates XII through XV illustrate clearly the homogeneity of style of the Royal Portal. The entire repertory of abstract motifs appears on the short columns beneath the jamb statues (Plates XII, 2, and XIII, 3). The patterns may be described as follows:

1. Fluted column (Plate XII, 2, CP.R.4)
2. Four-leaf clover (Plate XIII, 3, CP.L.3)
3. Stepped meander (Plate XIII, 3, CP.L.5)
4. Folded ribbon or band (Plate XIII, 3, CP.L.1)
5. Double-axe (Plate XIII, 3, CP.L.2)

The degree of modeling is uniform throughout. As already indicated in the preceding chapter, several of these patterns are plastic versions of motifs which appeared on the plinths at Saint-Denis (see Plate III).

Although the weathered surfaces make it hard to discover any marked differences in quality, it is clear that some of the columns on the embrasures LP.R and RP.L are left unfinished on the sides facing the entrances (see motif 2 on LP.R.4, Plate XVIII, 1, and the same motif on RP.L.3 and 4, Plate XVIII, 2). In addition, there appears to be a relative lack of crispness of detail such as in the carving of the abstracted leaves of motif 2 or the knobs which act as fillers (Plate XVIII, 1).

With the exception of that on the capitals and outer archivolts, all the floral decoration is located on the colonnettes between the jamb statues. Only one colonnette, LP.L.2 (Plate XVIII, 2), which is decorated with the Labors of the

---

[40] Lefèvre-Pontalis, "Les Façades successives," p. 283.

[41] See Appendix II for complete list, description, location, and measurements of all ornament on colonnettes and columns on the façade.

Months, has any iconographical significance.[42] All the other motifs have as their basis some form of vine, either singly or in pairs. These floral patterns appear alone or else combined with humans or animal figures. Some of the basic types are as follows:

1. Undulating vine with floral fillers (Plate XVI, 1, LP.L.2, middle piece, and Plate XIII, 3, CP.L.3).

2. Undulating vine embracing figures (Plate XIV, 1, 3, LP.L.1, middle piece).

3. Pair of climbing vines with floral fillers (Plate XIII, 1, 2, CP.R.2, lower section).

4. Hybrid undulating vines with floral fillers (Plate XV, 4, LP.R.1, bottom).

5. Pair of vines with addorsed birds (Plate XV, 1, LP.L.1, bottom section).

6. Pair of vines entwining confronted beasts, with elaborate floral fillers (Plate XIV, 4, CP.R.4, bottom).

7. Heart-shaped units of paired vines with putto heads and leaves (Plate XIV, 2, CP.R.1, lower part).

8. Separate floral units joined by circlets (Plate XV, 3, RP.L.2, bottom section).

9. Spiral frieze of interlaced figures, animals, and vines bordered by bands (Plate XV, 2, LP.L.2, lowest piece).

As in the case of the abstract patterns, the floral designs exhibit the same amount of undercutting and the same plastic treatment of vines and leaves. The treatment of spiral motif 9 (Plate XV, 2) appears somewhat flatter, but this effect is largely produced by the sculptor's insistence on echoing the band in the carving of the vine.

From the point of view of quality in the colonnettes, there is a vast difference. Compare colonnettes with motifs 3 (Plate XIII, 1, 2) and 4 (Plate XV, 4). Even though the patterns are different, the delicacy of modeling of vines and leaves in motif 3 contrasts strongly with the crudeness and uncertainty of carving in motif 4. In the vitality of all its parts, motif 3 acts as a delightful and sparkling counterpart to the sternly vertical folds of drapery of the adjacent statues. On the contrary, motif 4 adds little to the total effect of the adjoining monumental sculpture (Plate XVIII, 1). It is worth noting that motif 4 starts out with a pair of vines flanking awkward addorsed birds and then shifts into a hybrid design as though the sculptor changed his mind.

If colonnettes with motifs 7 (Plate XIV, 2) and 8 (Plate XV, 3) are compared, a distinction in quality will be observed. Although the treatment of motif 8 is an improvement on 4, just discussed, it has a coarseness not apparent in motif 7 or in any other colonnette in Plate XIV.

Colonnettes with motifs 4 and 8, both having comparatively unskilled carving, are placed in the least important

splays of the entire Royal Portal, LP.R and RP.L. In discussing the ornament on the short columns, we have already discovered the same relative decline in quality on the same embrasures.

The finest ornamental carving is found on the right side of the central portal (Plate XIII, 1, 2, and Plate XIV, 2, 4). The colonnettes on the opposite embrasure (Plate XIII, 3) are nearly as fine, although they have suffered more from weathering. By contrast, the decoration on LP.R and RP.L seems mediocre. The motifs on RP.R (Plate XVI, 2) do not show the same delicacy of surfaces which appears on the colonnettes of the central portal, yet the ornament is superior to that on the RP.L.

Some of the ornament on the extreme left (LP.L, Plates XIV, 1, 3, and XV, 1, 2) is of the highest quality. This observation appears to injure our contention that the best ornament is concentrated on the central portal. A full discussion of the problem here raised appears at the end of this chapter.

The Royal Portal of Chartres thus possesses a wealth of ornament varying from the simple abstract patterns on pedestals and short columns to the more elaborate motifs on the colonnettes. Floral designs increase in variety and are often combined with human and fantastic figures in great complexity. As evidenced in Plates XVI, XVII, XVIII, which illustrate all the jambs, the rhythmic flow of patterns of the colonnettes, the subtle shadows of the undercut areas, and the small scale of the motifs — all force up the monumentality of the jamb statues. In their totality, the colonnettes act as an animated frame for the Patriarchs and Prophets of the Old Testament. This implies a high degree of sensitivity and artistic invention.

More ornament appears on the capitals and around the archivolts. The abaci above the capitals are decorated with a cavetto molding capped by a fillet (Plate XXI, 1). The surface of the latter is plain with the exception of one (RP.L.1) which is over the capital containing the Entombment and the Holy Women at the Sepulcher. Here a row of raised circular areas surrounded by narrow bands alternate with smaller dots. The concave sections of all the abaci are adorned with an acanthuslike pattern. This pattern is made either of seven or nine leaves or a cluster of five or eleven leaves flanked by smaller groups of three or five leaves. In the LP.L the leaves have a spiky, angular character which is not found in the more curved treatment of this motif on the central portal. These variations do not follow any order or sequence. The undercutting is slight, and the abaci as a whole have the appearance of a narrow horizontal band of ornament which echoes the friezelike capitals. The treatment of the ornament is quite different from the rendering of the colonnettes below. Here the relief is much lower and the

[42] The top of RP.L.2 depicts the Labors of the Month. Jean Adhémar, *Influences antiques dans l'art du moyen âge française* (London, 1939),

pl. XXXI, fig. 98, identifies a detail of LP.R.1 as Nessus and Deianira.

pattern simpler so that it will enhance and not disturb the small historiated capitals.

While the abaci are restored only in certain sections, the stringcourses framing the archivolts are entirely modern (see Plates XI and XXI, 2). A fragment of the original has recently been discovered, and according to the architect in charge of the cathedral, it corresponds to the molding now *in situ*. The motif consists of pairs of leaves and buds which frame heads alternating with similar leaves flanking floral fillers. The style is very similar to that of the colonnettes.

FIGURE STYLES ON THE ROYAL PORTAL

Because of the sheer amount of sculpture and the variety of styles it comprises, the Royal Portal must be the work of several sculptors. In an experimental period such as the mid-twelfth century, we should expect that artists would come from different regions of France and would demonstrate varied attitudes toward the representation of the human form. Many critics have attacked the problem of separating the various hands which appear on the three portals. Vöge was the first to distinguish individual sculptors and to attempt to locate their origin.[43] Lasteyrie discussed the sculpture in connection with later portals, while Mayeux divided the sculpture of Saint-Denis, Chartres, Étampes, and other portals into types and assigned to each division a date.[44] Priest, who based his conclusions on Vöge's observations and his own more detailed study of the Royal Portal, divided the sculpture into groups according to style and assigned them to individual artists.[45] Aubert has further discussed the various styles found at Chartres in relation to other twelfth-century portals.[46] In a recent article on Chartres and in a general book on medieval sculpture, the same author describes the different ateliers working at Chartres and divides the activity into two campaigns.[47]

The following study will consist of a detailed consideration of the monumental sculpture, but it will not include a discussion of all the figured sculpture.

Headmaster. The chief sculptor carved the tympanum, lintel, and jamb figures of the central portal (Plates XI, XVII). This attribution follows Vöge and Priest. A comparison of the majestic Christ in the mandorla (Plate XX, 1) with the head to the right in Plate XX, 3, clearly illustrates the stylistic unity of the central portal. The undulating curls of hair, and details of the beard, nose, and eyes are all identical in both heads. The delicately carved drapery of the Christ with its rhythmic spacing of folds and its suggestion of anatomy beneath the garments has numerous counterparts

in the jamb statues on the same portal (Plate XVII).

Three female figures on the central portal, R3, L3, and L5, are all garbed in wattled bodices, mantles, and long robes falling in straight folds to the feet. The arrangement of the costume varies in each figure, but all three have the same placement of hands and symbols. The statue on the right embrasure has an opened bodice and a skirt of many folds decorated with long tassels continuing the ropelike belt. The mantle covers the hair and cascades down to the feet making long folds over the arms. The simplified head (Plate XXI, 1) with its restrained facial expression, together with the delicacy of every detail of drapery, is characteristic of the subtlety of the Headmaster's style. Very similar is the jamb figure, CP.L.5, in which the upper part of the body is covered with a cloak, while most of the hair is hidden beneath the folds of a wimple (Plate XVII, 1). In the figure 3 of the same side, the bodice reveals the shape of the breasts. A striking contrast in texture is achieved by the braided hair next to the wattled garment. The hems of the costumes of all three figures are decorated with minute geometric patterns. The faces of the figures on the left embrasure exhibit refinement and restraint in expression and in modeling, while the rotundity of the shapes are echoed by the curved wimple or the sweep of the bodice.

All five male statues of the central portal display multitudes of small parallel folds, the graceful curves of the cloaks varying an otherwise strict verticality (Plate XVII). While in the female figures there is no attempt to designate the knees, here their location is suggested by a slight bend in silhouette and by a duplication of the folds. The hands and faces are boldly modeled. The eyes are clearly marked but kept close to the surface of the mass. The costumes show even more variety in arrangement. The mantles pass over the left shoulder of each figure, but the manner in which they are worn on the right side differs in each statue. On left figure 2, it passes around the body and is gathered over the left hand. A similar arrangement is seen on the right figure 2, but the cloak is buckled on the shoulder. The main folds fall in delicate diagonal zigzags. Another type of drapery is seen on figures left 1 and right 1 and 4 in which the outer garment is caught in a bunch by the left hand and falls in double folds. The tubular projection extending downward from the hand gives ample support to the scrolls which two of the three are holding. The same delight in the treatment of parallel folds and the same interest in suggesting anatomy through drapery is seen in the Christ of the central tympanum and the Apostles of the lintel (Plate XX, 1). All are surely the work of a single artist.

[43] Vöge, *Die Anfänge des Monumentalen Stiles im Mittelalter.*

[44] Lasteyrie, t. VIII. Mayeux, "Les Grands Portails du XIIe siècle et les Bénédictins de Tiron," *Revue Mabillon,* pp. 96–122.

[45] Priest, "The Masters of the West Façade of Chartres," *Art Studies,* I, 28–44.

[46] Aubert, *French Sculpture at the Beginning of the Gothic Period,* pp. 8–17.

[47] Aubert, "Le Portail royal," pp. 177–218; *La Sculpture française au moyen-âge,* pp. 182–188.

On the basis of a study of tympanum, lintel, and jamb statues of the central portal, it is impossible to agree with critics who argue that the figures on the left side of the right portal and on the right side of the left portal are by the Headmaster (Plate XVII).[48] The statues on the RP.L (Plate XVIII, 2) show strong connections with the ones just described, yet they exhibit certain new mannerisms. The quality of carving seems relatively inferior, perhaps even mechanical. Certain groups of vertical folds are given new emphasis, and elongated parabolic curves of drapery make their appearance (see RP.L.4). Meaningless zigzags of drapery are revealed on the second and third figures of the same embrasure. The flowing robes do not terminate above the feet in an architectural horizontal line. Although the three heads of the RP.L are very fine, some of the extreme delicacy of the chief sculptor's modeling, especially in the cheeks, is wanting. All three figures have the same pose, a similar abundance of small folds, and zigzag hems which catch the eye and detract from the total effect. From a critical analysis of the style it is possible to conclude that these three jamb statues were carved by an artist who approached but failed to capture the Headmaster's majestic quality.[49]

The attribution of the two figures on the right side of the left portal (Plate XVIII, 1) is a more difficult problem. Although the cross-legged arrangement of LP.R.2 resembles some of the Saint-Denis figures (especially Plate VII, 7), the detailed rendering of the drapery and the large oval fold below the left hand differs from any Saint-Denis statue. The other figure on this embrasure is badly damaged, but the style closely resembles that of its neighbor. These figures do not contain the mannerisms of the individual who carved the RP.L jambs just discussed. The quality seems better. The spacing of folds approximates the right leg of CP.R.2 (Plate XVII, 2). These two figures are probably the work of a more gifted sculptor working under the close supervision of the Headmaster.

The Style of Saint-Denis and Étampes. In contrast to the figures already described, the jamb statues on the outer extremities of the Royal Portal (Plate XVI, 1, 2) have many characteristics which are related to the lost jamb figures of Saint-Denis. Moreover, the south portal of Notre-Dame at Étampes contains figures, now headless, which are closely related to those of both Saint-Denis and Chartres. Omitting for the time being any consideration of chronology, a detailed comparison of the Chartres figures (Plate XVI, 1, 2) in relation to these other two monuments will show many common features of style.

Although the six figures which adorn the two embrasures at Chartres are by no means identical in style, they have features in common which distinguish them from the other jamb statues. An almost archaic awkwardness separates them from the sophisticated poise of the Headmaster's sculpture. They are at once squatter and more angular. The wrists are disjointed. Folds of the drapery curve more arbitrarily than in the other jamb figures. The shape of the original stone block is not emphasized by the position of hands, symbols, or garments.

As already pointed out, the figure RP.R.1 (Plate XVI, 2) bears a close affinity to several of the Saint-Denis statues, especially to the Montfaucon preparatory drawing in reverse (Plate VII, 5). In contrast to the regular, almost rectangular silhouette of the jamb statues of the central portal (Plate XVII), this figure has rounded shoulders. The elbows, which curve outward from the waist, extend beyond the hips. The width of the drapery just above the feet is narrower than it is across the hips. This figure shows relatively more articulation of anatomy than do the jamb figures of the Headmaster or those of his assistants, the masters of LP.R and RP.L.

Almost the same style is seen in the adjoining figure (RP. R.2, Plate XVI, 2). In contour, type, and treatment of drapery it is similar to Montfaucon's drawings of the Saint-Denis sculpture. Features such as the elaborate arrangement of double folds falling from the left arm and the ornate band across the thigh are not found in any Montfaucon drawing but do appear in the Étampes figures. The indication of the knees by concentric folds is closer to Étampes than to Saint-Denis. Like the head of the adjoining figure, the silhouette, curled hair, and eyes are related to one of the preserved Saint-Denis heads (Plate VIII).[50]

These statues should not be considered debased works of art. It seems more logical to describe them as the creations of sculptors with a different artistic heritage. Characteristics of the Saint-Denis and Étampes sculpture manifest themselves. The former work, however, exerts the stronger influence. The head (Plate XIX, 2) shows a striking resemblance to the Saint-Denis heads, but, at the same time, produces a less archaic effect. The linear emphasis seen in the Saint-Denis heads has been ironed out. Modeled surfaces flow in a relatively uninterrupted manner. These two statues bear

---

[48] Priest, p. 28. Also Vöge.

[49] Aubert, ("Le Portail royal," p. 198) argues that the RP.L.4 jamb (Plate XVIII, 2) is the product of the Saint-Denis atelier which had carved the two female statues on the extremities of the façade during the late 1140's and which around 1150 carved the two male figures, RP.R.1 and 2 (Plate XVI, 2). He also believes (pp. 204–205) that the other two figures of the RP.L are by the Headmaster and that the head of the statue nearest the door dates from the thirteenth century or later.

[50] Priest, pp. 30–34, attributes all the figures of the RP.R to the "Saint-Denis Master of Chartres." This conclusion seems correct. It is necessary to add, however, that there are some connections between these figures and the sculpture at Étampes. Aubert ("Le Portail royal," p. 198) assigns the two male statues to the Saint-Denis atelier, which, according to his argument, had carved the two female statues on the outside embrasures around 1145 and these figures around 1150, thus helping to establish the formula used by the Headmaster.

little relationship to the jambs of the central portal, yet, they possess an artistic integrity of their own.

The second and third figures LP.L (Plate XVI, 1) are so close in costume and style to Étampes figures (Plates XXIII and XXIV) that it is safe to assume they are the work of the same artist or atelier.[51] By comparing Chartres LP.L.3 with Étampes R.1 (Plate XXIII, 2) and Chartres LP.L.2 with Étampes L.2 (Plate XXIV), one can see that all four have the same crudeness, the same disjointed articulation, the same symbols of staff and scroll, the same costumes of bodice and cloak, and the same treatment of drapery with double folds emphasizing each leg. The feet splay out and rest on supports of three curved tiers. The arbitrary method of designating the extended stomach by repeated oval folds, and the straight fall of drapery down the legs in contrast to the vertical row of parabolic curves down the middle of each figure make it clear that the same artist or artists worked at both places. Like the head RP.R.1, this head (LP.L.2, Plate XIX, 1) is modeled in gradually curving planes. In shape of the head and arrangement of hair and beard it is very similar to one of the Baltimore heads from Saint-Denis (Plate IX, 1, 2).

Two jamb statues remain to be discussed: the female figures on the side embrasures (Plate XVI, 1, 2). These have certain characteristics in common as well as features similar to other statues on their corresponding jambs. In both, the garments fall from modeled stomachs in small parallel folds; they are enhanced by pairs of cordlike tassels extending almost to the feet. The stance, with frontal feet on a conical socle, is the same. The general silhouette is marked by sloping shoulders, projecting elbows, curved torsos, and drapery flaring outward above the feet. If these two figures are contrasted with CP.R.3 (Plate XVII, 2), it can be seen that the basic conception of the human form differs profoundly, although there are apparent stylistic parallels.

In spite of the similarities between these two figures, there is even more evidence for their connection with the other statues on their respective embrasures. For example, the head of the female on the right portal (Plate XVI, 2) exhibits the same treatment of eye, cheek, and neck as the adjoining figures. The mantle, covering the left breast and the left side of the figure, is modeled in the same fashion as that of the other two neighboring statues. The upper part of the female figure on the left portal shows an arrangement of bodice and cloak identical to that of the two figures on the same embrasure as well as that on the jamb statues at Étampes, even though the lower part of the torso and the arrangement of

the feet differ. Priest believes that the lower part of this figure was completed by the Headmaster but neither the subtle treatment of vertical drapery folds nor the rectangularity of silhouette seen in the jamb statues of the central portal is to be found here.[52] There is more evidence to conclude that these two female statues are the creation of the same master who did the rest of the statues on the same side of the two portals.

The remaining undiscussed sculpture of the royal portal has been assigned to different sculptors by Priest.[53] The angel of the sundial on the south tower must have adorned the central portal. Priest concludes that the Saint-Denis Master at Chartres carved the figures on several of the pilasters between the portals and flanking the entrances as well as several of the capitals. Priest attributes to the "Master of the Angels" and his three assistants the north and south tympana and the majority of the archivolts. To the work of the Étampes Master he adds several capitals. All these conclusions seem correct; for the purpose of this study a detailed discussion of this sculpture is unnecessary.

The only other unmentioned sculpture is the double lintel of the right portal. On the basis of the possible Provençal origin of this master Priest allots this sculpture to the "Little Master of Saint-Gilles" and, at the same time, points out the relationship between his figure style and that of the Headmaster.[54] The close affinity in headdress, handling of hair, and profile between several heads on both lintels and the heads of Christ and the jamb statues carved by the Headmaster (see Plate XX, 1, 3, 4) leads to the conclusion that the sculptor or sculptors who carved the double lintel were profoundly influenced by the Headmaster's style.[55]

ONE OR TWO CAMPAIGNS ON THE ROYAL PORTAL?

What is the explanation of the many different figure styles found on the Royal Portal at Chartres? Assuming that they are creations of different individuals, did these sculptors work at the same time but under the general supervision of a single master? Or are they the result of two campaigns of activity? The problem is very complicated if we attempt to include the provenance of the styles of the sculptors, their development as individual artists, and their relative age or generation. It is, of course, impossible to say exactly how much freedom of action and expression each sculptor enjoyed.

Two Campaigns. Several students of the problem believe that the sculpture of the Royal Portal was carved in two

[51] Priest, pp. 37–40, calls these figures the work of the Étampes Master, while Aubert ("Le Portail royal," p. 194) argues that they were carved around 1145 by the most conservative atelier which, in the face of competition, left Chartres and journeyed to Étampes.

[52] Priest, p. 40.

[53] Priest, pp. 28–44.

[54] Priest, pp. 40–44.

[55] M. Aubert ("Le Portail royal," pp. 206–207) states that the RP. tympanum and lower lintel (Nativity etc.) were carved around 1145 with Burgundian overtones; then the same atelier carved the LP. tympanum, lintel, and some of the Elders of the Apocalypse. Aubert also states that a second and different atelier carved the RP. upper lintel between 1150 and 1155.

campaigns. In an examination of the pros and cons of this solution, it will become apparent that there is little evidence to substantiate this theory.

One writer explains the stylistic discrepancies of the jamb figures by assuming that the statues on the extremities of the façade were carved around 1145 and the Headmaster's jambs were made in the 1170's.[56] This theory cannot stand because of the existence of the Le Mans portal, which is dependent on the Headmaster's sculpture at Chartres and was completed in 1158.

As already outlined, another writer argues that a smaller project including a central portal with jamb figures, trumeau, tympanum, and small unadorned flanking portals was first planned between the east piers of the towers.[57] Then, around 1150, according to this theory, it was decided to elaborate the ensemble and erect it in its present location. The decision to change the location around 1150 would provide the dividing line between the two periods of artistic activity. To the first campaign would belong the jamb statues on the extremities of the façade, the right-hand tympanum of the Virgin and the lower lintel of the right portal. All the rest of the sculpture would fall in the period 1150 to 1155.[58]

What are the arguments for and against the theory of two campaigns?

(1) The marked differences between the Étampes-like figures (LP.L) and the Saint-Denis-like jambs (RP.R) on the one hand as against the Headmaster's figures (CP) on the other seem to be explained on the basis of an evolution of style over a ten-year period (1145–1155). Thus, the Étampes Master would have carved the extreme two left statues (1145–1150) and then journeyed to Étampes, while the Saint-Denis Master would have carved the two females on the outside embrasures (1145–1150) and then, towards 1150, carved the two male figures RP.R, forecasting the style of the Headmaster. From 1150 to 1155 the Headmaster would have supervised the carving of the rest of the sculpture.[59] On the other hand, the very size of the program at Chartres implies the work of many sculptors. At Saint-Denis, as can be seen from a study of the three engravings in Montfaucon or in a contrast of the two Baltimore heads, several sculptors with quite distinct styles worked. At Étampes the single portal is harmonious stylistically. The two-campaign theory overlooks the importance of the individuality of the sculptors and the different heritages which they may represent. Is it necessary therefore, to conclude that the jambs by the Saint-Denis Master and the Étampes Master are earlier or can it be argued just as successfully that the Headmaster, presumably in charge of the whole project, had great respect for the artists who had worked on two very important earlier monu-

ments?[60] The latter argument would explain the differences in style between the extreme side jamb figures and those on the central portal.

(2) The theory of two campaigns might account for the difference in portal design between the central and the flanking portals (Plate XI). The use of crenelated canopies over the jambs of the first campaign (LP.L and RP.R, Plate XVI, 1, 2) seem to have been respected in the second campaign so that the inner flanks of the side portals have similar canopies. Equally valid, however, is the argument that the Headmaster allowed these two sculptors to cap their statues with elaborate canopies and then had his assistants conform to this scheme on the opposite embrasures (LP.R and RP.L, Plate XI).

(3) If the earlier project for portals between the east piers of the towers was abandoned around 1150 and the portals then erected in their present location with a vaulted narthex and gallery behind them, the stained-glass windows would have had protection from the fire of 1194 which consumed the whole eastern portion of the church. On the other hand, is it certain that the fire of 1194 would have destroyed the stained-glass windows if the portals were in a position equivalent to the first bay of the present nave? The vaulted porch built by Raimbaud (see the engaged columns marked X and Y on Lefèvre-Pontalis' plan, Plate XXXVIII, 1) would have protected the portals. Whether the gallery above the porch was also vaulted is not known. The extent of the fire is likewise unknown. It is not necessary, however, to argue that the three stained-glass windows of the façade must have been behind a vaulted area. The survival of the twelfth-century section of "La Belle Verrière," now preserved in the south ambulatory, is worth mentioning in this connection.

(4) This erection of the façade on its present site in the early 1150's might explain the lack of connection in moldings and masonry courses between the base of the north tower, begun in 1134, and the left portal (see Plates XI and XXI, 3). The south tower, which was under construction in 1145, would be contemporary with the three portals. This theory would account for the liaison between the south tower and the portals apparent in the continuity of moldings in the bases and in the courses of masonry in the spandrel above (Plate XXI, 2, 4). In spite of the fact that the masonry above the archivolts of the right portal (Plate XXI, 2) appear to establish the date for the erection of the portals in the middle of the century, there is more evidence to prove that the façade was put in its present position after most of the south tower had been completed. Some of the courses are carried around the angle separating the portal from the south tower. This suggests either that the stonecutters left blocks projecting

[56] Gardner, *Medieval Sculpture in France*, pp. 213–214.
[57] Aubert, "Le Portail royal," pp. 188–190.
[58] Aubert, "Le Portail royal," pp. 188, 192, 194–212.

[59] Aubert, "Le Portail royal," pp. 194–200.
[60] In Part III, I shall attempt to prove that Étampes is earlier than Chartres.

from the tower in expectancy of the construction of the portals or that the south tower and portals were built simultaneously around the year 1150. On close scrutiny of the masonry along the top of all three portals (see Plate XI), it can be seen that even courses of masonry of the same width extend across the façade from the apexes of the archivolts of the side portals. It is not surprising to find that the layers of masonry are uneven in the extreme left spandrel because we know that the north tower was approaching completion by 1150, but how shall we explain the same sort of unevenness in the courses of the extreme right spandrel if portals and tower were being constructed at the same time? From a study of the bases on the extremities of the Royal Portal (Plate XXI, 3, 4), the lack of harmony between bases and north tower is striking when contrasted with the apparent harmony of bases and moldings into the south tower. There are, however, certain details which disrupt even the apparent liaison between right portal and south tower. What is the function of the small base on the next to the top step (Plate XXI, 4)? Lefèvre-Pontalis points out that the molding extending around the base of the tower stops at this small *tablette*, which he explains as a slip in planning.[61] If the southwest and northwest corners of the south tower are compared (see façade, Plate B; plan, Plates XXXVIII, 3; and Plate XXI, 2, 4), we see that part of the wall buttress on the north side of the tower has been incorporated into the façade masonry. This fact explains the break in masonry in the extreme right spandrel because the blocks next to the convex angle of the tower are actually a part of the tower and the façade has been fitted into the tower.[62] Further, a study of the masonry between the south tower and the stained glass of the scenes from the Passion of Christ reveals the same relationship between tower and façade for a width of one block only. The remaining courses are continuous across the windows and are unrelated to the tower.[63] The moldings which divide the stories of the south tower end abruptly against the façade only to appear on the north elevation of the tower (see Plate XXXVIII, 5). On this basis of study, it appears that there is ample evidence to prove that the Royal Portal did not grow up on its present location concurrently with the south tower, and thus must have been moved to its present site after its completion.

(5) The erection of the portals around 1150, in their present position, would explain the cutting of an entrance on the south face of the south tower (Plate XXII, 5) to maintain adequate access to the crypt without entering the church itself.[64] On the other hand, one can argue with equal validity that this portal was constructed in order to provide more convenient circulation between the Hôtel-Dieu and the crypt.

In addition to the arguments discussed above, there are others which remain unanswered if the two-campaign theory is accepted.

(1) The theory of two campaigns does not explain the existing crowded character of the portals themselves and the absence of the border on the south edge of the right-hand stained-glass window. If the portals were erected in their present site around 1150, how can we explain the pinched effect of the central portal, especially noticeable on the ends of the lintel, the loss of ten centimeters of both lintels of the right portal, and the damage to the stained-glass window? There is no instance in all medieval sculpture of such serious miscalculations. If the sculptors desired to establish an alignment between the middle of the central portal and the main axis of the church, which is slightly to the south,[65] would not the south portal have been planned smaller to fit the space alloted?

(2) No ornamental sculpture exists which might conceivably have been part of an earlier campaign. All the bases below the jambs, all the ornamented colonnettes between the monumental statues, and all the abaci above the capitals exhibit a uniformity of style. This seems to indicate a single building campaign.

(3) The capitals constitute a unified iconographical scheme, although it is true that some of the scenes are out of Biblical order. In spite of this organized sequence of scenes from the New Testament, which must have been planned at one time, several of the capitals are related very closely in style to the Saint-Denis and Étampes masters, but the arrangement of capitals precludes their separation into two periods of time.

(4) A study of the lintels of the right portal proves that both reflect the Headmaster's style.[66] If we compare the head of the Christ of the central tympanum (Plate XX, 1) with figures of the Presentation of the Virgin (Plate XX, 2, 4), it is clear the sculptor who carved the upper lintel of the right portal was, to say the least, strongly affected by the Headmaster. Even more striking are the similarities in profiles, headdress, and treatment of hair in the Joseph of the Nativity on the lower lintel and the head of one of the Headmaster's jambs on the central portal, CP.L.2 (see Plate XX, 3, 4). It would be difficult to argue that the monumental character of the Headmaster's sculpture grew out of the small size and narrative character of the right portal lintels.

---

[61] Lefèvre-Pontalis, "Nouvelles Études," p. 480.

[62] See Lefèvre-Pontalis' detail of the reconstruction of this area ("Nouvelles Études," p. 479, fig. 14).

[63] Lefèvre-Pontalis, "Nouvelles Études," pl. IX shows detail of junction of windows and tower.

[64] Aubert, "Le Portail royal," p. 191.

[65] Aubert, "Le Portail royal," pp. 192–193.

[66] Aubert (*ibid.*, p. 205) dates the RP. lower lintel 1145 and (p. 208) dates the upper lintel 1150–1155.

One Campaign. The weight of evidence seems to point to another solution: namely, that the Royal Portal was a single coöperative venture in which individual artists decorated sections of the façade under the general supervision of one sculptor.

A study of the ornament brings out strong evidence for the one-campaign theory. As already indicated, the differences in the ornamented colonnettes are only qualitative. The best ornament (Plates XII, XIII, XIV, 2, 4) decorates the Headmaster's sculpture on the central portal. The colonnettes LP.L flanking the jambs by the Étampes Master (Plates XIV, 1, 3, and XV, 1, 2) are of almost as fine quality. A falling off is seen on the extreme right embrasure, while the poorest ornament (Plates XVIII, 1, 2, and XV, 3, 4) decorates the jambs carved by the Headmaster's assistants on the LP.R and RP.L.

On the basis of this evidence, several possible theories of workshop procedure can be cited. First, the artist who carved the jamb statues for one section of the portals also carved the accompanying ornament. Following this assumption, the Headmaster would have carved the ornament of the central portal, while his assistants would have been responsible for the colonnettes as well as the jamb statues on the LP.R and RP.L. The discrepancies in quality might be explained equally well by a different assumption: that the best ornamental carvers worked for the Headmaster, while the less skilled ones aided his assistants. A third possibility is that the ornamented colonnettes were carved en masse and the best ones were chosen by the Headmaster to decorate his jamb figures while his assistants were left with the least successful ones (Plate XV, 3, 4).

The fine quality of the ornament flanking the jambs by the Étampes Master is of little help in choosing one of the three theories outlined above. The Étampes Master represents an older yet respected tradition. He could have carved the colonnettes himself (Plates XIV, 1, 3, and XV, 1, 2); or he could have delegated this work to an able assistant; or he could have had second or sharing choice with the Headmaster from all the colonnettes in the *chantier*.

More important than all this hypothesizing is the inescapable fact that all the ornament is homogeneous stylistically. The carving of all the colonnettes manifests a more plastic treatment of motifs first employed at Saint-Denis.

In this mid-twelfth-century formation of a new type of portal with integrated jamb statues, a considerable diversity in attitude should be expected, especially since Chartres seems to have been a point of convergence for artists from different parts of France. In the thirteenth century, however, a decided uniformity of spirit comes into being. The transept portals at Chartres provide clear examples. Yet, how is one to explain the quite exceptional variation in the sculpture of the west portals of Reims — the Annunciation as opposed to

the Visitation groups? The sculptor who carved the Visitation was inspired by Roman sculpture of which Reims abounds, while the other manifests the main attitude of the thirteenth century. A close scrutiny of the Parthenon sculpture likewise reveals, especially in the metopes, many hands of varying degrees of quality.

The one-campaign argument implies, of course, that the portals were completed either in their present location, or between the east piers of the towers, or in the first bay of the present nave. The evidence already cited eliminates the first solution. Again, close study of the ornament adds further evidence. The upper segments of the jambs exhibit fragments of colonnettes with the same motif, without small moldings to indicate tops and bottoms. This suggests the removal of the façade from an original emplacement to its present one (see Plate XVI, 1, LP.L). In several instances, colonnette has been put in place upside down (for example, see CP. L.2 top, Plate XVII, 1; and Plate XXI, 1).

Not only is there insufficient width between the eastern piers of the towers for the three portals, but there is also no evidence of an adequate subfoundation in this area. Thus the portals must have been constructed originally in the first bay of the thirteenth-century nave, as Lefèvre-Pontalis maintained (Plate XXXVIII, 2). His reconstruction is not altered by Fels's discovery of the foundations of an eleventh-century central tower. The twelfth-century architects merely employed the eastern part of the old foundations to support the Royal Portal and its stained-glass windows. The width of this area was ample for the façade as Lefèvre-Pontalis' plan clearly indicates. The present liaison in moldings between the south tower and the base of the south portal would also have existed in the easterly location in the nave, assuming as we may that both the façade and the tower were being constructed simultaneously.

When were the portals moved to their present westerly position? The claim that the finished façade was moved after the middle of the century or in the 1180's does not account for the difficulty of vaulting the area between the towers, a fact which Lefèvre-Pontalis brought out clearly.[67] All of the bases and the remnants of columns and capitals on the inside faces of the towers are related to the towers proper and bear no evidence of having supported vaults.

The fire of 1194 and the consequent construction of the Gothic cathedral afford good and sufficient reason for the moving of the original façade. The only objections which can be cited against this argument are the fact that the glass has survived and the presence of a new doorway cut into the south side of the south portal. The unknown extent of the fire and the unknown character of the gallery over Raimbaud's porch make it difficult to settle this question.

[67] Lefèvre-Pontalis, "Nouvelles Études," pp. 464–472.

The south doorway might have been cut in to increase circulation, thus having no bearing on the problem whatever. Finally, the general appearance of the small twelfth-century façade (see Plate B), crammed between the west faces of the soaring towers, is far removed from the powerful and harmonious effect the entire edifice would have if the portals remained east of the towers until the conflagration of 1194 necessitated the building of the High Gothic cathedral.[68]

[68] See Kenneth Conant's reconstruction in his book, *Early Medieval Church Architecture* (Baltimore: Johns Hopkins Press 1942), Plate L.

PART THREE

THE SOUTH PORTAL OF NOTRE-DAME AT ÉTAMPES

THE CHURCH of Notre-Dame at Étampes possesses one of the most interesting portals of the twelfth century (Plate XXIII, 1). Because of its close relationship to the west portals at Chartres, critics have attempted either to establish the priority of Étampes or to consider it a provincial reflection of Chartres sculpture.[1] If the jamb figures of Étampes are compared to the two on the extreme left side of the Royal Portal at Chartres (Plate XVI, 1), the intimate connection between the two monuments becomes so evident that one must believe the same sculptor worked in both places. A somewhat cruder treatment in the Étampes sculpture has been interpreted as signifying that the portal was inspired by Chartres. On the other hand, this difference might be as readily explained on the grounds that Étampes represents an earlier experiment. Unfortunately, there are no documents to help solve the problem.

To arrive at a definite conclusion, the Étampes portal must be examined from several points of view. The importance of Étampes in the history of twelfth-century France far exceeded its present role as wheat market to the regions lying south of Paris. The residence of royalty at Étampes and the many religious councils held there are of primary concern for this discussion. The iconography as well as the design of the portal must be analyzed. A comparative study of ornament and figure style in relation to the dated portals of Saint-Denis and to the sculpture of Chartres, presumably begun around 1145, is essential before any satisfactory solution can be reached.

ÉTAMPES IN THE TWELFTH CENTURY

The history of Étampes in the twelfth century suggests greater reason for the appellation *Portail Royal* for the single portal of its church of Notre-Dame than does the history of Chartres for the elaborate triple portals of its cathedral.

Neither the town of Chartres nor the twelfth-century construction of the cathedral was under royal patronage, whereas the whole church of Notre-Dame d'Étampes manifests the religious enthusiasm of the kings of France.[2] Founded in the first half of the eleventh century by Robert II, the church grew rapidly during the following century as a result of the financial backing of Louis VI, *le Gros* (1108–1137), and Louis VII, *le Jeune* (1137–1180).[3] In their time the town of Étampes seems to have been not only the favorite retreat for the royal court, but also served as the meeting place for great councils which attempted to solve the religious disputes threatening the very backbone of the church.

The church of Notre-Dame was built almost entirely by donations of the kings of France, who concerned themselves with many of its administrative problems.[4] Their patronage was not confined to the church of Notre-Dame. It is known that Robert II, son of Hugues Capet, patronized the whole town of Étampes.[5] Louis VI and his son, Louis VII, built a huge château on the hill overlooking the town. The road which still passes along the southern side of Notre-Dame led directly to the royal residence. Seats for the royal entourage were located in the choir. As a result of the construction of the south portal it was possible to enter the church without disturbing worshippers congregated in the nave,[6] a convenience of access for the court which was probably the reason for this portal.

In the first three decades of the twelfth century Louis VI had strongly curbed the power of the vassals. With the help of the clergy and the townspeople, he fought against the feudal powers of the individual barons. Communes were given their freedom. Étampes seems to have remained outside but profited from the revolutions which brought about these fundamental social changes. In a charter of 1123 Louis VI exempted a whole district of Étampes from taxes and from compulsory military service in order to balance the

---

[1] Summary of conclusions. Lefèvre-Pontalis, "Étampes," p. 26: portal about 1150 in the Chartres school. Lefèvre, *Le Portail royal d'Étampes*, pp. 112–113: portal finished before 1130. Aubert, *French Sculpture at the Beginning*, pp. 25–27: *ca.* 1150, one of the oldest portals based on Chartres. Priest, pp. 37–40: Étampes earlier than Chartres, mostly on iconographical grounds. Aubert, "Le Portail royal," p. 194: sculptors carved two extreme left figures at Chartres and then went to Étampes. Aubert, *La Sculpture française*, pp. 191–192: carved towards 1150.

[2] Lefèvre, p. 111.
[3] Lefèvre-Pontalis, *Les Campagnes de construction de Notre-Dame d'Étampes*, p. 7.
[4] Lefèvre, p. 1.
[5] Maxime de Mont-Rond, *Essais historiques sur la ville d'Étampes* (1836), p. 41.
[6] Lefèvre, p. 111.

regulations which required these people to furnish all the cooking utensils for the court.[7] In 1137 at the beginning of his reign, Louis VII granted other privileges to the people of Étampes.[8] The freedom of Étampes lasted until 1189 at which time it was revoked by Philippe-Auguste because of abuses by clergy and nobles.[9]

Councils were held in Étampes in 1048, 1092, 1112, and 1130. Pope Calixtus II consecrated the nearby Abbey of Morigny in 1119.[10] The National Council of 1130 met at Étampes to end the schism which followed upon the death of Honorius II. All the prelates and royalty of France discussed the relative merits of the two contestants claiming the papal throne, Innocent II and Anacletus II.[11] Louis VI, Suger, Abélard, Geoffroy of Chartres, Bernard of Clairvaux, and many other dignitaries were present. Partly as a result of Bernard's eloquence Innocent II was proclaimed Pope and the church of France, led by Bernard, later confirmed him. Innocent journeyed from Chartres to spend four days in Étampes, January 18 to 21, 1131.[12] It is possible that these historic discussions were held in the church of Notre-Dame.

One of the most exciting moments in the history of Étampes was the Assembly convoked by Louis VII in 1147. The meeting was held in the royal residence on February 16, and the final plans for the Second Crusade were laid. Suger was against the launching of the crusade, but was overruled. Later in the day, he was elected Regent of France.[13]

It is clear that Étampes played a vital role in state and religious affairs during the twelfth century. Why Étampes was selected ahead of such places as Chartres, Paris, Sens, or Orléans it is difficult to say. Étampes was centrally located in the prosperous royal domain, and yet detached from the more strenuous life of Paris. This atmosphere was probably considered more suitable for religious debates.

In his study of the iconography of the portal of Notre-Dame at Étampes, Lefèvre believes the portal itself was constructed either as a result of the Council of 1130 or, more probably, before that time. He considers that the high point in the history of Étampes came in that year and that the portal may have been done as early as the 1120's.[14] This contention is based on merely general considerations. In discussing the subject matter and its relationship to the teachings of Saint Bernard, he points out that Henri de France, brother of Louis VII and Abbot of the Chapter from 1140 to 1146, was a close friend of Bernard of Clairvaux.[15] In spite of all the evidence of royal patronage and religious enthusiasm at Étampes, there is nothing definite to assist in dating the portals. Yet the fact that so many decisions of paramount importance for the whole future of France were made within its walls should remind us that Étampes must not be passed off as the small provincial town it now is and that, therefore, its portal is not necessarily a reflection of Chartres.

ICONOGRAPHY OF THE ROYAL PORTAL OF ÉTAMPES

The theme of the south portal at Étampes is usually thought to be the Ascension (Plate XXIII, 1). Lefèvre, however, believes that it is not an Ascension but an Apocalyptic scene.[16] The fact that the Christ of the tympanum is standing still and not mounting toward heaven helps to justify his conclusion. The standing Christ represents the human personality of the Son of Man — the Lamb of God. In his teachings and writings Saint Bernard makes a clear distinction between the character of the seated as opposed to the standing Christ. According to Lefèvre, the whole portal represents the glorification of the Lamb which, through its connection with the Eucharist, symbolizes the Redemption. The Elders of the Apocalypse occupy the archivolts, and on the lintel appear the twelve Apostles with Saint John the Baptist on the left and the Virgin on the right. The Apostle next to the Virgin turns away from the scene above and makes a gesture toward the Virgin who is present to see her Son glorified. All these figures offer themselves to Christ in sacrifice and at the same time glorify Christ as Savior and Redeemer.[17]

This subject matter, if accepted,[18] illustrates how monumental sculpture reflected the religious ideas of the time. Bernard of Clairvaux was preaching the doctrine of redemption in an age struggling against heresy. The very existence of the Old Testament figures on the jambs and scenes of both Testaments on the capitals (Plate XXIII, 4, 5), together with the Church as symbolized by the Apostles, is an indication of the attempt on the part of the leading prelates to reëstablish the power and glory of Christianity. Bernard, the man and his teachings, in spite of the fact that he denounced excessive ornamentation, seems to be reflected in this portal at Étampes.

CONSTRUCTION AND PORTAL DESIGN

The history of the building campaigns of the church does not furnish any significant facts which help date the portal.

---

[7] Mont-Rond, pp. 84–89.

[8] Alliot, *Cartulaire de Notre-Dame d'Étampes, documents publiés par la Société Historique et Archéologique du Gatinais III* (1888), p. 126.

[9] Mont-Rond, p. 85.

[10] Mont-Rond, pp. 103, 110–111.

[11] Mont-Rond, pp. 111–116.

[12] Lefèvre, p. 80 and n.

[13] Mont-Rond, pp. 120–122.

[14] Lefèvre, pp. 1–92. On the basis of the history of Romanesque sculpture, it is difficult to agree with Lefèvre's conclusion.

[15] Lefèvre, p. 83.

[16] Lefèvre, pp. 49–74, also his *Le Portail royal d'Étampes et la doctrine de Saint-Irénee sur la Redemption*.

[17] Lefèvre (1908), pp. 51–63.

[18] These conclusions on the iconography of Étampes are directly opposed to the reasoning of Alan Priest in his article. Priest believes that the scene in the tympanum is an Ascension, while the fourteen figures on the lintel include two extra men who witnessed this event. He identifies the central figure on the lintel with the starred halo as the Virgin (pp. 37–40).

At some time early in the second quarter of the twelfth century, the narthex, nave, and part of the north transept were constructed.[19] According to Lefèvre-Pontalis, the portal, leading into the second bay of the nave, was erected toward the middle of the century. Finally, with the addition of the south transept later in the century, its right side was partially cut off. As a result, the jamb figures of Saints Peter and Paul which once occupied the positions on the extreme sides of the portal were removed to a chapel inside the church (Plate XXIII, 3).[20] A standing figure, corresponding to that beyond the angel on the left spandrel, has been lost.

From the point of view of construction, the Étampes portal (Plates XXIII, 1 and XXIV, 1) exhibits greater affinity with Chartres than with Saint-Denis. The pedestals supporting the jamb figures have the same arrangement of blocks as at Chartres, and each tier of masonry contains the same type of moldings (Plate XXIV, 1). The profiles of the moldings, however, especially on the bases directly below the jamb figures, are more archaic at Étampes. They do not bulge and hang over the concave molding below as at Chartres (Plate XIII, 3). The addition of a considerable amount of concrete makes it impossible to study the joints of masonry below the paneled areas. A cross section at the level of the bottom of the jamb statues shows the same arrangement of alternating large and small reëntrant angles filled with columns and connecting moldings as at Chartres.

The pointing of the archivolts does not, of course, help determine the date. When the arch is dissociated from any structural function in connection with ribbed vaults, its form varies greatly. At Saint-Denis the arches are almost round, whereas at Chartres and Étampes they are pointed. Yet Le Mans, completed in 1158, has a round arch.

The design of the whole portal shows features which are related to both Saint-Denis and Chartres. The problem at Étampes is entirely different, however, for, like the Miègeville door of Saint-Sernin at Toulouse, it is a single portal opening into the south aisle. Naturally, its sides must be more prominent since it cannot depend on flanking portals or wall buttresses. The general proportions resemble the Chartres portals, although the bases are higher in relation to the total height of the jambs (Plate XXIII, 2). In contrast to Saint-Denis, where the jamb statues filled the whole area between bases and capitals, here there are elaborate canopies and sections of undecorated columns above the figures. This same arrangement is found on the right and left portals at Chartres (Plate XVI, 1, 2), but the jamb figures stand on short columns and do not rest directly on the bases. Because the pedestals at Chartres are so small in relation to the jambs and because the figures are placed almost in the middle of the jambs, the statues give the appearance both of being

hung from above and, at the same time, upholding the superstructure. At Étampes, the figures occupy the lower three-quarters of the jambs and give the impression of being supports. The jambs flanking the door are unadorned and support the capitals which, in turn, sustain the lintel and tympanum. This feature is not found at Chartres, but is seen on all three portals at Saint-Denis. In contrast to Saint-Denis, however, these first jambs are decorated only by paneling and not by elaborate scenes surrounded by ornament. The awkwardness of the relationship between ex-lintel, first jamb, and capitals, noted at Saint-Denis, is eliminated here.

These points of similarity between Étampes and Saint-Denis which are not found at Chartres might lead to the conclusion that Étampes is earlier than Chartres. The flat first jambs of Étampes might, however, be explained just as readily by their connection with the undecorated jambs on the extremities of this portal. Thus the different nature of the problem itself may be the cause of this treatment of the first jamb just as much as any direct influence from Saint-Denis.

ORNAMENT

Étampes does not possess the degree of elaborate ornamental decoration which is found at Saint-Denis and at Chartres. Ornament is confined to the pedestals below the jamb figures, to the abaci above the capitals, to the border encircling the outer archivolt, and to the horizontal cornice at the top of the portal (Plate XXIII, 1, 4, 5). All this decoration bears a striking resemblance to Chartres.

The pedestals below the monumental figures (Plate XXIV, 1) are paneled as are the corresponding areas at Chartres, but lack the elaborate borders with circular indentations and the moldings punctuated by rows of squares and elongated rectangles. Contrast a detail of Chartres (Plate XIII, 3) with one of Étampes (Plate XXIV, 1). Does it necessarily follow that Étampes is a reduction or simplification of the Chartres pedestal? Chartres might just as well represent the elaboration of the experimental stage of Étampes. Several other portals of a date later than Chartres, Saint-Germain-des-Prés in Paris, Nesle-la-Reposte, Châlons-sur-Marne, and a portal preserved in the west façade of Rouen Cathedral, all have pedestals which are ornate versions of those on the west portals of Chartres. From the general development in the twelfth century, it might be concluded that on the basis of the treatment of the bases Étampes is the earliest of the series.

The acanthuslike motif found on the abaci is identical with that on the archivolt and cornice above the tympanum (Plate XXIII, 4, 5). It is composed of oval areas filled with ten leaves arranged in fan-shaped fashion, alternating with

[19] Lefèvre-Pontalis, "Étampes," pp. 7–8.
[20] Saint Peter measures 2.35 meters and Saint Paul 2.40 meters. These

measurements correspond to the average height of the jamb statues.

groups of leaves which, curving out and over, project slightly from the concave surface of the molding. In the abaci, the flaring parts appear on the projecting and reëntrant angles of each jamb and in the middle of the sides; elsewhere, this alternation of flat and projecting areas has no structural significance. At Chartres, this same design decorates the abaci above the capitals of all three portals. There is, however, more variety in the actual treatment of the leaves at Chartres. As stated earlier, the leaves on the extreme left embrasure are stiffer and more angular than those on the central portal (Plate XXI, 1). The leaves filling the main unit vary in number on the Chartres portals from five to eleven leaves. At Étampes the fan-shaped areas are uniformly filled with ten leaves. Is this difference a case of moving from uniformity to complexity or vice versa?[21]

FIGURE STYLE I: RELATIONSHIP TO CHARTRES

The relationship of the monumental sculpture of Étampes and Chartres presents a complicated problem. The style of the figures at Étampes is cruder and more archaic than the closely related statues at Chartres (Plate XVI, 1), yet certain mannerisms appear in this sculpture which are not found at Chartres.

In the discussion of the various individual artists who participated in the decoration of the west portals of Chartres, the similarities existing between certain figures, especially the LP.L.2 and 3 and the jamb statues of Étampes, were mentioned. It was pointed out that not only the stance, costume, and position of limbs, but also the treatment of drapery were so close as to lead to the conclusion that at least one sculptor worked at both places. The differences, however, should now be emphasized. In general, there is a thickness and ropelike quality in the drapery in contrast to the more delicate carving of folds in the Chartres figures.

The proportions of the majority of the Étampes jamb figures (Plates XXIII, 2, and XXIV) are different from the two figures at Chartres: at Étampes, about five heads high; at Chartres, nearly six. In silhouette, the curves of shoulders, elbows, and wrists appear in both monuments, but most of the Étampes figures do not taper down to narrow hips, knees, and ankles, as do the two figures from Chartres (Plate XVI, 1). Within the outlines, the arrangement of the parts of the body is the same. Broken wrists, disjointed elbows, and angular hands are seen in all figures. In contrast to the architectural arrangement in the central portal at Chartres, the hands and symbols of the Étampes figures and those on the side embrasure at Chartres do not emphasize the main axes. Several, however, hold staffs which divide the figures in the middle.

The male costume, consisting of an undergarment covered with a cloak falling in a loop in the center of the figure and forming double folds extending to just above the knees, is found on the two Chartres figures and on the so-called Moses, David, and Solomon of Étampes, L.2 and R.1 and 2 (Plates XXIV and XXIII, 2). The first statue on the left and the Saints Peter and Paul, now inside the church (Plate XXIII, 3), exhibit a different arrangement in which the mantle breaks into double folds over one leg and then curves down across the other leg. The strictly symmetrical adjustment of drapery in this type is broken, and the knee on the side with more drapery is designated by elaborate circular folds (see detail Plate XXIV, 4). The figures in the tympanum and the statue flanking the spandrel are of the first type, while the two spandrel angels in their three-quarter poses follow the second (Plate XXIII, 1).

The two female figures on the extreme sides of the portal wear garments with three sets of vertical folds separated by curved folds. The bodices, with circular folds emphasizing the breasts, are enhanced by geometrically patterned borders and by the strands of braided hair.

From an examination of the drapery certain differences in style between the Étampes and Chartres figures become clear. Instead of the many small, cascading folds of the Chartres figures (Plate XVI, 1), the drapery stands out more prominently in relation to the figures as a whole (Plate XXIV, 3, 4). The rugged stiffness of such Étampes statues as the Elders of the Apocalypse (Plate XXIII, 4) in the archivolts or the spandrel angels or the figures on the jambs is loosened up in the two Chartres statues. The almost excessive linear quality of Étampes is seen to better advantage in the Saint Peter (Plate XXIII, 3) which has been protected from weathering since the late twelfth century. Stark crispness of drapery is also found in the Saint Paul (not illustrated).

A comparison of details of the figures of both monuments helps bring out these differences. The treatment of drapery over the left leg of both Chartres jambs, as seen in illustrations depicting the ornament (Plate XV, 1, 2), when compared with Plate XXIV, 3, clearly illustrates a definite stylistic change. The method of indicating the knee, the horizontal band in the ornamented pattern, the accentuation of the general shape of the leg by the double cascade of folds on each side, and the repetition of oval shapes down to the hem of the garment — all are the same, yet at Chartres instead of eight oval sweeps of drapery down the leg there are twelve. More important than the increase in units is the difference in surface treatment. The boldness of the carving of Étampes is softened down and made more delicate and subtle at Chartres. Another detail of the handling of the cloak over

---

[21] In the Museum of Étampes is a fragment of an engaged colonnette decorated with a four-leaf-clover pattern like several of the short columns at Chartres. The width of the carved area, .22 meter, corresponds to the dimensions of the undecorated colonnettes between the jamb figures on the portal. There is therefore a possibility that this piece may be all that is left of the ornament which originally decorated the jambs, and that the colonnettes on the portal are nineteenth century.

the shoulders in the Chartres figure is illustrated in Plate XIV, 1.

Certain mannerisms seen in the Étampes figures do not appear at Chartres. The knees of the second male type and the two female figures are very much accentuated by repeated curved folds. Secondly, little circular twists of drapery appear between the ankles on the second male type, L.1 and R.2, and on Saint Peter (Plates XXIII, 2, and XXIV, 2, 4). Thirdly, on the statues of Saints Peter and Paul (Plate XXIII, 3) the vertical folds remain connected at intervals. None of these features are found in the related Chartres figures. In the two male figures on the RP.R at Chartres the knees are designated by round folds of drapery, but are not emphasized to the same extent as at Étampes.

FIGURE STYLE II: RELATIONSHIP TO SAINT-DENIS

Important for this discussion are the relationships between the Étampes statues and the jamb sculpture of Saint-Denis. The Saint-Denis figures have the same relatively squat proportions of the Étampes sculptures. Several from the central portal of Saint-Denis are clothed in garments arranged similarly to those on the Étampes statues. The lower right-hand jamb in plate xvii of Montfaucon and the preparatory drawing (Plate VII, 6) show a figure holding a staff bisecting the lower part of the torso, while the drapery falls in double folds over the left leg. This same treatment is found on the second type at Étampes and in the statue of Saint Paul.

The two female statues at Étampes (Plates XXIII, 2, and XXIV, 2) are connected with several Saint-Denis figures, such as the first, third, and fourth on the top row and the first and second on the bottom row in plate xvii of Montfaucon (Plate VII, 4). The general shape of both legs is revealed beneath the cascading folds of the garments of the figures from both monuments, while the central axes are accentuated by vertical cords and tassels. A corresponding treatment of knees is seen in two of Montfaucon's drawings. The symmetrical mantles covering the upper parts of the female figures at Étampes are similar to two Montfaucon drawings of the Saint-Denis jambs (Plate VII, 4). One of the drawings (Plate VII, 4) shows the same protruding stomach which is found on both Étampes female figures. Thus from the point of view of costume and rendering of certain parts of anatomy, there is a general affinity between the sculpture of Étampes and the figures of the central portal of Saint-Denis. These stylistic common denominators between Étampes and the Saint-Denis portals, finished in 1140, are further proof that Étampes antedates Chartres.

CONCLUSION

Since the history of Étampes reveals that it was one of the most important towns of France in the twelfth century, it would be a mistake to consider that the Royal Portal of Notre-Dame of Étampes is the work of a backward group of sculptors who retreated after losing out in competition at Chartres. There is no definite evidence, either in the history of Étampes or in the architecture of the church or in a study of the iconography, which would allow the assigning of an exact date, yet the great friendship between Bernard and Abbot Henri may be significant.[22] It is necessary to rely on a comparative study of this portal in connection with other monuments which can be more or less dated. From the point of view of construction, profiles of moldings, and decoration Étampes is very close to Chartres. At Étampes the moldings are more archaic and the pedestals are less elaborately decorated. All these considerations are useful in the contention that Étampes antedates Chartres.

Following the conclusion that the Royal Portal of Chartres is a coöperative artistic expression carried out in one campaign, it would be difficult to believe that the so-called Étampes Master came from Chartres to Étampes without bringing with him some features of the Headmaster's style. Furthermore, the only monumental sculptures at Chartres which can be assigned to the "Master of Étampes" are the LP.L jambs, while the RP.R figures have certain related details. In the case of the latter, their affinity to Saint-Denis is more marked than their superficial connection with Étampes.

Even the LP. L. 2 and 3 of Chartres (Plate XVI, 1), figures which are almost identical with two Étampes statues, display a more refined type of carving. Greater delicacy is seen in the treatment of folds of drapery, and the proportions have been heightened. The presence at Chartres of a superior sculptor has had its effect to the extent that a general process of smoothing out the ropelike surfaces of the Étampes figures has taken place. In the LP.L.1 the Étampes Master has actually tried to copy the Headmaster's work, such as his CP.R.3 (Plate XVII, 2). The lower part of this figure, LP.L.1, carries overtones of the Headmaster's treatment of the human form. It is difficult to agree with Priest that this part was actually carved by the Headmaster.[23]

A final reason for concluding that Étampes is earlier than Chartres is the fact that in all the portals which grow out of Chartres, such as Le Mans, Provins, Angers, Bourges, Saint-Loup-de-Naud, and others, there is no instance in which the Étampes style is reflected. Thus after the middle of the century the Étampes Master disappears from sight. It is hard to believe, if Étampes were later than Chartres — dating, that is, from the end of the 1140's or the early 1150's — that some other portals would not reflect this individual style, especially when it was available in so important a place as Étampes. The best way of explaining its lack of progeny is to assume that it was submerged in and surpassed by the art of Chartres.

---

[22] Lefèvre (1908), pp. 81–82.

[23] Priest, p. 40.

TRENDS IN THE SECOND HALF OF THE TWELFTH CENTURY LE MANS, SAINT-AYOUL AT PROVINS, SAINT-LOUP-DE-NAUD, SENLIS

How can we explain the tremendous artistic outburst in the Île-de-France and its environs in the second half of the twelfth century? In contrast to Burgundy, Provence, Languedoc, and other regions of France, the Île-de-France produced little Romanesque sculpture. The lack of any strong regional tradition which might reassert itself accounts, at least negatively, for the uninterrupted evolution of sculptured portals in the second half of the century. The greater concentration of wealth and power in the hands of Louis VII, the establishment of free communes, and the resulting decline of the prestige of feudal barons established the Île-de-France as the focal region for the dissemination of political and artistic ideas.

In the area within a hundred-mile radius of Paris, one finds portals with jamb figures in great abundance. These monuments cover an area resembling an opened fan with its pivotal point resting on Paris. Portals are found south and southwest of Paris in the departments of Sarthe, Eure-et-Loir, and Seine-et-Oise. Others are located to the southeast and east in the departments of Seine-et-Marne and Marne, while several are situated north of Paris. In the same area and at the same time, four-storied Gothic churches like Laon, Noyon, Paris, and Châlons-sur-Marne, and a smaller number of three-storied Gothic churches like Sens and Saint-Germain-des-Prés were constructed.

It is evident that the Royal Portal at Chartres, which provided a synthesis of the experimental portals of Saint-Denis and Étampes, became the major inspirational force behind later designers and sculptors. Saint-Denis exerted an independent influence second in importance only to Chartres. The portal of Notre-Dame at Étampes remained an isolated artistic phenomenon which affected, as far as existing monuments are concerned, only three jamb statues at Chartres.

In this section discussion will be confined to a limited number of portals which illustrate the stylistic evolution of the second half of the twelfth century. Starting with the south portal of Le Mans, finished in 1158, the portals of Saint-Ayoul at Provins and Saint-Loup-de-Naud, will then be considered. Senlis, which can be dated in the 1180's, serves as the end of the development.

An analysis of portals exhibiting the spread of the Chartres style to Burgundy and other outlying provinces is outside the scope of this present section. The portals at Bourges and Avallon, for example, represent an entirely different problem. Local characteristics asserted themselves with such force that influences coming from the Île-de-France were greatly altered.

The subtle combination of structurally conceived figures and abundant ornament prevented Chartres itself from becoming academic, but it does not follow that this high point in artistic achievement can be maintained elsewhere. On the other hand, new forces may conceivably transform the original impulse into a new expression.

HISTORICAL BACKGROUND OF THE PORTALS

Because the majority of dwellings of Le Mans were on the south side of the cathedral, the south portal (Plate XXV, 1) was and still is the principal entrance.[1] The date of the addition of porch and portal is controversial. The nave was rebuilt and vaulted by Bishop Guillaume de Passavant, and dedicated April 28, 1158.[2] During the early years of his service, from 1143 on, he had the difficult task of raising money for the building program necessitated by the disastrous fires of 1134 and 1137. Henry II of England, as Count of Anjou and Maine, gave money as did the bishop himself. Important relics were sold to help finance the project.[3] Fleury's claim that the portal was constructed before 1145 is based on the fact that the archivolts of the portal are round, while the arches of the porch are pointed.[4] He also believes that there is a lack of liaison between porch and portal. Be-

---

[1] Ledru, *La Cathédrale du Mans, Saint-Julien* (1923), p. 27.
[2] Lefèvre-Pontalis, *Étude historique et archéologique sur la nef de la Cathédrale du Mans* (1889), p. 16.

[3] Perrigan, *Recherches sur la Cathédrale du Mans* (1872), pp. 86–87.
[4] Fleury, *Le Cathédrale du Mans* (1910), pp. 86–87.

cause of the connection between the chevrons and clover motifs which decorate the diagonal ribs of the porch vault (Plate XXV, 1) and those on the vaults of the nave, he concludes that the porch was constructed in the 1150's under Guillaume de Passavant and that the portal was built before the death of Bishop Hugues of Saint-Calais in 1145. Ledru, writing at a later date, claims that the slight bits of evidence for different dates for portal and porch are actually the result of restorations made early in the nineteenth century. He believes that both were built in the 1150's under Guillaume de Passavant but offers no other reasons for his disagreement with Fleury.[5] A study of the joints between porch and portal reveals that many new blocks as well as a considerable amount of concrete have replaced the original masonry. The thoroughness of the nineteenth-century restorations might easily be misleading. Fleury's argument collapses if one considers the ample precedent for interchangeable use of round and pointed arches when no structural problem is involved. The Le Mans portal is framed by round archivolts which are echoed by the arches and vaults of the nave, whereas the pointed arrangement in the porch has structural significance. The continuity of the moldings of the bases of the portal and those on the piers of the porch (Plate XXV, 1) favors Ledru's conclusion. A band of four-leaf clover units arranged diagonally decorates the stringcourse which frames the archivolts. The same motif treated in similar fashion is seen on the ribs of the porch and of the nave.[6] Since the nave vaults were completed by 1158, this similarity is further proof of the contemporaneousness of all three: porch, portal, and nave vaults.

On the basis of this evidence we can conclude that the portal of Le Mans was executed in the 1150's.[7] Evidence will be brought out in the following discussion to show that the Le Mans sculpture is a reflection of the west portals of Chartres. The date of 1158 will thus serve as a *terminus ante quem* for the Royal Portal of Chartres.

The sculpture of the west façade of Saint-Ayoul at Provins, Seine-et-Marne (Plate XXV, 2), is an example of the dis-

semination of Chartres style to the southeast of Paris and directly east of Chartres. In many aspects these portals seem to be the counterpart of Le Mans in a different region. The general similarity of the jamb figures of the two monuments is quite striking.

The wealthy counts of Champagne played important roles in the life of the region. Under the rule of Thibault-le-Grand (died 1152), Provins prospered greatly.[8] Henri-le-Libéral, his son, not only augmented the commercial importance of the town but also became a stronger protector of the churches and clergy than his father. In all he founded thirteen churches and thirteen hospitals.[9] The existence of a charter of 1153 in which Henri-le-Libéral turned over to the clergy of Saint-Ayoul all powers of dispensing justice during the week of fairs proves his connection with this church.[10] The fire of 1157 which destroyed most of the church of Saint-Ayoul, establishes a *terminus post quem* for the carving of the portals.[11] The Marquise de Maillé uses the date of 1167 for the portal of the priory of Saint-Loup-de-Naud as a *terminus ante quem*,[12] while Aubert believes that the jambs were executed between 1160 and 1165.[13] In the following discussion an attempt will be made to determine the date of the Saint-Ayoul portals on the basis of their connection with the sculpture of Chartres and Le Mans.[14]

The little priory of Saint-Loup-de-Naud stands a few kilometers southwest of Provins. A single portal under the western porch is decorated with six jamb figures, a trumeau figure of the sainted Bishop Loup, and a tympanum portraying Christ with the symbols of the four Evangelists (Plate XXV, 3). The lintel contains eight Apostles and a statue of the Virgin, while the archivolts represent angels and miracles performed by Saint Loup.[15] The priory, originally dependent on the Abbey of Saint-Pierre-le-Vif in Sens, is first mentioned in 980.[16] According to Salet, the choir, the transept, and two eastern bays of the nave were constructed toward the end of the eleventh century, while the rest of the nave and the porch were built after 1167.[17] In that year Count Henri-le-Libéral turned over to Saint-Pierre-le-Vif and Saint-Loup-de-Naud

[5] Ledru, p. 29.

[6] Lefèvre-Pontalis, *Étude historique*, p. 37.

[7] Gardner, pp. 200–201. He refuses to accept either Ledru's or Fleury's conclusions, and thus is undecided whether or not Le Mans is earlier than Chartres.

[8] Bourquelot, *Histoire de Provins* (1839), I, 101.

[9] Bourquelot, p. 112: "Henri . . . méritait en Champagne par son opulence, ses dons, la fondation de treize églises, de treize hôpitaux et de plusieurs autres établissements, le titre de personnage magnifique, vir magnificus."

[10] Bourquelot, pp. 117–118: ". . . pendant les sept premiers jours des foires, sur toute la ville et châtellenie de Provins, la justice grande et petite, haute et basse du brigandage, du vol, de l'homicide, des champions, de la vente, et tous autres forfaits, amendes et autres choses justiciables . . . au serment corporel."

[11] Maillé, *Provins, Les Monuments religieux*, vol. II, p. 86, p. 12. Until this study of Saint-Ayoul (1939) and the article by J. Godefroy, "L'Histoire du Prieuré de Saint-Ayoul," *Revue Mabillon* (1938), pp. 29–48, the date of the fire could only be narrowed down to the interval between the years

1147 and 1162. These two writers dated a letter of consolation written by John of Salisbury to Abbot Pierre de Celles of Saint-Ayoul in the year 1157.

[12] Maillé, p. 86. Salet in his article, "Saint-Loup-de-Naud," *Bulletin monumental* (1933), p. 166, dates the portal in 1167.

[13] Aubert, *French Sculpture at the Beginning*, p. 36.

[14] Maillé, pp. 90–91. The Marquise discusses the relationship between Chartres and Provins. Both towns were part of the same domain until the death of Thibaut II in 1152. Thibaut's son, who was Count of Blois and Chartres, kept in close contact with his brother Henri-le-Libéral who controlled the Champagne region. The latter aided Saint-Ayoul extensively. Directly after the fire of 1157, Abbot Pierre de Celles of Saint-Ayoul sought the advice of the Bishop of Chartres (p. 12 and n. 3).

[15] Bourquelot, *Notice historique et archéologique sur le Prieuré de Saint-Loup-de-Naud* (1840–1841), II, 244–271. Saint Loup was Bishop of Sens in the seventh century (*ibid.*, p. 251).

[16] "Église de Saint-Loup-de-Naud," *Congrès Archéologique de France* (1902), p. 82.

[17] Salet, pp. 136ff.

all the rights of the land around the neighborhood of the priory, and, at the same time, gave them two houses in Provins.[18] Salet believes that the increase in revenue made the second campaign possible, and that this campaign included the portal. He dates the portal after 1167, toward the years 1170 to 1175.[19]

The portal between the western towers of the cathedral of Senlis illustrates the final development from the Saint-Denis–Chartres style. Senlis, although north of Paris, is nevertheless in the heart of the Île-de-France. The portal was carved in the 1180's and was finished by the time of the dedication of the cathedral on June 16, 1191.[20] The iconography and style of the portal represents both a continuation of and a definite break with earlier portals.

PORTAL DESIGN AND CONSTRUCTION

Although in general design and construction the south portal of Le Mans Cathedral (Plate XXV, 1) is very similar to the Royal Portal of Chartres, many features are at variance. The elaborate pedestals of Chartres are replaced by unadorned bases of two tiers of masonry. The same overlapping of blocks in the jamb bases which we observed at Saint-Denis, Étampes, and Chartres is found at Le Mans. Like Saint-Denis, but in contrast to Chartres (Plate XI) and Étampes (Plate XXIV), the jamb figures extend up to the capitals. The capitals at both Saint-Denis and Le Mans are ornamented, but at Chartres and Étampes they are historiated. This difference in the decoration of the capitals may explain the change in the portal design. At Le Mans many of the scenes which adorn the capitals and tympana of Chartres and Étampes appear in the archivolts.

Another feature which distinguishes this portal from the Chartres portals is the treatment of the inner jambs. Instead of a uniform system of statues, the jambs flanking the portal are decorated with reliefs of Saints Peter and Paul under a canopy. The presence of these two personages in this place has a precedent in several High Romanesque portals such as Moissac. The treatment in relief of the jambs supporting the lintel recalls Étampes and Saint-Denis. At Étampes these first jambs are relieved by panels, and the figures of Saints Peter and Paul appeared originally on the extreme sides of the portal. Because it is constructed under a small porch the Le Mans portal necessarily excludes the Étampes arrangement.

Instead of projecting from the walls the jamb figures have been pushed into the masonry (Plates XXVI, 1, and XXIX,

2). The colonnettes between the statues are closer to the front plane of each embrasure than at Chartres and Étampes. Unlike Chartres, these intermediate columns are undecorated and extend up between the capitals. The latter feature results in the relative isolation of each capital.

Scenes from the life of Christ, which appeared on the capitals at Chartres, decorate the archivolts (Plate XXV, 1). Most of the archivolt blocks contain more than one figure, in contradistinction to those monuments previously studied. At Chartres the V-shaped projection of each pedestal is carried up through jamb figures, capital, abacus, and around the archivolt. No such continuity appears at Le Mans. Here, each archivolt block is decorated with a scene; no part projects further than another, and the archivolts become curved pilasters decorating the slanting walls which frame the tympanum. The flatness or rather the uniform projection of each archivolt reflects the lack of projection in the jamb figures themselves.

In general proportions the Le Mans portal is much squatter than the Royal Portal. From the point of view of over-all portal design, Le Mans resembles Chartres, but it exhibits certain elements which are found in the portals of Saint-Denis and Étampes, and notably the former.

Because of the very badly battered condition of the portals of Saint-Ayoul of Provins it is difficult to visualize the sculpture as it was originally conceived. The central portal (Plate XXV, 2), with its eight now headless jamb statues and lacking its lintel and half its tympanum, is a mere reflection of its former state.[21] In addition to this damage, some of the decoration, especially on the left portal, was destroyed during the application of wall buttresses to the façade.[22] Remnants of an acanthus frieze, flanking the capitals on the sides of the central portal (Plate XXVI, 2), suggest a former shallow porch.[23] The left portal has either lost its side jambs or was built differently from the right portal, for only four instead of five columns exist today. It is hard to determine how these portals were originally joined. The fact that the top of the abaci of the central portal is .62 centimeter higher than those of the flanking doorways makes the liaison between the ornamental borders, existing today in fragmentary condition, very problematical. The question arises automatically as to whether the side portals were constructed at the same time as the central doorway.

Evidence of a close relationship with Chartres is exhibited in almost every detail of the portals. Although many of the joints have been repaired with concrete, it is still possible to

---

[18] Salet, p. 132 and n. 3.

[19] Salet, p. 166.

[20] Aubert, *French Sculpture at the Beginning*, p. 65.

[21] Maillé, p. 75. The destruction of the trumeau, lintel, and part of the tympanum took place in 1792 after parts of an organ had been transported from the Abbey of Jony, when, following the installation of this new acquisition at the entrance of the nave, it was apparent that more light

was needed in the west end of the church.

[22] Maillé, p. 73. Buttresses were added in the sixteenth century.

[23] Maillé, p. 73. I arrived at this conclusion before learning of the books by the Marquise de Maillé. The Marquise believes that the outer molding of the central portal is the formeret of the porch which may have been crowned by a tower (p. 74). She also believes that the porch was pulled down in the sixteenth century (p. 74).

make out the method of construction (Plate XXVI, 2). The alternation in direction of courses of overlapping masonry follows the precedents of Saint-Denis and Chartres. In the central portal the fourth row of masonry projects outward in the same manner as the corresponding part at Chartres and Étampes. In contrast to earlier portals, no decoration of any sort adorns these members. The projecting angles of the walls are not decorated with carved colonnettes, as at Chartres, or plain ones, as at Étampes and Le Mans. Here they are simply shaved off. It might, however, be supposed that these areas were originally filled with engaged colonnettes, but an examination of the lowest sections of the moldings shows that they terminate in clearly defined points which would not support an additional member. Between the third and fourth jamb figures on each side of the central portal (Plates XXVI, 2, and especially XXVII, 2), the protruding angles of the walls are left untouched.[24] Capitals, abaci, and archivolts follow the structural system of Chartres.

From the point of view of portal design the central doorway of Provins bears an affinity to that of Le Mans. The general height of the figures is approximately the same as at Le Mans, although in the latter the statues rest on short decorated columns, whereas the supports at Provins are the several rows of masonry which form the bases. Both Provins and Le Mans exhibit a squatness in distinct contrast to the verticality of Chartres.

From both the iconographical and stylistic standpoints, the connection between this portal and those of Chartres and Le Mans is very clear. It is not necessary to consider that Provins is a reflection of Le Mans. With equal validity we may treat it as a parallel manifestation of the extension of Chartres style to another region of France.

The sculpture of the portal of Saint-Loup-de-Naud (Plate XXV, 3) exhibits once again a strong dependence on the Chartres style, while some of the individual characteristics of the Le Mans and Provins portals are intensified. The general design of the portal of Saint-Loup-de-Naud is connected with that of Provins (Plate XXV, 2). Both monuments have plain bases. In both, the first jambs are undecorated and the figures fill the entire area between the bases and capitals, which in both portals are unhistoriated. In contrast to the elongated jambs of Chartres, this portal is relatively squat, like Le Mans and Provins. The relationship between the sculptural and architectural members of the portal is likewise similar to that at Le Mans and Provins. The jambs seem squashed into the masonry; but here they have greater bulk and bear a closer affinity to Chartres.

The same methods of construction in horizontal courses of masonry persist (Plate XXVI, 3). As at Provins, the bases are crowned with a projecting series of moldings consisting

of a torus which separates two concave areas. Above this is a plinth and then a base which is crowned by two small torus moldings which in turn uphold the conical supports for the jamb statues. This resembles the arrangement at Chartres, but the surfaces are not perforated. In contrast to all earlier monuments, the projections of the walls between the jamb figures are treated with neither decorated nor plain columns nor even by concave moldings but are left untouched. This same bold treatment is found between the third and fourth jambs on each side of the central portal at Provins (Plate XXVII, 2).

The west portal of the cathedral of Senlis (Plate XXV, 4) is at once reactionary in style and prophetic of Gothic portals to come. The entire design reflects the portals of Saint-Denis (Plate I, 1, 2, and Plate A). From a study of Senlis it is possible to visualize the original appearance of the Saint-Denis façade with its high unadorned bases and its small colonnettes on the first jambs supporting the low lintel. The measurements of the portals of the two monuments are practically identical. There are also connections between the figure sculpture of Senlis and Saint-Denis, but these are rather superficial. At Senlis, a decidedly new freedom of movement appears in the jambs, the tympanum, and the lintel. The sculpture is no longer subservient to the architecture.

EVOLUTION OF FIGURE STYLE

The jamb statues and the tympanum of Le Mans (Plates XXVI, 1, and XXVII, 1) are reminiscent of the sculpture by the Headmaster of Chartres and his pupils. Many of the jambs are almost replicas of figures on the Chartres central portal, while others are combinations of different parts of several statues. The stone used at Le Mans has weathered badly and some details of the modeling have disappeared. The greatest difference between figures of the two monuments, other than that of quality, is found in their relationship to the columns behind them. At Chartres, almost three quarters of the column is preserved and the figure, a part of the same block, grows out from the remaining quarter. At Le Mans, the reëntrant angles of the embrasures are not occupied by the columns but by both column and figure. Little if any of the column remains so that the statues themselves seem pressed into the angles of the portal, while at Chartres they stand out in full projection and state emphatically their architectonic role.

Most of the Le Mans figures seem to be flattened-out versions of Chartres statues. Most of the figures on the right side of the Le Mans portal (Plate XXVI, 1) with the exception of the relief of Saint Peter, are modeled on statues from the Chartres central portal (Plate XVII). The second jamb is

---

[24] Maillé, p. 87, mentions this in discussing the lack of unity between the figures. The fact that the sculpture is carved in stone different from the local material (p. 75) has led to her conclusion: "L'œuvre ne fut pas sculpté sur place."

a copy of Chartres CP.R.4, with the exception of the open hand which is like Chartres RP.L.4 (Plate XVIII, 2). Details such as the tube-like double folds over the left leg and the curved sweep of drapery over the right knee are similar. The wattled right sleeve resembles that on one of the Chartres female figures, CP.L.3 (Plate XVII, 1). The fourth and fifth figures of the right embrasure are replicas, with slight variations, of Chartres CP.R.2 (Plate XVII, 2) and CP.L.2 (Plate XVII, 1) respectively. The head of the latter is similar to Chartres CP.R.1. As in the other Le Mans jamb, the open hands increase the flatness of the statues. Details of drapery are less crisply rendered than at Chartres. The female figure, R.3, is related to Chartres CP.L.5 (Plate XVII, 1); the strong verticality of the Chartres statue is blocked, to a certain extent, by the sloping shoulders and outward flare of folds at the bottom. The undecorated arm lying across the stomach is only slightly modeled.

On the left embrasure, the jamb statues (Plate XXV, 1) do not follow Chartres models as closely, although the female figure resembles Chartres CP.L.3. The fourth figure is copied after Chartres LP.R.4 (Plate XVIII, 1), while the second and fifth are variations which include features of the fourth Le Mans statue plus details from other figures of the two monuments. The more closely the jambs follow their Chartres models, the more successful they are.

The general contour of these figures with elbows projecting beyond hips, together with a less architectural conception of the human form, is much closer to the style of the sculpture by a pupil or pupils of the Headmaster on Chartres LP.R and RP.L. There are none of the mannerisms such as little zigzag folds of drapery or parabolic curves of garments which distinguish the jambs of Chartres RP.L, yet the style of the LP.R.4 jamb seems closest to all the Le Mans statues from the point of view of proportions, silhouette and treatment of drapery.

The tympanum (Plate XXVII, 1) exhibits a coarsening in technique and style when compared to its model at Chartres. The majestic posture of the Chartres Christ (Plate XX, 1) is cheapened in the stubby replica. In every detail of drapery the Le Mans artist attempts to imitate the Headmaster of Chartres. The symbols of the Evangelists, particularly the lion of Saint Mark, are likewise relatively debased in rendering. Again the difference is one of degree.

The archivolts are decorated with angels and scenes of the life of Christ (Plate XXV, 1). Instead of the derivative forms found on the jambs and tympanum, these figures, like the ornament, exhibit a different style. Some of the characteristics, such as the V-shaped and angular folds seen on the jamb statues which do not echo Chartres models directly, are found on these small voussoir figures. Here the sculptors were confronted with a new problem, the representation of elaborate scenes on the curved surfaces of archivolts. Having

no models, the sculptors were free to develop in new directions. The Visitation on the right-hand archivolts (Plate XXVIII, 1), when contrasted with the same scene on the lintel of the Chartres right portal (Plate XX, 2), shows the transformation which has taken place. Wind-blown draperies and greater movement replace the static and rigid rendering of the Chartres figures. Other scenes above, such as the diagonally arranged Last Supper, show these same characteristics. The sensitive equilibrium and balance of monumental sculpture and ornament at Chartres is now partially lost as the jambs become flatter and the ornament and elaborate archivolts assume an importance of their own.

Like the jamb statues of Le Mans, the figured sculpture of Saint-Ayoul of Provins (Plate XXVI, 2) is strongly related to the west portals of Chartres. The process of flattening the jamb figures into the splays is carried further at Provins. From the point of view of the shape of the block (in cross section) and the silhouette, the similarity between the Le Mans and Provins jambs is very striking. Garments flare out slightly at the bottom, while sagging shoulders are different from the squared-off character of the Chartres figures.

In spite of the obvious connection between these two portals there are important differences which can be explained on the basis of the respective origins of the figures of the two monuments. Both portals are inspired by Chartres, yet features appear at Provins which prove that these jambs reflect Chartres directly and are not based on the disintegrated Chartres style found at Le Mans. The eight jamb figures at Provins are influenced by statues which are located on all three west portals of Chartres, whereas the Le Mans sculpture is related only to the central portal and the adjoining sides of the side portals. This difference would seem to lead to the conclusion that Provins and Le Mans are independent and possibly contemporary manifestations of the spread of the Chartres style.

One of the two female figures at Provins, R.3 (Plates XXV, 2, and XXVII, 2), is based on Chartres CP.R.3 in the prominent stomach and the folds of the drapery, while remnants of a wimple suggest a relationship to the Chartres CP.L.5. In contrast to the Chartres female statues, this figure presents a flat-chested appearance, and the shoulders slope considerably. The other female figure, L.3 (Plate XXVI, 2), exhibits a definite connection with Chartres RP.R.3 (Plate XVI, 2). None of the Le Mans jambs are modeled on those of this splay of the west portals of Chartres. As in the Chartres figure, the mantle covers three quarters of the upper part of the body and falls in a single fold down the center of the lower half of the figure. The braided hair and the small folds of the skirt are also similar details. The unusual varying contour of the Chartres figure is not found on this statue, which has something of the rectangular silhouette of the Headmaster's style. The sensitive carving of the Chartres statue, however, does not carry over.

While at Le Mans several of the male statues are close copies of Chartres figures, at Provins the greater number are related only indirectly. One, L.1 (Plate XXVI, 2), is a copy of the Chartres CP.R.2 (Plate XVII, 2). The R.1 is similar to the same Chartres figure, except that the V-shaped folds across the chest are new features also found several times at Le Mans. The adjoining jamb, R.2, is a combination of two figures from Chartres, RP.R.2 and CP.L.1. The upper half, with the cloak hiding most of the chest and passing down over the arm, follows the former; the truncated folds over the left leg derive from the latter.

The remaining three male jambs are not so closely related to Chartres prototypes. The R.4 is shorter than the other figures. The arrangement of garments is similar to Provins R.1, but the low position of the hands, the treatment of the curving drapery, and the slight increase in the bulk of the figure give this jamb a unique character. These differences suggest that another sculptor might have carved it. The L.2 (Plate XXVI, 2) with its long flowing mantle is not modeled on any Chartres figure. The arrangement of the garment in the area between the now damaged hands is unusual. Somewhat similar is L.4 in which the cloak covers the other side of the figure. The parabolic curves of the garb across the chest have no counterpart on this or the Le Mans portals, but are found on the Chartres RP.R.1 (Plate XVI, 2).

The single fragment which remains of the heads, R.4 (Plate XXVII, 2), is a smoothed-down version of Chartres examples.[25] The eye is very close to the surface of the block, and the subtleties of the changing planes in the Chartres heads are partially lost. The sculptor repeats lines around the eye and in the hair which flatten out the roundness of the head as a whole.

The archivolts and the tympanum at Provins have suffered more severely than the jambs. It is possible to get some idea of the style by a study of the remaining fragments. In the tympanum (Plate XXV, 2) all that is left after the eighteenth-century mutilations is half of the Christ in a mandorla, the Saint Matthew angel, and the Saint John eagle. The innermost archivolt is decorated with ten angels, and the next two with elders of the Apocalypse, and the outermost one with scenes of Paradise and Hell. The extreme flatness of the Christ in the tympanum, with the folds of his garments rendered like ropes applied to the surface of the block, is very similar to the general style of the jambs.[26]

The portals of Saint-Ayoul at Provins represent a decline

in quality.[27] As at Le Mans, the monumental character of the Chartres sculpture has been reduced, but new ornamental notions appear in the exuberant capitals. Because of the general similarities to Le Mans and because the figures do not derive from Le Mans, it may be concluded that Provins is roughly contemporary with Le Mans and was created in the late 1150's or early 1160's after the fire of 1157.

The six jamb figures of the portal of Saint-Loup-de-Naud (Plate XXVI, 3) depend on the sculpture of the west portals of Chartres Cathedral. In contrast to Le Mans and Provins, where the Chartres-type figure has become academic, these statues preserve the massiveness seen in the Royal Portal. The sculptor or sculptors who worked at Saint-Loup-de-Naud seem to have gained direct inspiration from Chartres, especially from its central portal, without being affected by the intermediate portals of Le Mans and Provins.

In spite of the strong resemblance between these jambs and the Chartres sculpture, a definite stylistic transformation has taken place. The proportions have changed from six or seven heads high to five or less. Because of their stockier appearance some of the monumentality of the prototypes is lost. The nearly rectangular silhouette of the Chartres figures is preserved, but a linear movement in the drapery ruffles the majestic calm of the Headmaster's creations. The staggered, geometric folds of drapery which at Chartres appear to have been pressed into the curved surface of the block, here project and terminate in undulating lines. The expression is more fluid, almost suggesting bronze sculpture. The staring eyes surrounded by repeated lines and the furrowed brows give a more particularized flavor to the faces. The whole emphasis is more naturalistic.

Two of the jamb statues are based directly on Chartres models; Saint Peter, R.1 (Plate XXVI, 3), follows CP.L.2, and R.2 derives from CP.R.4 (Plate XVII). Both figures exhibit the same arrangement of drapery and similar positions of hands and arms. The head of R.1 resembles CP.R.1 at Chartres. The third figure (R.3) is a variant of Chartres CP.R.2. The lower part of this figure is very close to the Chartres model, but the double folds over the left shoulder are a new feature. The head (Plate XXIX, 4) echoes closely CP.L.1 at Chartres.

On the left side of the portal, the first and third jamb statues do not derive from any single Chartres figure, although the lower part of the mantles and the undergarments are arranged like R.3, discussed above. The female figure, L.2, is similar to CP.R.3 of Chartres, but lacks the subtly curved shape of abdomen and breasts of the figure on the

---

[25] This head does not appear in Pl. 33 of Aubert's *French Sculpture at the Beginning.*

[26] It is difficult to follow Aubert's contention (*French Sculpture*, pp. 34–35) that the upper part of the portal is roughly twenty years later than the jamb figures. It is certainly true that a greater sense of plasticity is

found in the voussoirs, yet any parallelism between this sculpture and the Porte St.-Anne in Paris is doubtful (p. 34).

[27] Maillé, p. 91. From the point of view of quality, it is impossible to agree with the Marquise's enthusiastic claim: "Ce que Chartres suggérait, Provins le réalise."

Royal Portal. All these statues have ornamental borders on the hems of garments which are wider and more elaborate than those on the jamb figures at Chartres.

The finest sculpture on the portal is the trumeau statue of Saint Loup (Plates XXIX, 3, and XXVII, 3) in whose honor the priory was constructed. He is portrayed in ecclesiastical robes as Bishop of Sens, blessing with his right hand and holding a cross, now destroyed, in his left. The entire figure produces a strongly monumental and columnar effect, from the bird-supports up through the solid body to the bulky head. The face is an imaginary portrait (Saint Loup lived in the seventh century), yet the artist, who was undoubtedly the sculptor in charge, has endeavored to create an individual whose features are close to nature. The detailed treatment of nose, eyebrows, and beard, suggesting the presence of actual hair, are all new features in twelfth-century art. The trend toward Gothic here unfolds. Neither the archaic directness of the Saint-Denis heads nor the classic repose of the Chartres heads is seen here. This powerful image suggests a different age, an age in which the attitude toward humanity has changed.

The tympanum depicts Christ and the symbols of the four Evangelists (Plate XV, 3). The arrangement is the same as at Chartres, Le Mans, and Provins. Of the three this representation is most closely allied to Chartres. Neither the flatness of Provins nor the relative coarseness of Le Mans appears here. Instead, the sculpture is an elaboration of the central tympanum of Chartres. The Christ derives directly from Chartres, with the same pose and arrangement of drapery. Differences in detail include the introduction of more minute parallel folds.

The lintel (Plate XXV, 3) consists of eight Apostles under canopied battlements similar to those at Le Mans. The presence of the Mother of Christ directly below her Son, a new iconographical feature, forecasts her future role in the life and art of the thirteenth century. The Virgin is still conceived symbolically rather than as a woman, yet some of the stiffness of the Chartres Virgin (RP) has vanished. Many of the Apostles on the lintel are modeled after those on the lintel of the Chartres central portal. The first four from the left are based respectively on the second, fourth, fifth, and seventh Chartres Apostles, while the other four are close variants. Like the jambs, the figures are proportionately shorter.

The scenes depicted on the archivolts (Plates XXV, 3, and XXVIII, 4) demonstrate a new tendency. Outside the first rim, which is decorated with angels in the traditional manner, appear the miracles of Saint Loup himself. This iconographical treatment was partially achieved at Le Mans where scenes from the Passion of Christ adorn the voussoirs. At

Saint-Loup-de-Naud the process of humanization has progressed further. In contrast to Le Mans, where scenes elaborated with many figures tend to flatten out the V-shaped projections of the archivolts, the miracles of Saint Loup do not disrupt the shapes of the voussoirs.

The portal of Saint-Loup-de-Naud establishes the preeminence of Chartres as the inspirational force behind the sculpture of the Île-de-France into the 1170's. At the same time, the figures, especially that of Saint Loup, show a more pronounced interest in approximating actuality.

The monumental sculpture of the west portal of Senlis (1180's; Plate XXV, 4) is a stylistic paradox. On the one hand, the tendency toward increasing verisimilitude of natural appearance, observed in the portal of Saint-Loup-de-Naud, is intensified while, on the other hand, Senlis figures are transformations of Saint-Denis prototypes (1140).[28] In contrast to the strong Chartrain character of Le Mans, Provins, and Saint-Loup-de-Naud, the Senlis jambs have contorted poses, swirling drapery, and disjointed articulation. In the discussion of portal design it was noted that Senlis is based directly on Saint-Denis. The connection becomes clearer when the jambs (Plate XXVI, 4) are compared with the Montfaucon drawings and engravings (Plates VII and X, 2). Yet the resemblance is only superficial. In both compositions jambs stand on animals and grotesques; one figure is cross-legged and the drapery is intricately organized (compare Senlis L.4 and figures in the Saint-Denis bas-relief of Plate X). In all instances, the poses resemble Saint-Denis, but the treatment of folds and the irregular silhouettes differ noticeably. A new spirit of restlessness pervades the forms themselves. Baroque Romanesque reaches its apogee at Senlis and in the Mantes sculpture and the north portal of Saint-Benoît-sur-Loire.

The vitality of this sculpture is best seen in the scenes of the Death and Resurrection of the Virgin (Plate XXV, 4), with angels fluttering about her reclining figure. The Ancestors of Christ are arranged in many varied poses on the deeply undercut archivolts. The Virgin and Christ in the tympanum have voluminous, rhythmic draperies. Curves and countercurves disrupt the calm majesty and aloofness of the Chartres central tympanum. The scene of the Coronation, a subject associated with Gothic culture, is set in a hollowed-out niche.

If the head of Christ (Plate XXVII, 4) is contrasted with that of the central tympanum of Chartres (Plate XX, 1), we see two different attitudes. One expresses a symbol of spiritual power; the other, a human being. Sunken cheeks, furrowed brows, and staring eyes animate the Senlis head. None of the abstract, almost archaic ruggedness of the Saint-Denis heads (Plates VIII, IX) remains. The interest in

---

[28] The heads of the jamb statues (Plates XXV, 4, and XXVI, 4) are modern. See Porter, *Romanesque Sculpture of the Pilgrimage Roads*, ills. 1505–1506, engravings of portal; ill. 1508, casts of jambs prior to restoration.

detailed rendering of features shown in the head of Saint Loup (Plate XXVII, 3) is further intensified at Senlis. Garments no longer force up the relation of statue to portal and façade but take on a new, even a violent life of their own.

EVOLUTION OF ORNAMENT

The ornamental decoration of the Le Mans portal contains many motifs which are found on the Royal Portal of Chartres. The style exhibits a trend away from the delicate and refined treatment of the Chartres designs to a coarser, more slipshod rendering. The plastic floral ornament, restricted to the unstructural sections of the Chartres portals, now spreads itself over architectural members (Plate XXVI, 1).

The short columns supporting the jamb statues (Plate XXVI, 1) and the flat areas below the two relief figures are decorated with geometric patterns as on similar areas of the central portal at Chartres (Plate XIII, 3). While most of these blocks are modern, the designs are twelfth century. The four-leaf-clover pattern appears on L.3 and R.1. The ribbon or band motif is seen on R.5 in a modern column placed upside down. The double axe also appears on a modern column. Several restored blocks have vertical and spiral paneling. One column, L.2, contains a spiral of floral heart-shaped units separated by a band of four-leaf clovers (Plate XXIX, 1). This motif is very similar to the ornament of the spiral column from Saint-Denis in the Musée de Cluny (Plate V), but the direction of movement is downward. Both the subtle flatness of the Saint-Denis motif and the rhythmic flow of the plastic vines and leaves of similar patterns at Chartres, such as CP.R.1 or 2 (Plate XIII, 2), are lost in the flabbiness and coarseness of this ornament.

The inner faces of the pilasters immediately flanking the entrance are decorated with large panels of ornament. On the right side is a fretwork pattern (Plate XXVI, 1), a motif found on several Romanesque portals but not at Saint-Denis or Chartres. On the left side, the pilaster is adorned with paired vines interlaced with floral fillers and confronted birds (Plate XXIX, 2). The design resembles the two fragments of columns in the Musée de Cluny (Plate VI, 2), which may come from Saint-Denis, and such Chartres colonnettes as the bottom parts of LP.L.1 and CP.R.4 (Plate XV). Again the motif lacks the sensitivity of the Chartres ornament. In its ponderousness and lack of variety there is the unavoidable suggestion of a mechanical copy by an unimaginative sculptor.

The capitals of Le Mans (Plate XXVIII, 1) consist of staggered tiers of acanthus leaves culminating in volutes at the reëntrant angles and at the point of greatest projection. They are separated by plumes of floral leaves crowning the colonnettes between the jamb figures. Unlike those at Chartres and Étampes with their historiated scenes, these capitals

resemble the ones on the west portals of Saint-Denis. In contrast to the latter monument, their separation by the pointed plumes results in an interruption of the friezelike character of the Saint-Denis capitals. The style of these capitals bears the closest relationship to those in the south tower at Chartres (Plate XXII, 4). The carving of the leaves is of much finer quality than the ornament just described.

The treatment of the abaci (Plate XXVIII, 1) exhibits the greatest transformation of ornamental style. In place of the undecorated panels at Saint-Denis and the flat acanthus-like abaci of Étampes and Chartres, these have various types of undulating vines, groups of leaves and birds, and other floral patterns. The modeling destroys the surface of the structural blocks. At Chartres and Étampes the abaci act as crowning members of the capitals and as springboard to the archivolts. Here, because of the variety of motifs and the much more extensive undercutting, they attain almost the same importance as the capitals. Several of the motifs are very similar to patterns on the plinths of the Saint-Denis portals and the Chartres colonnettes. Typical of this relationship is the curving vine with floral offshoots which decorates the fourth abacus on the left. The same design is seen on the LP.L.1 at Saint-Denis and several colonnettes at Chartres, but it is carved much more deeply. Many of the patterns which appear on the vertical columns of Chartres now run horizontally on these abaci. There is a strong tradition in western France, in such monuments as Aulnay and Parthenay, for the employment of floral patterns of different varieties on this part of a portal, but in this instance, most of the motifs seem to be inspired by the designs of Saint-Denis and Chartres.

The ornament at Le Mans presents a new wealth of uniform plasticity. At Saint-Denis it is subordinated to the surface of the wall in the tradition of High Romanesque art. While the Chartres ornament becomes partially free from the bonds of architecture, this is true only in portions not important structurally. At Chartres the somewhat unstructural treatment of the intermediate columns is more than offset by the very great monumentality of the jamb figures. The abaci, because of their strategic location, are decorated with very shallow relief. Even though Le Mans never did possess decorated colonnettes between the jamb statues, the ornament tends to vie in importance with the figure sculpture; capitals and abaci manifest an even greater ornamental, uncontrolled exuberance. From the point of view of ornament alone and its relation to Saint-Denis and Chartres, it is impossible to believe that the Le Mans doorway is earlier than either of those two monuments.

The ornamental decoration of the portals at Provins shows many analogies to the twelfth-century sculptures at Chartres. The concave surfaces of the abaci of the side doorways are adorned with acanthus designs resembling very closely the patterns which adorn these members at Chartres and Étampes. This pattern continues on the sides of the shallow porches, although most of this part has been destroyed by the addition of the wall buttresses. The motif itself is exactly the same as that decorating the abaci of Étampes and Chartres, yet in the latter monument the design shows a greater variety. It is quite possible that the abaci of the central portal were originally decorated with this same design. The very marked curve of the unadorned molding and the smoothness of the present surface give rise to the assumption that the restorer has been at work.

The capitals of the central portal (Plate XXVIII, 2), consisting of two staggered tiers of acanthus leaves, are similar to those at Le Mans. The Le Mans capitals of three rows of leaves are more elongated and more elaborate than these. Although the surfaces at Provins have suffered from weathering, it is possible to see some of the delicate details of the curved leaves. As on the capitals of the south door and inside the south tower of Chartres (Plate XXII, 4, 5, 6), a definitely plastic quality is achieved. In the side portals, the capitals are occupied by human figures, birds, and grotesques. In general, their character remains Romanesque, yet they are far removed from the capitals of Vézelay and Autun.

The Provins ornament represents a further tendency away from the controlled character of earlier monuments. Again there is a definite affinity in certain details with the portal at Le Mans, yet many features, especially the abaci, are less exuberant than those at Le Mans and much closer to Chartres.

The ornament at Saint-Loup-de-Naud is confined to capitals and abaci (Plate XXVIII, 3, 4). Since 1140, when the Saint-Denis portals were finished, a new notion of ornamental design had evolved. In place of a type of decoration which hugs the wall, the surface of the blocks are here undercut to such an extent that the architectural members are partially dissolved in light and shade. The baroque elements which appear in an embryonic state at Chartres are more apparent at Saint-Loup-de-Naud than at Le Mans and Provins.

The capitals (Plates XXVIII, 3, 4, and XXIX, 4) are decorated with paired animals and birds combined with floral background. Similar capitals are found at Saint-Denis and on the side portals of Provins, yet here more of the original surfaces have been cut away, with an increased sense of the third dimension. At Provins, foliated backgrounds for the figures are exceptional; at Saint-Loup-de-Naud, they are the rule. The projecting angles of the capitals are accentuated by small volutes or paired tips of leaves or heads of animals. In each one, the central axis is marked by vines which split into secondaries giving off leaves. The bodies of birds and animals occupy the sides of the capitals, while wings or leaves act as fillers.

The capitals flanking the door are decorated with staggered rows of acanthus leaves which are capped either with volutes or pairs of floral offshoots. This motif is also found at Le Mans and in the south tower of Chartres. Here the leaves project less than at Chartres, yet more planes in depth are suggested. The second and third capitals on the left side of the portal (Plate XXVIII, 3) contain frontal birds with grotesque heads separated and embraced by vines and leaves. The same design is found on several colonnettes between the jambs at Chartres, such as LP.L.1 (Plate XV). In the latter monument the motif is piled up vertically, while at Saint-Loup-de-Naud individual sections of this continuous pattern are arranged horizontally, one on each capital. Thus not only the location of the design has changed but also the treatment of the surface. At Chartres the undercut surfaces do not minimize the structural sense of the portal as a whole because they are located between the monumental jamb statues, while at Saint-Loup-de-Naud they are given a prominent position on the capitals.

The abaci on the right side of the portal (Plate XXVIII, 4) are covered with the same motif of acanthus groups found at Chartres and Étampes and on the side portals at Provins. The pattern is essentially the same in all four monuments, but the treatment at Saint-Loup-de-Naud is different. Here, the three-dimensional overtones give the appearance of an elaborately decorative horizontal frieze nearly equal in importance to the capitals (see Plate XXIX, 4). On the other side, the abaci are enhanced by vines which weave across the jambs forming occasional spirals (Plate XXVIII, 3). Many of these patterns originally adorned the vertical columns at Chartres.

At Senlis (Plates XXV, 4, and XXVI, 4) the double capitals project from the flat embrasure to a marked degree. They are decorated with heavy frontal floral motifs, addorsed birds, or elaborate battlements. The patterns are not based on Chartres prototypes nor do they evolve out of Le Mans, Provins, or Saint-Loup-de-Naud. Some of the motifs are related superficially to designs on the capitals of the portals and in the narthex of Saint-Denis (see Plate I, 1, 2). The ornament is much thicker at Senlis, and the greater projection of the capitals causes dramatic contrasts of light and dark.

Crowning small columns between the jamb statues we find floral capitals which are isolated from the large capitals over the figures (see Saint-Denis, Plate I, 1, 2, for contrast). These small capitals are a fancy variant of the "plume" motif of Le Mans (Plate XXVI, 1). Floral borders frame the Labors of the Months which cap the pedestals. In every aspect the ornament at Senlis reinforces the undercut character of the entire portal.

Senlis marks the end of the period in which the Saint-

Denis–Chartres tradition was the inspirational force behind twelfth-century portals. In spite of the fact that it is the end of a long stylistic evolution and, oddly enough, combines features of the earliest of the series (Saint-Denis) with baroque tendencies developed in the 1160's and 1170's, Senlis does not influence High Gothic sculpture. Instead, early-thirteenth-century works such as the Chartres transept portals seem to be transformations of the style of the Headmaster of the Royal Portal into more human terms.

A THEORY OF ORIGINS OF THE ORNAMENTAL AND MONUMENTAL SCULPTURE OF SAINT-DENIS AND CHARTRES

THE PROBLEM of the geographic spread of artistic ideas in the Middle Ages is, by its very nature, conjectural. The organization of the medieval workshop, the training of sculptors, and the growth and development of individual artists — all are unknown factors and can only be surmised by hypothesizing after study of the monuments. The Île-de-France produced no great regional Romanesque as did Burgundy, Provence, Languedoc, and western France. Thus when Suger in the late 1130's set out to rebuild Saint-Denis, he was forced to import artists foreign to the royal domain. Suger, whose artistic sensibility is made clear in his journals, had ample opportunity in his numerous travels to see churches just completed or nearing completion. The western portals of Saint-Denis and Chartres contain much sculpture which, when compared with other Romanesque regions, may give some evidence of the possible origins of the Saint-Denis–Chartres style. An attempt will be made to study the relationships, or the lack of them, between the ornament of geographic areas which conceivably could have affected the great mid-twelfth-century artistic outburst in the Île-de-France. Discussion of the ornamental similarities may in turn suggest certain stylistic analogies between the monumental sculpture of these regions and Saint-Denis and Chartres.

In discussing such an ambiguous subject as origins, certain difficulties immediately arise. Romanesque ornament has been neglected in favor of historiated capitals and portals. Studies of Romanesque manuscripts are limited in number and scope. There is no clear understanding of the relationship between manuscripts and sculpture. Ideas could easily be transmitted via manuscripts, yet there is a danger in forgetting the importance of traveling workshops of sculptors and in failing to realize that the artistic achievement of a single sculptor could easily span fifty years. Another difficulty is the lack of dated monuments in some regions of France, especially Languedoc and western France. Because of outside influences the development of Romanesque sculpture in one given area did not necessarily follow that of another. A final difficulty is the role of the individual patron. How much of Saint-Denis is the result of the dictates of Abbot Suger?

All these qualifications make it necessary to proceed cautiously. The ornament of Languedoc, western France, and Burgundy will be contrasted with Saint-Denis–Chartres and then, following tentative conclusions on the source of inspiration for the ornament, the possible origins of the jamb figures and monumental sculpture will be studied.[1]

I

Languedoc

The flowering of Romanesque art in the region around Toulouse during the late eleventh and twelfth centuries can best be studied in such monuments as Saint-Sernin at Toulouse, Moissac, Saint-Étienne at Toulouse, and the cloister of La Daurade (Plates XXX and XXXI). Much of this sculpture is still in place, but many of the capitals and figures have been assembled in the Musée des Augustins at Toulouse.[2]

None of the ornament resembling that at Saint-Denis decorates monuments which can be accurately dated by documents. The difficulty produced by this situation has been

[1] Books on Romanesque sculpture are as follows: Deschamps, *French Sculpture of the Romanesque Period;* Focillon, *L'Art des sculpteurs romans;* Porter, *Romanesque Sculpture of the Pilgrimage Roads.*

[2] The most complete book on Languedoc is Rey, *La Sculpture romane Languedocienne.* A more recent work on the La Daurade sculpture is

Lafargue, *Les Chapiteaux du cloître de Notre-Dame La Daurade.* A small but complete catalogue of the Musée des Augustins is very useful: Rachou, *Musée des Augustins de Toulouse, pierres romanes de Saint-Étienne, La Daurade et Saint-Sernin.*

increased by the tendency of scholars to establish a date of 1135 to 1140 as the *terminus ante quem* for all important sculpture in the region.[3] If this arbitrary dating is followed, one is forced to conclude that the second series of La Daurade capitals and the portal of the chapter house of Saint-Étienne, both now in the Musée des Augustins, are earlier than Saint-Denis.[4] The importance of Languedoc as the source of inspiration for mid-twelfth-century sculpture in the Île-de-France is always stressed, and it is thereby implied that the relationship with the Île-de-France is the reason for the earlier dating of Languedoc sculpture.

The earliest sculpture in Languedoc contains an abundance of ornament, but none of it shows any relationship to Saint-Denis and Chartres. We must, however, describe the character of this ornament in order to clarify the evolution of style important to this study. Parallel manifestations in Spain will be omitted, since no Spanish ornament during this period bears any resemblance to Île-de-France monuments.[5]

SAINT-SERNIN AT TOULOUSE AND MOISSAC CLOISTER

The late-eleventh-century Corinthian-like capitals of the ambulatory of Saint-Sernin have flat, brittle, metallic leaves suggestive of antique models. They bear little or no relation to the capitals of Saint-Denis and Chartres. The strong influence of Gallo-Roman sculpture is especially noticeable in the bas-reliefs now attached to the ambulatory walls of Saint-Sernin and in the Moissac cloister reliefs (reproduced in Porter, ills. 262–273 and 296–305).[6] This same combination of crisp acanthus leaves and formal, flat, palmette patterns appears on capitals in the gallery and nave of Saint-Étienne of Toulouse.

In the Moissac cloister, which can be dated around 1100 by documents, there are seven floral capitals based on Corinthian or Composite forms.[7] If two of the capitals are compared (Plate XXX, 1, 2), it can be seen that the abaci are treated similarly, one with flat palmettes and the other with vines and floral fillers. The abacus of Plate XXX, 2, in spite of the actual connection between the units of design, is made up of separate unrelated patterns. The bells of these two capitals show interesting differences: Plate XXX, 1, is a subtle transformation of a Roman form, while Plate XXX, 2, is more two-dimensional and is probably an interpretation in stone of a Spanish textile. Other abaci are decorated with frontal birds and grotesques. None of the ornament in the Moissac cloister has any relationship to nature, either in motif or in the sense of growing forms. All the floral patterns are formal and frontal; they enhance but never interfere with the Biblical scene depicted.

CAPITALS FROM LA DAURADE, FIRST SERIES

The eight capitals of the first series from La Daurade, now in the Musée des Augustins, are close in style to the Moissac cloister.[8] The quality of the La Daurade sculpture is clearly inferior. The chronological relationship of the two monuments, however, rests on the difficult problem of "primitive" versus "provincial." [9] If the abaci of the two Moissac capitals are compared to two from La Daurade (Plate XXX, 3, 4), the similarity in motif and carving is obvious.[10]

CAPITALS FROM LA DAURADE, SECOND SERIES

As the twelfth century unfolds, ornament plays an increasingly important role in the design of capitals and portals. The second La Daurade series comprises twenty-two capitals in the Musée des Augustins. Thirteen of these depict scenes from the life of Christ, one the Four Rivers of Paradise, and eight are unhistoriated.[11] Sixteen of the abaci, now placed on top of capitals from both of the La Daurade series and also atop the capitals from Saint-Étienne, can be singled out.[12] All of them are crowned by triple paneled fillets. If the abaci of Plate XXX, 5 and 7, are compared to those from La Daurade, first series, and the Moissac abaci, Plate XXX, 1–4, a new sense of natural growth appears. Undulating, plastic vines with raised lines accenting ribs replace the more static and abstract ornament of the earlier monuments. The floral fillers, instead of consisting of flat, flangelike leaves, are plastically treated. The isolated character of each unit of design is transformed into a continuous organic rhythm which is not found in earlier monuments.

---

[3] Rey groups all the sculpture between the late eleventh century and 1140, while Lafargue sets the date of 1135 for the Saint-Étienne portal.

[4] A further difficulty in studying this sculpture is the confusing arrangement of sculpture in the Musée des Augustins itself. Abaci and capitals from La Daurade (second series) and Saint-Étienne have been interchanged. Lafargue's book when used in conjunction with Rachou's catalogue is of tremendous help in clarifying this situation.

[5] A study of illustrations in Georges Gaillard, *Les Débuts de la sculpture romane Espagnole* (Paris, 1938), in Arthur Kingsley Porter, *Spanish Romanesque Sculpture* (2 vols. Florence: Pantheon, 1928), and in Porter, *Pilgrimage Roads*, vol. V: Catalonia and Aragon, and vol. VI: Castile, Asturias, and Galicia, makes it clear that there is no connection between the ornament of Spain and Saint-Denis–Chartres.

[6] Compare Moissac reliefs with a Gallo-Roman low relief of a woman in the Musée de Niort, in Émile Espérandieu, *Recueil général des bas-reliefs de la Gaule romaine* (Paris, 1907), t. I, no. 1426, p. 317.

[7] For complete photographs and iconographical and stylistic analysis of all the historiated capitals see Schapiro, "The Romanesque Sculpture of Moissac," *Art Bulletin* vol. XIII, no. 3, pp. 249–351, and vol. XIII, no. 4, pp. 464–532; also Porter, *Pilgrimage Roads*, ills. 274–287.

[8] Porter, ills. 288–295, and Lafargue, pls. II–IX.

[9] Lafargue believes that these capitals from La Daurade were carved by 1080. Forsyth's review of Lafargue's book, p. 391, opposes this conclusion.

[10] In the summer of 1939, on the basis of comparison with the Moissac capitals, I made a detailed study of the abaci in the Musée des Augustins. My list of abaci belonging to the first La Daurade series agrees with Marie Lafargue's list which appears in her pl. IX.

[11] These capitals are illustrated in Lafargue's pls. XI–XXX and Porter's ills. 464–473. Lafargue has added three capitals, nos. 396, 397, and 398 to La Daurade. Rachou connected them with Saint-Étienne de Toulouse. Lafargue's addition is backed up by measurements and scientific tests of the stone (p. 82).

[12] See Lafargue, pls. XIX and XX.

Did this change in style result from the normal evolution of the art of Languedoc or was it due to influences coming from outside the region? If the ornament on the Moissac portal, dated about 1115, is examined, the new sense of organic growth accompanied by strongly three-dimensional overtones will be found on the archivolts (see Plate XXXI, 2). The fact that the monumental sculpture of the Moissac portal exhibits strong influences from Burgundy suggests the possible conclusion that Burgundian ornament may have influenced the main stream of Languedoc sculpture.[13] It should be noted, however, that at Moissac the vines are treated simply and the dependent leaves with arbitrary concave surfaces.

The abaci of the second series of La Daurade capitals include several motifs found on the plinths of Saint-Denis. The single vine with floral fillers (Plate XXX, 5) can be compared with the worn plinth (Plate III, 6) and with the vertical border beside the Wise and Foolish Virgins (Plate III, 1, 2). The column in the Musée de Cluny (Plate V) gives a more accurate picture of the flat Saint-Denis ornament which almost completely envelops the column. These same differences can be seen if the La Daurade abacus (Plate XXX, 7) is compared with the same motif at Saint-Denis (Plate IV, 2). On the Saint-Denis plinths none of the floral patterns consist of paired vines interweaving, while on the La Daurade abaci four display a forward and backward movement of the paired stems. The folded ribbon motif (Plate XXX, 6) is similar to a Saint-Denis plinth (Plate III, 4), but in the latter the pattern remains on the surface.

The bells of the ornamental capitals of La Daurade, second series (Plate XXX, 4 not including abacus, and 5), show thick, well-rounded vines either entwining each other to create balanced patterns or encircling strange beasts. Animals and foliage have many fine lines incised on their surfaces in the same manner as on the figures of the historiated capitals. The generally loose character of these two capitals is in marked contrast to the flatter and more tightly conceived ornament and figures on the Saint-Denis column in the Musée de Cluny (Plate V). Thus from the point of view of style, the La Daurade ornament does not develop into that of Saint-Denis. When contrasted with Chartres ornament, all the La Daurade second series seems stiff and congealed and possesses none of the grace and flow of the Chartres colonnettes (see Plates XIII–XV).

The question now arises whether the La Daurade second series was necessarily carved before 1135 or 1137 and whether it therefore did affect Saint-Denis.[14] There are no documents to help in solving the problem although comparisons with more or less accurately dated monuments may shed new light. The capitals from the cloister of Saint-Sernin, now in the Musée des Augustins, (Plate XXX, 8), show strong connections in style with the capitals on the Saint-Sernin west façade, which was not completed until some time toward the middle of the century.[15] At the same time, these capitals (Plate XXX, 8) are very close in style to the two ornamented La Daurade capitals (Plate XXX, 4, 5) just discussed. The evidence would thus seem to point to at least the late fourth or, closer still, the fifth decade of the twelfth century. If this be the case, the La Daurade second series is later than Saint-Denis.

A double capital from La Daurade (Plate XXXI, 6) remains to be discussed.[16] The upper section displays a complex pattern of folded bands, while the lower part is covered with elaborately circulating vines from which grow plastic leaves. Interspersed among the foliage are small nude and draped figures and birds. The style of this ornament is in striking contrast to the delicate flatness of the Saint-Denis column in the Musée de Cluny (Plate V). It is somewhat reminiscent of a decorative column at Chartres (see Plate XIV, 1, 3), yet there is a rigidity and hardness about the La Daurade capital that is absent at Chartres. The heaviness of this ornament finds its closest parallel to Île-de-France sculpture in the capitals and abaci of Saint-Loup-de-Naud (Plate XXVIII, 3, 4) which were carved after 1167.

PORTAL FROM SAINT-ÉTIENNE AT TOULOUSE

The chapter-house portal from Saint-Étienne at Toulouse has been reassembled in the Musée des Augustins (Plate XXXI, 1, 3, 4, 5).[17] Some sections of this small portal, especially the abaci, do not appear to fit together harmoniously (for example, Plate XXXI, 3).[18] Most of the abaci are decorated with some variant of the palmette motif crowned by a banded molding. The relatively light handling of the vines is similar to the second La Daurade series and does not always seem consistent with the capitals. These abaci are completely different from the flat palmettes of Chartres and Étampes (Plates XII, 1; XIX, 1; XXIII, 4, 5) but in their

---

[13] Ansquetil, Abbot of Moissac (1085–1115), was a close friend of Saint Hugh of Cluny.

[14] Rey, pp. 213–234, dates this series 1125–1130; Lafargue, p. 86, places it earlier, 1115–25; but Porter, pp. 242–243, believes that the capitals were carved in the middle of the century, or even later because some of the figures are related to the jamb statues of the chapter-house portal of La Daurade which he argues was inspired by Chartres.

[15] Rey, pp. 290–291 and figs. 207–208, dates the Saint-Sernin façade capitals around 1140. He also dates the Saint-Sernin cloister capitals around 1150. Aubert in L'Église Saint-Sernin de Toulouse, Petites Monographies

des Grands Édifices de la France (Paris, 1933), p. 8, dates the façade toward the middle of the twelfth century.

[16] Lafargue, pp. 82 and 86, dates this capital slightly later than the second series from La Daurade, which she places between 1115 and 1125. Rey, pp. 330–331, believes that it was carved in the third quarter of the twelfth century.

[17] Rey, pp. 192–202, places this sculpture ca. 1120; Lafargue, p. 86, dates it after La Daurade, between 1125 and 1134; Porter, pp. 159–160 and ills. 434–449, argues that the portal is later than Chartres.

[18] The measurements are: 1.62 meters on both sides of the portal (from top of abaci to bottom of jamb figures).

plasticity do possess features common to Le Mans, 1158, and Saint-Loup-de-Naud (see Plate XXVIII, 1, 3, 4).

The ornament on the capitals consists of vines embracing leaves, animals, or humans. The stems are heavy and rope-like. In contrast to the fine quality of both the Saint-Denis and Chartres columns, this ornament seems uninspired (note especially right-hand detail, Plate XXXI, 3). The floral decoration gives the appearance of an overlay without regard for the structural clarity of the portal. If Plate XXXI, 4, 5, is compared to details of the Chartres portals (Plate XII, 1, 2), it can be seen that the Chartrain ornament clarifies the capitals and increases the architectonic character of the jamb statues, whereas the Saint-Étienne capitals detract from the monumental effect of the sculpture. This interest in pictorial effects with its resulting loss of structural clarity is reminiscent of Le Mans and Saint-Loup-de-Naud (see Plates XXVIII and XXIX). The thick vines and general heaviness of the foliage is close to Le Mans (see Plate XXIX, 2).

From a study of the ornament alone, it is difficult to see how either the La Daurade capitals of the second series or the sculpture from Saint-Étienne could be the seeds from which sprang the art of the Île-de-France.[19] Although there are certain simple motifs which appear at Saint-Denis and Chartres, the style of ornament and the relationship between ornament and portal are quite different. For the most part, the portal as a whole is closer in style to monuments in and near the royal domain, which were carved in the late 1150's into the 1170's.

The jamb figures of Saint-Étienne de Toulouse (Plate XXXI, 5) are related to both Saint-Denis and Chartres. Half of the Saint-Étienne statues have crossed legs, while at Saint-Denis seven out of twenty had crossed legs and at Chartres only one. The short proportions are like the Saint-Denis figures and the related statues at Chartres. None of the heads are frontal as in the Île-de-France monuments; all are turned from the main axis of the figures. Eyes are wide open in a frozen stare; hair and beards are extremely stylized. None of the humanity suggested at Saint-Denis and developed further at Chartres is to be found in these heads (see Plate XXXI, 5). All these differences would suggest, it is true, that the Toulouse figures are earlier than Saint-Denis and Chartres, but the strength and continuity of the Languedoc tradition must not be overlooked. For example, the strong impact of Burgundian style on the Moissac portals (ca. 1115) did not obliterate but merged with the Languedocien style. By studying the figure of Saint Andrew (Plate XXXI, 5, right-hand figure) one can understand how the flat pier figures of Moissac (ca. 1100) and the ambulatory reliefs of Saint-Sernin (ca. 1095) with their ample frame of columns,

capitals, and arches have been transformed into plastic statues framed by slender columns.

The figures of Saints Thomas and Andrew (Plate XXXI, 5), originally signed by Gilabertus, are the finest. Some of the statues exhibit a coarseness and crudity which marks them as the work of inferior sculptors. The drapery of the two saints, consisting of innumerable small folds, discloses portions of the anatomy, especially the legs and arms. The hands are coördinated with the main axis of the figures, as at Chartres, but not like the more varied gestures of Saint-Denis. Elaborately embroidered patterns decorate the hems of the garments. The ornament on the bottom of the hems is similar to the fragment of the tomb of Odo, Abbot of Saint-Remi of Reims, who died in 1157.[20] A similar but more chaste treatment of hems is found on the Saint-Denis jambs (Plate VII).

The Saint Andrew (right-hand figure in Plate XXXI, 5) is related to one statue at Saint-Denis (Plate VII, 5, drawing in reverse for Montfaucon). The bunched folds over the arms and the double cascade of drapery over the knees are similar, but the Saint-Étienne jamb displays a more complex sequence of double folds over the left leg and many shallow tight folds over the right leg. The drapery, proportions, gestures, and general treatment of folds find an even closer parallel in style in a Chartres figure (RP.R.1, Plate XVI, 2). The Chartres jamb has fewer folds and less ornamentation on the hems. It is in fact a statue-column and not carved back from the projecting corner of a square block. The elaborate treatment of drapery of the Saint Andrew resembles more closely the figures by the Chartres Headmaster, especially CP.R.2 and 4 (Plate XVII) and the Le Mans jambs (Plate XXVI, 1). The quality of carving is inferior to that of the Headmaster and nearer to the sculptor who carved the Le Mans portal.

As in the case of the relationship in ornament between Saint-Étienne and Saint-Denis–Chartres, this Languedoc sculpture shows a closer connection with Chartres and later monuments than with Saint-Denis. Since Chartres grew out of the earlier experiments at Saint-Denis, it is difficult to see how Saint-Étienne at Toulouse could have affected Saint-Denis. The quality of workmanship is inferior to that on either Île-de-France monument but it has an affinity with the less sensitive carving of Le Mans and Provins. The general effect of the Saint-Étienne portal, with its profusion of ornament and elaborately treated statues, closely parallels monuments of the late 1150's and 1160's, in a period just after the high point of artistic achievement reached at Chartres. These relationships between Saint-Étienne and portals in and around the royal domain would seem to in-

---

[19] Lafargue, p. 88: "Ainsi le cloître de la Daurade a été le point de départ d'une iconographie et d'un style qui se sont développés dans l'Île-de-France et à Chartres, berceau de la sculpture gothique."

[20] This relationship was pointed out by W. R. Tyler in an article "A Spanish Romanesque Column in the Fogg Art Museum," *Art Bulletin* (March 1941), XXIII, 51.

dicate that, toward and after the middle of the century, sculpture in widely separated areas in France was progressing in the same direction and has many similarities of style. Saint-Lazare at Avallon represents the same moment in Burgundian art as Saint-Étienne in Languedoc. The artistic impetus for this sculpture seems to be Chartres; this impetus affects regions in various ways depending on the strength of local traditions. The sculptors who carved the Saint-

Étienne portal appear to have grasped at some of the externals of this imported art and to have combined it with their elaborate ornamental background which had already passed through an extensive evolution. It is difficult to argue that out of this hybrid, which incidentally is of uneven and often poor quality, grew the masterpieces of Saint-Denis and Chartres.

II

Western France

The regions of Saintonge-Poitou, Angoumois, and Périgord are crowded with Romanesque churches. The architecture is largely dependent upon outside influences. The Poitevin churches, such as Notre-Dame-de-la-Grande at Poitiers, and Aulnay, Melle, and Parthenay, are small versions of the Pilgrimage Roads churches with high aisles buttressing the barrel-vaulted naves instead of galleries (Aulnay, Plate XXXII, 2). The domed churches of Angoumois and Périgord are based on eastern types like Saint Mark's, Venice, and are possibly inspired by Byzantine architecture in Cyprus. Another aisleless group in Saintonge is a further simplification of the above.[21] No progressive structural or spacial ideas were evolved that were later incorporated in Gothic. Perhaps to disguise their architectural inferiority complex, the Romanesque builders profusely decorated their churches. Decorative stringcourses, moldings, and archivolts were carved with an abundance of ornament.

Strong influences from these regions on the Île-de-France, especially in the treatment of archivolts, have often been suggested, yet the lack of dated monuments makes the study of origins difficult. Most of these churches are, however, late Romanesque and thus contemporary, more or less, with Saint-Denis.

ANGOULÊME AND POITIERS

Two monuments, Angoulême and Notre-Dame-la-Grande at Poitiers, have elaborately ornamented borders around the profusion of figured sculpture on their façades.[22] At Angoulême much of the ornament consists of rinceaux and animals interlaced, and palmettes in various combinations. The vines are thick and ponderous by contrast with those at Saint-Denis and Chartres. The heavy character of this ornament is clearly shown in the vine, double-axe, and folded-ribbon patterns at Poitiers. Although many of these motifs, practically universal within the limits of Romanesque, can be found at Saint-Denis and Chartres, their style is alto-

gether dissimilar. In both monuments ornament and figures are treated as an overlay.

SAINT-PIERRE AT AULNAY

Details of four monuments, shown in Plates XXXII and XXXIII, show various connections in style with Île-de-France sculpture. The chronological relationship between these churches and Saint-Denis is, however, difficult to solve. The south transept of Saint-Pierre at Aulnay (Plate XXXII, 1, 2) has an elaborate portal with radiating voussoirs of atlas figures.[23] The inmost archivolt has flat vines and animals strongly reminiscent of Hispano-Moresque textiles and Moorish ivories. The impact of Spain is constantly felt in the art of western France. The vines and griffons in the continuous frieze across the abaci (Plate XXXII, 1) have no counterpart at Saint-Denis or Chartres.

The three portals of the west façade of Aulnay portray the Crucifixion of Saint Peter on the left (Plate XXXII, 4) and Christ with the Virgin and Saint John on the right. The central portal has no tympanum but elaborate archivolts with the Zodiac, Wise and Foolish Virgins, and Angels. In contrast to the transept portal, there is some connection in style between the paired vines and fillers extending across the abaci and beneath the tympanum (Plate XXXII, 3, 4) and the ornament in the Île-de-France. At Saint-Denis the vines and leaves are much flatter (see column, Plate V). Similar motifs appear at Chartres, yet all the Chartres ornament is located on columns between the jambs, the abaci being decorated with simple, flat palmettes (see Plate XII). As in Languedoc, the Aulnay ornament in its role in the allover decoration of the portal resembles later Île-de-France monuments such as Saint-Loup-de-Naud (Plate XXVIII, 3, 4).

No documents are available for a proper dating of the Aulnay portals. The sculpture is similar to that of Chadenac which has a relatively modern inscription of 1140. It is argued that this inscription follows one contemporary with

---

[21] See Mendell, *Romanesque Sculpture in Saintonge* pp. 19–34.

[22] Porter, pp. 304–313 and ills. 929–940, argues that all the Angoulême sculpture was completed by the consecration date of 1128 and that

Poitiers (*ibid.*, pp. 320–323 and ills. 951–962) was finished around 1130 because of its stylistic connections with Angoulême.

[23] Porter, pp. 331–332 and ills. 979–986, dates this portal *ca.* 1130 purely on stylistic grounds.

the sculpture.[24] The same double undulating vine appears on the abaci to the left of the central portal.[25] The figures on the archivolts of the central portals of both monuments display flowing drapery of numerous flat folds reminiscent of Burgundy. Since the Saint-Denis portals were carved in the late 1130's, neither Aulnay or Chadenac could have affected Saint-Denis, assuming that the inscription of 1140 is valid. Although it is quite possible that these two monuments could have influenced Chartres, all the Chartres ornament, on the other hand, develops quite naturally out of the experiments at Saint-Denis. The Chartres motifs are either more plastic versions or new combinations of patterns already carved at Saint-Denis by 1140. None of the elaborate Chartres motifs can be found on any monument in western France.

NOTRE-DAME-DE-LA-COULDRE AT PARTHENAY

The sculpture of Notre-Dame-de-la-Couldre at Parthenay (Plate XXXIII, 1, 2, 4, 5, 6) is related to that of Aulnay and Chadenac.[26] In 1135 Saint Bernard converted Guillaume IX, Duke of Aquitaine, in front of a portal of a church in Parthenay. It is not clear, however, whether this document refers to Notre-Dame-de-la-Couldre or to Parthenay-le-Vieux; nor is it at all certain how near completion the church was in 1135. Again, the chronological relationship between this sculpture and Saint-Denis remains doubtful. It is difficult to reconstruct its elaborate sculptural composition (Plate XXXIII, 1). The upper half of the façade has been destroyed. What is left of the monumental sculpture is now in the Louvre (Plate XXXIII, 6) and in Fenway Court, Boston.

The most elaborate ornament is found on the outer border of the archivolts and the continuous frieze at the level of the abaci (Plate XXXIII, 1, 2, 4). The wide, flat vines of the archivolts are dissimilar to any of the Saint-Denis ornament and appear thicker than any floral patterns at Chartres. The frieze extending from the central across the right portal consist of a basket-weave pattern, a motif which is common in western France but never appears in the Île-de-France. The frieze running from the central portal to the left (Plate XXXIII, 2, 4) consists of a double rinceau forming heart-shaped ovals. This pattern is like the floral spiral of the Saint-Denis column in the Musée de Cluny (Plate V, 3). The vines are treated similarly, but the undercutting is more extensive at Parthenay with the result that ornament stands out in relief against a dark ground. At Saint-Denis, the leaves are only slightly concave in the center and rounded on the edges in contrast to the distinctly concave treatment at Parthenay. A similar pattern at Chartres (Plate XIII, 1, 2), with its subtle variation of relief, differs from the two-dimensional character of the Parthenay frieze. As at Aulnay, the ornament acts as a unifying agent for the whole façade and attracts as much attention as the figured archivolts. This relationship of ornament to the total ensemble is unlike the subordinate role of ornament at Saint-Denis and at Chartres. The flank of a later church, Saint-Hilaire at Melle (Plate XXXIII, 3), shows how floral motifs extend over every available molding.

The figured sculpture at Parthenay shows some connections with the Île-de-France but is closer stylistically to earlier Burgundian monuments such as Vézelay, Autun, and fragments from the destroyed portal of Cluny. The archivolt figures of Parthenay (Plate XXXIII, 2) are elongated, unlike those at Saint-Denis. The freedom with which the voussoirs are handled is more reminiscent of Le Mans (completed by 1158; see Plate XXV, 1), while the treatment of drapery in relatively wide, flat folds is strongly Burgundian. The larger sculpture (Plate XXXIII, 6), which has been much restored, lacks the monumentality of the jambs at Saint-Denis and Chartres.[27] Does it follow that their more archaic character necessarily makes them earlier? The pointed heads with flowing hair and ample beards and the drapery in large curved folds seem Burgundian in character.

The head in the Fogg Museum, probably from Parthenay, has lost a great deal of its original surface.[28] When compared with Saint-Denis (Plates VIII and IX) and Chartres (Plates XIX and XX), it can be seen that in silhouette the head is closer to Saint-Denis. The birdlike shape of the head is like one of the Baltimore heads from Saint-Denis (Plate VIII). On the other hand, the more fluid treatment of hair and beard is closer in style to the second Baltimore head (Plate IX) and the Chartres heads (Plate XIX). It is impossible to establish any chronological relationship in this instance, especially when there is the possibility of a common source both for this head from western France and those from Saint-Denis and Chartres.

CLOISTERS OF SAINT-AUBIN AT ANGERS

In the cloisters of Saint-Aubin at Angers there is a large amount of ornament which, at first glance, bears a strong

---

[24] Porter, p. 317 and ills. 1034–1040, believes that the inscription is based on one which is contemporary with the sculpture. Because of the stylistic relationships between Chadenac and Aulnay, he dates the latter around 1140. Mendell places Chadenac after 1140.

[25] See Mendell, p. 102, fig. 6d, for diagram of motif.

[26] Porter, p. 334 and ills. 1045–1057, thinks that the lower half of the façade was carved between 1135 and 1140.

[27] The lower half of the Louvre and Fenway Court figures are modern, as proved by Sadoux's engravings (Porter, ills. 1053, 1055–1056). In an

article entitled "The Restored Twelfth Century Parthenay Sculptures," *Technical Studies*, Fogg Art Museum (January 1942), pp. 122–130, James J. Rorimer published for the first time photographs of this sculpture taken at Parthenay about 1900 before the restorations (see Plate XXXIII, 6, for two examples). A comparison of these photographs and the sculpture as it exists today in Fenway Court and the Louvre reveals the extensive cleaning and the resulting damage to the surfaces.

[28] The Fogg Museum head from Parthenay was first published by James Rorimer in the above article on Parthenay, fig. 6.

similarity to the plinths of Saint-Denis (Plate XXXII, 5, 6; compare Plate IV). The shape of the voussoirs and the relatively low relief are, however, the only common denominators, for the Angers sculpture is largely made up of patterns governed by an elaborate interweaving process foreign to Saint-Denis. The actual carving of the rinceaux lack the subtlety and finesse of the Saint-Denis column in the Musée de Cluny. Another type of sculpture in the same cloister, consisting of a frieze and capitals, possesses a freedom of handling which resembles Chartres (see Plate XXXII, 6). In contrast to the other Saint-Aubin sculpture, this would appear to be later in date. The general character of this ornament suggests an elaboration of motifs found at Aulnay and Parthenay; the relation to the Île-de-France is only tentative.[29]

In spite of the apparent similarities between the ornament and some of the figured sculpture of western France and the Île-de-France, the relationship remains superficial. All the ornamental motifs which have counterparts at Saint-Denis and Chartres are of the type which is common to the Romanesque vocabulary. None of the monuments can be dated earlier than Saint-Denis (1140). Furthermore, it seems superfluous to argue that the Chartres sculpture could not have developed out of Saint-Denis sculpture without influence from western France. In all instances, the total impact of the portal — ornamental sculpture in relation to figured sculpture — is entirely different. Strong influences from Burgundy on both areas would help explain some of the apparent stylistic affinities. In spite of the captivating charm of western-French churches, it would be strange and unusual if the monumental portals of Saint-Denis and Chartres grew out of this relatively backward region.

III

Burgundy

In contrast to Languedoc and western France, many of the Burgundian monuments can be dated by documents earlier than the mid-1130's and thus before Suger's portals of Saint-Denis. Ornamental decoration found on capitals and portals, as well as in Burgundian manuscripts, have counterparts to Île-de-France sculpture both in type of motifs and style. Affinities in style between the figure sculpture of these two regions are more difficult to discover.

The precociousness of Burgundian architecture is seen in the tenth-century narthex vaults of Tournus, the groin-vaulted nave of Vézelay, and the ninety-nine-foot pointed barrel vaults, rising above a clerestory, of Cluny III. No region of France, or of all Europe, developed an architecture which so definitely presaged the Gothic. Although Norman architecture contributed six-part ribbed vaults and embryonic flying buttresses to the development of Gothic construction, the masses and spaces of Norman Romanesque do not challenge the soaring and daring character of Cluny and Paray-le-Monial. Burgundian sculpture has a richness and variety which is in complete harmony with its architecture. Manuscripts produced by Cluniac and Cistercian monks are among the most beautifully ornamented in the twelfth century. These manuscripts contain many similarities to Burgundian sculpture.

ABSTRACT ORNAMENT IN BURGUNDIAN SCULPTURE

On the transept portals of Paray-le-Monial several abstract motifs appear which are found at Saint-Denis and at Chartres. The north portal (Plate XXXIV, 1) is framed by channeled pilasters supporting an arched cornice.[30] The column on the left, the top of which can be seen in Plate XXXIV, 1, is ornamented with a four-leaf-clover pattern. This motif appears on several short columns beneath the jambs at Chartres (see Plate XVII).[31] The undercutting is similar. The leaves are arranged diagonally at Paray-le-Monial.

The right-hand columnar jamb and the rounded archivolt are adorned with the double-axe pattern, a motif of antique origin uncommon in Romanesque times except in Burgundy. This motif appears on a Chartres column (CP.L.2, Plate XIII, 3) and at Saint-Denis (plinth, RP.L.3, Plate III, 5). At Saint-Denis the pattern is incised on the block in small scale, whereas at Chartres the depth of relief is similar to that of Paray-le-Monial, perhaps because the problem is the same, that is, the decoration of a columnar surface. The voids are ornamental, with drill holes at Paray-le-Monial and single knobs at Chartres. The badly worn surface of the Chartres column makes the comparison difficult, yet the projection of lobes and the crispness of the carving are identical in style.

The south transept portal of Paray-le-Monial (Plate XXXIV, 2), partly destroyed by subsequent construction, is even more elaborately decorated. The folded-band motif on the outer border is found at Chartres on the two columns flanking the central portal (Plate XVII). At Saint-Denis this motif appears in much lower relief on a plinth running horizontally (Plate III, 4). The outer jamb and its archivolt display an alternating concave and convex meander pattern

---

[29] Porter, p. 341, dates the cloister about 1145 on stylistic grounds.
[30] Mâle suggests an Islamic influence. See Émile Mâle, "Les Influences arabes dans l'art roman," *Revue de Deux Mondes* (November 15, 1923),

p. 315. Some of the motifs, however, seem closer to Roman ornament.
[31] This motif decorates the following columns at Chartres: CP.L.3, CP.R.2, CP.R.3, LP.R.4, RP.L.2, and RP.L.3.

which zigzags laterally across the column. At Chartres this motif climbs up in steps on three of the short columns below the joints.[32] The modeling is like that of the damaged Chartres RP.L.4 column (Plate XVIII, 2).

All four of these abstract motifs found at Paray-le-Monial have parallels at Chartres. Two appear at Saint-Denis, but they are carved in lower relief on plinths which have an architectural function different from the members decorated at Paray-le-Monial and at Chartres. All these patterns have their own further development in Burgundy, notably in the Brionnais region to the south of Paray-le-Monial. The double-axe motif is found on archivolts of portals at Montceau-l'Étoile and Semur-en-Brionnais.[33] The folded band decorates the archivolts of Semur-en-Brionnais and also flanks the outer portal at Charlieu.[34] The ornament in these three monuments is an elaboration of the Paray-le-Monial portals. The patterns have become more complex with additional details carved on borders. Crispness of carving yields to sinuous curves. The profuse ornament covers the entire portals and partly disguises the structural members. Saint-Denis and Chartres, especially the latter, are related to the earlier style of the Burgundian evolution, represented by Paray-le-Monial, and not to the later monuments.

CORINTHIAN CAPITALS

Many pseudo-Corinthian capitals are found in the narthex and choir of Saint-Denis and in the south tower of Chartres (Plate XXII). In an effort to determine the possible origin of these Roman-looking capitals, which had not appeared in the Île-de-France prior to 1140, one is forced to turn to Burgundy (Plate XXXIV, 3, 4, 6). Any discussion of Corinthian or Composite capitals is complicated by the fact that France is filled with Roman ruins which could and did serve as models for Romanesque carvers. Nevertheless, each region of France interpreted the Roman forms in its own way. In Provence, in such a monument as Saint-Gilles, the leaves and scrolls are heavy and deeply undercut. They bear no stylistic relationship to Saint-Denis and Chartres.[35] Monuments in southwestern France, such as Moissac (see Plate XXX, 1) and Saint-Sernin at Toulouse, possess many such capitals, but none display the same delicacy found both in Burgundian and in Saint-Denis–Chartres capitals. The leaves in the Languedocien capitals are relatively flat and flange-like.

Corinthian capitals appear in Burgundian monuments over a period of half a century. The earliest of the series — Cluny, ambulatory, 1088–1095; Cluny transept, *ca.* 1100 — had little or no effect on the design of capitals in the Île-de-France.[36] Most of the Cluny capitals have three tiers of acanthus leaves capped by volutes at corners and rosettes in the center. The leaves remain close to the bell of the capitals.

In contrast to those at Cluny, Burgundian capitals of the 1120's and early 1130's with plastically conceived leaves resemble those of Saint-Denis and Chartres. In fact, there is no closer parallel outside the Île-de-France. Such examples as a capital from Vézelay (Plate XXXIV, 6) or the two from Saulieu (Plate XXXIV, 3, 4), which can be dated soon after 1119, are very similar to those in the south tower of Chartres (Plate XXII, 4).[37] At Chartres greater attention is given to the detailed carving of individual leaves (compare Plate XXXIV, 3, 4, with the right-hand capitals of Plate XXII, 4). Some stylistic analogies between Saint-Denis and Burgundian capitals may be seen, especially in the crispness of the carving (see Plate XXII, 2).

It is quite clear that Burgundy exerted no influence on the sculpture of the north tower of Chartres, begun after the fire of 1134 (see Plate XXII, 3). The impact of Burgundy began to appear at Saint-Denis in the narthex of 1140 and the chevet of 1144 (see Plate XXII, 1, 2). The full strength of this impulse, however, was felt in the south tower of Chartres (Plate XXII, 4), which was under construction by 1145, and in the south portal of this tower, which was cut into it during the 1150's (Plate XXII, 5, 6). It can be argued, therefore, that the effect of Burgundy on the evolution of sculpture in the Île-de-France is not an isolated or momentary artistic phenomenon but rather increases in intensity.

ORNAMENT IN BURGUNDIAN MANUSCRIPTS

Burgundian manuscripts provide the most important source for the ornamental motifs of Saint-Denis and Chartres. All the Cistercian manuscripts which are related to monuments of the Île-de-France can be dated between 1098, when the order was founded, and 1134, the year in which the restrictive rules of Saint Bernard were put into effect.

The Cistercian order was founded March 21, 1098, in protest against the luxuries of the Cluniac order. A group of monks led by Abbot Robert and Étienne Harding left Mo-

---

[32] See Chartres CP.L.5 (Plate XIII, 3), RP.L.4, and CP.R.4 (modern).

[33] Porter, ill. 143.

[34] Porter, ills. 108–110. Elizabeth Sunderland, "The History and Architecture of the Church of St. Fortunatus at Charlieu in Burgundy," *Art Bulletin* (March 1939), vol. XXI, figs. 17, 18, 21.

[35] Porter, ills. 1315–1317, 1321, 1323.

[36] In an article, "The Date of the Ambulatory Capitals of Cluny," *Speculum*, vol. V, no. 1 (January 1930), pp. 77–94, Kenneth Conant proves conclusively that these capitals were in place when the sanctuary of the church was dedicated by Pope Urban II. For the date of the transept and

its capitals see Conant, "Drawings and Photographs of the Transept of Cluny," *Speculum*, vol. IV, no. 3 (July 1929), pp. 291–302. Note especially pls. I–III.

[37] Porter, p. 113, dates the Saulieu capitals soon after the translation of relics in 1119. Another series of Burgundian capitals from Moutier-Saint-Jean and now in the Fogg Museum can be dated before 1133 (Porter, p. 114). These capitals show strong connections in style with the Île-de-France. A capital from Moutier-Saint-Jean was recently purchased by the Lawrence Art Museum, Williams College.

lesme and went to the forests of Cîteaux to live in the spirit of Saint Benedict's original teachings.[38] The asceticism of Cîteaux attracted Saint Bernard in 1112. Surprisingly enough, in spite of the strictness of the rules, so much attention was paid to the study of the classics, to the development of libraries, and to the illumination of manuscripts that it is difficult to distinguish between Cistercian and Cluniac illuminations. Plate XXXV illustrates pages from the Légendaire de Cîteaux and the Cluniac Bible of Saint-Bénigne de Dijon. It can hardly be argued that the one is a reaction against the lavishness of the other; in fact, the same monk might easily have illuminated both pages.

The Cistercian order developed rapidly during the early years of the twelfth century. By 1151 there were 330 Cistercian monasteries in western Europe. The role of Cluny was being overshadowed. And it must not be forgotten that, as a result of the spread of the Cistercian order in the late twelfth century, Gothic construction was carried to Spain, Italy, England, and Germany.

In 1134 detailed statutes were promulgated forbidding the use of ornament in manuscripts. Other stringent rules governed sculpture.[39] Assuming that these rules were obeyed, the date of 1134 establishes a *terminus ante quem* for the Cistercian manuscripts under discussion.

While there are certain relationships to Saint-Denis and Chartres in the earlier manuscripts of this group, they become more apparent in the later manuscripts. In the Bible of Saint-Étienne Harding, which can be dated between 1098 and 1109, occur initials composed of vines embracing fantastic beasts, reminiscent of the column in the Musée de Cluny.[40] The remarkable freedom of pose and movement and the feeling for natural growth in trees and branches, which can be seen in the Creation of Adam forming the initial *A*, links this manuscript art to Burgundian Romanesque sculpture, specifically to such ambulatory capitals of Cluny as the Rivers of Paradise.[41] The figures of the Church and the Synagogue in the initial *O* bear a strong resemblance to the Christ in the wall paintings of Berzé-la-Ville.[42] In the Moralia in Job, completed in 1111, the initials depicting scenes from everyday life have the same freedom and expressive character found in the Cluny and Vézelay capitals.[43]

The illuminations in later Cistercian manuscripts are more restrained and precise. The ornament is light against a dark ground, and the modeling of stems and vines is effected by delicate shading.

Although there are eight manuscripts in the group, only the Légendaire de Cîteaux (Plate XXXV, 1) will be discussed here.[44] The frontispiece of the Légendaire (Plate XXXV, 1) exhibits an abundance of ornament related to the Saint-Denis–Chartres sculpture.[45] The initial *T* is filled with vines, monsters, and birds. The problem of decorating a rectangular panel does not exist in the Saint-Denis and Chartres sculpture. On the other hand, some of the motifs and their style resemble the Saint-Denis column in the Musée de Cluny (Plate V). In the manuscript and the column, the relationship between solids and voids and the controlled but never frozen character of the ornament is the same. The way in which vines embrace animals and birds and at the same time flatten them against the ground is seen in the initial and in the Saint-Denis column (compare the lower left corner of the initial and Plate V, 2, 6).

Many of the Chartres colonnettes have figures, vines, and leaves in various combinations (Plate XIV, 1, 3).[46] The ornament in the initial is more controlled; voids consist of smaller units. The relative complexity of the Burgundian ornament resembles Chartres, yet the drawing of the tightly rolled leaves and the general flatness of the whole decoration is closer to Saint-Denis.

The borders of the frontispiece of the Légendaire de Cîteaux and of the page from the Bible of Saint-Bénigne de Dijon (Plate XXXV, 1, 2) are decorated with combinations of vines and leaves organized in frontal patterns and in spirals.[47] Although the motifs are not identical with those on the plinths and columns at Saint-Denis and the colonnettes at Chartres, there is ample evidence to suggest that the sculptors were familiar with these or similar manuscripts. The upper section of the right-hand border of both manuscripts is found in a somewhat different combination of leaves on a Saint-Denis plinth (CP.L.1, Plate III, 2) and decorating the heart-shaped patterns on the column in the Musée de Cluny (Plate V, 3). The leaves are treated similarly with accented midribs and rolled extremities. One notices the sense of flatness which is created by the uniform lightness of the vines against the dark ground in the manu-

---

[38] See Oursel's excellent book for analysis of the Cistercian manuscripts and for brief account of the formation of the order: Charles Oursel, *La Miniature du XIIe siècle à l'Abbaye de Cîteaux d'après les manuscrits de la Bibliothèque de Dijon* (Dijon, 1926).

[39] This condemnation of ornament was first pronounced by Saint Bernard in 1125 in his "Apologie à Guillaume de Saint-Thierry." See Oursel, p. 50 and n.

[40] Bible de Saint Étienne Harding (Dijon Mss. 12 to 15); Oursel pls. III–XXI; note especially initial *I* in pl. III.

[41] Creation of Adam, Dijon Ms. 14 (fol. 76). See Oursel, pl. X.

[42] Initial *O*, Dijon Ms. 14 (fol. 60) in Oursel, pl. VIII.

[43] Moralia in Job, Dijon Mss. 168, 169, 170, and 173. See Oursel, pls. XXII–XXIX.

[44] Légendaire de Cîteaux consists of five volumes. Dijon Mss. 638, 639, and 640 were written in the thirteenth century; Dijon 641 is intact; 642 is unfinished. See Oursel, pp. 35ff and pls. XXXII–XXXVI.

[45] Frontispiece of Légendaire, Dijon 641 (fol. 2 verso): .36 x .26 meters. All the photographs of the Dijon manuscripts were taken under the supervision of Jack Savacool who made a study of the Cistercian and Cluniac manuscripts in Dijon.

[46] Also compare central medallion of left (Plate XXXV, 1) with Chartres LP.L.2 top (Plate XVI, 1) and with Chartres CP.L.3 bottom and middle piece (Plate XVII, 1) and with Chartres RP.R.1 top (Plates XVI, 2, and XIX, 2).

[47] Bible de Saint-Bénigne de Dijon, Dijon 2. Initial *I* (fol. 2 verso) with frame measures .40 x .14 meters.

scripts and the shallow relief of the sculpture (note especially Plate V). The relative lack of modeling in vines and leaves is seen in both the manuscripts and the Saint-Denis sculpture.

This same motif (upper right-hand border of both manuscripts, Plate XXXV, 1, 2) combined with climbing vines appears at Chartres (LP.L.2 top, Plate XVI, 1, and CP.L.3, Plate XVII, 1). The foliage in the Chartres colonnettes — seen more clearly in a different pattern (Plate XIII, 2) — is conceived in more plastic terms. The Chartres ornament manifests a new freedom and elasticity. The ornament of Languedoc and western France exhibits some connections with Chartres and later monuments and none with Saint-Denis. These Burgundian drawings, on the other hand, resemble the Saint-Denis sculpture.

Another motif, which has counterparts at both Saint-Denis and Chartres, is the spiraling pattern on the lower right-hand section of the border of both manuscripts (Plate XXXV, 1, 2). The jeweled band framing the spiral is similar to the border flanking the Labors of the Month at Saint-Denis (Plate II); it is also found on the spiral column in the Musée de Cluny (Plate V). The treatment of the floral fillers is closer to Saint-Denis than to spiral colonnettes at Chartres (LP.L.2, Plate XV, 1).

The arbitrary flatness of the Saint-Denis sculpture gives the impression that the whole idea of the decoration had originally been conceived as light drawings against a darker ground. One would like to conclude that Abbot Suger was the owner of a Burgundian manuscript and had the sculptors use it as models for the Saint-Denis ornament.

FIGURE STYLE IN BURGUNDIAN MANUSCRIPTS

There are certain general connections in style between the manuscripts and the monumental sculpture of Saint-Denis and Chartres. There is no instance, however, in which the sculptors of Île-de-France monuments utilized figures directly from manuscripts. The transformation from drawings to sculpture in the round is, of course, a more difficult problem than the change from drawings to low-relief ornament.

Many of the initials of the Cistercian manuscripts (Plate XXXVI, 3, 4) incorporate columns with attached figures. Since this is painting, not architecture, the illuminator is free to decorate both ends of the column with capitals, and to enhance the column itself with floral ornament. It has been suggested that these initials may have inspired the idea for columnar jamb statues, first used on a monumental scale at Saint-Denis.[48]

When the drawings of the Saint-Denis jambs (Plate VII) are compared with the Burgundian manuscripts (Plate XXXVI), we find some interesting similarities. The outer silhouettes of statues and initial figures taper inward from

the widest section where the drapery envelops the elbows. In the Cistercian manuscript (Plate XXXVI, 2, 3, 4, 5), the drapery flares outwards at the bottom hems. This detail is different from the Saint-Denis jambs in which the narrowest width is reached just above the feet. Some of the figures of the Cluniac manuscript, especially the two right-hand ones (Plate XXXVI, 1), are similar to the Saint-Denis drawings in their outer contour lines. This same characteristic of tapering silhouette is found at Étampes (Plates XXIII, XXIV) and at Chartres in the jambs related to Saint-Denis and to Étampes (Plate XVI, 1, 2). It is not seen on the statues by the Headmaster of Chartres and his assistants (Plates XVII, XVIII).

Another characteristic common to the manuscript figures and to the jambs of Saint-Denis, Étampes, and those at Chartres related to Saint-Denis and Étampes is the disjointed anatomy. This feature is most apparent in the treatment of elbows and wrists. The eighteenth-century draftsman employed by Montfaucon smoothed out the awkward wrists of the Saint-Denis figures, yet the jumpy anatomy is clearly seen in the Saint-Denis bas-relief (Plate X). Gestures are uncoördinated with the central axis of the figures. The Headmaster of Chartres (Plate XVII) makes smoother the transitions from shoulder to arm and forearm to hand; he aligns hands and symbols along the center of the figures. As in the case of the silhouettes of jambs and manuscript figures, the connection is between Burgundy and Saint-Denis and Étampes and not between Burgundy and the Headmaster of Chartres.

In several of the illuminated figures (see Plate XXXVI, 5), the position of the knee is indicated by an elliptical curve. This feature is found on several Saint-Denis statues (see Plate VII, 5). A variant on this characteristic in which the knees are emphasized by curves of drapery is seen in several Saint-Denis figures (Plate VII, 1, 2, 3).

Certain details of drapery, moreover, are roughly similar. In some of the initials (Plate XXXVI, 2, 3, 5) the mantle covers the left hand and cascades down the left leg in a double fold. This motif is found at Saint-Denis (Plate VII, 5, drawing in reverse for engraving) and on one of the figures by the Saint-Denis Master at Chartres (Plate XVI, 2, RP.R.1). In other figures, the mantle forms a broad circular loop across the middle of the body, passes over the forearm and falls in a simple fold at the left side. Note the upper left-hand and lower right-hand figures in the canon table of the Cluniac Bible (Plate XXXVI, 1) and the Saint-Denis jamb figure (Plate VII, 2). The position of hands and symbols in all the figures in the reproduced page of the Bible of Saint-Bénigne de Dijon is similar in the Saint-Denis jambs (Plate VII).

Evidence of the influence of Burgundian *ornament* in sculpture and manuscripts on the monuments of the Île-de-

---

[48] Both Oursel and Porter mention this possibility.

France is apparent. No such clear connections in style can be found in comparing *figures* in the Burgundian manuscripts with the sculpture of Saint-Denis, Étampes, and Chartres, yet there are several common characteristics which disclose a similarity of point of view.

BURGUNDIAN MONUMENTAL SCULPTURE

There are apparently no instances to indicate direct copying by the Saint-Denis and Chartres sculptors from Burgundian portal figures. In certain features of articulation of the human body and in the treatment of drapery, parallels in style do exist which are worth exploring.

Before discussing affinities between Burgundian sculpture and the Île-de-France monuments, we must first investigate the general evolution of Burgundian Romanesque and attempt to ascertain what period in the Burgundian development might have influenced Saint-Denis and Chartres. The tympanum of the inside portal of Charlieu (before 1094), with its Christ in a mandorla held by two angels, displays a flatness and static quality in spite of the zigzag folds of drapery.[49] The ambulatory capitals from Cluny III, completed before the dedication of 1095, exhibit a dynamic movement which is at variance with the sculpture at Charlieu and is derived from a different source, possibly Ottonian.[50] The wind-blown draperies of the Vézelay tympanum, after 1120 (Plate XXXVII, 1, 2), intensify the restlessness of the Cluny capitals, yet a new interest in displaying anatomy beneath these fluttering garments is revealed.[51] As Professor Koehler has pointed out, this emphasis on articulation can be traced directly to the influence of Byzantine art of the Second Golden Age.[52] The figures Peter and Paul flanking the Christ have thighs and knees fully displayed by the tight-fitting draperies. In each instance, however, the Burgundian sculptor has transformed Byzantine models into a more nervous, elongated, and dramatic kind of expression. The effect is strongly North European. The same interest in articulation can be found in Burgundian manuscripts and in the frescoes of Berzé-la-Ville of the early twelfth century.[53]

The portals of Saint-Lazare of Avallon, 1150's or later (Plate XXXVII, 3), represent the end of the Burgundian development. Ornament which had remained subservient to the figured sculpture at Vézelay and Autun assumes a new importance. Spiral columns and elaborately decorated bases,

jambs, and archivolts produce a baroque flavor which has certain affinities with the portals from Saint-Étienne at Toulouse (Plate XXXI, 1, 3, 4, 5), Saint-Loup-de-Naud (Plate XXV, 3), and Senlis (Plate XXV, 4). Along with the exuberant ornamental treatment, a single jamb statue appears (Plate XXXVII, 3). This is one of the earliest instances of the influence of the Saint-Denis–Chartres style on Burgundy. This figure is closely related to the Chartres jamb, CP.R.2 (Plate XVII, 2), yet the head remains Burgundian. It descends directly from the Vézelay Christ (Plate XXXVII, 2). The sculpture at Avallon thus remains within the stream of Burgundian art, and illustrates the impact, at that time, of the Île-de-France. This portal would seem to be the Burgundian counterpart of the Languedocien portal of Saint-Étienne at Toulouse. Both were carved toward the end of evolutions in their respective regions and both show the influence of the Saint-Denis–Chartres style.

The only period in the Burgundian development which might have influenced the sculpture of Saint-Denis and Chartres is represented by Vézelay (1120–1125), Autun 1119–1132), and the destroyed portal of Cluny (1109–1115).[54] Professor Koehler has pointed out the effect of the international Byzantine style on the portals of Chartres (see his figs. 21, 22, 23, comparing Byzantine manuscripts and the Angel of the Virgin Portal at Chartres).[55] One can only wonder what was the role of Burgundy in the dissemination of these international and vaguely classic ideas. There are, to be sure, some general affinities in style between Vézelay and Chartres. If the Saint Paul of Vézelay (figure to the right of Christ, Plate XXXVII, 1) is compared with the Christ of the central tympanum of Chartres (Plate XX, 1) or some of the figures on the central lintel of Chartres (Plate XI, second apostle from the right), similarities will be observed. In both instances, the drapery is pulled tightly across the legs and accentuates the location of anatomy. The double folds falling down the left legs of all those figures force up the articulation.[56] Some of the jamb figures of Saint-Denis (note especially Plate VII, 5) show this same interest in indicating knees and legs. The Saint-Denis and Chartres sculpture, however, possesses none of the nervous, linear tensions of the Vézelay figures. In every respect the Île-de-France sculpture is calmer, more majestic, and more human. The relationship between the monumental sculpture of Burgundy and Saint-Denis–Chartres is a tenuous one in spite of the

---

[49] Porter, p. 71 and ill. 4, relates this tympanum to other dated eleventh-century monuments. See also Sunderland, pp. 61–88 and figs. 15, 29.

[50] See Porter, ills. 5–10, and the two articles by Conant.

[51] See Salet, "La Madeleine de Vézelay, notes sur la façade de la nef," *Bulletin monumental*, XCIX (1940), 223–237, for analysis of two campaigns at Vézelay. In his book, *La Madeleine de Vézelay* (1948), pp. 147–148, Salet dates the tympanum before 1125. See Katzenellenbogen, "The Central Tympanum at Vézelay, its Encyclopedic Meaning and its Relation to the First Crusade," *Art Bulletin*, XXVI (1944), 141–151, for excellent analysis of the iconography.

[52] Koehler, "Byzantine Art in the West," *Dumbarton Oaks Papers*, Number I, pp. 63–87.

[53] See Focillon, *Peintures romanes des églises de France, cent trente photographies de Pierre Devinoy*, pls. 105–112.

[54] Conant, "The Third Church at Cluny," *Medieval Studies in Memory of A. Kingsley Porter*, pp. 335–338.

[55] Koehler, figs. 21–23.

[56] Koehler, pp. 80–81, has indicated certain relationships between the Christ of Vézelay and the Christ of Chartres.

fact that the connection between the ornamental style of the two regions is fairly direct.

Interesting evidence for this discussion of artistic exchanges between Burgundy and the Île-de-France is offered by the transept portals of the cathedral of Bourges (Plate XXXVII, 4). Located between Burgundy and the royal domain, Bourges exhibits in its two portals strong influences from both regions. The exuberant floral ornament is roughly similar to that a Avallon (Plate XXXVII, 3), while abstract motifs such as the four-leaf clover, the meander, and the pin-wheel may be an elaboration of motifs found either at Paray-le-Monial (Plate XXXIV, 1, 2) or at Chartres. The

allover elaborateness of the portals seems closer to Avallon than to any monument in the Île-de-France. Although some features such as accentuation of knees by oval folds and scrolls extending down legs (see SP.L.2, 3) are similar to Saint-Denis figures, the jamb statues are all related to Chartres.[57] The three statues reproduced in Plate XXXVII, 4, are all connected with the central portal of Chartres. All the figures from Bourges are shorter than the Chartres statues, and the garments flare out at the bottom. In both these characteristics Bourges resembles the jamb statues on the cathedral of Angers which are also dependent on the Royal Portal.[58]

IV

Conclusion

This search for possible origins of the Saint-Denis–Chartres style has led us to Burgundy. Burgundian ornament in sculpture and in manuscripts which can be dated before 1134 seems to have inspired the sculptors of Saint-Denis. The connection between the figure sculpture of Burgundy and of the Île-de-France is, however, more tenuous.

How were Burgundian forms transported to the royal domain? An attempt to answer this question leads us directly to the role of Abbot Suger, whose passionate interest in rebuilding and redecorating Saint-Denis caused him to summon artists from many regions of Europe. As Mâle and Panofsky have clearly indicated, Suger was largely responsible for the establishment of a new iconography which presages the complex High Gothic portals of Reims, Amiens, and the transept portals of Chartres.[59] Suger's "De Administratione" reveals ample evidence of his absorption in the task of making Saint-Denis a religious symbol worthy of the French monarchy. In reading Suger one is impressed by his keen interest in the construction of the narthex (1140) and the chevet (1144) and his vain delight in the new stained glass, enamels, and goldsmith work. His greatest pleasure seemed to center around the costliness and glitter of precious objects. It is small wonder, as Panofsky has pointed out, that his sole reference to the sculpture of the west portals concerns the inscription on the lintel of the central portal and the inclusion of himself worshiping the Christ of the Last Judgment.[60]

Did Suger import sculptors from Burgundy? Did he have a Burgundian manuscript in his possession? Did he dictate in detail the entire ensemble of the three portals? It is impossible to answer these questions. We need not overlook, however, the ample opportunity which Suger had to observe many of the greatest Romanesque monuments. In 1107 he attended the dedication of the Cluniac Abbey of La Charité-sur-Loire.[61] He made five trips to Italy, in 1112, 1121–22, 1123, 1124, and 1129, presumably passing through some part of Burgundy en route.[62] Between October 24 and November 3 of 1130 he was at Cluny.[63] He made two trips to Germany and the Low Countries, to Mainz in 1125 and to Liège in 1133.[64] In 1137 he went to western France to arrange and attend the marriage of Louis VII to Eleanor of Aquitaine, and in the following year he made an extensive trip through Burgundy.[65] It is not certain how far the sculptural program for Saint-Denis had progressed before these last two trips. From the standpoint of Suger's travels, Burgundy is the region in France which he knew the best.

Both Suger's detailed preoccupation with Saint-Denis and the direct influence of Burgundy are apparent in his Eagle Vase now in the Louvre.[66] Panofsky offers the interesting idea that "the transformation of a Roman porphyry vase into an eagle suggests the whim of an abbot rather than the invention of a professional goldsmith."[67] Joan Evans has discovered that Suger utilized a capital from La Charité-sur-Loire for the eagle itself.[68] As already stated, Suger was

[57] The lower drapery of the no. 1 jamb resembles Chartres CP.R.3; the no. 2 figure is very close to Chartres CP.R.2 with the scroll similar to Chartres CP.R.4; the head of no. 3 resembles CP.L.2, while the drapery is based on Chartres CP.L.1.

[58] It is difficult to follow the argument of Gardner, pp. 189–190, that Bourges was carved 1140–1150 and is earlier than Chartres.

[59] Mâle, *L'Art réligieux du XIIe siècle en France*, pp. 151–185, and his "La Part de Suger dans la création de l'iconographie du moyen-âge," pp. 91–102, 161–168, 253–262, 339–349.

[60] Mâle, "Le Part de Suger," p. 165.

[61] Cartellieri, *Abt Suger von Saint-Denis*.

[62] Cartellieri, p. 128 (14), p. 129 (19, 20), p. 131 (34, 36), p. 132 (40), p. 135 (63).

[63] Cartellieri, p. 135 (66, 67).

[64] Cartellieri, p. 133 (46), p. 137 (80).

[65] Cartellieri, p. 139 (92–96), p. 139 (99).

[66] Panofsky, ill. 26.

[67] Panofsky, p. 36.

[68] Evans, "Die Adlervase des Sugerius," pp. 221–223. Miss Evans writes in conclusion: "We have thus another instance of the interdependence of the iconography of the various arts in the Romanesque period, when they are dominated by the taste and fancy of such men as Suger rather than by the less eclectic traditions of craftsmen."

at La Charité for its consecration and probably revisited the abbey on his trips to Rome.[69]

Lombardy has been suggested as a possible source of the columnar jamb statues which first appeared in quantity and in a unified composition at Saint-Denis.[70] The Lombard monuments which might conceivably have influenced Saint-Denis exhibit many features which are dissimilar to Île-de-France sculpture. All the figures are either a part of door jambs or else a part of convex, triangular jambs, not columns. The statues have squat proportions and occupy a small fraction of the total height of the splays. The closest parallels — but they are later than Saint-Denis — appear to be the stocky figures of the cathedral of Verona, begun in 1139 by Niccolò, pupil of Guglielmo da Modena.[71] Two jamb statues on the portal of the cathedral of Ferrara show some similarity to Saint-Denis, but the figures remain part of the wall. Also the completion date of the portal, 1135, is open to question.[72]

Both Porter and Oursel have mentioned the importance of initials in Cistercian manuscripts as possible forerunners of jamb statues. As can be seen by studying Plate XXXVI, 2, 3, 4, there is some evidence for this assumption, especially since the ornament of Saint-Denis and Chartres seems to be inspired by these illuminations and by Burgundian abstract and floral patterns.

The possible importance of goldsmith work in relation to the origin of Saint-Denis–Chartres ornament as well as monumental sculpture has often been mentioned but never documented. Mâle argues that Godefroy de Claire was at Saint-Denis and was greatly affected by Suger.[73] None of Godefroy's work can be dated early enough to have influenced the west portals. Most of the interior embellishments were finished for the consecration of the chevet (1144), according to Suger's "De Administratione" which he wrote between 1144 and 1148-49.[74] Suger's sardonyx chalice, now in the National Gallery in Washington (see Panofsky, ill. 24) exhibits only a vague connection in style with the Saint-Denis ornamental sculpture. The stylistic relationships with Burgundian ornament are much closer.

Although one may claim that Suger was impressed by Burgundian art, especially ornament, many questions of origins remain unanswered. Did the sculptors of Saint-Denis necessarily come from Burgundy? Or, did artists with quite different artistic backgrounds become inspired by Suger's sensitivity? Any discussion of origins tends to forget or ignore the inventiveness, originality, and evolution of individual artists. Can we discover the origin of the Headmaster of Chartres? Does he evolve out of Saint-Denis or is he essentially Burgundian? Unfortunately for us and for the individual, anonymous sculptors of the twelfth century, many artistic phenomena remain unexplained.[75]

---

[69] Panofsky, p. 78 (33/34, "De Administratione"). Suger's own reactions to the vase emphasize his interest in color and precious materials. The verse on the vase reads: "This stone deserves to be enclosed in gems and gold. It was marble, but in these (settings) it is more precious than marble."

[70] Porter, p. 225: "It is therefore entirely within the bounds of possibility that the jamb sculptures of Saint-Denis came from Lombardy. On the other hand, it is certain that Saint-Denis was much influenced by pilgrimage art." By pilgrimage art he is referring to Santiago de Compostela.

[71] Porter, *Lombard Architecture* (New Haven: Yale University Press, 1917), I, 277; III, 469; vol. IV, pl. 217.

[72] Porter, *Lombard Architecture*, I, 277; II, 407. The cathedral was moved in 1135. Porter dates the sculpture of the west portal before 1135 (pp. 420–422) on stylistic grounds.

[73] Mâle, "La Part de Suger," p. 164.

[74] Panofsky, p. 144. Mâle, "La Part de Suger," p. 98 and n. 3, states that Eugène III dedicated the huge gold cross in 1147. He dates the cross between 1145 and 1147.

[75] Just before this book went to press, the following article was called to my attention: Hermann Giesau, "Stand der Forschung über das Figurenportal des Mittelalters," *Beiträge zur Kunst des Mittelalters, Vorträge der Ersten Deutschen Kunsthistorikertagung auf Schloss Brühl 1948,*

Berlin (1950), pp. 119–129. Giesau's conclusions are as follows: Saint-Denis is earlier than Chartres; Bourges (1140–1150 or earlier) antedates Chartres; Le Mans (1158) is inspired by both Bourges and Chartres; Saint-Loup-de-Naud and Angers grow out of Bourges; Étampes is earlier than Chartres; Saint-Lazare at Avallon is similar to two tympana from Saint-Bénigne at Dijon (1137–1145) and was carved in the 1130's and is therefore earlier than Saint-Denis; Ferrara sculpture (1135) may be related to Saint-Denis; the portal of Saint-Étienne de Toulouse antedates Saint-Denis. His conclusions that Saint-Denis and Chartres are not the earliest portals with monumental columnar figures are based almost entirely on the relationship between jamb statues and their architectural backgrounds. He argues that the sculpture at Avallon and Bourges remains relatively encased in the façade and that the emancipation of the statue-columns finally occurred at Chartres. He fails to note that the portals carved in the late 1150's and 1160's after Chartres, such as Le Mans, Provins, and Saint-Loup-de-Naud, are closely related to Avallon and Bourges and late Burgundian monuments. When compared to Chartres, all these portals exhibit jamb statues which have been pushed back into the embrasures. Also, these monuments plus the portal of Saint-Étienne de Toulouse are elaborately decorated with a profusion of ornament which is stylistically later than Saint-Denis and Chartres.

APPENDICES
AND
BIBLIOGRAPHY

Catalogue of Ornament, Saint-Denis West Portals

WEST FAÇADE: Plinths (motifs on crowning surfaces of bases). The measurements of plinths vary slightly. The average is .34 × .10 meter on the north or south side of each jamb and .43 × .10 on the west.

I. ABSTRACT MOTIFS (Geometric)

(1) Geometric motif of squares with centers recessed: CP.L.4

(2) Diamond pattern: CP.R.2 (Plate III, 3)

(3) Diamond pattern with centers undercut: RP.R.4

(4) Ribbon or band motif (pairs of folded bands running horizontally): CP.R.3 (Plate III, 4)

(5) Double-axe pattern: RP.L.3 (Plate III, 5)

II. ORGANIC PATTERNS (Floral)

A. Undulating Vine with Simple Floral Fillers

(1) Running vine with dependent rolled fillers: CP.L.3 (Plate IV, 1)

(2) Elaboration of (1) with extra leaves entwining the main stem: LP.R.4

(3) Undulating vine with partially rolled leaves alternating in axial direction: LP.R.1 (Plate III, 6; LP.L.4 is similar but badly mutilated)

(4) Running vines giving off pairs of shoots which converge and form oval fillers: RP.L.1 (Plate II, 4)

(5) Undulating vine from which stem elaborate floral fillers: LP.L.1 (Plate IV, 2)

(6) Running vine with floral offshoots resembling birds' wings: LP.R.3 (CP.R.1 a modern copy)

B. Undulating Vine with Complex, Independent Floral Fillers

(1) Separate units of fillers of seven leaves entwining undulating vine: CP.L.1 (Plate III, 2)

(2) Floral fillers of seven and two leaves embracing a broken, running vine: CP.L.5 (modern copy)

C. Floral Patterns of Separate Units

(1) Frontal units of paired leaves growing out of a banded base and encircle buds: RP.R.1 (Plate IV, 3)

(2) Four vines, each giving off three leaves, growing from the center of rectangular units: RP.L.4 (Plate I, 3)

(3) Squares of four three-leafed sections, alternating with four buds, radiating from the center of the unit: CP.R.5

(4) Squares of four tonguelike leaves and circular fillers growing toward the center of the unit: LP.R.2 (north side only) and LP.L.3 (modern)

(5) Palmette motif of nine leaves: CP.L.2 (Plate III, 2; only north part of west face is original)

(6) Rosettes of eight leaves: RP.L.2 (Plate I, 3)

III. COMBINATIONS OF ABSTRACT AND ORGANIC AND MISCELLANEOUS

(1) Double row of small leaves flank a chain of circles: CP.R.4 (Plate IV, 5)

(2) Elongated S-shaped objects resembling leaves flowing from right to left, "blind leading the blind": RP.R.3 (Plate IV, 4)

(3) Elaborate folded bands decorated with incised squares and abstract leaves: RP.R.2 (Plate IV, 6; LP.L.2 is modern)

WEST FAÇADE: Ornament on first jambs running vertically from bases to capitals.

(1) Jeweled border (flanking medallions containing the Occupations of the Months), alternating ellipses and pairs of dots: RP.R.1, RP.L.1; The Occupations of the Months are framed by bundles of vines (Plates I, 3, and II; All with exception of lower part of bottom units recarved in the nineteenth century)

(2) Undulating rinceau from which grow rolled leaves (.09 meter wide) bordering the Wise and Foolish Virgins: CP.R.1 and CP.L.1 (same motif as plinth, LP.R.1, yet runs vertically). This motif stops halfway up the right first jamb (See Plates I, 1; III, 1, 2, and V, 4)

(3) Horseshoe-shaped floral units arranged vertically framing the Signs of the Zodiac; each unit has three pairs of leaves: LP.L.1 and LP.R.1

MUSÉE DE CLUNY: SCULPTURE FROM THE FAÇADE OF SAINT-DENIS

I. SPIRAL COLONNETTE: served as model for three nineteenth-century copies which flank all three portals on the left side (Plate V)

Measurements: 1.47 meters high; .43 in circumference; bands separating spirals, .04 meters wide; spiral motifs .14 meters wide; depth of relief .01 to .015 meter

Description: two spiral motifs separated by two bands making one and three-quarter revolutions to the right

Bands: slightly concave, bounded by thin raised borders and decorated with oval floral objects alternating with pairs of small knobs (Plate V, 5)

Floral Spiral: pairs of decorated vines forming heart-shaped units which are entwined by seven leaves (Plate V, 3)

Figured Spiral: undulating vine grows out of a dragon's mouth; secondary leaves and stems embrace five putti, two birds, and two griffins (Plate V, 2, 5, 6)

II. TWO FRAGMENTS OF COLONNETTES (much restored): may have been located originally between the jamb statues of Saint-Denis.

Fragment 1: .79 meter high and .42 in circumference; vines and addorsed birds: pairs of climbing vines, joining in elaborate knots, forming oval spaces which are filled by addorsed birds and griffins (Plate VI, 2)

Fragment 2: .80 meter high by .42 in circumference; paired birds flanking putti: pairs of birds, whose tails grow out of rectangular knots, facing each other and embraced by frontal putti supported, in turn, by formal floral fillers (Plate VI, 2)

LOUVRE: TWO FRAGMENTS OF COLONNETTES FROM SAINT-DENIS

Louvre nos. 41 and 42: two colonnettes which originally decorated the R.1 jambs of Saint-Denis and served as models for nineteenth-century columns now in place (Plate VI, 1)

Description: two floral bands in spiral separated by borders of rosettes; undulating vine with elaborate floral fillers (see Saint-Denis motif II, A (5), LP.L.1. plinth, Plate IV, 2)

APPENDIX II

Catalogue of Ornament, Chartres Royal Portal

I. ORNAMENT ON SHORT COLUMNS SUPPORTING JAMB FIGURES (height of columns varies from .70 to .90 meter)
  A. Fluted column
    (1) CP.R.4 (Plate XII, 2)
  B. Four-leaf clover
    (1) CP.L.3 (Plate XIII, 3)
    (2) CP.R.2 (Plate XII, 2)
    (3) RP.L.2 (Plate XVIII, 2), south side unfinished
    (4) RP.L.3 (Plate XVIII, 2), south side unfinished
    (5) LP.R.4 (Plate XVIII, 1), north side unfinished
    (6) CP.R.3 (Plate XII, 2), units smaller than above
  C. Stepped meander
    (1) CP.L.5 (Plate XIII, 3)
    (2) RP.L.4 (Plate XVIII, 2)
    (3) CP.R.5, modern (Plate XII, 2)
  D. Folded band or ribbon, running vertically
    (1) CP.L.1 (Plate XIII, 3)
    (2) CP.R.1 (Plate XII, 2)
  E. Double-axe and pin-wheel motif
    (1) CP.L.2 (Plate XIII, 3)

II. ORNAMENT ON COLONNETTES BETWEEN JAMB STATUES
  A. Undulating vine with floral fillers (motif 1 in text)
    (1) LP.L.2 (middle piece 1.03 meters): secondary stems form medallions which are filled with leaves and buds (Plate XVI, 1)
    (2) CP.R.2 (top piece 1.27 meters): climbing vine forming medallions with rosettes as fillers (Plate XXI, 1)
    (3) CP.L.3 (bottom 1.63 meters): similar to (1) (Plate XIII, 3)
    (4) CP.L.3 (middle piece 1.21 meters): same as (3) (Plate XVII, 1)
    (5) LP.L.2 (top piece, no top molding, .78 meter): same as (3) (Plate XVI, 1)
  B. Undulating vine embracing figures (motif 2 in text)
    (1) LP.L.1 (middle 1.52 meters): climbing vine giving off secondary stem which entwines nude figures (Plate XIV, 1, 3)
    (2) LP.R.1 (upper section, but not top piece, 1.42 meters): same as (1) except vine embraces beasts and grotesques (Plate XVIII, 1)
    (3) CP.L.1 (top piece .55 meter): same as (1) and (2); here vine entwines birds and an erotic figure (Plate XVII, 1)
    (4) RP.R.1 (top piece, which does not extend up to the capital, .90 meter): vine forming medallions which encircle a winged boy, human head, and a monster's head (Plates XVI, 2, and XIX, 2)
  C. Pairs of climbing vines with floral fillers (motif 3 in text)
    (1) CP.R.2 (bottom section 2.30 meters): two pairs of vines with floral fillers (Plate XIII, 1, 2)
    (2) LP.L.1 (top fragment, base but no top, .24 meter): interlocking paired vines with secondary stems and floral fillers (Plate XVI, 1)

(3) LP.R.1 (top fragment, top but no bottom, .41 meter): same as (2) (Plate XVIII, 1)
(4) LPR.2 (third fragment from bottom, top border but no bottom border, .79 meter): same as (1) and (2) (Plate XVIII, 1)
(5) CP.L.3 (top fragment .76 meter): same as (4) except top sixth seems to be a different motif, a spiral; this section may be another piece of colonnette (Plate XVII, 1)
(6) LP.R.2 (middle piece .83 meter): pair of undulating vines interlocking in center of colonnette and giving off floral fillers (Plate XVIII, 1)
(7) CP.L.2 (middle 1.44 meters): complex pattern of paired vines with secondary stems and fillers of leaves and buds (Plate XVII, 1)
  D. Hybrid undulating vines with floral fillers (motif 4 in text)
    (1) LP.R.1 (lower section 1.75 meters): undecorated vine with secondary stem and floral fillers; bottom unit contains pair of vines framing addorsed birds (Plate XV, 4)
    (2) CP.L.4 (top piece 1.21 meters): pair of vines giving off elaborate fillers from their point of tangency (Plate XVII, 1)
  E. Pair of vines with addorsed birds (motif 5 in text)
    (1) LP.L.1 (bottom section 1.78 meters): pairs of climbing vines creating oval areas which are filled with paired birds and leaves (Plate XV, 1)
    (2) LP.R.2 (bottom 1.75 meters; top units destroyed): similar to (1)
  F. Pair of vines entwining confronted beasts, with elaborate floral fillers (motif 6 in text)
    (1) CP.R.4 (bottom section 2.27 meters): vines growing vertically creating heart-shaped areas which are filled with beasts and leaves growing downward (Plate XIV, 4)
  G. Heart-shaped units of paired vines with figured fillers (motif 7 in text)
    (1) CP.R.1 (lower section 2.28 meters): pairs of vines forming inverted heart-shaped units; leaves and putto heads serving as fillers (Plate XIV, 2)
    (2) CP.R.1 (upper section 1.31 meters): like (1) except individual units are smaller (Plate XXI, 1)
    (3) CP.R.3 (lower section 2.40 meters): pairs of vines forming heart-shaped areas in which leaves, paired birds, and grotesque animals act as fillers (Plate XVII, 2)
  H. Pairs of climbing vines with elaborate figured fillers
    (1) RP.R.2 (middle piece 1.07 meters): pair of vines climbing the center of colonnette with birds and figures decorating the sides (Plate XVI, 2)
    (2) CP.R.4 (top piece 1.30 meters high): pair of climbing vines framing oval areas filled with bearded figures embracing secondary vines (Plate XXI, 1)
    (3) RP.P.2 (top piece, not extending up to capital, .90 meter): elaborate climbing vines with grotesque heads filling the areas around the knots binding the stems (Plate XVI, 2)
    (4) LP.R.3 (bottom 1.57 meters); four climbing, interlacing vines with froglike creatures (Plate XVIII, 1)

(5) CP.L.2 (lower section 1.63 meters): similar to (4) except more modeling of vines (Plate XIII, 3)

(6) RP.L.3 (top piece 1.11 meters): two sets of interweaving vines with figures as fillers (Plate XVIII, 2; amplification of CP.R.1, motif 7)

(7) RP.R.2 (bottom section 1.58 meters): similar to (6) above (Plate XVI, 2)

I. Separate floral units joined by circlets (motif 8 in text)

(1) RP.L.2 (bottom section 1.30 meters): separate units of paired vines and floral fillers joined by circlets (Plate XV, 3)

J. Spiral frieze of interlaced figures and vines bordered by bands (motif 9 in text)

(1) LP.L.2 (lowest piece 1.73 meters): vines entwining humans and animals climbing in spiral separated by an elaborate band (Plate XV, 2)

(2) CP.L.1 (bottom piece 1.70 meters): similar to (1) (Plate XIII, 3)

(3) CP.L.1 (middle section 1.34 meters): similar to (1) and (2) except vines form medallions decorated with floral fillers

(4) CP.L.2 (top piece, bottom molding but no top, .53 meter): similar to (3) (Plate XVII, 1)

(5) CP.L.4 (lower piece 2.21 meters): similar to (1) above, spiral frieze rising at a steeper angle (Plate XVII, 1)

(6) CP.R.3 (top section, no bottom molding, 1.19 meters): like (5) above; separating band is decorated with rosettes (Plate XXI, 1)

(7) LP.R.2 (top fragment, no bottom molding, .20 meter): like (6), possibly part of (6) (Plate XVIII, 1)

K. Miscellaneous

(1) RP.L.2 (top 2.26 meters): series of unconnected sections containing the Labors of the Months (Plate XVIII, 2)

(2) RP.L.3 (bottom 1.65 meters): folded pair of ribbons or bands with one or two full-length figures (Plate XVIII, 2)

APPENDIX III

Saint-Denis Bas-Relief

In June 1947 Professor Sumner McK. Crosby discovered a bas-relief (Plate X, 1) during his excavations in the south transept of Saint-Denis.[1] He has an extensive monograph under preparation on this beautifully preserved relief. Since the ornament is similar to fragments from the west portals of the abbey and since the figures are related to the Montfaucon drawings and engravings of the lost jamb statues, a brief description and analysis of the bas-relief is included herewith. According to Crosby there are no documents which would explain its use or date.

The bas-relief measures 2.05 meters long by 52 centimeters high and contains twelve Apostles under an arched colonnade. From left to right, they can be identified tentatively as follows: James Minor, Thomas, John the Evangelist, Simon, Andrew, Peter, Paul, Matthew, James Major, Philip, Bartholomew, and Matthias (substituting for Judas).

The unfinished end of the relief (Plate X, 4) illustrates the preliminary stages in the carving of ornament. In the left section of vine, four leaves, and bud, the sculptor engraved the main silhouettes of the motif on the block. Undercutting is carried further in the next three units; vines and buds are blocked out and two planes emerge, the front plane of the block and the background. The subtractive process is continued in the right-hand unit. Squareness of vines is softened and details of leaves and buds make their appearance. The border on the front (see detail in Plate X, 3) represents the final, finished stage, with midribs accented by rows of squares and more detailed carving of leaves. The whole procedure from the initial step of transferring the pattern to the block to the final modeling is portrayed.

Ornament plays a significant role in this relief. It is found on the enframement, arches, spandrels, capitals, columns, bases, and hems of drapery of the figures. Many of the motifs such as on the fourth column from the left (see Plate IV, 4) and folded bands on the eighth (see Plate III, 4) are similar to plinths on the façade. The main border is the most important for this brief analysis. The motif (Plate X, 1, 3), leaves and buds growing from a vine, is like the plinth LP.L.1 (Plate IV, 2) and the Louvre fragments (Plate VI, 1). The degree of relief is closer to the plinth, while the motif more closely resembles the columns in the Louvre. The ornament of the Louvre pieces exhibits more variety of arrangement and more clarity and assurance of carving. The difference in quality is more apparent if the ornament is contrasted with details of the Musée de Cluny column (Plate V, 3).

In spite of their stocky character the twelve Apostles are clearly related to the jamb figures of the right portal of the façade (see Plate X, 2, Montfaucon pl. xviii). So close is the affinity between Apostles and monumental jamb statues in arrangement of drapery, carving of folds, and general articulation of forms that one is forced to conclude that the sculptor utilized the right portal as model for the bas-relief. At Chartres the artist of the double lintel of the right portal (Plate XX, 2, 4) owed a great debt to the Headmaster who carved the Chartres central portal jambs and tympanum (see Part II, section II, and Plate XVII). In both the bas-relief and the Chartres

RP lintel the smaller figures are more squat and more freely posed variants of the major theme of the jamb statues. The discovery of the bas-relief, like the identification of the Baltimore and Fogg heads, gives further proof of the relative accuracy of the drawings and engravings made for Montfaucon.

Only vague stylistic connections are revealed when the Apostles (Plate X, 1, 3) are compared with seven drawings of jambs from the central and left portal (Plate VII). On the other hand, the left-hand six Apostles are based on the six right-portal jambs (Plate X, 2). The right-hand six Apostles seem to be associated with or to be alterations of the other Apostles. Thomas, no. 2 from the left, has the same treatment of drapery as RP.L.2 (middle top figure, Plate X, 2) in folds across the right leg and break in mantle beside the left leg. The position of hands is reversed but the relationship to the tablet is similar. John, no. 3 (Plate X, 3), is even closer to the model from the portal (RP.L.1, top right hand in Plate X, 2); the entire bottom half of the figure is the same with the exception of the crossed legs on the jamb statue. The mantle sweeps across from the right hip starting with a small fold on the thigh and ending over the left ankle. Above the left ankle is another flattened fold which breaks the straight drop of the cloak. The undergarments have analogous terminations above the feet. Even the V-fold over the right foot of the jamb figure is repeated in the same area in John the Evangelist. In the jamb the presence of crossed legs results in a different treatment of the cloak over the knees. John's left hand holds a scroll, not a box, and the right hand is raised in blessing, yet the handling of the mantle over the left shoulder and the sleeve of the right arm is related to the jamb statue. Since these two Apostles, 2 and 3, are modeled on RP.L. jambs, it can be argued that the first figure, James Minor, was based on RP.L.3 of which only a fragment remained when the drawings were made for Montfaucon. The remaining drapery is similar to that of the jamb statue.

The next three Apostles, Simon, Andrew, and Peter are modeled on the RP.R. jambs (Plate X, 2, bottom row). Simon, no. 4 (Plate X, 3), has the unusual feature of an outer garment gathered in his left hand as on jamb 3 (Plate X, 2, lower right figure). The Apostle's drapery is pulled up from the right leg and not across the hips as in the jamb. The folds over the left foot are identical. The connection between Andrew, no. 5, and RP.R.2 (Plate X, 2, middle lower figure) is not as close, yet if the Apostles' garments are reversed, the same handling of hand and scroll and falling drapery of right forearm (left on jamb figure) can be observed. The keys of Peter, no. 6, change the character of the upper half of RP.R.1 (see Plate X, 2, left-hand bottom row), but the symmetrical folds over legs as well as the pronounced V-shaped sleeve over the right wrist can be seen in both. On the basis of the strong affinity between Apostles and jamb statues, it can be reasoned that the sculptor of the bas-relief not only was inspired by the right portal jambs but also proceeded from left to right for the first three Apostles and from right to left on the right splay for the next three.

The right-hand six Apostles are modifications of the left six with some decline in quality. Paul, no. 7, depends on no. 1 and no. 2: fold over right arm like no. 2 and left fold like no. 1. No. 8, Matthew, is reminiscent of no. 3, only reversed. James Major, no. 9, is similar

[1] Sumner McK. Crosby, "Fouilles exécutées récemment dans la basilique de Saint-Denis," *Bulletin monumental*, CV (1947), 179–181.

to no. 2 except for the ambiguous drapery over the right foot. Philip, no. 10, is related to nos. 2 and 3 and also exhibits some vague similarity to LP.R.3 jamb (see Montfaucon pl. xvi, lower right). Bartholomew, no. 11 is no. 3 reversed with the same three accentuated folds over the feet. The last Apostle, Matthias, is connected with no. 5.

The uncrowned heads of the Apostles are squarer than the preserved portal heads or drawings for Montfaucon. If John's and Simon's heads (Plate X, 3) are compared with the Baltimore head (Plate VIII), the more pointed silhouette and greater sense of rugged power can be seen in the latter. The heads from the jambs exhibit more sensitivity in the treatment of eyes, lips, and beards.

The small amount of sculpture preserved from Suger's façade and the extraordinary state of preservation of the bas-relief make its discovery an important event. Until more fragments are unearthed, this relief, the heads and columns in museums, parts of the central tympanum, sections of the ornament on the façade, plus the Montfaucon drawings and engravings must suffice to establish the Saint-Denis style. The Apostle bas-relief would seem to date from the late 1140's and possibly be part of a project left unfinished at Suger's death in 1151.

BIBLIOGRAPHY

GENERAL BOOKS AND ARTICLES

Aubert, Marcel, *French Sculpture at the Beginning of the Gothic Period*, Pantheon Series (New York: Harcourt, Brace, 1929).

Aubert, Marcel, *La Sculpture française au moyen-âge* (Paris: Flammarion, 1946).

Deschamps, Paul, *French Sculpture of the Romanesque Period*, Pantheon Series (New York: Harcourt, Brace, 1930).

Fleury, Gabriel, *Études sur les portails imagés du XIIe siècle, leur iconographie et leur symbolisme* (Mamers, 1904).

Focillon, Henri, *L'Art des sculpteurs romans* (Paris: Leroux, 1931).

Gardner, Arthur, *Medieval Sculpture in France* (Cambridge: The University Press, 1931).

Lasteyrie, P. de, "Études sur la sculpture française au moyen-âge," *Académie des Inscriptions et Belles-lettres, Fondation Piot*, Paris (1902), VIII.

Mâle, Émile, *L'Art religieux du XIIe siècle en France* (Paris, 1922).

Mayeux, André, "Les Grands Portails du XIIe siècle et les Bénédictines de Tiron," *Revue Mabillon*, Paris (1906), pp. 96–122.

Porter, Arthur Kingsley, *Romanesque Sculpture of the Pilgrimage Roads* (Boston: Marshall Jones, 1923).

Vöge, Wilhelm, *Die Anfänge des Monumentalen Stiles im Mittelalter* (Strassburg, 1894).

SAINT-DENIS

Suger and Saint-Denis

Cartellieri, Otto, *Abt Suger von Saint-Denis* (Berlin, 1898).

Evans, Joan, "Die Adlervase des Sugerius," *Pantheon* (July 1932), X, 221–223.

Mâle, Émile, "La Part de Suger dans la création de l'iconographie du moyen-âge," *Revue de l'art Ancien et Moderne* (1914–1915), XXXV, 91–102, 161–168, 253–262, 339–349.

Panofsky, Erwin, *Abbot Suger on the Abbey Church of St.-Denis and its Arts Treasures* (Princeton: Princeton University Press, 1946).

Monographs
(listed chronologically)

Doublet, Jacques, *L'Histoire de l'abbaye de St.-Denys* (Paris, 1625).

Félibien, Michel, *L'Histoire de l'abbaye royale de Saint-Denis en France* (Paris, 1706).

Flamand-Grétry, L., *Description complète de la ville de Saint-Denis, depuis son origine jusqu'à nos jours* (Paris, 1840).

Viollet-le-Duc, Eugène, "L'Église impériale de St.-Denis," *Annales Archéologiques* (1846), Vol. V.

Guilhermy, Ferdinand, Baron de, *Monographie de l'église royale de Saint-Denis* (Paris, 1848).

D'Ayzac, Mme. Felicie, *Histoire de l'abbaye de Saint-Denis en France* (Paris, 1860–61), 2 vols.

L'Église impériale de Saint-Denis et ses tombeaux par les auteurs de la monographie de Saint-Denis (Paris, 1867).

Varaville, Jules de, *Histoire de l'abbaye de Saint-Denis* (Paris, 1903).

Vitry, Paul, and Gaston Brière, *L'Église abbatiale de Saint-Denis et ses tombeaux* (Paris, 1908).

Vitry, Paul, and Gaston Brière, *L'Église abbatiale de Saint-Denis et ses tombeaux* (Paris, 1925).

Crosby, Sumner McK., *The Abbey of St.-Denis* (New Haven: Yale University Press, 1942), vol. I.

Restorations of Saint-Denis

Debret, François, Monuments Historiques, Dos. 41–76.

Didron, Adolphe, "Achèvement des restaurations de Saint-Denis," *Annales Archéologiques* (1846), V, 110.

Papiers du Baron de Guilhermy, Bibliothèque nationale, Dép. des Mss. Nuov. acq. françaises, Nos. 6121–6122.

Léon, Paul, *Les Monuments historiques, conservation, restauration* (Paris, 1917).

"Saint-Denys: Restauration de l'église royale," *Annales Archéologiques*, I (1844), 232.

Viollet-le-Duc, Eugène, *Monuments Historiques Dos.*, (1841–1876), pp. 109–110.

Saint-Denis and the National Museums of France
(listed chronologically)

Lenoir, Alexandre, *Musée des Monumens Français* (Paris, 1800).

Lenoir, Alexandre, *Description historique et chronologique des monumens de sculpture réunis au Musée des Monumens Français* (Paris, 1803).

Lenoir, Alexandre, *Musée impérial des Monumens Français, histoire des arts en France, et description chronologique* (Paris, 1810).

Sommerard, Alexandre du, *Notices sur l'Hôtel de Cluny et sur le Palais des Thermes* (Paris, 1834).

Musée des Thermes et de l'Hôtel de Cluny, catalogue et description des objets d'art (Paris, 1849). Other editions in 1855 and 1859.

Sommerard, E. du, *Musée des Thermes et l'Hôtel de Cluny: catalogue* (Paris, 1877).

Courajod, Louis, *Alexandre Lenoir, son journal et le Musée des Monuments Français* (Paris, 1878–1887), 3 vols.

Sommerard, E. du, *Musée des Thermes et de l'Hôtel de Cluny: catalogue et description des objets d'art* (Paris, 1881). Another edition in 1883.

Lenoir, Albert, *Le Musée des Thermes et de l'Hôtel de Cluny: documents sur la creation du Musée d'Antiquités Nationales suivant le projet exposé au Louvre en 1833* (Paris, 1882).

Haraucourt, Edmond, and François de Montremy, *Musée des Thermes et de l'Hôtel de Cluny, catalogue général I: la pierre, le marbre et l'albâtre* (Paris, 1922).

Haraucourt, Edmond, *L'Histoire de la France expliquée au Musée de Cluny; guide annoté par salles et par séries* (Paris, 1922).

Musée de Cluny, guide officiel (Paris, 1935).

Literature dealing with the monumental sculpture of the Saint-Denis portals
(listed chronologically)

Montfaucon, Bernard de, *Les Monumens de la monarchie françoise* (Paris: Julien-Michel Gandouin, 1729–1733), t. I, pl. XVI–XVIII, pp. 195ff.

Montfaucon drawings, Bibliothèque nationale, Dép. de Mss. fr. 15634 fol. 33ff.

Ross, Marvin C., "Monumental Sculptures from St.-Denis, an Identification of Fragments from the Portal," *The Journal of the Walters Art Gallery* (Baltimore, 1940), III, 91–109.

Ross, Marvin C., "Two Heads from St.-Denis," *Magazine of Art* (December 1940), XXXIII, 675–679, 706.

Aubert, Marcel, "Têtes de statues-colonnes du portail occidental de Saint-Denis," *Bulletin monumental* (1945), CIII, 243–248.

BIBLIOGRAPHY

CHARTRES

Monographs and general articles

Bulteau, L'Abbé, *Monographie de la Cathédrale de Chartres*, Société Archéologique d'Eure-et-Loir, Chartres (1887–1892), 3 vols.

Buisson, Pierre, et P. Bellier Chavignerie, *Tableau de la Ville de Chartres en 1750*, Société Archéologique d'Eure-et-Loir (Chartres, (1896).

Durand, Paul, *Monographie de Notre-Dame de Chartres* (Paris, 1881).

Lassus, Jean, *Monographie de la Cathédrale de Chartres* (Paris, 1842); Paul Durand, *Explication des planches* (Paris, 1861); also *Annales Archéologiques*, XXVII, 18.

Merlet, René, *La Cathédrale de Chartres*, Petites Monographies des Grands Édifices de la France (Paris: Laurens, 1929).

Houvet, Étienne, *Cathédrale de Chartres; portail occidental ou royal, XIIe siècle* (Chelles: Faucheux, 1919).

Mâle, Émile, *Notre-Dame de Chartres, cent cinquante-quartre photographies de Pierre Devinoy* (Paris: Hartmann, 1948).

Documents

Bouquet, Dom Martin, *Recueil des historiens des Gaules et de la France* (Paris, 1738–1755), 21 vols.

Delisle, Léopold, "Chronique de Robert de Torigny," *Société de l'Histoire de France*, Rouen (1872), I, 238.

Mortet, Victor, et Paul Deschamps, *Recueil de textes rélatifs à l'histoire de l'architecture et à la condition des architectes en France au moyen-âge* (Paris, 1929), 2 vols.

Articles dealing with twelfth-century Chartres
(listed chronologically)

Merlet, René, and Abbé Clerval, *Un Manuscrit Chartrain de XIe siècle*, Société Archéologique d'Eure-et-Loir (Chartres, 1893).

Lanore, Maurice, "Reconstruction de la façade de la Cathédrale de Chartres au XIIe siècle," *Revue de l'Art Chrétien* (1899), pp. 328–332, and (1900), pp. 32–39, 137–145.

Lefèvre-Pontalis, Eugène, "Les Façades successives de la cathédrale de Chartres au XIe et XIIe siècle," *Congrès Archéologique de France*, Chartres (1900), pp. 256–307. Same article in *Mémoires de la Société Archéologique d'Eure-et-Loir* (1901–1904), XIII, 1–48.

Mayeux, A., "Réponse à M. Eugène Lefèvre-Pontalis sur son article," *Mémoires de la Société Archéologique d'Eure-et-Loir* (1901–1904), XIII, 414–433.

Lefèvre-Pontalis, Eugène, "Nouvelles Études sur les façades et les clochers de la Cathédrale de Chartres: réponses à M. Mayeux," *Mémoires de la Société Archéologique d'Eure-et-Loir* (1901–1904), XIII, 434–483.

Priest, Alan, "The Masters of the West Façade of Chartres," *Art Studies* (Cambridge: Harvard University Press, 1923), I, 28–44.

Aubert, Marcel, printed extract of lecture delivered at 15th International Congress of the History of Art, July 25, 1939, in London, entitled: "Les deux États successifs du portail royal de Chartres au milieu du XIIe siècle."

Aubert, Marcel, "Le Portail royal et la façade occidentale de la Cathédrale de Chartres, essai sur la date et leur exécution," *Bulletin monumental* (1941), C, 177–218.

NOTRE-DAME OF ÉTAMPES

Alliot, l'Abbé, *Cartulaire de Notre-Dame d'Étampes, documents publiés par la Société Historique et Archéologique du Gatinais III* (Paris, 1888).

Lefèvre, L. Eugène, *Le Portail royal d'Étampes* (Paris, 1908), 2e éd.

Lefèvre, L. Eugène, *Le Portail royal d'Étampes et la doctrine de Saint-Irenée sur la Redemption* (Paris, 1915).

Lefèvre-Pontalis, Eugène, "Étampes," *Congrès Archéologique de France*, Paris (1919), pp. 6–29.

Lefèvre-Pontalis, Eugène, *Les Campagnes de construction de Notre-Dame d'Étampes* (Caen, 1909).

Mont-Rond, Maxime de, *Essais historiques sur la ville d'Étampes* (Étampes, 1836).

Saint-Paul, Anthyme, "Notre-Dame d'Étampes," *Gazette Archéologique* (1884), pp. 211–223.

LE MANS

Fleury, Gabriel, *Le Cathédrale du Mans*, Petites Monographies des Grands Édifices de la France (Paris, 1910).

Ledru, Ambroise, *La Cathédrale du Mans, Saint-Julien* (Le Mans, 1923), 2e éd.

Lefèvre-Pontalis, Eugène, *Étude historique et archéologique sur la nef de la Cathédrale du Mans* (Mamers, 1889).

Perrigan, l'Abbé, *Recherches sur la Cathédrale du Mans* (Le Mans, 1872).

SAINT-AYOUL AT PROVINS

Bourquelot, Félix, *Histoire de Provins* (Provins, 1839–40), 2 vols.

Fleury, Gabriel, "Le Portail de Saint-Ayoul de Provins et l'iconographie des portails du XIIe siècle," *Congrès archéologique de France* (1902), pp. 458–488.

Maillé, Mise Aliette de, *Provins, les monuments réligieux* (Paris: Les Éditions d'Art et d'Histoire, 1939).

"Séances générales tenues à Troyes et Provins," *Congrès archéologique de France* (1902), pp. 74–76.

SAINT-LOUP-DE-NAUD

Bourquelot, Félix, *Notice historique et archéologique sur le Prieuré de Saint-Loup-de-Naud*, Bibliothèque de l'École des Chartes (Paris, 1840–41), II, 244–271.

"Troyes et Provins, sixième excursion: Église de Saint-Loup-de-Naud," *Congrès archéologique de France* (1902), pp. 82–85.

Salet, Francis, "Saint-Loup-de-Naud," *Bulletin monumental* (1933), pp. 129–169.

FRENCH ROMANESQUE OF LANGUEDOC, WESTERN FRANCE, AND BURGUNDY

Conant, Kenneth, "The Date of the Ambulatory Capitals of Cluny," *Speculum* (January 1930), vol. V, no. 1, pp. 77–94.

Conant, Kenneth, "Drawings and Photographs of the Transept of Cluny," *Speculum* (July 1929), vol. IV, no. 3, pp. 291–302.

Conant, Kenneth, "The Third Church at Cluny," *Medieval Studies in Memory of A. Kingsley Porter* (Cambridge: Harvard University Press, 1939).

Focillon, Henri, *Peintures romanes des églises de France, cent trente photographies de Pierre Devinoy* (Paris: Paul Hartmann, 1938).

Forsyth, William, review of Lafargue's *Les Chapiteaux* in the *American Journal of Archaeology* (1945), vol. XLIX, no. 3.

Katzenellenbogen, Adolf, "The Central Tympanum at Vézelay, its Encyclopedic Meaning and its Relation to the First Crusade," *Art Bulletin* (September, 1944), XXVI, 141–151.

Koehler, Wilhelm R. W., "Byzantine Art in the West," *Dumbarton Oaks Papers*, Number 1 (Cambridge: Harvard University Press, 1941), pp. 63–87.

BIBLIOGRAPHY

Lafargue, Marie, *Les Chapiteau du cloître de Notre-Dame la Daurade* (Paris, 1940).

Mendell, Elizabeth, *Romanesque Sculpture in Saintonge* (New Haven: Yale University Press, 1940).

Oursel, Charles, *La Miniature du XIIe siècle à l'Abbaye de Cîteaux d'après les manuscrits de la Bibliothèque de Dijon* (Dijon, 1926).

Rachou, Henri, *Musée des Augustins de Toulouse, pierres romanes de Saint-Étienne, La Daurade et Saint-Sernin* (Toulouse, 1934).

Rey, Raymond, *La Sculpture romane Languedocienne* (Toulouse: Édouard Privat, 1936).

Rorimer, James J., "The Restored Twelfth Century Parthenay Sculptures," *Technical Studies*, Fogg Art Museum (January 1942), X, 122–126.

Salet, Francis, *La Madeleine de Vézelay* (Melun, 1948).

Salet, Francis, "La Madeleine de Vézelay, notes sur la façade de la nef," *Bulletin monumental* (1940), XCIX, 223–237.

Schapiro, Meyer, "The Romanesque Sculpture of Moissac," *Art Bulletin* (1931), XIII, 249–351, 464-532.

Terret, Victor, *La Sculpture Bourguignonne aux XIIe et XIIIe siècles, ses origines et ses sources d'inspiration, Cluny* (Autun, 1914).

A   RECONSTRUCTION OF THE FAÇADE OF SAINT-DENIS

B   FAÇADE OF THE CATHEDRAL OF CHARTRES

1 CP

2 RP

3 RP.L

I SAINT-DENIS

1 RP.L.1

2 RP.L.1

3 RP.L.1

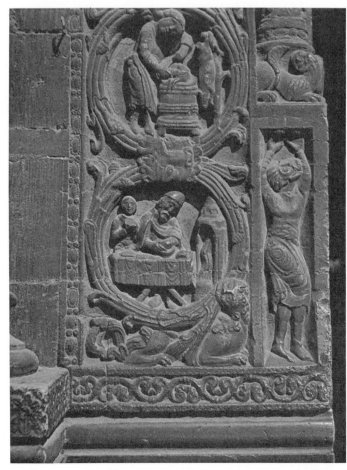

4 RP.L.1

II SAINT-DENIS

1 CP.L.1

2 CP.L.1

3 CP.R.2

4 CP.R.3

5 RP.L.3

6 LP.R.1

III SAINT-DENIS

1 CP.L.3

2 LP.L.1

3 RP.R.1

4 RP.R.3

5 CP.R.4

6 RP.R.2

IV SAINT DENIS

1

2

3

4   19th-century copy *in situ*   5   6

V SAINT-DENIS   *Column in Musée de Cluny*

1 Louvre fragments

2 Musée de Cluny fragments

VI SAINT-DENIS

CP.L.1 (in reverse)

2 CP.R.1

3 LP.L.1

CP.L.4

5 CP.R.3 (in reverse)

6 CP.R.4

7 LP.L.3 (in reverse)

VII SAINT-DENIS *Drawings for Montfaucon*

1

2

3

4

VIII SAINT-DENIS *Head from Walters Art Gallery*

1 Walters Art Gallery

2 Walters Art Gallery

3 Fogg Museum of Art

4 Fogg Museum of Art

IX SAINT-DENIS

1 Bas-relief

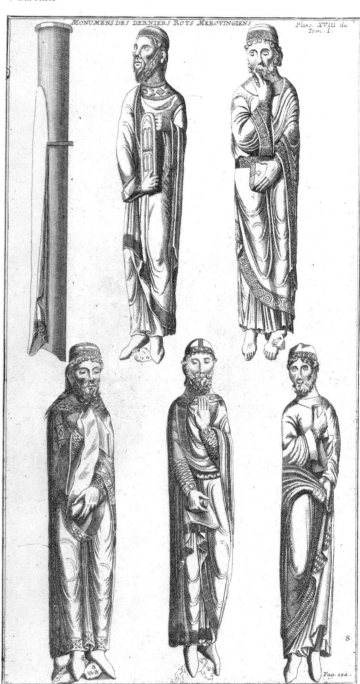

2 RP (Montfaucon)

3 Bas-relief (detail)

4 Bas-relief (detail)

X SAINT-DENIS

LP.L   LP.R   CP.L   CP.R   RP.L   RP.R

XI CHARTRES *The Royal Portal*

2 CP.R

1 CP.R

XII CHARTRES

1 CP.R.2

2 CP.R.2

3 CP.L

XIII CHARTRES

1 LP.L.1

2 CP.R.1

3 LP.L.1

4 CP.R.4

XIV CHARTRES

1 LP.L.1

2 LP.L.2

3 RP.L.2

4 LP.R.1

XV CHARTRES

2 RP.R

1 LP.L

XVI CHARTRES

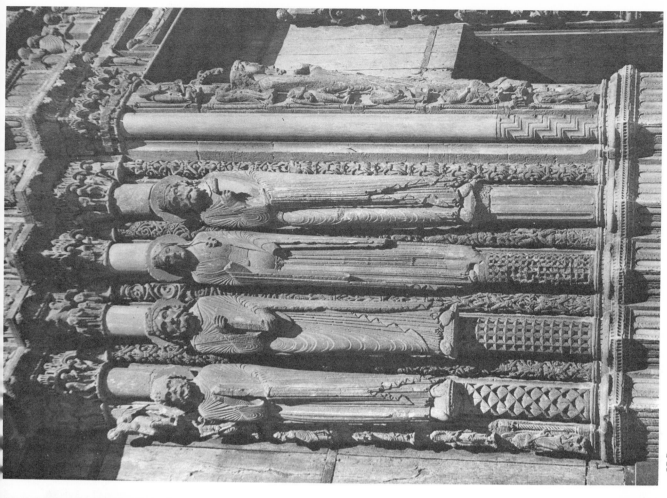

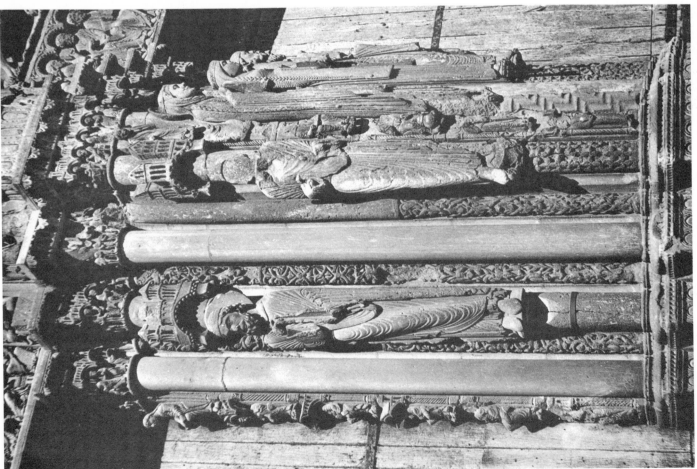

1 LP.L.2

2 RP.R.1

3 CP.R.2

4 CP.R.2

XIX CHARTRES

1 CP tympanum

2 RP

3 CP.L.1,2

4 RP lintels

XX CHARTRES

1 CP.R

2 RP spandrel

3 LP.L

4 RP.R

XXI CHARTRES

1 Saint-Denis narthex

2 Saint-Denis chevet

3 Chartres north tower

4 Chartres south tower

5 Chartres, south portal of south tower

6 Detail of 5

1 Portal

2 R

4 R capitals

3 Saint Peter, inside church

5 L capitals

XXIII ÉTAMPES

1 L

2 L

3 L.2,3

4 L.1

XXIV ÉTAMPES

1 Le Mans

2 Provins

3 Saint-Loup-de-Naud

4 Senlis

XXV

1 Le Mans

2 Provins

3 Saint-Loup-de-Naud

4 Senlis

XXVI

1 Le Mans, Christ

2 Provins, CP.R.4

3 Saint-Loup-de-Naud, Saint Loup

4 Senlis, Christ

2 Provins

1 Le Mans

3 Saint-Loup-de-Naud

4 Saint-Loup-de-Naud

XXVIII

1 Le Mans

2 Le Mans

3 Saint-Loup-de-Naud, St. Loup

4 Saint-Loup-de-Naud

1 Moissac

2 Moissac

3 La Daurade, 1st series

4 La Daurade, abacus 1st series, capital 2nd series

6 La Daurade, 2nd series

5 La Daurade, 2nd series

8 Saint-Sernin, Toulouse, cloister

7 La Daurade, 2nd series

XXX LANGUEDOC

1 Saint-Étienne, Toulouse

2 Moissac portal

3 Saint-Étienne, Toulouse

4 Saint-Étienne, Toulouse

5 Saint-Étienne, Toulouse

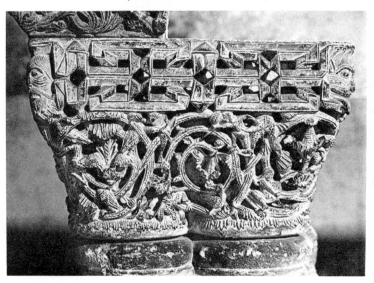

6 La Daurade

XXXI LANGUEDOC

1 Aulnay, south transept

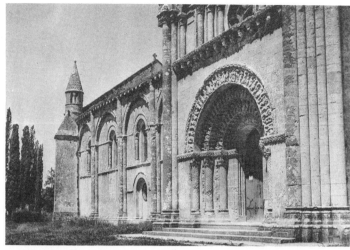

2 Aulnay, south transept

3 Aulnay, LP.L

4 Aulnay, LP

5 Angers, Saint-Aubin, cloister

6 Angers, Saint-Aubin, cloister

1 Parthenay, Notre-Dame-de-la-Couldre

2 Detail of 1

3 Melle, Saint-Hilaire

4 Detail of 2

5 Fogg Museum of Art

6 Parthenay (now Louvre)

XXXIII WESTERN FRANCE

XXXIV BURGUNDY

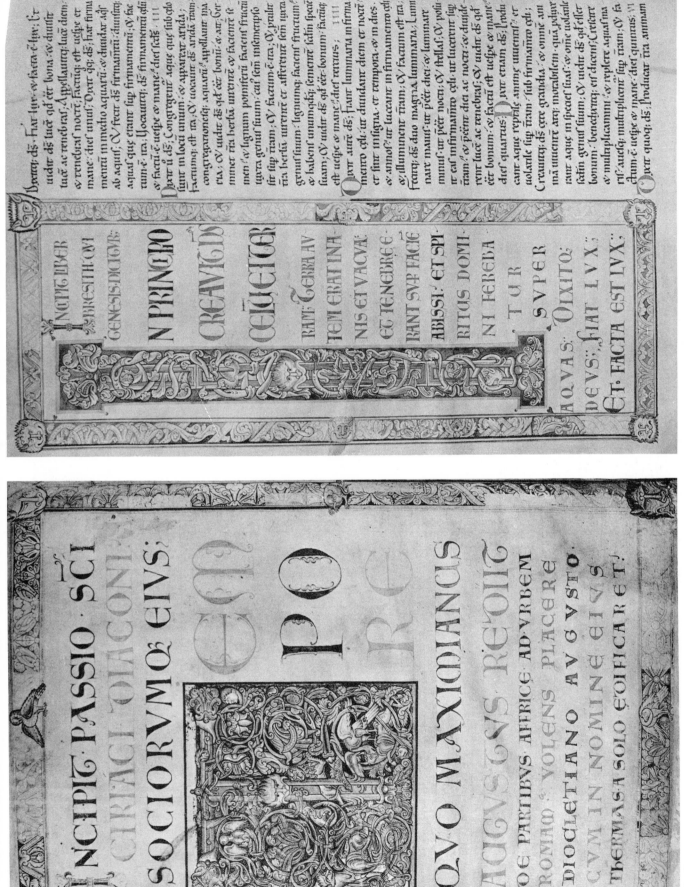

1 Légendaire de Cîteaux   2 Bible of Saint-Bénigne de Dijon

XXXV BURGUNDY

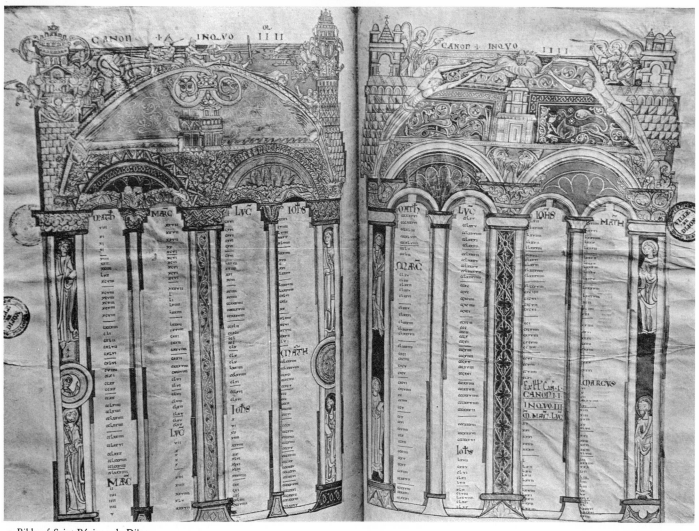

1 Bible of Saint-Bénigne de Dijon

2   2–5 Légendaire de Cîteaux   3   4   5

1 Vézelay

2 Detail of 1

3 Avallon

4 Bourges

XXXVII BURGUNDY

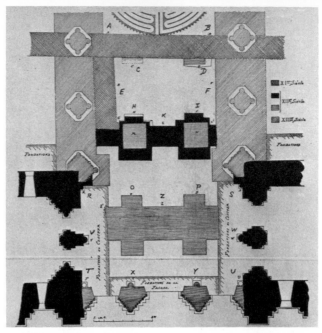

1 Lefèvre-Pontalis, excavations of 1901

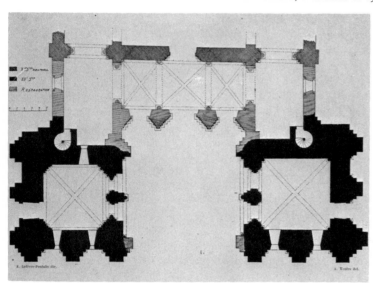

2 Lefèvre-Pontalis, reconstruction of façade, *ca.* 1160

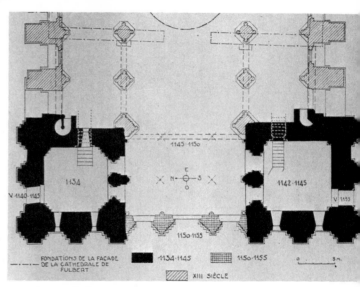

3 Aubert, reconstruction of façade, 1145–1150 and 1150–1155

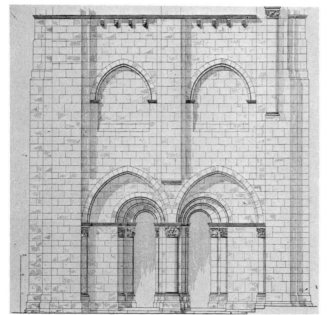

4 Lefèvre-Pontalis, south elevation of north tower

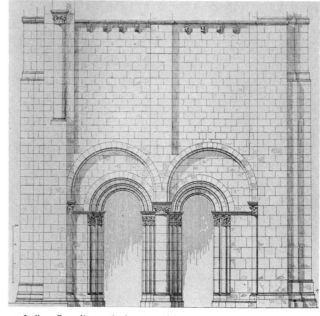

5 Lefèvre-Pontalis, north elevation of south tower

XXXVIII CHARTRES

SCULPTORS OF
THE WEST PORTALS OF
CHARTRES CATHEDRAL

Their Origins in Romanesque
and Their Role in Chartrain Sculpture

CONTENTS

CONTENTS

ILLUSTRATIONS

All illustrations are from photographs by the author unless otherwise indicated. The author wishes to thank the following for permission to reproduce photographs: James Austin; Foto-Marburg; Arch. Phot./S.P.A.D.E.M., Paris/V.A.G.A., New York, 1985; Sandak Inc.

Parts of portals are typically designated as follows: LP.L1 is left portal, left side, jamb nearest doorway; CP.R4 is central portal, right side, fourth jamb from door.

PART I

THE WEST PORTALS
OF SAINT-DENIS

INTRODUCTION

During the past thirty years, knowledge about the west portals has increased markedly. Careful cleaning and study of the superstructure of the central portal was begun by Sumner Crosby in 1947. At that time it was evident from photographs that much original sculpture was preserved beneath accumulated grime. This sculpture was not discussed (W.S.S., 1952, 3, fn. 16.). Several summer campaigns from 1968 through 1971, conducted by Sumner Crosby and Pamela Blum, resulted in an extensive article on the tympanum, archivolts, and door jambs of the central portal. This study (Sumner McKnight Crosby and Pamela Z. Blum, "Le Portail central de la façade occidentale de Saint-Denis," *Bulletin monumental,* 131, 1973, 209–66) allows a more detailed analysis of the entire central portal, including the Baltimore head and the Paris head, discovered by Léon Pressouyre ("Une tête de reine du portail central de Saint-Denis," *Gesta,* XV, 1976, 151–60).

Paula Gerson ("The West Façade of St.-Denis: An Iconographic Study," Ph.D. dissertation, Columbia University, 1970, microfilm) has carefully studied the alterations of the façade and Abbot Suger as iconographer, including sources of his ideas both from travels in Italy, Germany, and France and from medieval texts. By concentrating on detailed analysis of each portal such as the central portal with statue-columns, Wise and Foolish Virgins on door jambs, trumeau, bronze doors, and Last Judgment in the tympanum, she has discovered a more unified and more complex meaning. Taken together with the writings of Suger, studies of Saint-Denis glass by Louis Grodecki, and research on the liturgical objects and on the architecture of narthex and chevet, this study gives an added dimension and greater focus to the extraordinary role of Abbot Suger as patron, iconographer, and luminary unique among churchmen of his day. It is hoped that Paula Gerson's thesis will soon become available in printed and illustrated form.

Identification of the small statue-column in The Metropolitan Museum of Art, New York, with a drawing and engraving for Montfaucon of the cloister of Saint-Denis (Vera K. Ostoia, "A Statue from Saint-Denis," *Bulletin of The Metropolitan Museum of Art,* XIII, 10, June 1955, 298–304) makes it possible, when augmented by capitals from

the cloister and the Crosby relief of the Apostles, to study further the post–1140 sculpture of Saint-Denis.

Finally, the splendid exhibition at The Cloisters in the spring of 1981 (Sumner McKnight Crosby, Jane Hayward, Charles T. Little, and William D. Wixom, *The Royal Abbey of Saint-Denis in the Time of Abbot Suger (1122–1151),* 1981) assembled four heads from the jambs, three Louvre heads from the central portal, ornamental colonnettes from the Musée de Cluny, the cloister figure from The Metropolitan, the Crosby relief from Saint-Denis, capitals from the church and cloister, and stained glass and objects from the treasury. This exhibition and the attendant superb symposium offered an exciting opportunity to reevaluate Suger's enormous contribution to the birth of Early Gothic art.

CONDITION OF THE PORTALS:
RESTORATIONS

(See W. S. Stoddard, 2–3; Plates I, II, 2)

On the basis of careful scrutiny of the bases and inner jambs of Saint-Denis in the summer of 1939, together with an interpretation of the heated debate over the nineteenth-century restorations on the façade, I concluded that the inward slant of each portal from about .93 meters above the present pavement level was the result of recarving and that no original sculpture remained, with the exception of parts of the tympanum and archivolts of the central portal. Study of the inner jambs and superstructure by Crosby and Blum from scaffolding, revealing considerable twelfth-century sculpture in spite of recarved sections and insertions of new heads, has proved that my conclusions were wrong (Crosby and Blum, 1973). Further, Louis Grodecki in his review of my book pointed out my erroneous interpretation of this inward slant of the portals and called attention to documents in the Archives des Monuments historiques, which enumerate the recarved and replaced sections of the sculpture (Grodecki, *Bulletin monumental,* III (1953), 312–15).

By studying a drawing (1600–1630) of the façade and the excavations (1846–1847) of Viollet-le-Duc in front of the Abbey and by using the known dimensions of Suger's bronze doors (melted down in 1794) on the central portal, Paula Gerson was able to estimate the height of the lintels ("The Lintels of the West Façade of Saint-Denis," *Journal of the Society of Architectural Historians,* Vol. XXXIV, 3, 1975, 189–97). The left portal lintel under the mosaic in the tympanum was practically nonexistant (.01 meters to .05 meters high), while the central portal one was sufficient for Suger's inscription (.13 to .17 meters). Only the lintel of the right portal (.42 to .47 meters) originally contained sculpture. Before Gerson's article appeared, it had been assumed that large lintels were supported visually by the small colonnettes in the doorjambs (Plates A, I, 1, 2). Without the large lintel on the central portal, greater prominence was given to Suger's bronze doors.

FRAGMENTS OF COLONNETTES IN THE MUSÉE DE CLUNY

by W. S. Stoddard 6–7; Plate VI, 2

Four sections of colonnettes in storage in the Musée de Cluny (Plate VI, 2) have been questioned. The fact that a uniform wash covers the surfaces, giving the appearance of plaster, has led scholars to argue that they are nineteenth-century forgeries. Indeed, two are modern. In the summer of 1939, I washed the surfaces of the other two with water (Plate VI, 2) and discovered that over half the surfaces are original. Their stylistic relationship to the two columns from the inner jambs of Saint-Denis, both now in the Musée de Cluny (Plates V, VI, 1), and their more compact composition and lower relief, when contrasted with Chartres ornament, points to the plausible conclusion that these fragments served as decorative foils for the jamb figures. Thus Suger and his team of sculptors created a new portal design with columnar jamb statues together with framing, ornamental colonnettes, which accentuate the architectonic character of each splay. This portal design was repeated with variations through the twelfth century and into the High Gothic period.

MONTFAUCON (1729): DRAWINGS AND ENGRAVINGS

Since Marvin Ross in 1940 connected two heads in the Walters Art Gallery, Baltimore, and a head in the Fogg Art Museum, Cambridge, with jamb figures on the left and central portals of Saint-Denis on the basis of drawings made for engravings in Bernard de Montfaucon's *Les Monumens de la monarchie françoise* (1729, I, Plates XVI–XVIII), the use of both drawings and engravings to identify monuments has increased as more Early Gothic sculpture has been discovered. Of the three sets of drawings (Paris, Bib-

liothèque Nationale, Ms. français, 15634), the original pencil drawings with wash made by Antoine Benoist are obviously the best evidence for identifying the heads. Two sets of copies, the second reversed for the engraver, are very close to the original, especially in the treatment of drapery. The engravings (central portal, fig. 2) exhibit the same treatment of costume, arrangement of folds, and awkward articulation as the drawings. The greatest change from the original drawings to engravings appears in details of faces. In spite of the fact that a lot of the surface of the column figure from the Saint-Denis cloister in the Metropolitan (The Metropolitan Catalogue, 4, 1981) has been recarved, the close resemblance between statue and both drawing and engraving (Montfaucon, Plate X) suggests that it is feasible to use cautiously the engravings to analyze figure style. Incidently, jamb figures and fragments of jambs discovered in 1977 and now in the Musée de Cluny in Paris, which originally decorated the Sainte-Anne portal of Notre-Dame in Paris, were identified by studying the Montfaucon engravings (Montfaucon, Plate VIII).

SCULPTURE OF SAINT-DENIS

by W. S. Stoddard with John Wetenhall

Extensive damage has greatly impaired the task of sorting out the different sculptors who worked on the west façade of Saint-Denis. Nevertheless, since the original publication of this book, significant progress has been made by Crosby and Blum in separating original work from restoration and in grouping sculptural styles in the tympanum, archivolt, and door jambs of the central portal. Enough scattered evidence remains so that further groupings can be attempted, particularly concerning the sculptors of the now destroyed jamb fixtures.

FOUR HEADS FROM THE JAMB STATUES

The head of a queen in Paris, Collection Jean Osouf (fig. 3), was identified by Léon Pressouyre (*Gesta,* 1976, 151–60). This head belonged to the second jamb on the right side of the Saint-Denis central portal (CP.R 2, fig. 2) The original drawings, when compared with multiple views of the head and its stylistic, dimensional, and geological similarities with the Baltimore head (Plate VIII), prove beyond any doubt that the Paris head belonged to the Saint-Denis central portal and that the same sculptor carved both heads. Treatment of the jewelled crown, hair, stark eyes with large, round irises, cheek, and upper lip accented by marked planes are very similar stylistically. The oval shape of the two heads, capped by cylindrical crowns, together with the abstracted, anatomical features, portray a marked monumentality of the highest quality. In 1952, I differed with the identification by Marvin Ross in 1940 of the Baltimore head (Plate VIII) with "Clothaire III" (Plate VII, 2) and attributed it to "Clovis II" (Plate VII, 1). Pressouyre (1976) and the authors of The Metropolitan Catalogue (1981) have argued for "Clothaire III" (Plate VII, 2). By careful scrutiny of the remaining parts of the crown, the pointed beard terminating in two, not four, knobs, the rhythmic, spacing, and number of curls of the beard lead us to believe that the Baltimore head belongs to the figure of "Clovis II," as I originally argued.

Two heads from the left portal of Saint-Denis (fig. 1), one in the Walters Art Gallery, Baltimore, and the other in the Fogg Art Museum, Cambridge (Plate IX), were carved by a different sculptor. The general shape of the left portal heads is more triangular, with slightly wider crowns and its silhouette tapering to a point. Surfaces of foreheads and cheeks are more animated by shifting planes, while hair and beards are treated with more sinuosity. The forceful archaic ruggedness of the heads from the central portal is in marked contrast to the more animated and softer surfaces of the left portal heads.

JAMB STATUES

Time and history have left none of the original jambs except the four heads just discussed, and also the eighteenth-century drawings and engravings for Montfaucon. As evidence, the drawings and engravings can be contested as uncertain blends of eighteenth-century style, but, without insisting on ambiguous nuance, points of validity do appear: first, details such as ornament are accurate enough for the four original heads to be attributed to a specific jamb figure; and second, when a particular trait appears in the figures of one portal to the exclusion of the other two, we may deduce that it is not of the eighteenth century but a characteristic peculiar to the figures of that portal and, in all likelihood, an identifying characteristic of a specific, individual sculptor.

The same stylistic differences that distinguish the heads of the central and left portals can be seen if the jambs of the two portals are compared (figs. 1, 2). Although many features such as jewelled borders of garments and somewhat disjointed anatomy are common characteristics of the sculpture of both portals, a certain rigidity and lithic quality permeates the central portal figures, while a greater litheness is portrayed in the jambs on the left portal. The fact that five of the six figures on the left portal are cross-legged, whereas only one is on the central portal may accentuate these differences. If the cross-legged figures (CP.R no. 2, fig. 2) is contrasted with five on the left portal (fig.

1), it is clear that there is more graceful movement in the figures on the left portal. Decorative hems and borders appear to blend into the more detailed surfaces of drapery on the left jambs. Heads on the left portal are either frontal or slightly turned, whereas those on the central portal bend forward. It would thus appear that two different sculptors were responsible for the jamb figures of the left and central portals.

The right portal (Plate X, 2 and fig. 11) can be separated from the other two on grounds of relative anatomical correctness. Although slightly attenuated, the left and central portal figures conform to a logicality based on the human body. The right portal jambs are conspicuous in their Romanesque awkwardness: both upper and lower center figures have noticeably disjointed wrists and no indication of elbows, while the drapery of the upper right-hand figure hardly conforms with the crossed legs beneath. Wide ornamental bands decorate the diagonal hems of mantles. Heads of the right portal are more pointed in silhouette and possess more freely curled beards. Even with liberal concessions to eighteenth-century draftsmen, significant differences exist in the engravings, leading to the conclusion that the jamb figures of each portal were carved by different sculptors. Willibald Sauerländer (Gothic Sculpture in France 1140–1270, London, 1972, 381) stated that three different sculptors were responsible for the jambs on the three portals.

CENTRAL PORTAL: TYMPANUM, ARCHIVOLTS, INNER JAMBS

To complete the attribution of the central portal to different sculptors, we must summarize the conclusions of Crosby and Blum (1973), who, through cleaning, detailed photography, and careful observation, distinguished original sculpture from recut areas and modern additions or replacements. On the basis of their study, three different personalities were identified.

To the Master of the Apostles they attributed the lower two-thirds of the tympanum, including the Apostles and the raising of the dead but not the Christ (fig. 4—see Crosby and Blum, 1973, 220–29, Plates V and VI for the relatively small areas recut and the modern replacements, including all the heads). His figures reveal attention to human anatomy, natural proportions in lively and plausible poses, and resistance to cramped groupings despite limitations of space. Stylized drapery folds contrast with a realism of detail in decorative borders and hems that tend to bind groups of figures together. Details such as hands and feet are soft, rounded, and delicate. Treatment of drapery is quite different from that of the jambs of the central portal (fig. 2), but exhibits some stylistic relationships to the statues of the

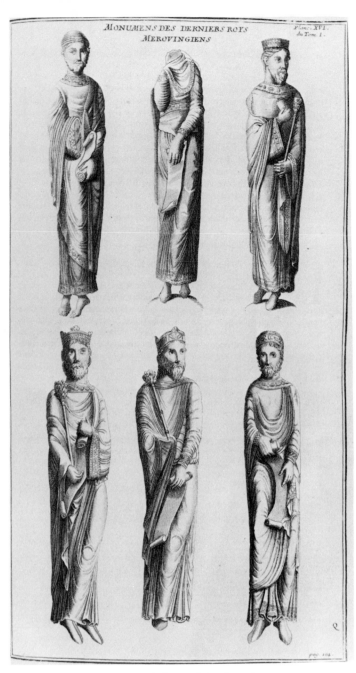

1. Saint-Denis, LP jamb figures (Montfaucon)

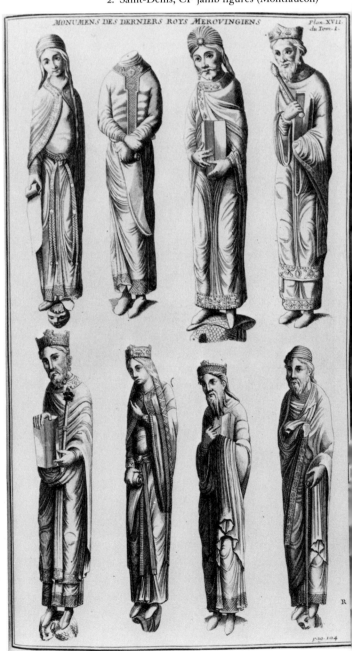

2. Saint-Denis, CP jamb figures (Montfaucon)

3. Saint-Denis, CP.R2 head, Paris, Collection Jean Osouf, 37 cm by 20 cm (Sandak)

4. Saint-Denis, CP tympanum, Last Judgment

5. Saint-Denis, CP tympanum, detail

6. Saint-Denis,
third Patriarch on right,
second archivolt

7. Saint-Denis, Double heads from central tympanum
(18 cm x 16 cm), Louvre (Sandak)

8. Saint-Denis, Head of Patriarch from second archivolt
(25 cm), Louvre (Sandak)

left portal (fig. 1). Those connections are seen in the organization of drapery over thighs and knees of the Apostle and angel on the right, as well as in the treatment of hems and feet. However, the double head of Apostles on the left side of tympanum (fig. 7), to be discussed later, does not exhibit the subtlety of surface of the Baltimore and Fogg heads from the left portal (Plate X).

The work of the Angel Master, who is credited with the upper third of the tympanum (fig. 5), inner archivolt and the centermost areas of the other archivolts, and the inner door jambs (Crosby and Blum, 1973, 229–49, Plates III, IV, VII, VIII, XVII, XVIII), is less dexterous. Feet are often awkward and hands too large and stiff. The main distinctive characteristic of this sculptor is his conception of drapery: folds are created by twin, parallel incisions on a flat surface, which forms patterns of concentric curves, always maintaining a U-shape and never merging into V's.

The Master of the Patriarchs, to whom Crosby and Blum give the outer archivolts and Christ of the tympanum (figs. 4, 6—1973, 254–64, Plates IX–XII, figs. 18, 19), creates drapery in folds rather than by grooves. Most noticeable is the tension between more stylized, heavier, rhythmic folds over torsos and arms and the delicate, varied, and agitated drapery below the knees. His more angular, V-shaped folds, as seen on the Christ of the tympanum and on most of the Patriarchs, further remove him from both the Angel Master and the Master of the Apostles.

Four heads in the Louvre (Marcel Aubert and Michèle Beaulieu, *Musée National du Louvre: Description raisonnée des sculptures du Moyen Âge, de la Renaissance et des temps modernes I: Moyen Âge,* Paris, 1950, No. 52–54) have been connected with specific figures on the central portal by Crosby and Blum (1973, Plates XIX, XX). The condition of the double head by the Apostle Master (fig. 7, and Metropolitan Catalogue, 1981, 1a), which originally belonged to the left two Apostles, does not allow for subtle comparisons and contrasts. In general, the heads are cruder than both those from the central jambs (Plate VIII and fig. 3) and the two heads from the left portal (Plate IX), as seen in the treatment of hair and beards. Curving eyelids and bulging eyeballs are closer to the left portal heads.

One of the three Louvre heads by the Patriarch Master (fig. 8, and Metropolitan Catalogue, 1981, 1b) lacks the crispness of carving of the heads from the central portal jambs, but, at the same time, exhibits a different treatment of eyes, moustache, and beard when contrasted with the double head by the Apostles Master.

Three different sculptors seem to have carved the jamb figures of the west portals. It is hoped that more study of the remaining sculpture of the side portals and discovery, by chance or excavation, of torsos of jamb figures will lead to clearer determination of the number of sculptors involved in the completion of the Saint-Denis façade. The façade of Saint-Gilles-du-Gard was carved by five sculptors, and the Chartres west portals were the work of four artists with assistants.

POST-1140 SAINT-DENIS SCULPTURE

by W. S. Stoddard

Sculpture carved after the dedication of narthex and west portals in 1140 consists of capitals in crypt and chevet (1144), a column figure of a king from the old cloister, now in The Metropolitan Museum of Art, New York (1981, Metropolitan catalogue, 4, 45–46), capitals from the cloister in the Louvre, the Musée de Cluny, Rouen, and Saint-Denis (1981, catalogue, 8a, b, 47–49), impost blocks with acanthus decorations (1981, catalogue, 8 a–d, 55–57), and the relief of twelve Apostles, discovered in 1947 by Sumner Crosby in the south transept of Saint-Denis (Sumner McKnight Crosby, *The Apostle Bas-Relief at Saint-Denis,* New Haven and London, 1972, and 1981, catalogue, no. 6, 50–53). Acanthus capitals in the chevet (1144—Plate XXII, 2) are more freely organized in three dimensions as compared with the flatter, spikelike capitals of the narthex (1140—Plate XII, 1). Obviously, two different workshops were responsible for narthex and chevet.

That the capitals and column figure of a king from the old cloister of Saint-Denis were carved at the same time is revealed by comparisons of heads of capitals with the battered head of the king. It was suggested by Pressouyre in the Saint-Denis Symposium of 1981 (to be published) that the relationship between the Saint-Denis cloister sculpture and the capitals in Saint-Germain-des-Prés reveal a date in the early 1160s rather than a date before Suger's death, in 1151. Since the Metropolitan king appears to be influenced by the Headmaster's sculpture on the Chartres central portal, which was completed in the mid-1140s (see Part II), a date of around 1150 or in the late 1140s is certainly plausible.

Sumner Crosby graciously allowed me to publish the twelve Apostles relief (1952, Appendix III, 60–61, Plate X), even though he disagreed completely with my interpretation. His extensive monography (*The Apostle Bas-Relief at Saint-Denis,* 1972) contains the history of the discovery and a detailed analysis of ornament and figure style. Because the sculptured side of this relief was placed face downward on a thirteenth-century tomb, its condition is pristine. Its unfinished state can be verified not only by the partially carved ornamented side but also by the omission of drilled irises on all the Apostles except Peter and Paul and the lack of delineation of toenails on several figures.

The main stylistic problem with the relief is its lack of quality when compared with the sculpture on and from the façade. Its ornament, which covers every available space, does not possess the crispness of the two earlier colonnettes from the west portals, now in the Musée de Cluny (Plate V). Indeed, the undulating vine with floral fillers, which frame the Apostles, is relatively crude when contrasted with either the colonnettes (Plates V, VI) or with the weathered ornament on the plinths (Plate II, 4).

Apostles exhibit none of the complexity of drapery folds nor the implied anatomical articulation of the CP. lintel of Chartres (Fig. 46), carved by the Headmaster. Further, if compared to the narrative cycle of the Chartres RP. lintels (figs. 47–49), the Apostles appear flat, disjointed, and repetitive. Heads of the Apostles are less forceful and less sensitively carved than the four heads from the central and left portals (Plates VIII, IX and fig. 3). Several scholars have noted connections between the Apostle relief and Chartres as well as with the Last Supper tympanum of Dijon (Metropolitan catalogue, 1981, 53; Lapeyre, 1960, 115).

The Dijon tympanum is of higher quality and owes a debt to both Saint-Denis and Chartres, while the twelve Apostles can be derived directly from the Saint-Denis west portals.

As described in detail (1952, W.S.S., 60–61 and Plate X), the poses, gestures, and arrangements and style of drapery of the six Apostles on the left are free adaptations of the six jamb statues of the right portal of Saint-Denis (Plate X), reading from left to right on the upper tier and right to left on the lower range of the Montfaucon engraving. Symbols are similar, with the exception of Peter's keys, although hands are reversed in the second and fourth Apostles. The six right-hand Apostles appear to be variations of the six left-hand Apostles. Thus, it seems highly plausible that this relief is a belated extension of the Saint-Denis west portals. Its unfinished state points to the time of Suger's death in January 1151 and was perhaps planned for Suger's tomb.

PART II

THE ROYAL PORTALS
OF CHARTRES CATHEDRAL

Since 1952, the west portals of Chartres have been discussed in numerous articles and books. Most of these publications have concentrated on the iconographical interpretations of the portals within the context of the School of Chartres. This new addition, however, is an attempt to distinguish the individuality of the sculptors who created this entire extraordinary ensemble.

In 1956, Otto von Simson (*The Gothic Cathedral: Origins of Gothic Architecture and the Medieval Concept of Order,* New York, 1956) stressed the importance of measure and light in Gothic design and delineated the roles of Suger, Geoffrey of Chartres, Henry of Sens, and others in the formation of Gothic art. Peter Kidson discussed the design of the portals, their original emplacement, and their iconographical interpretation, including fifty illustrations of the west façade and tower capitals (*Sculpture at Chartres,* London, 1958). In 1959, Adolf Katzenellenbogen (*The Sculptural Programs of Chartres Cathedral: Christ-Mary-Ecclesia,* Baltimore, 1959) explained the total meaning of the nine portals by specific references to liturgical texts, literary sources, and contemporary theological and political concepts and, at the same time, placed the Early Gothic west portals and the High Gothic transept portals in the historical stream of the evolving Middle Ages. His conclusions on the west portals are summarized in my book (*Monastery and Cathedral in France,* Wesleyan University Press, 1966, 153–55).

In a 1959 article, Louis Grodecki raised and analyzed the problems of research in Gothic sculpture ("La 'première sculpture gothique,' Wilhelm Vöge et l'état actuel des problèmes," *Bulletin monumental,* CXVII, 265–89). In 1960, André Lapeyre published his extensive research on all the known twelfth-century portals (*Des Façades Occidentales de Saint-Denis et de Chartres aux Portails de Laon*). Three years later, Grodecki published a monograph on Chartres, with handsome plates in color and black and white (*Chartres,* New York: Harcourt Brace). Adelheid Heimann's article on the subject of the capital friezes at Chartres and their origins appeared in 1968 ("The Capital Frieze and Pilasters of the Portail Royal, Chartres," *Journal of the Warburg and Courtauld Institutes,* Vol. 31, 73–102), and René Crozet's response to the Heimann article came out in 1971 ("À propos des chapiteaux de la façade occidentale de

Chartres," *Cahiers de civilisation médievale,* XIV, 159–65).

In a volume in the Norton Critical Studies in Art History, Robert Branner edited *Chartres Cathedral* (New York, 1969). In addition to Branner's introductory essay, the text includes translations of medieval documents and important studies of Chartres by Vöge, Focillon, Bony, Priest, Henry Adams, and others. In 1970, Willibald Sauerländer published a large book with extensive notes and text and with splendid photographs by Max Hirmer (*Gotische Skulptur in Frankreich 1140–1270;* an English edition appeared in 1972 (*Gothic Sculpture in France 1140–1270*). Jean Villette in 1971 proved that the lintel of the central portal was originally supported by a trumeau depicting John the Baptist ("Le portail royal de Chartres a-t-il été modifié depuis sa construction?" *Bulletin des Sociétés Archéologiques d'Eure-et-Loir,* Vol. 115, 1971, 255–64). Jan van der Meulen, with Nancy W. Price, published a book on the left tympanum of the west portals (*The West Portals of Chartres Cathedral, Vol. I, The Iconology of the Creation,* Washington, D.C., University Press of America, 1981). Finally, van der Meulen and Jürgen Hohmeyer published *Chartres. Biographie der Kathedrale* (Köln, 1984). All these books and articles will be referred to in the following pages.

In the summer of 1939, my research at Chartres was concentrated on the construction, ornament, and jamb figures of the west portals. Detailed stylistic analysis of tympana, lintels, and archivolts, as well as figured reliefs of the inner jambs and capital frieze was not included in my dissertation (1941) nor in its subsequent publication, which was delayed by World War II. In rewriting the dissertation, I paid more attention to the styles of jamb figures. Further, it was argued that the LP.R and the RP.L jamb figures, as well as the double lintel of the right portal, were carved by assistants of the Headmaster, the sculptor of the CP jambs, lintel, and tympanum.

This new edition will attempt both to refine these conclusions and to include an analysis of all the sculpture of inner doorjamb and pilasters (forty-eight reliefs), of the capitals (twenty-two), and tympana, lintels, and archivolts of all three portals. The foldout drawing of the west portals shows the distribution of the work of the four sculptors and their assistants whose individual styles can, it is hoped, be identified.

JAMB STATUES

Since January 1967, the following jamb statues have been replaced by copies: LP.R 4, CP.L 5, RP.L 4, RP.R 2 and 3 (1970, Chadefaux). The originals, including the angel with a sundial, are now exhibited in the crypt. The cleaning and conservation of the portals is now completed (LP 1981, CP 1982, and RP 1983).

In 1952 (W.S.S., 12–13 and 20–22), it was argued that of the original twenty-four jamb figures, the nineteen that are preserved were carved by five sculptors. Perhaps detailed photographs of each splay since the cleaning, together with more study of inner jambs, capital-frieze, tympana, lintels, and archivolts, will help support this conclusion. Three of the five sculptors of the jamb statues carved sections of the superstructure, while the other two were responsible for most of the sculpture on doorjambs, pilasters, and capitals.

THE ÉTAMPES MASTER

The Étampes Master, the sculptor of the south portal of Notre Dame of Étampes (see Part III), carved the two extreme left-hand jamb figures. Since the cleaning of the left portal, the stark rigidity, tapering silhouettes, disjointed but delineated anatomy, and deeply undercut surfaces of LP.L 2 and 3 by the Étampes Master are even more apparent (Plate XVI, 1 and fig. 9a). Wide bands with geometric patterns, accented by drill holes, animate the hems, while similar horizontal bands decorate the plain, curved surfaces between the knees and ankles. Knees are revealed by narrow bands of drapery at their bottoms and the scalloped folds of the mantle at their tops. Lower parts of legs are articulated by parabolic ridge-folds with thicker, vertical ridge-folds between the legs beneath the staffs, which are broken off in both statues. The drapery of mantles consist of parallel raised ridge-folds, often with horizontal connections. Stomachs are marked by oval folds, while upper mantles are open to reveal elaborately carved bodices. The female head of LP.L 3 (Plate XVI, 1) is placed on a male figure and does not fit, and the LP.L 2 head (Plate XIX, 1) appears to be carved from a different colored limestone, with several breaks in the joints to make it fit the body.

The relationship of these two statues to those on the portal of Notre-Dame at Étampes will be discussed in detail in Part III. Suffice it to say that the same sculptor carved these two jamb statues at Chartres and the majority of the sculpture at Étampes. Stylistic evidence points to the conclusion that Étampes predates Chartres.

The authorship of the LP.L 1 jamb has been debated extensively (figs. 9, 9b). The jamb's elongated silhouette, with drapery flaring over the frontally posed feet, is clearly different from that of both LP.L 2 and 3, by the Étampes Master, and all the monumental sculpture on the Étampes portal. However, in spite of these differences, there are many stylistic characteristics that relate this jamb statue to the work of the Étampes Master. First, the rounded ridge-folds (fig. 9b) resemble the folds of the upper mantle on the adjacent jambs. The oval stomach is treated somewhat differently than in the Étampes figures, but the double cords, falling from waist to ankles, are a more three-dimensional variant of the cords on R 3 jamb of Étampes. Although the upper bodice resembles those of the two female figures at Étampes, breasts are not accented as they are in the Étampes jambs. Articulation of wrists is less awkward than in the other figures on the LP.L splay. The treatment of the folds in the hems resemble that in the other Étampes Master figures at Chartres. The head appears too small for the body, and a marked break between torso and head suggests this head is a replacement. On balance, it can be argued that, indeed, LP.L 1 is by the Étampes Master and was probably carved after LP.L 2 and 3. The discussion in Part IV of the Burgundian origins of the Étampes Master will verify the attribution of LP. LI to this sculptor.

THE SAINT-DENIS MASTER

Although certain stylistic common denominators, such as awkward anatomy and curving silhouettes, exist between statue-columns by the Étampes Master (LP.L 1, 2, 3) and those by the so-called Saint-Denis Master (RP.R 1, 2, 3—figs. 10, 10a, b, c and Plate XVI, 2), it is abundantly clear that the RP.R jambs were carved by a different sculptor.

The designation of the sculptor of the RP.R 1, 2 jambs of Chartres (Plate XVI, 2 and fig. 10 a, b) as the Saint-Denis Master of Chartres is based on the slightly tapered bodies, the mannered sense of anatomy beneath the drapery, particularly emphasized by swirls around the knees, and by rhythmic folds that call to mind the figures of Suger's façade (figs. 1, 2, and Plate X, 2), as suggested by Alan Priest ("The Masters of the West Façade of Chartres," *Art Studies*, I, 1923, 28–44). The elongated heads with high cheek bones, wide, somewhat bulbous, eyes, stylized hair, and tapered beard (especially RP.R 1—Plate XIX, 2), when compared with the Saint-Denis heads, further suggest a connection between the two monuments (W.S.S., 1952, 12–13, 21–22). With the existence of the four heads from the jamb figures of Saint-Denis, the Louvre heads from the superstructure of the central portal, and the remaining, original sections of tympanum and archivolts on the central portal, is it possible to identify the specific sculptor, out of the six already identified, who worked at Saint-Denis?

Although all existing Saint-Denis heads exhibit some

9a. Chartres, LP.L2, 3 (detail)

9. Chartres, LP.L1, 2, 3

9b. Chartres, LP.L1 (detail)

10a. Chartres, RP.R1 (detail)

10. Chartres, RP.R1, 2, 3 (Austin)

10b. Chartres, RP.R2 (detail)

125

superficial relation to the Chartres RP heads, there are none that appear to have been carved by the Chartres sculptor. The two Saint-Denis heads from the CP jamb statues (Plate VIII and fig. 3) possess cheeks and eyebrows animated by edges and large, drilled irises framed by evenly curving eyelids, while the Chartres heads (Plates XVI, 2 and XIX, 2) exhibit uninterrupted curving planes and eyes with double eyelids, which countercurve at corners, and with no irises. The two heads from the Saint-Denis LP (Plate IX), carved by a different hand than the CP heads, also reveal a general archaic starkness and emphasis on edges, separating planes, which is somewhat different from the Chartres heads. The Louvre heads from the superstructure of Saint-Denis CP (figs. 7, 8) are crudely carved, with bulging eyeballs and starkly delineated beards and hair that is quite different from the Chartres heads, with their more subtle transition of planes and greater sinuosity of beard and hair. Thus, from the point of view of comparisons with existing heads from Saint-Denis, the RP.R heads of Chartres do not appear to have been carved either by the sculptors of the jamb statues of the LP or CP or by the sculptors of the heads of the CP superstructure.

If comparisons of heads of the Saint-Denis CP and LP with those of the Chartres RP appear to be inconclusive, it follows, by the process of elimination, that if there had been a Saint-Denis sculptor in the Chartres *chantier,* it would have to have been the RP Master of Saint-Denis (Plate X, 2 and fig. 11). Unfortunately, no original sculpture remains from the jamb figures of this portal. However, several similar characteristics can be found in the Chartres RP figures and in the drawings and engraving of the Saint-Denis RP. Very disjointed anatomy at the elbows and wrists, which distinguishes the RP of Saint-Denis from the other two Saint-Denis portals, is exhibited in the Chartres RP jamb statues. Folded, ornamented hems of mantles appears only on the Saint-Denis RP and the RP.R 1, 2 jambs at Chartres (figs. 10a, b). Treatment of drapery above the ankles of Chartres RP.R 1, 2, with parabolic loops accenting legs and vertical folds terminating in serrated hems, is closest stylistically to the Saint-Denis RP, especially the right-hand figure (fig. 11). Both the Chartres RP.R 1 jamb (fig. 10a) and the Saint-Denis drawing (fig. 11) exhibit an unusual detail of a hand extending up from the supporting corbel and grasping the foot. The right legs of both Chartres statues (figs. 10a, b) are animated by raised, loop-folds or spirals, which merely suggest the location of knees. The irregular intervals between the folds are in marked contrast to regular, rhythmic folds of the statues by the Étampes Master and are more complex than the drapery on any of the drawings or engravings of the Saint-Denis jambs. The bodice and left side of RP.R2 of Chartres (fig. 10b) are decorated with curving, double- or triple-ridge folds, which resemble the double folds in the legs of the Saint-Denis RP (Plate X, 2). Granted that the attribution of the RP.R1, 2 Chartres figures to the Saint-Denis RP Master is a tenuous assertion, at least there does appear to be sufficient stylistic similarities to suggest this possibility.

The identification of the RP.R Chartres figures is further complicated by the fact that they appear to be influenced by the Étampes Master. Crenellated canopies, which did not exist at Saint-Denis (see the left-hand statue in fig. 11), separate heads from capitals, while wide, ornamented bands, which animate the lower legs of LP.L2, 3 by the Étampes Master, decorate the thighs of the RP.R1, 2 by the so-called Saint-Denis Master. Thus there would appear to be some attempt on the part of the RP.R Master, within the constraints of his individual style, to conform to the splay being carved by the Étampes Master. Influence of the Étampes Master may possibly explain the greater complexity of drapery of the Chartres RP.R1, 2 jambs when compared to the Saint-Denis sculpture.

The female figure, RP.R3 (fig. 10c and Plate XVI, 2), has certain features, such as tapering silhouette, oval protruding stomach, and long braided hair, that are similar to LP.L1 (fig. 9b and Plate XVI, 1), but if these two jambs are compared in detail, it is clear that two different sculptors are involved. Shape, modelling, and crown of the RP.R3 head resembles that of the RP.R2 head, while the treatment of the mantles of the two is very similar. The drapery over the legs of the RP.R3 (fig. 10c) with parallel ridge-folds is related to the folds between the legs of RP.R2 (fig. 10b) and markedly different from the drapery of LP.L1 (fig. 9b), in which the ridges are separated by relatively wide concavities. Thus the RP.R3 was carved by the sculptor responsible for RP.R1 and 2, and this sculptor probably came from Saint-Denis.

With the discovery in 1977 of a large amount of sculpture from Notre-Dame in Paris, now installed in the Musée de Cluny, it is possible to study fragments that comprised part of the jamb figures of the Sainte-Anne portal, the right-hand portal of the façade, until its destruction in 1793 (François Giscard d'Estaing, Michel Fleury, and Alain Erlande-Brandenburg, *Les Rois Retrouvés, Notre-Dame de Paris,* Paris, 1977, and Alain Erlande-Brandenburg, *Les Sculptures de Notre-Dame de Paris au Museé de Cluny,* Paris, 1982). Some of these fragments are so close stylistically to the RP jambs of Chartres that it can be assumed that the same sculptor worked at both Chartres and Paris. Another Chartres sculptor also worked at Paris. Discussion of the chronology, Chartres to Paris or Paris to Chartres, will be included in Part V.

10c. Chartres, RP.R3 (detail)

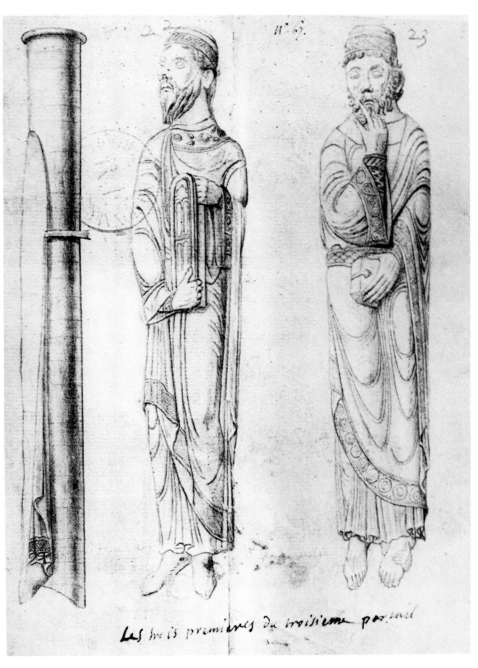

11. Saint-Denis, RP jambs
(drawing for Montfaucon)

12a. Chartres, CP.L5 (detail)

12. Chartres, CP.L1, 2, 3

12b. Chartres, CP.L2 (detail)

128

13a. Chartres, CP.R1, 2, 3, 4

13c. Chartres, CP.R4 (detail)

THE HEADMASTER

The Headmaster of Chartres carved the remaining eight jamb statues of the central portal (Plates XVII, 1, 2 and figs. 12, 13a), the tympanum of the central portal, and its lintel. In contrast to the Étampes Master's and Saint-Denis Master's jambs, the Headmaster preserved more of the original vertical block, which was square in section. The back corner of the square was transformed into a column, while much of the front corner was preserved on the central axis by hands holding symbols and by frontal heads (see Plate XX, 3). In contrast to curving silhouettes of arms and legs of jambs by the Étampes and Saint-Denis masters, the Headmaster's figures, with square shoulders and straight sides, exhibit a static, frontal grandeur. Multiple ridge-folds animate mantles, while interlocking loop-folds suggest legs (see CP.L2 and CP.R2 and 4). All of the vital awkwardness of the Étampes and Saint-Denis statues is replaced by a majestic calm. The squared, expressionless heads (Plates XIX, 3, 4; XX, 3; XXI, 1) are set back against halos and do not bend forward like the Étampes and Saint-Denis heads. This style is thus distinctly different from that of the sculptors of LP.L and RP.R.

Details of the central portal jambs help clarify the marked divergence in style between that of the Headmaster and the Étampes and Saint-Denis masters. The finely carved drapery of CP.L5 (fig. 12a) in bundles of vertical folds of varying degrees of depth is totally different from that of the two female figures on the outer embrasures (figs. 9b and 10c). The same complexity of types of folds and undecorated, folded hems in male figures (see CP.L2—fig. 12b) exhibits the uniqueness of the style of the Headmaster.

On the right splay of the central portal (figs. 13a, b, c) the same variety of drapery folds is intensified. The rounded ridge-folds are less apparent in the three male figures, while the female jamb (CP.R3—fig. 13a) continues the bundles of ridge-folds seen in CP.L5 (fig. 12a). Surfaces in the CP.R jambs are often animated by the edges of multiple folds (see CP.R2—fig. 13b), while bottom hems become more complicated (see CP.R4—fig. 13c). On the basis of study of details it can be argued that CP.L jambs were carved before CP.R jambs, not including CP.R3, but all eight of the ten jambs are clearly the work of one sculptor, the Headmaster.

ASSISTANTS OF THE HEADMASTER

The jamb statues of RP.L2, 3, 4 (Plate XVIII, 2 and figs. 14, 14a, b) are related to those of the CP in their strict, rectangular silhouette; placement of feet on conical socles; arrangements of arms, hands, and symbols; general treatment of drapery in upper sections; and in the format of the heads. Figures are shorter and are surmounted by canopies in order to harmonize with the opposite splay (RP.R), by the Saint-Denis Master. Folded collars of mantles are similar to those of CP.R2, 3, while loop-folds animating sleeves occur on CP.L1, 2 and CP.R 1, 2, 4.

In spite of these stylistic connections with the central portal jambs, important differences are apparent. Feet are more precariously placed on the conical socles, and hems of garments over ankles are not arranged in a general horizontal format with a slight lowering of folds on the left side of CP.L jambs and the right side on CP.R statues. Instead, the hems are completely horizontal in RP.L2 and 4 and raised over the left ankle of LP.L3, revealing wattled stockings. The major differences between RP.L and CP jambs occur in the treatment of drapery over thighs and legs. Narrow strips of folded drapery, which accent the sides of the figures, are more prominent in RP.L jambs, while the central sections are animated by a thin panel of loop-folds framed by decorated and folded hems (RP.L2, fig. 14a). In RP.L3 (fig. 14a), three loop-folds at the same height and a small zigzag fold counteract the vertical folds. None of these small elements possesses the sweep, consistency, and monumental scale of the central portal jamb figures. Although the RP.L heads resemble those of the CP (Plate XXI, 1), they appear stiffer. The RP.L3 head appears to be a flatter version of CP.R1, while the two beardless heads (LP.L2, 4) seem to be modelled on the female heads of the central portal.

Because of these differences, including the mannerisms of folds, which visually jump out of context, and the general lack of crispness of carving when contrasted with the CP jambs, it can be safely argued that the RP.L jambs were carved by an assistant of the Headmaster. The fact that this first assistant also carved the lower lintel of the right portal (to be discussed later) in a narrative style related to the Headmaster's is further evidence that an assistant carved the RP.L statues. In this instance, it is clearly a qualitive difference that distinguishes the RP.L jambs from the CP jambs. Regarding the Étampes and Saint-Denis jamb figures, it is not a case of relative quality but rather a different point of view emerging from different traditions. The first assistant was attempting to imitate the Headmaster, but partially, and not completely, failed.

The two remaining jambs of LP.R (Plate XVIII, 1 and figs. 15a, b, c) are also related to the style of the Headmaster, but exhibit higher quality than the RP.L jambs. If the legs of LP.R2, the so-called Moses, were uncrossed, the figure would resemble CP.R2 in reverse (fig. 13a). In spite of shorter size, this jamb is thinner, with the head off axis, countering the crossed legs. Curving folds over the left foot with uneven terminations (fig. 15a) are different from the

14a. Chartres, RP.L2, 3 (detail)

14. Chartres, CP.R1, 2, 3, 4 and RP.L2, 3, 4 (Marburg)

14b. Chartres, RP.L4 (detail)

15a. Chartres, LP.R2 (detail)

15c. Chartres, LP.R4

15b. Chartres, LP.R2 (detail)

lower sections of the Headmaster's jambs, while the head (fig. 15b) is more oval and less square than the CP heads (Plate XXI, 1). The border of the mantle, as it loops from the right shoulder under the right arm, is undecorated, in contrast to the elaborately ornamented hems of the CP figures.

The badly eroded and faceless LP.R4 (Plate XVIII, 1 and fig. 15c) exhibits the same articulation of the right leg through drapery and the same unevenness of drapery over feet. The thinness of the figure is accentuated by the inward tapering of the silhouette from waist to ankle. All these characteristics differentiate it from the CP jamb statues.

These two LP.R jambs are somewhat closer to the Headmaster's style than are the RP.L jambs. The probability that this assistant of the Headmaster carved most of the upper lintel of the right portal further helps identify him as a different personality. If these conclusions are correct, five sculptors were responsible for the nineteen preserved jamb statues out of the original twenty-four.

RELIEFS OF INNER DOORJAMBS AND PILASTERS

by Nancy Sojka

A total of forty-eight small statues (figs. 16–31), arranged in vertical groups of six (with each statue numbered 1 at the top to 6 at the bottom), flank each of the inner doorjambs of the west portals and decorate the two thin buttresses separating the central from the lateral portals. In a general sense, these figures can be divided into two major stylistic categories. They display features associated with the monumental jamb sculpture attributed to either the Étampes Master or the so-called Saint-Denis Master. However, the division between these two styles is one of degree. Complicating this distinction are possible crosscurrents of influence between the major masters, in addition to the evolution of their styles and the likely presence of their assistants. The purpose of this essay is to discuss these stylistic variables, with the major concern being the identification of individual sculptors' "hands." (See foldout.)

Representing the group most closely related to the Étampes style are the statues of the LP.L inner jamb (figs. 16, 17). All these figures are seated in stiff, frontal poses similar to those of the archivolts at Étampes (figs. 73–76). In terms of quality, no. 2 and no. 4 are as skillfully rendered as the large jamb figures of the LP.L (Plate XVI, 1 and fig. 9a). However, as will be the case on the other jambs, minor inconsistencies can be found here among alternating statues, indicating that more than one sculptor was responsible for their carving. While no. 2 and no. 4 are dressed in costumes of an indisputably Étampes type,

wearing robes characterized by rhythmic, symmetrical folds, no. 3 and no. 5 tend toward a looser drapery style somewhat like that associated with the first large jamb figure of the RP.L (Plate XVI, 2 and fig. 10a). There is a quality of softness and animation in the cloaks of no. 3 and no. 5, as well as a roundness in the rendering of anatomy, as in the shoulders, which cannot be found in no. 2 or no. 4. Indeed, the absolute rigidity that characterizes no. 2 and no. 4 is absent in no. 3 and no. 5. Because of the strong resemblances they bear to the large jamb figures of this embrasure, no. 2 and no. 4, as well as no. 1 and probably no. 6, can be attributed to the Étampes Master (this last figure, no. 6, is too badly damaged for us to be certain). The hand responsible for no. 3 and no. 5 belongs to an assistant of the Étampes Master. This hand conforms to the overall design principles of the LP.L jamb sculpture, but deviates just enough to enable us to identify a separate personality. Additional work by this assistant appears in the capital-frieze, to be discussed later.

In order to find the inner jambs most like Saint-Denis in nature, it is necessary to traverse the entire façade. All six figures of the RP.R (figs. 18, 19) are by the Saint-Denis Master. Like the large jamb statues of this jamb (Plate XVI, 2 and figs. 10a, b), no. 1 and no. 4 are cloaked in robes characterized by convexly carved drapery swirls. The outer garments of these costumes are tightly drawn around the right side of each figure and emphasize the curve of their hips. On the left, the robes fall away in straight pleats from a bent arm and end in a border of ripples. All the figures are characterized by a robustness of anatomy. The whirling motion of their clothing enhances some part of the body by implying a swelling of muscles, such as in the shoulders and legs of no. 2 and no. 3.

Added to these six reliefs by the Saint-Denis Master are the figures on the buttresses between the central and lateral portals (figs. 20–23). Evidence for this attribution rests in the resemblence of no. 1 on the left pilaster (fig. 20) to the RP.R 1 jamb figure (Plates XVI, 2 and XIX, 2). It is in the carving of facial details and the schematization of the bony structure of the hands that striking similarities are revealed. Along with the beast represented on the controversial "Rogerus" block of the right pilaster (no. 1, fig. 22), a study of the eye structure reveals nearly the same degree of curve in the double lids and deep incisions at their corners. In their flat, planar brows, high cheeks, and tapered noses, no. 1 of the left pilaster and RP 1 are nearly identical. Robes of swirling, convexly articulated folds cloak bodies characterized by softly sculpted shoulders, nipped waists, and rounded hips. In comparison to the left pilaster no. 1 and its counterpart on the right pilaster, the remaining ten pilaster statuettes conform to the type just described. In comparison to the RP.R1 jamb figure and the RP.R inner jamb

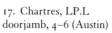
17. Chartres, LP.L
doorjamb, 4–6 (Austin)

19. Chartres, RP.R
doorjamb, 4–6 (Austin)

16. Chartres, LP.L
doorjamb, 1–3 (Austin)

18. Chartres, RP.R doorjamb, 1–3

20. Chartres, pilaster figures between LP and CP, 1–3 (Austin)

21. Chartres, pilaster figures between LP and CP, 4–6 (Austin)

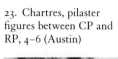

22. Chartres, pilaster figures between CP and RP, 1–3 (Austin)

23. Chartres, pilaster figures between CP and RP, 4–6 (Austin)

24. Chartres, CP.L
doorjamb, 1–3 (Austin)

25. Chartres, CP.L
doorjamb, 4–6 (Austin)

26. Chartres, CP.R
doorjamb, 1–3 (Austin)

27. Chartres, CP.R
doorjamb, 4–6 (Austin)

29. Chartres, LP.R
doorjamb, 4–6 (Austin)

31. Chartres, RP.L
doorjamb, 4–6 (Austin)

28. Chartres, LP.R
doorjamb, 1–3 (Austin)

30. Chartres, RP.L
doorjamb, 1–3 (Austin)

figures, these buttress statuettes display a greater flexibility in pose and a softer, more molded quality in the manner in which their bodies are depicted. They appear to represent the evolution, a growing range in ability, of the hand of the Saint-Denis Master.

The most stylistically complicated doorjamb figures are those of the central portal (figs. 24–27). Although at first glance it might appear that several sculptors were involved, a visual comparison of each figure to the next indicates that what in fact occurs here is the evolution of the Étampes Master's style. With the exception of CP.R no. 2 (fig. 26), all the remaining eleven figures can be attributed to him. The principal Étampes-like feature present in each central portal statuette is the sense of sophistication associated with the LP.L work previously assigned to this master. The seated figures relay the same sense of rigidity present in their LP.L counterparts. In the standing figures this rigidity does not disappear, but is tempered by a quality of gracefulness, as displayed by the large jamb statues of the LP.L. Other outstanding Étampes-like qualities developed on the CP include the use of rhythmic folds as decorative elements and the plastering of very lively drapery against the back plane of the reliefs. Complicating the analysis of these figures but indicative of the evolution of their style is the presence in some of the lower figures, and invading the upper ones, of the looser, more softly molded anatomy associated with the Saint-Denis style. Serving as an indirect explanation for this combination of Étampes and Saint-Denis-like characteristics is the fact that the CP is the literal meeting ground of the distinctive west façade sculptural styles and therefore a very logical place to unite them visually by carving statuettes in which their features are blended. Two of the CP statuettes appear to be unique. While CP.L no. 5 (fig. 25) wears a costume that is definitely of the Étampes type, the figure displays an overall quality of awkwardness. Although this awkwardness would appear to distinguish this figure from the other reliefs on the portal, its stylistic connection with the spandrels reliefs at Étampes (fig. 72) confirms its authorship by the Étampes Master. However, CP.R no. 2 (fig. 26) is clearly not by the Étampes Master.

The final two inner jambs, LP.R and RP.L (figs. 28–31), are the most problematic. The top three figures of the LP.R, together with CP.R2 (fig. 26), are unique in their extreme simplicity. Although their drapery is minimally defined, with folds being represented by a series of simple slashes and unarticulated hemlines, their facial features and hands display a considerable degree of sophistication. Regarding the lower three figures (fig. 29), a link can be made between LP.R no. 4 and LP.L no. 5 (fig. 17), which was associated with the Étampes assistant. Figures no. 5 and no. 6 of the LP.R (fig. 29) are clearly stylistic misfits on this jamb. They belong to the group of figures on the lower CP elaborately carved by the Étampes Master. Thus, the six LP.R reliefs appear to have been carved by three sculptors: no. 5 and no. 6 by the Étampes master, no. 4 by the Assistant of the Étampes Master, and no. 1, no. 2 and no. 3 by a third sculptor. Work by this last individual can be found in two capitals on the right portal frieze; the sculptor is identified as the Assistant of the Saint-Denis Master and is discussed in the following section.

Compared with the jambs already discussed, the statuettes of the RP.L are the least coordinated (figs. 30, 31). No clear group relationship is evident among them; rather, each figure is an individual representation of one of the several hands already identified. No. 2 bears a striking resemblance to CP.L no. 1 (fig. 24), a work by the Étampes Master. It is a magnificently carved figure. By contrast, no. 3, directly below, is a statue dressed much like CP.L no. 3, but rendered so crudely, as in the tubular definition of the lower body and nondescript drapery enveloping the legs, that it cannot be given to the same hand. This relative lack of quality continues in no. 4. No. 5 resembles no. 3 and no. 5 of the LP.L (figs. 16, 17). Because they conform in overall type, these four lower figures are assigned to the Assistant of the Étampes Master. In its unconventional costume type, RP.L no. 1 (fig. 30) resembles the buttress reliefs and is therefore assigned to the Saint-Denis Master. Thus, like the LP.R reliefs, three sculptors were involved in carving the RP.L inner jamb: no. 1 by the Saint-Denis Master, no. 2 by the Étampes Master, and nos. 3, 4, 5, and 6 by the assistant of the Étampes Master.

The study of the inner jamb and pilaster statuettes, together with an analysis of the statue columns, suggests a collaborative workshop procedure with some type of overall supervision in operation during the carving of the west façade. Following the pattern established by the large jamb statues, the purest manifestations of the Étampes and Saint-Denis hands also occur in the inner jamb statuettes of the extreme left and right splays (LP.L and RP.R). After having completed the large jamb figures, it appears that these two sculptors continued to work on the reliefs: the Saint-Denis Master was responsible for the more evolved sculpture on the pilaster-buttresses between the portals, while the Étampes Master carved the more developed inner jamb statuettes of the central portal.

The LP.R and RP.L splays are areas of stylistic compromise. On the LP.R the two extant jamb statues were carved by the second assistant of the Headmaster, while three of the six statuettes were sculpted by the Assistant of the Saint-Denis Master, two by the Étampes Master, and one by the assistant of the Étampes Master. On the RP.L, the first assistant of the Headmaster was responsible for the three large jamb statues, and the statuettes were the work of the Étampes Master (no. 2) and his assistant (nos. 3 through 6), with one assigned to the Saint-Denis Master (no. 1). The hybrid nature of these two splays is explained by the fact that the majority of the sculpture was carved by assistants. The marked decline in sensitivity on these splays is also evident in the study of their ornament, which has been explained as piecemeal, at best (W.S.S. 18–19, Plates XIII–XV).

In spite of the hybrid nature of the LP.R and RP.L splays, when considered as a whole, all the jamb sculpture exhibit an overall consistency in design. Several patterns are evident that indicate that combining the work of the distinct individual masters into a cohesive visual program was a consciously pursued principle. The bottom figures of each inner doorjamb are frontal and in low relief, while the upper figures project more from the block and twist in space. Sculpture by each of the three major masters appears on some portion of the central portal. The Headmaster's jamb statues are framed on their inner sides by the Étampes Master's statuettes and on their outer sides by those of the Saint-Denis Master, while the outer embrasures are entirely of the Étampes or Saint-Denis style. Even the problematic splays display a pattern with the work of assistants, by one master opposing the work of the other; the assistant of the Saint-Denis Master carved the upper three statuettes of the LP.R opposite the Étampes splay, while the Étampes Master and his assistant completed major portions of the RP.L jamb opposite the Saint-Denis splay.

Thus, the Headmaster, identified as such only because he was the author of the jamb statues of the central portal as well as tympanum and lintel, to be discussed later, might well have directed the Étampes and Saint-Denis masters to complete the sculpture of the major portal after they had finished the outer, LP.L and RP.R, splays, although such a direct hierarchy of command is not suggested here. What is suggested, as the very least, is a relatively joint division of labor among the three major sculptors. Because the Headmaster was responsible for so much of the central portal sculpture, it is tempting to designate him as the executive supervisor, but it is equally plausible to view the design and carving of the façade as a collaborative agreement between him and the Étampes and Saint-Denis Masters.

SUMMARY BY PORTAL

LP.L 1, 2, 4, 6—Étampes Master; LP.L 3, 5—Assistant of the Étampes Master (figs. 16, 17)

RP.R 1 through 6—Saint-Denis Master (figs. 18, 19)

Pilaster between LP and CP 1 through 6—Saint Denis Master (figs. 20, 21)

Pilaster between CP and RP 1 through 6—Saint-Denis Master (figs. 22, 23)

CP.L 1 through 6—Étampes Master (figs. 24, 25)

CP.R 1, 3 through 6—Étampes Master; 2—Assistant of the Saint-Denis Master (figs. 26, 27)

LP.R 1 through 3—Assistant of the Saint-Denis Master (same as CP.R2); 4—Assistant of the Étampes Master; 5, 6—Étampes Master (figs. 28, 29)

RP.L 1—Saint-Denis Master; 2—Étampes Master; 3 through 6—Assistant of the Étampes Master (figs. 30, 31)

SUMMARY BY SCULPTOR

Étampes Master: LP.L 1, 2, 4, 6; CP.L 1 through 6; CP.R 1, 3 through 6; LP.R 5, 6; RP.L 2   Total 18

Assistant of Étampes Master: LP.L 3, 5; LP.R 4; RP.L 3 through 6   Total 7

Saint-Denis Master: RP.R 1 through 6; Pilaster between LP and CP, 1 through 6; Pilaster between CP and RP, 1 through 6; RP.L 1   Total 19

Assistant of Saint-Denis Master: CP.R 2; LP.R 1, 2, 3   Total 4

(See foldout drawing)

CAPITAL FRIEZE

by W. S. Stoddard with John Pultz

The historiated frieze consists of twenty-two blocks that overlap on a north-south axis. Twenty-two blocks of acanthus abaci interlock on an east-west axis and, together with the capitals, create solid support for lintels and archivolts. Side portals have three blocks on each splay, while each splay of the central portal contains four. Two capitals surmount the pilaster-buttresses, separating the central from side portals.

The capital frieze not only creates a narrow, horizontal band that crowns the monumental jamb figures and echoes the geometric bases below, but also coordinates the alternation of the columnar figures and the much smaller, ornamental colonnettes. The capitals, flanking each doorway, extend from the rectangular inner jamb over both the first jamb statue and the first colonnette (fig. 32). The second and subsequent blocks on each splay crown one jamb figure and its adjacent colonnette. Convex projections of the floral abaci are aligned with the center of each jamb figure, while the concave angles of the abaci cap the transitional, reentrant sections of the capitals, which rise above the intermediate colonnettes. The result is an extraordinary synthesis of horizontality of capital frieze and vertical sequence of bases, statue columns, colonnettes, capitals, and archivolts.

Scenes from the Life of the Virgin and the Infancy of Christ extend from the central portal, left (CP.L) to the LP.L, while the Passion of Christ is illustrated from the

CP.R to the south tower. In her excellent article, Adelheid Heimann described forty-two scenes on twenty-two capitals and established the source of some of the scenes (1968, 73–102). The cycle of the early Life of the Virgin (CP.L 1–4, figs. 32–34) is the earliest in Western Europe, according to Heimann, and originated in the East in the Greek *Protevangelium of St. James,* of which no illustrated copies survive. However, two early twelfth-century Constantinopolitan copies of a later Greek manuscript, the *Homilies* of monk Jacobus Kokkinobaphos, are preserved in Paris and the Vatican (see Heimann, 77–78, fig. 35 d–f). Since the unusual subjects and arrangement of scenes are so clearly related, it must be assumed that one of these manuscripts or a similar one, now lost, was in the possession of the Chartres clergy and available to the sculptors. If the relief of the Chartres capital (CP.L1), depicting, from right to left, Joachim's and Anna's gifts being refused by the priest because they are childless, Joachim and Anna turning back, and Joachim among his flock with an approaching angel who announced that Anna will bear a daughter, is compared with a Byzantine illumination in the Vatican (figs. 32, 69 and Heimann, fig. 35), the iconographical dependence of the refusal episode on the Byzantine model is abundantly evident. This capital was carved by the Étampes Master, who began his career in Burgundy (to be discussed later) and was responsible for most of the portal of Notre-Dame at Étampes before coming to collaborate with three other major sculptors at Chartres. The Infancy of the Virgin cycle, part of the program conceived by the clergy for the most important monument in the West dedicated to the Virgin, was thus derived from Byzantine models, undoubtedly at Chartres, but depicted in a totally different style. Crozet (1971, 159–65), in his generally favorable reaction to Heimann's article, offered slightly different identifications of some of the scenes. Our concern is not a discussion of the iconography of the capitals, but rather an attempt to attribute these capitals to individual sculptors.

Although the Chartres capitals have generated discussions of iconography and possible sources of program, little has been written about the style of the capitals since Priest's article of 1923. Priest identifies two sculptors: the Master of Saint-Denis and the Master of Étampes. He sees the hand of the former in many of the capitals of the south half of the frieze, specifically in the Presentation in the Temple (CP.R 1), the Temptation (CP.R 3), the Last Supper (above the buttress between the central and right portals), the three Maries at the Sepulcher (RP.L 1), and the Supper at Emmaus (RP.R 2) (Priest, 1923, 30). Regarding the Master of Étampes, Priest either attributes or finds his "touch" in all the capitals, from the Sacrifice of Joachim and Anna (CP.L 1) to the Magi before Herod (LP.R 2). According to Priest, the remaining capitals on the left por-

tal cannot be ascribed to either the Saint-Denis Master or the Étampes Master, but some of the heads suggest to him the style of his "Little Master of St.-Gilles," who carved the lintels of the right portal. He believes that the seated Herod (LP.L 1) is unique. Priest's stylistic analysis is generally accurate, but further study of the capitals makes it possible to refine, supplement, and occasionally correct his observations.

The two most obvious sculptors, involved in carving the capital frieze, are the Master of Étampes and the so-called Master of Saint-Denis, each of whom created three monumental jamb statues on the outer splays of the façade (Plate XVI, 1, 2). The archaic awkwardness and squat and angular bodies with disjointed elbows and wrists of these six jambs differentiate them from those by the Headmaster on the central portal (Plate XVII, 1, 2) and from the jambs by the Headmaster's two assistants on LP.R and RP.L (Plate XVIII, 1, 2). In spite of certain common denominators of style, these two sculptors have distinct personalities. On figures by the Étampes Master, drapery of multiple, sharply raised folds fits tightly over legs, arms, and stomachs, while drapery on jambs by the Saint-Denis Master falls more freely, in gentle curves, swirls, or loops. Feet splay outward on the Étampes jambs, but are frontal on the Saint-Denis statues.

These two sculptors are largely responsible for carving the capital frieze: the Étampes Master, the left half, and the Saint-Denis Master, the right half. Figures on the capitals are approximately one-tenth the size of the jamb statutes and obviously are not restricted in pose to conform to the column jamb. Thus distinctions of style are complicated by size and by purpose, which goes from iconic to narrative. (See foldout elevation.)

The Étampes master seems to have sculpted three of the four capitals on the left splay of the central portal (CP.L 1, 3, 4—figs. 32, 33). The innermost capital (fig. 32) depicts, from right to left, Joachim's and Anna's offerings refused by the priest, Joachim and Anna turning back in distress, and Joachim and his flock. Loop-folds descending over legs, horizontal, decorated bands across legs, accented knees, straight hems, and splayed or parallel feet are all stylistic characteristics, which are clearly revealed on capitals, spandrels, lintel, and jambs at Étampes (Plates XXIII, XXIV) as well as on the Chartres jambs by the Étampes Master (LP.L—fig. 9).

The third capital (CP.L 3—fig. 33), including, from right to left, Joachim and Anna accompanying Mary to the temple, Mary mounting steps of the temple, and four priests, has the same characteristics as the first capital. Drapery folds and heads are identical. However, the capital between these two (CP.L 2—figs. 32, 33) is not the work of the Étampes Master, but, because of references to the style of the Étampes Master, would appear to be by his assistant.

32. Chartres, CP.L1 capital (R. to L.) Joachim's and Anna's offerings refused, Joachim and Anna turn back in distress, and Joachim and his flock

33. Chartres, CP.L2, 3 (R. to L.), Joachim and Anna embracing, Bath of the Virgin, Joachim and Anna (CP.L2); Joachim and Anna accompanying Mary, Mary mounting steps to temple (CP.L3) (Austin)

34. Chartres, capital over pilaster separating CP and LP (R. to L.) Annunciation, Visitation, Nativity

35. Chartres, LP.R1, 2 (R. to L.), Magi before Herod and Adoration of Magi

36. Chartres, LP.L1 (R. to L.), Flight into Egypt, Massacre of Innocents

37. Chartres, LP.L2, 3, Massacre of Innocents

The folds of the mantles of the seated and embracing Joachim and Anna are thicker and heavier. The same relative crudeness is visible in the next two scenes, of the Bath of the Virgin and Joachim and Anna considering Mary's entry into the temple. The most apparent differences between this capital and the adjacent capitals by the Étampes Master are the turned-up hems beside or between ankles and the totally dissimilar baldachin over the figures. The Étampes master projects the feet of figures almost to the bottom of the torus molding, while his assistant has them resting nearer the top of a more bulbous molding.

The Assistant of the Étampes Master, who carved the CP.L 2 capital (figs. 32, 33), is the same sculptor to whom seven reliefs on the inner jambs have been attributed. If the seated figures of Joachim and Anna on the capital are compared to the LP.L 3, 5 figures (figs. 16, 17) or to RP.L 5 (fig. 31), it is abundantly clear that the capital and reliefs are by the same hand. Loose drapery with wide hems bounded by raised folds and raised hems between and adjacent to the feet are identical.

Although only the left section of CP.L 4 (fig. 34), which displays Joseph taking Mary home, is illustrated, this capital is also by the Étampes Master because of treatment of drapery and configuration of heads, which is similar to that of CP.L 1 (fig. 32).

The abraded capital, crowning the pilaster-buttress separating the central from left portals (fig. 34), includes, from right to left, the Annunciation in the presence of Joseph, the Visitation, and the Nativity. When contrasted to figures by the Étampes Master in the adjacent capital, these figures are stockier and have larger, squarer heads. Curving, soft drapery extends over the ankles, terminating in raised oval folds at the hems. This treatment is identical to that in the CP.L 2 capital by the Assistant of the Étampes Master (figs. 32, 33). In both capitals, feet are placed on top of the molding. The twisting and overlapping drapery of Joachim and Anna resembles that of the Virgin and Joseph. The head of the Virgin in the Annunciation is similar to the Virgin's head in the Bathing scene. The baldachins of the two capitals are similar and quite different from those crowning capitals by the Étampes Master. Again, the drapery style of these two capitals is related to the seven statuettes by this sculptor on the inner doorjambs.

The three capitals on the right splay of the left portal (LP.R 1, 2, 3—Adoration of the Magi, the Magi before Herod, and the Annunciation to the Shepherds—fig. 35) are identical in drapery, poses, and heads to the CP.L 1, 3, 4 capitals, by the Étampes Master (figs. 32, 33).

On the left splay of the left portal (figs. 36, 37), all three capitals, with the exception of the Flight into Egypt, over the doorjamb, depict scenes from the Massacre of the Innocents. The LP.L 1 capital (fig. 36), which includes Herod on the left and the Flight on the right, is by a third sculptor. Because of the complicated poses, rubbery articulation, expressive gestures, feet overlapping the molding, and extensive drill-work on hems of mantles and bodices, together with a totally different baldachin—all characteristics that are unique on the façades as a whole—it is tempting to see this capital and another one, to be discussed later, as the work of an itinerant sculptor whose provenance awaits discovery.

The remaining two capitals (LP.L 2, 3—figs. 36, 37), illustrating more events of the Massacre of the Innocents, appear to be the work of the Assistant of the Étampes Master, who carved CP.L 2 (fig. 33) and the pilaster capital (fig. 34). All four capitals exhibit the same turned-up folds at the hems. The distraught mother on the left of LP.L 2 (fig. 37) is very close stylistically to the female columnar figure under the LP.L 2 jamb (Plate XVI, 1 and fig. 38), which is related to the Étampes Master's style. However, drapery, descending in oval folds approaching V-folds, distinguishes this figure from capitals by the Étampes Master. It would seem that the same Assistant of the Étampes Master carved these capitals and the female figure below the jamb statue. Since the cleaning of the left portal in 1981, the figures beneath the jamb statues have a gray caste, which is different from the yellow-orange of the larger statues.

Capitals of the right half of the frieze depict the youth and Passion of Christ (figs. 39a–44). Heimann (1968, 81–82) argued that the scene to the left of the Presentation in the Temple (CP.R1—fig. 39a) represents Elizabeth and her son John the Baptist hiding and that it, along with the Infancy of the Virgin and the extended Massacre of the Innocents (LP.L1, 2, 3), originated in the Greek *Protevangelium of St. James*. Crozet (1971, 159–65) accepted Heimann's identification of Elizabeth and John the Baptist but mentioned three scenes of the Infancy of John the Baptist in the Apocalypse: the escape of Elizabeth and John from the massacre, Elizabeth and John hiding, and the killing of Zaccharias, all appearing in Greek manuscripts. Jean Villette (1971, 255–64) reasoned that these three episodes could have been originally on the capital above the trumeau of John the Baptist. He interpreted the scene of Elizabeth and John (CP.R1) as representing John the Baptist on a high chair assisting in the Presentation scene, with the trumeau capital serving as transition from the Massacre of the Innocents (LP.L) to the Passion of Christ. Basing his work on a study of the iron bracing underneath the three lintels, the absence of the Lamb of God in the keystone of the central portal, and the potential inclusion of episodes in the early life of John the Baptist on the trumeau capital, Villette made a convincing argument that the Chartres central portal originally had a trumeau of John the Baptist with the Lamb.

38. Chartres, LP.L,
female figure beneath LP.L2

39a. Chartres, CP.R1, 2 (L. to R.) (1) Elizabeth and John the Baptist, Presentation of Christ in the Temple;
(2) Christ among the Doctors, Mary and Joseph take Jesus home, John in the Wilderness

39b. Chartres, CP.R2, 3, 4 (L. to R.) (2) Mary and Joseph take Jesus home; (3) Temptation; (4) Simon
and Andrew, Bribing of Judas

40. Chartres, capital over pilaster separating CP and RP, Last Supper, Peter smites Malchus (RP.L3)

41. Chartres, RP.L2, 3 (L. to R.) Betrayal, Entry into Jerusalem (Austin)

145

Although the right half of the capital frieze is largely the work of the Saint-Denis Master and his assistant, two capitals were carved by the Étampes Master and one by the itinerant sculptor. The first two capitals on the right splay of the central portal (CP.R 1, 2—fig. 39a) exhibit the marked differences between the Saint-Denis and Étampes masters when both sculptors are carving small narrative scenes. CP.R 1 (fig. 39a), which depicts Elizabeth and John the Baptist, and the Presentation of Christ in the Temple, is clearly the creation of the Saint-Denis Master. The treatment of drapery with multiple folds, revealing legs and implying movement, is in marked contrast to the static poses and projecting folds of CP.R 2 by the Étampes master (fig. 39a), who portrays from left to right, Christ among the Doctors, Mary and Joseph taking Jesus home, and John in the Wilderness. CP.R 2 reveals close parallels to capitals by the Étampes Master (figs. 32, 33, 35) as well as the LP.L jambs (Plate XVI, 1), while the preserved heads in the Presentation (CP.R 1—fig. 39a) are very similar to those of the RP.R jamb figures (Plate XVI, 2) and extremely close to the head on a pilaster relief by the Saint-Denis Master (fig. 20). Differences in pose, position of feet, treatment of drapery, and implied movement exhibit how different these two sculptors are when the freedom of narrative statements replaces the restrictions of the format of statue-columns.

The next capitals (CP.R 3, 4—fig. 39b) portray from left to right, the Baptism and Temptation of Christ (no. 3) and Simon and Andrew and the bribing of Judas (no. 4). Treatment of splayed feet and heads connects capital no. 3 with those by the Étampes Master. However, the next capital, no. 4, resembles the CP.R 1 capital, carved by the Saint-Denis Master. The Last Supper (fig. 40), which crowns the buttress-pilaster between central and right portals, is clearly related to CP.R 1 and CP.R 4 by the Saint-Denis Master. The swooning John the Evangelist and the kneeling Judas reveal the sense of graceful movement that is absent from the two capitals by the Étampes Master. Thus the middle two capitals of this splay (CP.R) were carved by the Étampes, while the outer two and the Last Supper were created by the Saint-Denis Master.

The scenes of Peter cutting off the ear of Malchus (right side—fig. 40) and the Betrayal (left side—fig. 41) comprise the LP.L 3 capital. Extensive drill-work on hems of sleeves, bodices, and mantles, awkward anatomy, and heavy folds relates this capital to one depicting the Flight into Egypt and beginning of the Massacre of the Innocents (LP.L 1—fig. 36) by the itinerant sculptor. These two capitals appear to be unique to the sculpture of the entire façade. The next two capitals (RP.L 2, 1—figs. 41, 42) narrate clearly and subtly the Entry into Jerusalem, the Entombment, and the Holy Women at the Sepulchre. Heads, treatment of folds, placement of feet, rhythms of movement—all connect these two capitals with the Presentation and the Last Supper (figs. 39, 40), by the Saint-Denis Master.

On the right splay of the right portal (figs. 43, 44) there appears to be one capital by the Saint-Denis Master and two by his assistant. RP.R3 (fig. 44), which includes, from left to right, Christ commanding Peter to "Feed my sheep," the Mission of the Apostles (Heimann, 1968, 88) or the Doubting Thomas (Crozet, 1971, 163), and three Apostles leaving on their mission, is identical in style to the scenes of the Entry into Jerusalem and the Entombment, on the opposite splay (figs. 41, 42). However, the two inner capitals (RP.R1, 2—fig. 43), which include Christ washing the Apostle's feet, Christ meets his Disciples on road to Emmaus, Supper at Emmaus, and the Denial of Peter, contain heads that resemble the RP.R jamb statues, but the quality of carving, found on the Saint-Denis Master's capitals, is lacking. The drapery and the baldachins are somewhat crudely treated when contrasted with those of RP.R3. Thus these two capitals would appear to have been sculpted by an assistant of the Saint-Denis Master.

Since the Assistant of the Étampes Master carved four capitals and seven figures in relief on the inner jamb, is it possible to link the Assistant of the Saint-Denis Master (RP.R1, 2—figs. 43, 44) with any of the jamb reliefs? There are some stylistic common denominators between the two capitals by the Saint-Denis Master Assistant and the fourth hand, who seems to be responsible for the reliefs (LP.R1, 2, 3—fig. 28 and CP.R2—fig. 26). Both capitals and jamb reliefs display heavy drapery folds covering squat bodies. The interlocking hook-folds on the tablecloth in the Supper at Emmaus resemble the treatment of the right leg of LP.R2 relief (fig. 28). Also, the heads of capitals and reliefs are similar and both are derived from those of the jambs (RP.R) by the Saint-Denis Master.

Thus a study of the capitals reveals the fact that the collaboration between the Étampes and Saint-Denis masters, established in the carving of the doorjamb statuettes, continues in the capital frieze, with the jambs of the Headmaster on the central portal virtually surrounded by sculpture by the Étampes and Saint-Denis masters.

SUMMARY OF CAPITALS BY PORTAL
(FROM LEFT TO RIGHT)

Left Portal, left: L1—Itinerant Sculptor; L2 and L3—Assistant of the Étampes Master (figs. 36, 37)

Left Portal, right: R1–3—Étampes Master (fig. 35)

Pilaster capital between LP and CP: Assistant of the Étampes Master (fig. 34)

Central Portal, left: L1, 3, 4—Étampes Master; L2—Assistant of the Étampes Master (figs 32, 33)

Central Portal, right: R1, 4—Saint-Denis Master; R2, 3—Étampes Master (figs. 39a, 39b)

42. Chartres, RP.L1 (L. to R.)
Entombment, Holy Women at
Sepulchre (Austin)

43. Chartres, RP.R1, 2 (L. to R.) (1)
Christ Washing the Apostles' Feet;
(2) Christ on road to Emmaus,
Supper at Emmaus, Denial of Peter
(Austin)

44. Chartres, RP.R3 (L. to R.) Christ
Commanding Peter "Feed my sheep,"
Mission of the Apostles, three Apos-
tles leaving (Austin)

Pilaster capital between CP and RP: Saint-Denis Master (fig. 40)

Right Portal, left: L1, 2—Saint-Denis Master; L3—Itinerant Sculptor (figs. 40–42)

Right Portal, right: R1, 2—Assistant of the Saint-Denis Master; R3—Saint-Denis Master (figs. 43, 44)

SUMMARY OF CAPITALS BY SCULPTORS

Étampes Master: LP.R1, 2, 3; CP.L1, 3, 4; CP.R2, 3
                                               Total 8

Assistant of Étampes Master: LP.L2, 3; CP.L2; capital between CP and LP   Total 4

Saint-Denis Master: CP.R1, 4; capital between CP and RP; RP.L1, 2; RP.R3   Total 6

Assistant of the Saint-Denis Master: RP.R1, 2   Total 2

Itinerant Sculptor: LP.L1; RP.L3   Total 2

SUMMARY OF DOORJAMB RELIEFS AND CAPITALS

	Reliefs	Capitals	Totals
Étampes Master	18	8	26
Saint-Denis Master	19	6	25
Assistant of the Étampes Master	7	4	11
Assistant of the Saint-Denis Master	4	2	6

It is interesting to point out that the Étampes and Saint-Denis masters each carved three jamb statues and almost exactly the same number of capitals and reliefs.

SCULPTURE OF THE SUPERSTRUCTURE

by Minott Kerr

The intention of this essay is to reopen the examination of the different hands that carved the superstructure of the west portal of Chartres Cathedral. In no way, however, does this pretend to be a definitive statement concerning such investigations. The task is made difficult by the fact that the Chartres portals are nearly 850 years old and have suffered the ravages of weather, vandalism, and restoration. This is especially evident in the apices of the archivolts, where the sculpture has been eroded to such a degree as to preclude almost any detailed discussion of its style. Fortunately, most of the more than 130 figures of the tympana, lintels, and lower archivolts are well preserved, and suggest that six sculptors worked on the superstructure in three distinct styles: that of the Headmaster, that of the so-called Angel Master, and that of the lower lintel of the left portal. (See foldout elevation.)

The central portal tympanum and its lintel and the majority of the two lintels of RP are in the style of the Headmaster (figs. 45–49). In general, these figures have oval faces with rounded features. Often the faces are modeled with articulated cheekbones. Eyelids are heavy, and bags appear beneath the eyes. The drapery of these figures seems thin and relatively light in weight. Its folds are expressed by raised lines either in a series of radiating concentric curves, or in closely packed parallel rows. Where the drapery is pulled across the body, such as at the knee or thigh, there are smooth, flat areas between the raised lines. While the drapery conforms to the shape of the body beneath, the fold lines often form a surface pattern, rather than depict natural folds. The variation among the figures carved in this style suggests that they are not all the work of the Headmaster, but also the work of two of his assistants, probably the two who worked with the master on the jamb figures below them.

The central tympanum and lintel are the work of the Headmaster himself (figs. 45, 46). This is especially apparent when the head of the Christ is compared to that of CP.L1 (fig. 45 and Plate XX, 1, 3). The Christ head has a subtlety of modeling similar to the head below it. In both, the cheekbone is articulated. Eyebrows consist of flattened arcs that create a strong outline across the brow and make a pronounced pocket of shadow beneath it. Both figures have wavy hair pulled back over their ears. The tympanum head, however, has eyes with drilled-out pupils and more prominent bags beneath.

As with the drapery of the jamb figures by the Headmaster, that of the Christ (fig. 45) is defined by a multitude of tightly grouped ridge-folds, which form either a series of concentric curves or straight rows. The latter tend, on both the Christ and the jamb figures by the Headmaster, to end either by forming a diagonal series of flat angular folds, as is found running upward from the left to the right between the legs of Christ, or by simply stopping abruptly at the figure's feet. Sometimes this abrupt halt at the bottom of a figure is mediated by small butterfly-shape folds. In all cases, the drapery edges on both the Christ and the jamb figures have a jagged or crinkly quality. This trait can also be seen in the drapery of the angel of Saint Matthew. The drapery of this smaller figure suggests that it, like its larger neighbor, was carved by the Headmaster.

At a first glance, figures on the lintel below seem quite different (fig. 46). A closer examination shows that these fourteen figures, the twelve Apostles and Enoch and Elijah, are the work of the Headmaster as well. The smaller format and the fact that figures are enclosed in an arcade and grouped tightly together—the limitation of being forced to fit so many figures on the single block—may account for the initial differences.

The similarities between the tympanum figures and those on the lintel become apparent when the second lintel figure

45. Chartres, CP, Christ and Symbols of four Evangelists (tympanum), twelve Apostles (lintel) (Austin)

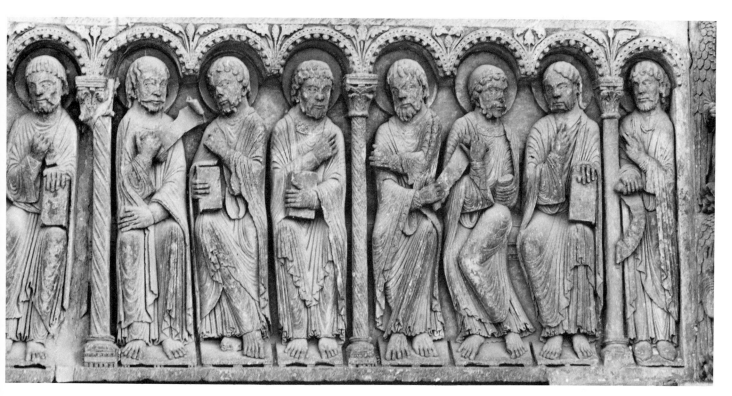

46. Chartres, CP, lintel (detail) (Austin)

149

47. Chartres, RP, Virgin and Child Enthroned (tympanum), Presentation in the Temple (upper lintel), Annunciation, Visitation, Nativity, Annunciation to Shepherds (lower lintel) (Austin)

48. Chartres, RP, detail of lintels: Presentation, Annunciation, Visitation, Nativity (Austin)

from the right is compared to the Christ. In fact, except for the turn of his head and the position of his right hand, this Apostle is almost a miniature version of the Christ. Both sit with their upper body facing forward, with their left hand holding a book on their left knee. Each figure's left thigh is set perpendicular to the torso so that it points in the same direction as the upper body. The other leg points diagonally to the figure's right. Even more important than the close relationship between the two figures' poses are the similarities between their faces and the manner in which draperies have been rendered. Note the series of thin, raised lines across both figures' right legs and the smooth areas over the knee and thigh on the same leg. The drapery on the other knee are closely packed parallel lines that fall vertically to the foot. Both the Christ and the lintel figure also have the flat, diagonally arranged, angular folds running upward left to right between their legs. Such folds are typical of the Headmaster. These figures also have the Headmaster's jagged drapery edges.

When the two figures' heads are compared, one finds they have wavy hair brushed back behind their ears. Both have faces with thin-lipped mouths, articulated cheekbones, and sharply outlined ridges of flattened arcs for eyebrows. These features, like the drapery, suggest that the Headmaster carved the smaller figure as well as the Christ. The thirteen other central portal lintel figures are all closely related to the one discussed here. Although the two outside ones show some differences—they stand, and do not sit, wear shoes, and have a more simplified drapery—all are variations on a single theme, and are all the work of the Headmaster.

The two right portal lintels (figs. 47–49), except for the outer figures of the upper one, are probably by the two assistants of the Headmaster. The figures of the lower lintel are more elongated and have more slender proportions than those carved by the Headmaster. Their heads consist of thinner ovals. Modeling of the faces is less defined, so that the cheekbones are hardly articulated and the cheeks are not as round. The eyebrows are also flatter and, if arched like those carved by the Headmaster, they are softer and have a marked puffy character. Furthermore, all figures on the lower lintel have drilled pupils. Bags beneath their eyes are slightly less pronounced. Their hair is also thinner and much more finely cut.

The drapery is more varied, and while it is formed by parallel lines and concentric curves, folds are generally flatter and come to more pointed edges as seen at the feet of the Virgin Annunciate (fig. 48). That of the adjacent Gabriel shows a similar fold pattern between his legs. The incised lines of his thighs are very shallow and quite different from those carved by the Headmaster. Also typical of the drapery found on the lower lintel is the wattling on the sleeves and stockings of Joseph and the shepherds and the strange narrow loop-folds on Joseph's right thigh. These two latter traits point to the first Assistant of the Headmaster, who carved the RP.L jamb figures (Plate XVIII, 2 and fig. 14a).

In contrast to the slender proportions of the lower lintel figures, those on the upper one are much stockier. Indeed, their heads seem almost too big for their shorter but broader bodies. Faces are broader as well, with somewhat wider noses. Eyes are sometimes set deeper, and eyebrows are often more softly modeled than those of the figures below. The bags beneath their eyes are a little smaller. Despite these differences, the upper lintel figures are still closely related to those carved by the Headmaster. They are, however, neither by him or by the first assistant, who carved the lower lintel.

Although drier, less animated, and heavier, their draperies show many traits of the Headmaster. The incised hook-folds, which usually overlap similar ones from the opposite side, suggest the second assistant, who carved the LP.R jamb figures (Plate XVIII, 1 and figs. 15a, b, c). Wide, smooth areas between these folds and the slight suggestion of the hip beneath also point to the work of this assistant. The two figures at either end of the upper lintel, which are separate blocks, are neither by this assistant nor in the style of the Headmaster. Instead, they are by the master who carved most of the remaining superstructure sculpture, the Angel Master.

The four figures of the right tympanum, the Virgin and Child and Angels, are also the work of the sculptor whom Priest (1923) called the Master of the Angels, because he was responsible for all the angels on Chartres West (figs. 47, 50). The heads of these four figures are abraded, and wear intensifies their blocky nature. Their sides and chins are only slightly rounded and their faces are rather flat. The abrasion tends to exaggerate the eyelids and makes the hair seem more like an awkwardly worn wig rather than natural, growing hair.

In comparison to drapery carved by the Headmaster and his two assistants, that of the Angel Master is much bulkier. It seems thicker and possesses more weight. Though the folds create a surface pattern rather than a true interplay among body, material, and gravity, more attention is paid to the fall of the material over the body of these four figures than to those by the Headmaster. The fold lines are wider and tend, especially on the shoulders and upper arms, to be more layered and overlap more than is typical of the style of the Headmaster. A very important aspect of the Angel Master's style is the contrast between two different ways the drapery is handled below the knees. Over the shin, the drapery is usually a series of curved lines, often alternating with wide, smooth areas. Between the legs, however, the drapery consists of tightly grouped parallel

49. Chartres, RP, detail of lintels,
Music and Pythagoras (inner archivolt),
Grammar and Priscian (outer archivolt)
(Austin)

50. Chartres, RP, tympanum,
Virgin and Christ enthroned (Austin)

ridges. Unlike figures by the Headmaster, on which the curved folds across the knee and shin often become straight parallel lines between each figure's legs, the two types of drapery carved by the Master of the Angels are kept completely separate. These two different types establish a rhythm of drapery found on most of this master's figures.

The same sculptor carved the left portal tympanum, the Ascension (fig. 51, 51a). Again, the features of the faces have been worn away, but the figures have the same blocky heads and awkward hair. Drapery here is more refined, but there is still the same contrast between curved folds and smooth areas on thighs, knees, and shins, and parallel lines between their legs as found on the right tympanum. The two left tympanum angels are more dynamic. Their bodies curve and their heads turn away from the ascending Christ. The four angels on the lintel below were also carved by the Angel Master (figs. 51, 51a). Their bodies bend like those of their counterparts above. Figures have heads and drapery closely related to the Virgin and angels on the right portal. Important, too, are the bits of drapery fluttering away from their bodies, which recall those behind the two angels on the right tympanum.

The archivolts of the left portal (figs. 53, 54) are also the work of the Angel Master. The two figures, which begin the two archivolts on the left, are fine examples of this master's style. Unlike the drapery of the figures carved by the Headmaster, the drapery here has wide, round folds conforming to the shape of the body beneath. The figure of April, although wearing an odd sort of culotte, has the typical Angel Master drapery (fig. 53). Over shins and knees are smooth, curved folds, which contrast with the narrow, linear folds along the inverted V between the legs. The heads of these two Labors of the Month are blocky and have broad, softly modeled features on their flatish faces. The cheekbones are only slightly articulated, and the eyebrows are much more softly modeled than are those of the Headmaster. The eyes are very shallow, with cut, almost incised, eyelids encircling them. Their hair is gathered in thick strands, while beards and flesh are separated by a strong outline.

Unfortunately, most of the other archivolt figures over the left portal are not as well preserved. What is left, however, suggests that they are also the work of the Angel Master. The two Zodiac figures, Libra and Virgo, have drapery close to that of the lateral tympana (fig. 54). Above Libra (not illustrated), the representation of November has drapery with the same thick, round folds of April and July. What remains of the drapery of March, May, June, August, September, October, and December indicates that the Angel Master was responsible for them as well. Since the animals of the zodiac have neither faces or drapery, they are difficult to compare to the human figures. The surfaces of Cap-

ricorn, Cancer, and Scorpio have the same texture as that of the pig being slaughtered in the representation of November. Aquarius has been destroyed and many of the other zodiac signs are too abraded to make a comparison with the other figures. The Angel Master must have been responsible for the representations of Pisces and Gemini found on the right portal.

The Angel Master also surely carved the figures of January (fig. 54) and February, as well as the three men writing on the lowest voussoirs of the right portal (figs. 47, 49). Their almost-incised eyes and eyelids, thick strands of hair, and heavy drapery with round folds are similar to other figures by this master. The female representations of Dialectic, Grammar, and Music, like the two figures on either end of the upper lintel, have the same stylistic traits (figs. 48, 49).

Closely related to all these figures are the four lowest Elders of the Apocalypse on the cental portal (figs. 55, 56). Again one finds blocky heads with flat sides and broad, softly modelled facial features. The drapery at their feet is typical of the master. Note the contrast between the smooth areas on the shins that have a few curving folds and the linear ridges between their legs. In the latter handling of the drapery, there is an up–down alternation of butterfly-shape folds that is a more refined version of the folds found at the feet of the right-hand tympanum Virgin. The central portal figures are also close to the Virgin in the way the drapery at their feet forms a smooth curve over each foot.

Among the remaining figures of the right and central portal archivolts (figs. 55–58) there is a wide range of quality, particularly in the handling of drapery. All these figures betray aspects of the Angel Master's style, but may not be the work of the master himself. The condition of some of the sculpture makes analysis difficult. Perhaps some sculpture was carved quickly to complete the project. The latter suggestion is surely a possibility, since these figures are the ones closest to the apices of the archivolts and would probably have been the last to be carved. The figures, deviating the most from the typical sculpture of the Angel Master, are probably the work of an assistant of this master. Such a situation would be analogous to the one proposed by Stoddard for the LP.R and RP.L jamb figures (figs. 14–15). As with the jamb figures below, the most important figures would have been the work executed by the more accomplished sculptor, while some of the rest would have been left to another under his supervision.

Priest was correct in calling the Master of the Angels the second most important sculptor of Chartres West (1923, 34–37). Indeed, the six angels surrounding the right tympanum and the lower six on the central portal gave this sculptor his name (figs. 47, 56). They all betray his stylistic

51. Chartres, LP, Ascension and Apostles (Austin)

51a. Chartres, LP, Ascension, tympanum (Austin)

52. Chartres, LP,
lower lintel, detail of Apostles
(Austin)

54. Chartres, LP.R archivolts, Labors of
Months and Signs of Zodiac, January and
October (Austin)

53. Chartres, LP.L archivolts, Labors of Months and
Signs of Zodiac, July and April (Austin)

55. Chartres, CP.L archivolts,
Elders of the Apocalypse (Austin)

56. Chartres, CP.R archivolts,
Angels and Elders of the Apocalypse (Austin)

57. Chartres, CP.R archivolts,
Angels and Elders of the Apocalypse (Austin)

58. Chartres, RP.L archivolts,
Angels, Rhetoric and Cicero (Austin)

traits. Priest was wrong, however, in assigning much of the sculpture of the superstructure of the three portals to as many as four of the Master's assistants.

Comparison of lower and upper voussoirs of the central portal (figs. 56, 57) reveal qualitative differences. It is clear that the four lowest angels and four standing Elders (figs. 55, 56) were carved by the Angel Master. When lower sections are contrasted with the upper areas (fig. 57), treatment of drapery is less sensitive and sometimes confused. Because of abraded surfaces, it is difficult to determine at what point the Assistant of the Angel Master took over the completion of the portal. It can be suggested, however, that the Angel Master carved the eight lowest Elders of the Apocalypse, four on each side, and his assistant was responsible for the remaining sixteen. Further, the six lowest angels, three on each side, appear to be of higher quality than the upper six angels.

If the upper voussoir figures of CP and RP are compared (figs. 57, 58), subtlety of carving and consistency of relief suggest that the RP archivolts were carved by the Angel Master. Thus sculpture attributed to his assistant would seem to be confined to the central portal.

The third and last style found in the superstructure of Chartres West is that of the left portal's lower lintel (fig. 52). All these Apostles sit on a continuously running bench, their bodies placed frontally, but their heads raised or turned. The heads are oval in shape and have deep-cut features, while the eyes are wide open and encircled by heavy eyelids. Their round shape is unlike that carved by the Angel Master. While these figures have bags beneath their eyes, these are heavier than those of the Headmaster. Each figure holds a book or a scroll or makes a rhetorical gesture. Both gestures and books break each figure's silhouette at the waist. Characteristic of the master is the disjointed turn of the head. Similarly, the hands are bent at acute angles. Like the drapery carved by the Headmaster, the drapery here is created by folds forming a surface pattern. The style of the left portal lintel is not found anywhere else on the west façade. Although perhaps related to the lintel at Moissac, these figures at Chartres are clothed in an entirely different drapery, which is not a series of overlapping flat folds, but rounded ones.

In summary, most of the sculpture of the Chartres superstructure was carved by the Headmaster and the Angel Master. To two assistants of the former can be attributed the two lintels of the right portal and to an assistant of the latter the upper archivolt of the central portal. The lower lintel of the left portal is unique and could conceivably be a *remploi*. Thus, of the six sculptors who completed the Royal Portals, three carved jamb statues, and three worked solely on the superstructure.

SUMMARY OF SCULPTURE OF SUPERSTRUCTURE BY PORTALS

LP: tympanum, upper lintel and archivolts—Angel Master (figs. 51–54)
lower lintel—Another hand
CP: tympanum, lintel—Headmaster (figs. 45, 46)
archivolts, lowest sections (six angels and eight elders)—Angel Master
archivolts, upper sections—Assistant of the Angel Master (figs. 55–57)
RP: tympanum, archivolts, and outer two figures on upper lintel—Angel Master (figs. 47–50, 58)
lower lintel—first Assistant of the Headmaster; he carved RP.L jambs
upper lintel—second Assistant of the Headmaster; he carved LP.R jamb

SUMMARY BY SCULPTORS

Angel Master: LP tympanum, upper lintel, and archivolts; CP lower archivolts; RP tympanum, archivolts, two exterior figures of upper lintel
Assistant of the Angel Master: CP upper sections of archivolt
Headmaster: CP tympanum and lintel
First Assistant of the Headmaster: RP lower lintel
Second Assistant of the Headmaster: RP upper lintel, except outer two figures
Sculptor of LP lower lintel

ONE OR TWO CAMPAIGNS BASED ON STUDY OF SCULPTURE

by W. S. Stoddard

In 1952, it seemed to me that evidence for one campaign for the completion of the portals greatly outweighed that for two campaigns (see 22–26). With further study of masonry and sculpture over the past years, it now seems impossible to argue that two campaigns ever existed. Since the so-called earlier sculptors, the Étampes and Saint-Denis masters, collaborated with the Headmaster on the central portal, with the Étampes Master carving the doorjamb reliefs and the Saint-Denis Master, the figures on the framing pilasters, and both responsible for the CP capitals, all three portals were created in one campaign involving four major sculptors: the Saint-Denis Master, the Étampes Master, the Headmaster, and the Angel Master. There were also five assistants, two working with the Headmaster and one with each of the other three major sculptors. As the foldout drawing of the portals indicates, the division of labor has a logic that precludes the possibility of designating any parts of the portals to an earlier campaign. The one exception is the LP lower lintel, which is probably *spolium*.

The Headmaster sculpted the jamb statues, tympanum, and lintel of the central portal, the Étampes Master was responsible for eleven of the small figures on the door jambs (CP.L1 through 6 and CP.R1, 3 through 6), and the Assistant of the Saint-Denis Master (CP.R2) made one figure. As stated, the pilasters, which separate the central from the side portals and frame the jamb statues, were created by the Saint-Denis Master, while the archivolts were carved by the Angel Master and his assistant.

This collaborative approach is clearly evident on the left portal. The LP.L jambs are by the Étampes Master, whereas the LP.R statues are by the second Assistant of the Headmaster. Reliefs of the inner door jambs were carved by three sculptors: the Étampes Master (LP.L1, 2, 4, 6 and LP.R5, 6), the Assistant of Étampes Master (LP.L3, 5, and LP.R4), and the Assistant of Saint-Denis Master (LP.R1, 2, 3). The upper lintel, the tympanum, and the archivolts of the left portal are the work of the Angel Master, while the lower lintel of Apostles is unique stylistically and was probably a piece in the Chartres chantier reemployed partially to balance the superstructure of the right portal.

The right portal jambs were carved by the Saint-Denis Master (RP.R) and the first Assistant of the Headmaster (RP.L), while the doorjamb reliefs were created by the Saint-Denis Master and the Étampes Master and his assistant: RP.R1 through 6 and RP.L1 by the Saint-Denis Master; RP.L2 by the Étampes Master; RP.L3 through 6 by the Assistant of the Étampes Master. The lower lintel was carved by the first Assistant of the Headmaster, the sculptor of the RP.L jamb figures, whereas the upper lintel, except for the two outermost figures on separate blocks, was sculpted by the second Assistant of the Headmaster, the author of the LP.R jamb figures. The Master of the Angels was responsible for the two end figures of the upper lintel, the tympanum, and archivolts.

Both side portals thus contain sculpture carved by assistants of the Headmaster and both the Saint-Denis and Étampes masters and their assistants.

The twenty-two capitals in the frieze were all carved by the Étampes and Saint-Denis masters or their assistants, with the exception of two (LP.L1 and RP.L3), which are unique on the façade and must have been carved by an itinerant sculptor. The majority of the capitals on the left-hand half of the frieze are by the Étampes Master (six capitals: CP.L1, 3, 4 and LP.R1, 2, 3) or his assistant (four capitals: CP.L2, capital over left pilaster, LP.L2, 3). However, two capitals on the right-hand side of the frieze were also created by the Étampes Master (CP.R2, 3). The remaining capitals on the right half are by the Saint-Denis Master (six capitals: CP.R1, CP.R4, the Last Supper over pilaster, RP.L1, 2, and RP.R3) or by the Assistant of the Saint-Denis Master (RP.R1, 2). The presence of two capitals by the Étampes Master above the right jamb of the

central portal further corroborates the evidence of collaboration displayed in the pilaster and inner jamb reliefs.

This disposition of individual hands on the façade (see foldout) points to the conclusion that all the sculpture was carved in one campaign. Since the Headmaster was responsible for the monumental sculpture of the central portal and his two assistants carved the jamb figures on the side portals and the two lintels on the right portal, it is possible to argue that the Headmaster was in charge of the *chantier* and was assisted by one sculptor from Saint-Denis and one from Étampes, plus the Angel Master and their assistants. The program of the portals was obviously conceived by the learned clergy in the School of Chartres.

ESTIMATE OF TIME INVOLVED IN CREATING CHARTRES WEST

With the majority of the figural sculpture attributed to individual artists, is it possible to determine the approximate length of time each sculptor worked at Chartres? Further, can the total amount of time to complete the Chartres West program be estimated? If long spans of time are allotted to each element of the portals, the breakdown of the three major sculptors of statue-columns, doorjambs, capital frieze, and tympanum and lintel of the central portal can be tentatively summarized as follows:

Headmaster

CP:	10 jamb statues (2 lost)	8 weeks each	80
	1 tympanum	20 weeks	20
	1 lintel	20 weeks	20
		Total	120 weeks

Étampes Master

LP.L:	3 jamb statues	8 weeks each	24
	18 doorjamb reliefs	4 weeks each	72
	8 capitals		
	2 large capitals	5 weeks each	10
	6 smaller capitals	4 weeks each	24
		Total	130 weeks

Saint-Denis Master

RP.R:	3 jamb statues	8 weeks each	24
	19 doorjamb & pilaster reliefs	4 weeks each	76
	6 capitals		
	4 large capitals	5 weeks each	20
	2 smaller capitals	4 weeks each	8
		Total	128 weeks

Using these figures, we see that the three sculptors each worked approximately two and one-half years and completed all the figurative sculpture on the splays of the portals and tympanum and lintel of the CP. The sculpture by their assistants breaks down as follows:

Headmaster's First Assistant

4 jamb statues (RP.L) (1 lost)	8 weeks each	32
1 lintel (RP. lower)	20 weeks	_20_
	Total	52 weeks

Headmaster's Second Assistant

4 jamb statues (LP.R) (2 lost)	8 weeks	32
1 lintel (RP upper)	18 weeks	_18_
	Total	50 weeks

Assistant of Étampes Master

7 doorjamb reliefs	4 weeks each	28
2 large capitals	5 weeks each	10
2 small capitals	4 weeks each	_8_
	Total	46

Assistant of Saint-Denis Master

4 doorjamb reliefs	4 weeks each	16
1 large capital	5 weeks each	5
1 small capital	4 weeks	_4_
	Total	25

The Headmaster's assistants and the Assistant of the Étampes Master each carved sculpture, which can be identified as their own, for almost a year, while the Saint-Denis Master Assistant carved sculpture for about half a year. Obviously these assistants worked simultaneously with their masters and were probably involved in preparing blocks for them.

What is missing from this estimate is ornamental sculpture: the elaborate bases, columns with geometric motifs, ornamental colonnettes, and abaci (see 11–12; 18–20; 24–25 and Plates XI–XV). As pointed out in 1952, the Chartres West ornament generally appears to be stylistically uniform, with differences being the result of varying degrees of quality. The finest ornament can be found on the Headmaster's central portal and the LP.L (Plates XII–XV, 1,2). The much-damaged colonnettes of the RP.R appear to be less crisp, while the obvious decline in quality is found in

the LP.R and RP.L splays, in which two assistants of the Headmaster were responsible for the statue-columns (Plate XV, 3, 4).

Without specific knowledge of workshop procedure, beyond the collaborative effort of the three Masters and their assistants to complete the six splays and their crowning capital-frieze, there appear to be three possible solutions of how the ornament was carved. 1. Ornament was sculpted en masse by specialists in the *chantier,* and each of the five sculptors selected colonnettes to frame his jamb statues, with the Headmaster selecting first and his assistants last. 2. Each of these sculptors had assistants who worked with them on their splays. 3. Each of the five sculptors of the statue-columns sculpted the ornament of his individual splay. The third option appears to be the strongest, since the crudely carved colonnettes are all found on LP.R and RP.L splays, by the two assistants of the Headmaster, in which the statue-columns reveal a decline in quality and on which eight of the twelve doorjamb reliefs were carved by assistants of the Étampes and Saint-Denis masters.

Even though the colonnettes appear stylistically unified, there are some discrepancies that suggest that different personalities were involved in their carving. The colonettes of CP.R (Plates XII, XIII, XIV, 2, 4) portray an extraordinary sense of plasticity in the rhythmic in-and-out movement of vines while preserving the shape of the block. By contrast, ornament on the LP.L (Plates XIV, 1, 3; XV, 1, 2; XVI, 1) emphasizes the outer surfaces of the colonnette, resembling the columns and fragments of colonnettes from Saint-Denis, in the Musée de Cluny (Plates V, VI, 1, 2). These differences are not qualitative. Furthermore, the undulating vine with figures and leaves as fillers (LP.L1—Plate XIV, 1, 3) exhibits heads that are similar to those on capitals by the Étampes Master (figs. 32, 35, 39b). It can thus be argued that the Headmaster did indeed carve the colonnettes of the central portal, while the Étampes Master was responsible for those on the LP.L.

Not all of the colonnettes of the LP.R splay by the Headmaster's second Assistant are crudely carved (see LP.R1—Plate XV, 4). The colonnette directly above LP.R1 (fig. 15b) is identical stylistically with LP.L1 (Plate XIV, 1, 3), by the Étampes Master. It should be noted that the three capitals directly above this colonnette are by the Étampes Master, although the three upper, adjacent doorjamb reliefs are attributed to the Assistant of the Saint-Denis Master (fig. 28). The LP.R and RP.L splays are thus hybrid constructs by masters and assistants.

Further, even though there is no possible way of estimating the relative speed of sculpting among individual artists, it is of interest that the Headmaster carved eight colonnettes, as opposed to three by the other four sculptors, which would even out the totals of the original estimates of the Headmaster—120 weeks, the Étampes Master—130 weeks, and the Saint-Denis Master—128 weeks.

If the time-spans assigned to different parts of the portals are valid, Chartres West, without the LP tympanum, upper lintel, and archivolts, CP archivolts, and RP tympanum and archivolts, could have been carved in three years. While all the statue-columns, capital-frieze, lintel, and tympanum of the central portal were being sculpted, the Master of the Angels was occupied with the rest of the superstructure. The contemporaneity of the RP tympanum and upper lintel is proved by the fact that the Angel Master carved the outer two figures of the lintel in the identical style of the tympanum. The breakdown of time-span for the superstructure is as follows:

Master of the Angels

LP and RP tympana	16 weeks each	32
LP lintel	14 weeks	14
RP upper lintel, 2 figures	3 weeks each	6
LP 22 voussoirs	4 weeks each	88
RP 22 voussoirs	4 weeks each	88
CP voussoirs		
4 large voussoirs	5 weeks each	20
16 smaller voussoirs	4 weeks each	64
	Total	312 weeks

By attributing all of the left portal and the tympanum and archivolts of the RP and the lower archivolts of the CP to the Angel Master, we see that he was employed for six years, with the first three of those years congruent with the rest of the Chartres West sculpture. The entire project appears to have been completed in six years, not ten years (1145–1155), as usually cited. If more of the sculpture of the superstructure, such as the upper archivolts of the LP, is attributed to his assistant and the amount of time alloted for the carving of each element is shortened, then the six years can be reduced to five years or less.

THE ARCHAEOLOGY OF TWELFTH-CENTURY CHARTRES

A. 1903–1984

The debate concerning the original emplacement of the Royal Portals began in the late nineteenth century and intensified in this century, following excavations by Lefèvre-Pontalis between the north and south towers and in the two western bays of the High Gothic nave (see 25–26 and Plate XXXVIII, 1). This debate involves three theories: 1. Portals were carved for and erected in their present location between the west faces of the north and south towers; 2. Portals were carved for the area between the eastern faces of the towers originally and the program was enlarged and moved to the present emplacement (Plate XXXVIII, 3); 3. Three portals were planned for or constructed in the first or second bay of the Gothic cathedral and moved at a later date to their present location (Plate XXXVIII, 1, 2).

The following list of pertinent facts precedes a review of this debate and an update of its evolution during the past thirty years.

1020—September 7–8, fire
1030—fire destroyed roof of Fulbert's church
1037—October 17, dedication of Saint-Fulbert's church (c. 1030, miniature of Fullbert's church).
Mid-eleventh century—porches added to façade and transepts by Canon Raimbaud.
1134—September 5, fire probably damaged west end since new campaign began with north tower.
1134 and 1138—donations of North Tower by Gautier and by Anegerius of Blois, who died between 1139 and 1142.
1145—two towers mentioned by Robert de Torigny, Abbot of Mont-Saint-Michel.
1194—June 10–11, Fulbert's church destroyed by fire but north and south towers and west portals with three stained-glass windows above were spared.

On the basis of the excavations of 1901 and 1903, Lefèvre-Pontalis placed the original location of the portals in the first bay of the nave (Plate XXXVIII, 1, 2—see W.S.S., 1952, 15–17 for detailed discussion and bibliography). The foundation A/B is designated as Fulbert's façade, C/D and E/F as Raimbaud's mid-eleventh-century porch, while the western part of Raimbaud's porch is reconstructed to support the portals (Plate XXXVIII, 1, 2).

Mayeux's attack in 1904 accused Lefèvre-Pontalis of not following his own plans, and Mayeux argued that the portals were built in their present location as a porch open to the west and south, following the campaign of the north tower. Then the south tower was constructed, which necessitated the dismantling and cutting down of the southern edges of the south portal. In his response to Mayeux, Lefèvre-Pontalis, employing more evidence from the excavations of 1903, strengthened his arguments and described the foundation O-Z-P as an abandoned project and reiterated his evidence for the impossibility of vaulting the area between the towers (see the south elevation of the north tower and north elevation of the south tower—Plate XXXVIII, 4, 5).

Excavations in 1937 and 1938 were carried out by Trouvelot inside the western towers. The pavement was lowered and the original entrances to the aisles of the crypt revealed. In 1938, Étienne Fels excavated the area between the towers. Unfortunately, these excavations were never published in detail. Marcel Aubert, in 1941, seems to have misinterpreted the findings of Fels and concocted a smaller Vézelay-narthex-type campaign between the eastern piers of the west towers in 1145–1150 and the enlarged campaign of 1150–1155 on the present location (Plate XXXVIII, 3). Since all three portals were carved in one campaign by four sculptors and their assistants, this two-campaign theory is untenable. Furthermore, Fels wrote me in 1947 that the foundations between the eastern piers of the towers were insufficient to support portals with jamb statues. Fels did discover that the large foundation between the middle of west towers, marked O-Z-P on Lefèvre-Pontalis' plan, extended under the foundations of both towers. In addition, he correctly interpreted this foundation as supporting the western face of the large western, central tower of Fulbert's church, as seen in André de Mici's illumination. Fels then argued that the west portals were designed and constructed for their present emplacement.

In 1955, Fels summarized his conclusions based on his excavations of 1938 ("Die Grabung an der Fassade der Kathedrale von Chartres," *Kunstchronik*, Vol. 8, 1955, 149–51). His discovery of the function of the large foundation O-Z-P as the west façade of Fulbert's early eleventh-century, central tower led him to interpret the two foundations in the first bay of the nave (H-K-I) and between the third, western gothic piers (A-B-C-D) excavated by Lefèvre-Pontalis, as the middle and eastern supports of a huge tower (Plate XXXVIII, 1). Thus this central tower would follow the eleventh-century tradition of churches between the Rhine and Loire, as exemplified by Saint-Benoît-sur-Loire. Although we really do not know the detailed nature of the masonry discovered by Lefèvre-Pontalis east of the towers, Fels' conclusions that all three north-south foundations originally supported a single tower seem plausible, but there is no reason to overlook the possibility that the middle foundation (H-K-I) was reused or programmed to support originally the Royal Portal, as Lefèvre-Pontalis believed.

Otto von Simson (1956, 148 and fn. 29) stated that the program of the sculpture of the three portals evolved gradually and that Lefèvre-Pontalis' theory of the moving of the portals was now untenable because of the excavations by Fels.

In 1958, Peter Kidson incorporated the findings of Fels concerning the original function of the three north–south foundations as supporting an early eleventh-century central tower, but outlined a new theory for the twelfth-century campaigns (8–9). He argued that, after the fire of 1134 and the start of construction of the north tower, a low porch was planned between the towers and extended eastward into the thirteenth-century nave, with the sculptured portals on its eastern side over the foundations of Fulbert's façade. To Kidson, the design of the south tower, built in 1145, exhibits no evidence of this porch; so he posited the theory that this first scheme with portals in the nave was abandoned before 1145 and the portals were erected in their present location, following their trimming as well as cutting back of the north tower and adapting of the south tower. He further suggested that the first scheme was not carried very far. Because of the difficulties of converting the remains of the eleventh-century tower into a porch-narthex, Kidson believed that the plan for a deep porch was jettisoned, the nave and aisles extended to join the towers, and a new smaller but taller narthex, with portals on the west façade and three stained-glass windows above, was erected. Kidson believed that a vaulted porch could have been planned but was not constructed.

Adolf Katzenellenbogen (1959, 5, 106, fn. 7, 8) argued that the Royal Portals were never erected on foundations east of the towers, following the conclusions of Fels. However, the many adjustments of portals to fit into their present location seems to him to prove that the portals were planned for a wider space in the nave. He disagreed with Aubert, who envisaged a smaller campaign without lintels between the eastern piers of the tower and a second campaign in which the RP lintels were carved but trimmed to correct the main axis of the central portal with the nave. Katzenellenbogen basically returned to the Lefèvre-Pontalis theory, but was not specific about the originally planned location of the portals. Instead, he believed that all the sculpture was carved for one site but erected on its present location in the 1150s, and not moved around 1180, as Lefèvre-Pontalis had reasoned.

In 1960, André Lapeyre (*Des Façades Occidentales de Saint-Denis et de Chartres aux Portails de Laon*, 1960, 27) followed Aubert's theory (Plate XXXVIII, 3). Louis Grodecki (*Chartres*, New York: Harcourt Brace, 1963, 27) claimed that the original intention was to join the north and south towers by a porch. By 1150, it was decided to place portals on the west face, but most of the sculpture had already been carved.

Robert Branner (1969, 75) essentially continued the Kidson–Katzenellenbogen–Grodecki theory of an open porch between the western towers for circulation from stairs in the towers through long corridors to the crypt. According to Branner, this porch was planned to support a chapel with three stained-glass windows. The sculpture was to be erected up against Fulbert's façade, or just east of the towers (see Plate XXXVIII, 1—A-B or H-K-I). The plan was then changed when the south tower was beginning to rise and the sculpture was put in its present location on a narrower emplacement, which necessitated the squeezing of the three portals.

Willibald Sauerländer (1972, 383–86) did not accept the compromise solution that the portals were planned and created in two campaigns. In an article in 1956 ("Zu den Westportalen von Chartres," *Kunstchronik,* Vol. 9, 155–57), he argued that side portals are of different widths and that the tympanum and lintels of the left portal are trimmed, as are the obvious trimming of the right portal. Based on these conclusions, he stated in his recent book, "The most likely supposition is that all parts of the Royal Portal were created between 1145 and 1155, but that when work started the intended site was wider than the one it occupies. Whether it ever in fact stood elsewhere, or whether the plan was changed during its execution is for the moment impossible to decide."

Jan van der Meulen, in an article published in 1975 ("Sculpture and Its Architectural Context at Chartres around 1200," *The Year 1200: A Symposium,* The Metropolitan Museum of Art, 509–60, esp. 512 and fn. 23, 530–31), disagreed with Sauerländer and argued that the tympanum and upper lintel of the left portal were not trimmed (fig. 51). Extremities of wings and the outer border of the central slab are missing, but a metal strut to the left of the deity and a socle on the right prove their original emplacement. The even juncture of the three blocks of tympanum and two blocks of the upper lintel prove that they have not been recut. Van der Meulen also stated that the right portal tympanum has not been trimmed (figs. 47–49), but points out that although both lintels of this portal have obviously been cut back on their right sides (fig. 49), a narrow filler block has been inserted on the left edge of the lower lintel "due only to a desire to move the composition out of axis" (fig. 48). He also suggested the possibility that the jambs LP.L2, 3 and RP.R1, 2 are earlier than the sculpture by the Headmaster, possibly resembling in style the lower lintel of the left portal (fig. 52), and that they could have been originally located on one or two portals without a tympanum. Because of the naturalism of the head of the Christ in the central tympanum and some of the heads on the central portal, he believed that they must have been recut after 1200. For proof of this recutting, he cited the better preservation of these heads compared to those by the Angel Master in the superstructure.

Van der Meulen's two-campaign theory does not stand up when the doorjamb figures, pilaster reliefs, and capitals are analyzed, since the majority of this sculpture was carved by the Étampes and Saint-Denis masters and their assistants. The recutting of heads after 1200 is also open to question when one compares the head of the tympanum with the heads of jambs and with the smaller ones of the right lintel (Plate XX, 2, 3, 5). One would have to assume that all these heads were recarved. Weathering as evidence is dangerous. The portals are approximately 840 years old, and one wonders if sixty years would account for appreciable differences. Sculpture in the upper superstructure often seems to deteriorate faster than jamb figures because of the overhang of the archivolts, which impedes the drying process.

In his book published in 1981, van der Meulen, with Nancy Price (4–6), concentrated on the left tympanum as Creation of the World, not an Ascension. In the opening chapter, he attributed the portal sculptures to a number of workshops and their masters as follows: Headmaster—CP tympanum and at least some jamb statues of the central portal; Atelier of Headmaster—CP lintel, LP.R and RP.L jambs; Angel Master—tympana of LP and RP and archivolts of all three portals; Little Master of Saint-Gilles or the Headmaster—RP lintels; Étampes Master—LP.L2, 3; Saint-Denis Master—RP.R1, 2 and LP lower lintel. The Little Master of Saint-Gilles as sculptor of the RP lintels is questionable since very few stylistic similarities between the reliefs of Saint-Giles-du-Gard and the Chartres lintels exist, and the two monuments are contemporary. Van der Meulen agreed with Sauerländer (1972, 385) that the LP.L1 jamb and the RP.R3 jamb are different from the Étampes and Saint-Denis masters and recalled the sculpture of Autun and the outer façade of Vézelay. Van der Meulen now believed that the six jamb statues (LP.L1, 2, 3 and RP.R1, 2, 3) are part of an earlier portal or portals.

Van der Meulen further stated that the present location of the portals, as their original emplacement, has not been conclusively proved. However, he stressed the adjustments of the lintels of north and south portals to their new architectural context and thus implied that some to the sculpture are *spolia* from an earlier campaign.

Jan van der Meulen and Jürgen Hohmeyer's book of 1984 concentrated on the original program of the cathedral and its transformations during the campaigns of construction. Because of deviations in axis, shifts in levels, and dimensions of bays in the nave, the authors proved that the master builders planned to replace the Early Gothic façade, towers, and portals, with a new High Gothic façade. When this plan was, fortunately, abandoned, parts of two portals, already carved for the west façade, were then placed on the expanded transepts (83–86). Although they located the Fulbert façade of the eleventh century between the eastern piers of the second bay of the present nave (85, fig. 83), the authors argued that, in spite of the lack of connection between the portals and the north tower and the merging of portals with south tower at jamb level, there is no evidence to prove or disprove another location of the Royal Portals further east (228). Further, the authors believed that some of the sculpture of Chartres West is earlier and that the heads of some of the Headmaster's figures on the central portal, especially CP.L1, were recarved in the thirteenth century (229–32).

B. Evidence in the Portals Confirming That They Were Designed for Another Location

The three portals in their present location are 15.92 meters wide, north tower to south tower at the level of the ovals in the bases. This dimension is approximately a meter shorter than the emplacement in the first bay of the nave, proposed by Lefèvre-Pontalis (see Plate XXXVIII, 1, 2). The question of what evidence there is on the three portals to prove that they have been cut down and narrowed to fit their present emplacement is summerized as follows.

The most obvious evidence appears on the double lintel of the right portal (figs. 47, 49). Over one-half, a shepherd and part of a lamb have been cut from the Annunciation to the Shepherds on the lower lintel, while part of the figure in the Presentation in the Temple on the upper lintel by the Angel Master has been eliminated. The presence of narrow, vertical filler-blocks on the left extremities of the lintels (fig. 48) does not negate the evidence that both lintels have been reduced in length to fit their present location. The doorway of the right portal is 1.85 meters wide, while the left doorway is 1.95 meters and the central portal is 3 meters wide. It is thus difficult to argue that these two lintels were carved for their present location.

The outer, floral archivolts are modern but were based, according to what I was told in 1939, on preserved fragments. An inventory of the depot in the upper sections of the cathedral, begun in June 1982, revealed approximately 600 fragments. Two voussoirs of the outer archivolt, two fragments of the torso (identified as Aquarius and reinstalled on the LP.R archivolt on September 22, 1982), and two fragments of drapery from one of the lost jamb statues of the CP were published by Marie-Anne Chevallier and Léon Pressouyre ("Fragments récemment retrouvées du Portail Royal," *Revue de l'Art,* 57, 1982, 67–72). The two voussior blocks must have come from the central portal, since the human heads, surrounded by spraying vines and supporting leaves and buds, resemble the nineteenth-century archivolt blocks on the central portal (fig. 57). The present archivolts end abruptly at the top of the second voussoir figures on the side portals, at the top of the first voussoirs of standing figures on the central portal (Plate XI, foldout elevation, and figs. 45, 47, 51). In the case of the CP and LP.R and RP.L, this floral archivolt is sup-

ported by thick, short pilasters that rest on the bases of the projecting responds that in turn articulate the three portals (figs. 54, 56 and Plate XI). Nothing sustains this archivolt on the extremities of the portals; the archivolts terminate over a void.

The lowest voussoir blocks of the side portals have been cut off at their bottoms (figs. 49, 53, 54). Since these blocks are vertical, only the height, and not the width, of the portals was affected by their reduction in size.

The tympanum of the central portal, consisting of five blocks, has not been trimmed (fig. 45). The undulating clouds on the periphery of the tympanum have been destroyed to the left of the Lion of Mark and the lower half of the Angel of Matthew, while the clouds have been badly worn to the right of the Eagle of John. However, the clouds are well preserved on top of the wings of the Angel and on the upper wing of the Eagle. The lintel, containing the twelve Apostles and Jacob and Elijah on one block, appears pinched (figs. 45, 46). Part of the arcade and outer frame is missing on the left, while the right-hand figure is contained by a column and an unfinished, narrow pilaster (fig. 46).

As already stated, the tympana of both side portals, each of three blocks, have not been cut back either on their outer sides or on the edges between the blocks (figs. 47, 50–52). The upper lintel of the left portal is untouched, while the lower one, with ten Apostles, and unique stylistically, is *spolium* and appears cramped. The use of sculpture from an older building campaign in a new context occurred often in the twelfth and thirteenth centuries, e.g., the cathedrals at Bourges, Paris, Reims.

The capital-frieze, which was created in one campaign mostly by the Étampes and Saint-Denis masters, has not been transformed in any manner. However, the extreme right-hand capital (fig. 44) displays two anomalies: 1. On the right edge, only half the turret of the baldachin is showing; 2. Part of the drapery of the third Apostle is visible in the matrix of the south tower. Part of a block of the south tower must have been cut away to make room for the capital to penetrate into it. It thus follows that the south tower was completed at the height of the capitals before this capital was imbedded into it. If the three portals were designed for their present location, one is forced to question this awkward solution.

In the zone of the jamb statues there are several features that suggest that the portals were designed for a wider space. The alignment of the jamb statues and the superstructure is slightly off, as can be seen in a frontal view of each portal (see Plate XI and foldout elevation). The door-jamb reliefs and the inner jamb statues support the lintel of each portal. However, the second jamb (CP.L2, CP.R2, etc.) also overlaps slightly the outer edges of each lintel; this results in a lack of exact alignment among jamb statues, capitals, abaci, and archivolts (see Plate XII, 2 and fig. 13a). It would appear that all three doorways were narrowed as jamb statues with their bases and capitals were moved closer together.

In all six splays of the façade there are small, undecorated sections of columns between jamb figures and capitals. Since the height of the jambs from bases to capital is established by the six doorjamb reliefs on each embrasure, one must assume that the sculptors consciously wished to separate the haloed heads with or without canopies from the historiated capitals, following the precedent of Étampes (Plates XXIII and XXIV and fig. 13a). At Saint-Denis (1140), Le Mans, Provins, Saint-Loup-de-Naud, Saint-Germain-des-Prés, Senlis, and many other places, the heads of the jamb statues extended directly up to the capitals, but in all these portals the capitals are decorative, not historiated.

Careful scrutiny of the ornamented colonnettes between the jamb statues reveals more evidence that the portals were not planned for their present location (see W.S.S., 18–20, and Plates XII–XVIII). The sizes and placement of the colonnettes vary considerably from splay to splay. The standard is set on the CP.R (Plate XVII, 2), in which the lowest colonnettes are between 2.27 meters and 2.40 meters in height and the top ones between 1.19 meters and 1.31 meters (see Appendix I in this book for measurements). On the CP.L (Plate XVII, 1) there are three blocks on each jamb, with the bottoms varying from 1.63 meters to 2.21 meters, middle pieces from 1.21 meters to 1.44 meters, and top ones from .18 meters to .76 meters. The CP.L4 top piece (.18 meters) is uncarved. On the LP.L (Plate XVI, 1), the two series of colonnettes consist of three blocks: LP.L1—1.78 meters, 1.52 meters, .24 meters from bottom to top, and LP.L2—1.73 meters, 1.03 meters, .78 meters. The top block of LP.L1 (.24 meters) has no top molding. Only one complete jamb of colonnettes is preserved on the RP.R (Plate XVI, 2), while RP.R1 has one top piece (.90 meters), which does not extend up to the capital.

The RP.L colonnettes (Plate XVIII, 2) are arranged differently, with a longer colonnette (2.26 meters) above a shorter one (1.30 meters) in RP.L2, with probably the same longer-over-shorter system in RP.L3, although the upper block is broken off. Even more variety is exhibited in the LP.R splay (Plate XVIII, 1), with the lowest blocks of 1.57 meters, 1.75 meters, and 2.58 meters in height, middle blocks of 1.42 meters and .79 meters, and top pieces of .41 meters and .20 meters. Again, the top pieces of LP.R1 (.41 meters) and of LP.R2 have tops but no bottom moldings.

The unfinished top piece (CP.L4) and the short, top blocks without moldings are further proof that the portals have been moved. The most consistent splay is the CP.R, in which the jamb statues were carved by the Headmaster. The most inconsistent splays from the point of view of the lengths of

the colonnettes are LP.R and RP.L, in which two assistants of the Headmaster carved the jamb figures. It is in these splays that we find the decline in quality of the carving in contrast to CP colonnettes or the LP.L colonnettes (Plates XIII–XV).

There seems to be much accumulated evidence for the conclusion that the three west portals were carved for a larger emplacement. Whether they were ever erected on this site is impossible to say, although it would appear that most of the sculpture was carved by the time that the change in location transpired.

C. Towers, Façade, and Narthex

What is the evidence in the design, construction, and masonry of the west towers, façade, and narthex that would ascertain whether or not the portals were planned for another location, and if they were moved, when did this change of plan take place? The north tower was designed in 1134 to be freestanding, as the window in its east side indicates (Plate XXXVIII). Its northwest pier-support (fig. 59) consists of pilaster buttresses on both the north and west faces and two responds between these buttresses. As viewed from the northwest, this diagonal corner presents four projecting edges and three reentrant, right angles (fig. 59).

The southwest corner of the north tower must have originally been identical to the northwest corner, but now only the west buttress and one respond are visible in LP.L (figs. 60, 61). This respond has been cut back considerably so that the bases, jamb figures, and capitals of the LP. could be set against the tower. Since buttress and responds are slightly narrower at the level of the upper arcade than at their bases, it was necessary to shave off some of the south face of the first respond to make it vertical for the addition of the portal (fig. 61 and detail, Plate XXI, 3).

In the spandrel above the left portal (fig. 60), the west face of the second respond of the north tower appears and continues up above the level of the springing of archivolts over the Tree of Jesse window. This respond is interrupted by the section of an arc that either supported the gable of the twelfth-century façade or was inserted in the early thirteenth century to strengthen the wall to sustain the High Gothic rose window. Above the arc, a section of this respond reappears and is capped by a molding that is continuous around the entire north tower. The top cornice, including the corbels above the pilasters, are from the thirteenth century.

Since the portals were carved later than 1134, it could be argued that they were designed and placed originally against the north tower, but one must question the planning of these portals if it required the extensive cutting back of one respond and the absorption of the southwest buttress into the matrix of the left portal as well as the many changes in the portals themselves.

The south side of the north tower (see elevation—Plate XXXVIII, 4), designed differently from the west and north faces (fig. 59), has two stages of blind arcades, with the lower one embracing two openings. These entrances are flanked by columns and were thus not meant to serve as barriers. The fact that no closing doorways were planned has led critics to argue that a porch for access to the north tower and, more importantly, to the crypt was conceived from the outset of the construction following the fire of 1134. Clearly, the façade and portals were added to and caused the transformation of the north tower. As originally designed, it would appear that the south side of the north tower was open to pilgrims with grilles somewhere inside controlling access to the crypt.

The south tower, being erected in 1145, exhibits the same architectural forms and system of construction on its south-west corner as does the north tower in its northwest corner, two buttresses, and two responds. One half of the north-western pier of the south tower vanishes inside the masonry of the right portal (fig. 60). Only the western wall buttress and western respond are visible and extend up to the top ballustrade between the towers. Again, the question arises as to whether the west portals would have been designed for their present location in such a manner that they incor-porated into their matrix large sections of the corner piers of both towers. However, if the portals were planned for another, wider location, their removal to a narrower site would obviously necessitate compromises.

If the junctures of the base of the façade and the north and south towers are compared, it is evident that the LP.L bases and jambs have no connection with the north tower in their courses of masonry, while in the RP.R there appears to be continuity between the south tower and the base under the jamb statues (Plate XXI, 3, 4). Not only has the respond of the north tower been cut back, as already stated, but also vertical plugs of stone have been inserted between the respond and the jambs. In the south tower, the respond to the right of the right portal, the masonry course, crowned by a scotia molding, is interlocked with the bases of the jambs, which have the same moldings. The next lower masonry course, capped by a torus molding, is interrupted at the juncture of the tower and the portals by a projecting section of a base (Plate XXI, 4). Even though the moldings continue from tower to portal, some ambiguities exist.

Masonry between the south tower and RP.R jamb fig-ures is only continuous for the first three courses above the bases (Plate XVI, 2 and fig. 62). Above that height there is generally a lack of alignment between the horizontal courses of tower and portals. As already pointed out, the RP.R3

capital (fig. 44) is inserted into the south tower, which obviously implies that the capitals were carved earlier and for another location. Continuity at the level of the bases and lack of same above suggests that, at the outset, the south tower and portals were being constructed at the same time, but work on the tower, at the upper section of the jambs and at the level of the capitals, preceded that of the portals. John James (*The Contractors of Chartres,* Doora-long, N.S.W., Australia, 1981) in 1983 pointed out to me that inside the narthex the masonry courses of the portals are bonded into and continuous with the south tower, although the column and capital that supported the six-teenth-century organ loft make it difficult to analyze. The decision to erect the portals on their present site must have occurred while the south tower was rising out of its foun-dations. The document of 1145 stated only that two towers were under construction, but gave no information concern-ing the height of the tower in 1145.

If the masonry between the outer archivolts of all the portals and the cornice supported by corbels is studied carefully, it is evident that the portals were planned for another location (see W.S.S., 23–24, Plate XI, and foldout elevation). In the extreme left-hand spandrel, the courses of masonry are not continuous between the façade and remains of the second respond. In the right spandrel of the right portal, masonry courses are continuous horizontally from tower to façade so that the portal and the tower are interpenetrated structurally and thus would appear to have been constructed simultaneously (Plate XXI, 2). However, the three upper courses of the spandrel are not aligned with the masonry across the rest of the right portal.

Courses of masonry are evenly spaced and uniform across the top of the central portal, through the articulated pilas-ters separating the central from the side portals, and end at the apices of the side portals. Above the apex of each side portal, small square blocks can be seen as well as coursing changes, as already stated, from apex to north tower and apex to south tower. The presence of the square blocks over both side portals, which appear incongruous, are per-haps explained by the cutting of the lowest archivolt blocks on both side portals and the resulting lowering of these two portals.

Since the system of construction of the pedestals of the portals, jamb statues, inner jamb figures, and capitals is uniform throughout the six splays, one could expect that the courses of masonry across the top of the portals would be consistant. Evidence in the masonry of towers and por-tals, however, taken together with the evidence in the por-tals themselves, points to the conclusion that the portals were carved for a different emplacement.

The north face of the south tower (see Plate XXXVIII, 5), like the south elevation of the north tower, was not

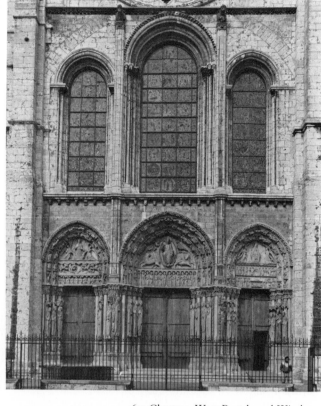

59. Chartres, North Tower, from the northwest

60. Chartres, West Portals and Windows

61. Chartres, North Tower and LP.L.

62. Chartres, RP.R and South Tower

65. Chartres, Masonry of façade and South Tower
above Passion Window

64. Chartres, Masonry of façade and South Tower
at upper level of Passion Window

63. Chartres, Masonry of façade and South Tower
at lower level of Passion Window

designed for closing doors. Since, as already stated, the lower walls of the south tower are bonded into the inner façade walls in the southwest corner of the narthex, and since the bases under the RP.R jamb statues are continuous with the south tower, it follows that the decision to erect the façade on their present site coincided with the emergence of the south tower from its foundations.

The masonry at the juncture of the south tower and the Passion of Christ window reveals the fact that the tower was completed up to the level of the molding before the façade wall (figs. 63, 64). Odd-shaped blocks abut the tower, while the left-hand edge of the molding (top of fig. 63) has been cut off and façade blocks of different size and shape have been placed against it. Thus from the level of the capital-frieze up through the tower molding (fig. 63) the tower was completed before the façade. The desire to complete the vaults of the south tower may lie behind the priority of tower over façade.

Masonry in the area between the tower molding and the cornice of the Passion of Christ window (fig. 64) also exhibits the fact that the south tower was complete at this level before the façade was erected. Above the cornice (figs. 63, 64), the relieving arc makes it difficult to ascertain the priority of tower or façade. However, courses of masonry do not extend from tower to façade in the lower sections, while blocks in the upper part appear to be attached to the tower in order to receive the penetrating ones of the façade (fig. 65).

Thus the only parts of the south tower and façade which were constructed simultaneously are the lower courses of the south tower and RP.R and the lower courses of the inner walls of façade and south tower in the southwest corner of the narthex. From the RP.R capital (fig. 44), which involved the hollowing out of one block of the tower, to the thirteenth-century cornice above the windows, the construction of the south tower proceeded that of the façade. The decision to incorporate the three portals into a western façade, creating a western narthex between the towers and controlling circulation to the crypt through the open sides of both towers, must have been made while the south tower was rising above ground level.

Many questions remain unanswered. Was the present narthex originally vaulted? John James (Vol. 1, 219–20 and Vol. II, 469–70) stressed the necessity of a vaulted narthex and gallery with a closing wall between the eastern piers of the towers to protect the three stained-glass windows from the devastating fire of 1194. His reconstructed narthex of nine bays, three in width and three in depth (see 471, fig. a), is problematical, since there are, according to Fels, no foundations of sufficient width between the towers to support the eastern wall of the narthex and the gallery, and the four freestanding piers of narthex are not aligned with

the foundations of the central, eleventh-century tower between the twelfth-century towers (Plate XXXVIII, 1). The only evidence of the possible existence of a gallery are the two engaged columns and capitals between the portals on the eastern face of the façade, but these half-columns could have been part of the earlier program to erect the portals, the gallery, and three stained-glass windows in the High Gothic nave.

Much of the argument for a vaulted narthex hinges on the theory that the existence of a vaulted gallery above a narthex saved the three lancet windows from the 1194 fire. The south transept windows of York Minster survived a fire on July 9, 1984 that burned the wooden roof. The small window in the gable above the rose window was destroyed and the rose window was damaged. One of the lancets was damaged by a falling timber (*New York Times,* July 10, 1984). The prevailing west winds at Chartres could have kept the flames from the three windows. Is it necessary to assume that the glass survived because of the existence of a vaulted gallery?

D. Conclusion

No detailed drawings or photographs of Lefèvre-Pontalis' excavations in the western bays of the Gothic nave exist to help determine the original, intended emplacement of the Royal Portals (Plate XXXVIII, 1, 2). His reconstruction may be correct. Certainly there is sufficient evidence in the portals themselves and the architecture of towers and narthex to prove that the majority of the sculpture was not carved for its present location.

A plausible scenario for the Chartres twelfth-century campaigns of architecture and sculpture is as follows:

1. The fire of September 5, 1134 damaged the west end of the eleventh-century cathedral.

2. 1134—the beginning of construction of the freestanding north tower with two open portals on the south and the doorway on north side.

3. Around 1143—the arrival of four major sculptors and their assistants at Chartres to execute the program conceived by the School of Chartres. One sculptor came from Saint-Denis, dedicated in 1140; a second came from Étampes, where he had carved the south portal of Notre-Dame between around 1140 and 1143 (three years—see Part III); the third, the Headmaster, came from Burgundy (see Part IV); and the fourth, the Angel Master. Together with five, identifiable assistants, these four sculptors began the collaborative task of implementing the sculptural desires of the clergy.

4. 1145—two towers a building, as mentioned by the Abbot of Mont-Saint-Michel.

5. 1145 or 1146—the decision to create a narthex between the towers to increase the security of entrances to the crypt from both towers and to protect pilgrims entering either the cathedral or the crypt. This change in architectural intent also involved installing the finished sculpture, which included all the sculpture, except some of the upper archivolts, on this new western façade, which was meant to rival Suger's façade of Saint-Denis.

The question of whether or not any of the sculpture carved for a wider emplacement in the western nave was ever installed must remain debatable. There are, however, some hints, such as the inconsistent installation of the ornamented colonnettes between the jamb statues and the presence of engaged columns and capitals on the inside of the portal, now supporting nothing, which suggest that the six embrasures may have been erected before being transferred to their present location.

6. 1145 or 1146—extensive cutting back of the southwest, corner pier of north tower to fit the portals, designed for wider emplacement, between it and the south tower, which was emerging from its massive footings and foundations. The lower courses of masonry interlocked the façade and the south tower (RP.R and south-west corner of narthex), and the rapid construction of the south tower preceded the erection of the façade.

7. 1147—the completion of the installation of all sculpture and stained glass.

Discussion of three twelfth-century stained-glass windows above the Royal Portals is beyond the scope of this revision. However, it is curious that the Passion of Christ window over the right portal is considerably narrower than the Tree of Jesse window over the left portal. The former window has a floral panel at the bottom similar to the borders completely framing the other two windows. In the Passion Window, ornament fills the outer voids between the rondels, and a beaded molding emerges to crop and frame the top two rondels. This window would seem to have been designed for a narrower space after the decision to move the location of sculpture and glass.

Obviously it is impossible to prove all the dates listed above, but five to six years is more than sufficient time to complete all the sculpture of the Royal Portals. The period 1143–1148 seems to be confirmed by the archaeology of towers, façade, narthex, and sculpture.

PART III

THE SOUTH PORTAL OF
NOTRE-DAME AT ÉTAMPES

The debate has continued since 1952 over whether Étampes is earlier or later than Chartres. Louis Grodecki ("La 'Première Sculpture Gothique.' Wilhelm Vöge et l'état actuel des problèmes," *Bulletin monumental,* CXVII, 1959, 265–89, esp. 278–79), having read André Lapeyre's thesis in manuscript, agreed with Lapeyre that Étampes was derived from Chartres. Lapeyre's book (*Des Façades Occidentales de Saint-Denis et de Chartres aux Portails de Laon,* 1960, 53–66) contains a chapter on the south portal of Étampes. Lapeyre argued that the sculptor of the Étampes tympanum was of Burgundian origin but also knew the sculpture of Languedoc since he was part of the Chartres workshop, which contained sculptors from southwestern France. He cited iconographic connections between the tympanum at Montceaux-l'Etoile, in Burgundy, and the Miègeville portal at Saint-Sernin, in Toulouse. Basing his arguments largely on iconographic considerations, Lapeyre believed that the Bathing of Christ (L3) was probably inspired by the Bathing of Mary, at Chartres and that the Holy Women at the Tomb (R2), Entry into Jerusalem (R4), and Last Supper (R3) were all based on Chartres capitals. It is difficult to agree with these conclusions when figure style, composition, and design of the baldachins are considered. Furthermore, the Chartres capitals he cited were not carved by the Étampes Master (Bathing of Mary, by the Assistant of Étampes Master— fig. 33; Holy Women and Entry into Jerusalem, by the Saint-Denis Master—figs. 41, 42; the Last Supper, by the Saint-Denis Master, fig. 40).

The baldachins crowning the capital scenes of Étampes are uniform, with arches surmounted by a horizontally arcaded superstructure and accented by small towers (fig. 68), whereas the baldachins at Chartres, on the capitals carved by the Étampes Master, contain gabled cornices and towers and decorated borders (fig. 69). Even the quite different baldachin of the CP.L2 capital, depicting Joachim and Anna embracing and the Bathing of the Virgin, which was carved by the Assistant of the Étampes Master, is more horizontally designed, like the Étampes canopies, but exhibits more animated moldings (figs. 32, 33, 68). It would appear that the evidence of different sculptors at work on the Chartres capitals, together with the evolution in design of the bal-

dachins, points to the conclusion that Étampes predates Chartres.

Lapeyre was correct in pointing out that I had stressed the fact that the Étampes style was limited to Chartres and Étampes, whereas it is evident that the sculpture at Châteaudun and possibly Saint-Ayoul at Provins was influenced by Étampes. This fact, however, does not help solve the question of the priority of Étampes or Chartres.

Charles Grosset ("Les sculptures du portail sud de Notre-Dame d'Étampes à propos du livre récent," *Cahiers de civilisation médiévale,* VII, 1964, 53–61) agreed, for the most part, with Lapeyre's general conclusions, but disagreed on the subject of Étampes. He observed that at first glance the south portal is homogeneous in concept and execution, but then pointed out that the lintel of twelve figures (his number) was originally designed to support a round-arched tympanum, with the figures of Enoch and Elijah on separate blocks added at a later date (figs. 70, 71). The Virgin (right) and Peter (left) appear directly beneath the Christ of the tympanum. Grosset proceeded to assign the sculpture to related ateliers according to their relative quality. The six jamb statues were carved by different sculptors, with the best figure, L3, early in the major master's career and R3 later. In contrast, the archivolt figures are considered monotonous and mechanical. A different group of sculptors gave less life to the Christ of the tympanum and the prophet adjacent to the left spandrel (fig. 72). The chief work of the atelier was the angels of the spandrels and tympanum, while the statues of Peter and Paul in a chapel inside Notre-Dame were originally placed on the sides of the portal but were probably not part of the original program.

With regard to the capitals of Étampes and Chartres, Grosset found a precise program at Étampes, with several capitals serving as models for those at Chartres. He saw a strong, sytlistic connection between Étampes and the north façade of Châteaudun that exists only in engravings (see Lapeyre, 1960, 68–69, figs. 37, 38). He hypothesized that the sculptor or his disciple, who carved the Étampes lintel for a round-head portal, carved the Châteaudun north façade between 1130 and 1140 and then either created the Chartres LP.L jambs at Chartres or had the Chartres statues sent from Étampes to Chartres. This sculptor, trained at Chartres, then took over the Étampes chantier between 1145 and 1150 and carved the Christ of the tympanum and the upper columnar prophet and also conceived the capital-frieze format, which was copied later at Chartres. Grosset's theory was based on two campaigns on Chartres west, following Aubert, with the result that the Chartres jambs, LP.L, are earlier than Étampes, but the Étampes portal as a whole was, according to Grosset, completed before the moving and enlargement of the Chartres west portals, between 1150 and 1155. Thus Grosset dated the lintel of Étampes earlier than Chartres, the LP.L Chartres statues earlier than Étampes, but the Étampes portal earlier than the expanded three portals of Chartres. Many of Grosset's conclusions are open to question and will be discussed later.

Sophie Baratte-Bévillard ("La sculpture monumentale de la Madeleine de Châteaudun," *Bulletin Archéologique du Comité des traveaux historiques et scientifiques,* 1972, 105–25) discussed both the north and south portals of Châteaudun. Engravings of 1733 of the north portals, before their destruction, depict thirteen statues in relief: six above the central portal, five on buttresses, and two above the right portal. As the author pointed out, some of the reliefs relate stylistically to the Wheel of Fortune window at Saint-Étienne, at Beauvais, while others are close to Chartres and Étampes. She dated the LP.L figures at Chartres toward 1145 and at Châteaudun between 1140 and 1150. Willibald Sauerländer (*Gothic Sculpture in France, 1140–1270,* London, 1972, 398) stated that the stylistic closeness of Étampes to Chartres (LP.L2, 3) makes it almost impossible to determine the priority of one over the other, but concluded, "This portal may have been executed c. 1140, shortly before Chartres."

Clark Maines ("Le Portail Ouest de St.-Pierre-au-Parvis, Soissons (Aisne): Reconstitution Iconographique," *Revue archéologique de Picardie,* No. 4, 1982, 178–98) has determined, on the basis of careful study of the badly damaged portal, that the tympanum is not a *Maiestas Domini,* as previous critics had argued, but rather an Ascension, with a standing Christ flanked by two standing and two kneeling angels. The lintel contained twelve standing Apostles, as determined by study of pre–World War I photographs, while the archivolts consisted of eight of the twenty-four Elders of the Apocalypse. He discovered the remains of an angel swinging censers in the spandrels, and identified the majority of scenes in the eight capitals. Since the Ascension, the Apostles on the lintel, the Elders in archivolts, angels in spandrels, and historiated capitals under baldachins all recall Étampes, Maines is correct in concluding that the portal of Saint-Pierre-au-Parvis, at Soissons, is iconographically a somewhat simplified version of Étampes.

Étampes has thirteen scenes on eight capitals, while Saint-Pierre exhibits ten episodes on eight capitals, with six of the ten repeating scenes of Étampes. Because of the condition of the portal at Soissons, Maines suggested certain stylistic connections with Étampes only in drapery style. He dated the portal between 1140 and 1155 and pointed out the strong role played by both Étampes and Soissons in the expanding Capetian monarchy, even though Soissons was outside the royal domain.

Further study of the portal at Étampes during recent summers has convinced me that my original conclusion that Étampes was earlier than Chartres was correct (1952, W.S.S., 27–31). When details of jamb figures and capitals of Étampes and Chartres are compared, this conclusion is confirmed.

The portal at Étampes is presently being cleaned and preserved. When the accumulated grime between folds of the Étampes statues is removed, the similarity of the Étampes L2 (fig. 66) and the recently restored Chartres LP.L3 (fig. 67) will be even more apparent. These two jamb statues were obviously carved by the same sculptor. Arrangement of loop-folds articulating legs, vertical folds and staffs between legs, wide bands with geometric patterns across legs, vertical double folds on the sides, knees accentuated by narrow bands at their bottom and the folded hem of mantles at their top, and mantles with serrated hems between legs—all are identical in both statues (figs. 66, 67). In the Chartres figure, the silhouette tapers inward from the knees to the ankles, while it remains rectangular in shape in the Étampes statue. At Chartres, drapery folds over the lower legs are increased in number, and vertical folds between the legs are more three dimensional and are connected at intervals by horizontal membranes. In the Étampes jamb, the lower hem terminates in an even horizontal band, whereas in the Chartres statue, the band is preserved but butterfly folds animate center and sides (figs. 66, 67). The Chartres figure is a subtle refinement of the Étampes jamb. It is impossible to argue that the Chartres figure is earlier than the Étampes jamb.

The historiated capitals of Étampes (Plate XXIII, 4, 5) appear stiffer, with more-pronounced ridge-folds than those of Chartres. If the L3 capital of Étampes, depicting the Nativity and the Bathing of Christ (fig. 68), is contrasted with Joachim and Anna capital (CP.L1—fig. 69, right capital), it is evident that although drapery forms with accented knees and thighs and splayed feet overlapping the torus molding are related, the Chartres capital is more subtly carved, with a greater variety of surface. Baldachins over the Étampes capitals (fig. 68) consist of arches supporting a horizontal arcade with turrets on the corners, outer edges, and centers of each face, while in the Chartres capital (CP.L1,

66. Étampes, jamb statue, L2

67. Chartres, jamb statue, LP.L3

68. Étampes, capital L3, Nativity and Bathing of Christ

69. Chartres, capital CP.L1, Joachim and Anna

70. Étampes, tympanum: Ascension, Second Coming; lintel: The Apostles (Austin)

71. Étampes, detail of lintel

72. Étampes, left spandrel (Austin)

fig. 69) the baldachin has pedimented arcades, with cornices decorated by circlets. As in the case of the jamb figures, greater complexity replaces the relative simplicity of the Étampes capitals. Incidently, the construction of the Étampes capitals and their abaci are the reverse of the Chartres capitals: Étampes capitals are interlocked perpendicularly to the portal, with abaci set laterally, which is the opposite arrangement of Chartres.

The tympanum, depicting the Ascension and comprised of five blocks, appears to be by the same sculptor who carved the considerably larger jamb statues (fig. 70). The standing Christ and two angels resemble the jamb statues in pose and drapery style. Flaring mantles, serving as backgrounds for figures, have their counterparts in the capitals, especially in the Adoration of the Magi on the left-hand frieze (Plate XXIII, 5).

The badly damaged lintel presently contains twelve figures, with the fifth and sixth, counting from the left, possessing slightly different designs on their halos (fig. 70). The fifth might be Peter and the sixth the Virgin, as Grosset remarked (1964). A detail of the right side of the lintel (fig. 71) shows either the remains of a thirteenth figure or else a section of the raised folds of the right Apostle. The lintel would appear to have been designed for a narrower, round-arched tympanum, and two blocks, probably containing Enoch and Elijah, were added to support the pointed tympanum. The lintel projects outward and creates a narrow ledge supporting the tympanum. Does this transformation of the lintel necessarily mean that the lintel is considerably earlier than the tympanum or did the design change occur when work had progressed to the beginning of the superstructure? The preserved lower sections of the Apostles of the lintel, which are approximately one-third the height of the jamb figures, exhibit the same style of drapery as both the jambs and the capitals.

The angels in the spandrels adjacent to the archivolts seem to be stylistically inseparable from the tympanum, lintel, capital and jambs (fig. 72). It is impossible to agree with Grosset, who believed that the Christ of the tympanum and outer column statue were by one sculptor, while a superior sculptor carved the angels of spandrels and tympanum (fig. 70, 72—Grosset, 55). Treatment of the drapery is identical; the poses are dissimilar. If the angles in the spandrels were straightened out and made vertical as part of a column, they would be indistinguishable from the six jamb statues or the high columnar figure. Since there seems to be no qualitative decline in the tympanum, lintels, and spandrels, it seems incorrect to divide the sculpture among different hands (see Grosset, 53–61).

In spite of the stylistic similarities of jamb figures, capitals, lintel, tympanum, and spandrels, subtle variations exist in all this sculpture. No two jambs statues are alike (Plates XXIII, 2 and XXIV). Differences in poses and arrangement of drapery are exhibited in the lintel (fig. 70), while the angels of the tympanum and spandrels are not copies in reversed position (figs. 70, 72). In the case of the thirty-six figures in the archivolts, twenty-four Elders of the Apocalypse and the Prophets (figs. 73–76), one finds much repetition and a distinct decline in quality. Although the archivolts are carefully planned as a unified ensemble, qualitative differences suggest the work of assistants under the supervision of the Étampes Master. On the left-hand side, the lowest three figures of the inner archivolt (fig. 73) appear to be the work of the Master, while the lower two figures of the second and outer archivolt appear to be close copies of the first three on the inner archivolt. These copies are squatter and relatively stiffer and more awkward. This same assistant seems to have carved the third and fourth blocks of the second archivolt and the third through fifth blocks of the outer archivolts (figs. 73, 74). The upper two figures of all three archivolts would seem to be by another assistant. In general, figures and surfaces are flatter and bodices and mantles are crudely carved. The most marked differences between the two assistants can be seen if the third and fourth blocks of the inner archivolt are contrasted (bottom two figures in fig. 74).

The right-hand archivolts appear to display a uniform mediocrity in all five inner voussoirs, in all six of the second, and in the lowest four of the outer archivolt (figs. 75, 76). Drapery over the stomachs is exaggerated. There appears to be a stylistic relationship between these fifteen voussoir figures and the six, the top two in each of the three archivolts, on the left-hand side (fig. 74) by the second assistant.

The top three of the right, outer archivolts numbers 5, 6, 7–fig. 76) seem to be by another assistant. The legs are placed frontally, in contrast to the diagonal placement in all but two of the other figures. Plain, wide hems of the mantle curve across the legs, while the upper torso is almost completely enveloped in the cascading mantle. Thus three assistants seem to have been involved in the completion of the archivolts with the Étampes Master carving three figures, the first assistant responsible for nine, the second assistant for seventeen, and the third assistant for three. The last's sculpture possesses certain common denominators with the inner doorjamb figures at Chartres, which are by the Assistant of the Étampes Master, but more detailed photographs from scaffolding are necessary to prove this suggestion.

The capitals on the right-hand embrasure, R1 The Expulsion and Temptation, R2 Holy Women at the Sepulchre and Christ appearing to Mary Magdalene, R3 The Last Supper, and R4 Entry into Jerusalem repeat the forms of the Master in a cruder fashion. Thick folds of uniform intervals lack the crispness and variety of surfaces

73. Étampes, left archivolts, 24 Elders of
the Apocalypse and Prophets (Austin)

74. Étampes, left archivolts, upper figures (Austin)

75. Étampes, right archivolts, lower sections (Austin)

76. Étampes, right archivolts, upper sections (Austin)

78. Étampes, Saint Peter (detail)

79. Étampes, Saint Paul

of those on the left side of the portal.

The statues of Peter and Paul inside Notre-Dame at Étampes have been questioned both concerning their authenticity and, if genuine, their original location (figs. 77–79, and Plate XXIII, 3). Since their placement in the chapel to the left of the choir in the second half of the twelfth century, new heads and hands have been attached and all surfaces have been covered with a yellow-orange wash. Both additions have led some critics to consider them fakes. In spite of the differences of opinion, there is no question that they once served as the statue-columns on the lower sides of the portals (Plate XXIII, 1). When the south transept was added, they were removed to the interior. Proof of their original location can be seen in a detail of Peter (fig. 77). Drapery, which articulates Peter's right leg, continues around onto the column. The same phenomenon occurs on the left leg of Paul. Since the portal projects outward from the south flank of Notre-Dame, the sides of the figures would be visible when one is approaching along the main route connecting the château and the royal church. Furthermore, the size of Peter and Paul relates to the jamb figures. The plain column to the left of the portal is 2.65 meters high, as are the jambs. Peter is 2.34 meters, Paul is 2.40 meters, and the jamb statues are all approximately 2.34 meters in height.

Peter, protected from the elements since the twelfth century, obviously has more original surfaces preserved than the jamb statues, yet when the jambs are cleaned like those of the LP.L2, 3 of Chartres have been (fig. 67), the stylistic differences between the figure of Peter and the jamb will be minimal. The diagonal, geometric bands of Peter are identical to the female jamb, L3 (fig. 78 and Plate XXIV, 2, 3), while Peter's left knee and the folds over his lower leg (fig. 78) are extremely close to that of L1 jamb (Plate XXIV, 4). Indeed, the entire statue of Peter is very similar to the jamb statue L1, if the staff is removed (Plates XXIII, 3 and XXIV, 2, 4).

The Paul statue column (fig. 79), which was obviously on the right side of the portal, as its design emphasizes, is basically a reverse image of the Peter. Stylistically, its relationship to the jamb, L1, is clear. The hands, symbols, heads, and halos must be overlooked.

Peter and Paul possess so many characteristics that relate them to the jamb statues that it must be argued that the Étampes Master carved all the monumental sculpture of the portal, while the majority of the archivolts and half the capitals were produced by assistants.

How long would it take the Master to carve the portal of Notre-Dame? If we assume that the relatively soft blocks of limestone were prepared for the sculptor, it is quite possible that the entire portal could have been carved in slightly more than three years. Since it took a sculptor approximately ten days to carve a large Corinthian capital in marble for the cloister of the Church of the Jacobins, in Toulouse in 1969, using no power tools, the following breakdown of the Étampes portal does not seem unreasonable (the same time allotments were used at Chartres):

	Time in Weeks	Number	Total Weeks
Jamb Statues	8	10 (1 lost)	80
Tympanum	18	1	18
Lintel	18	1	18
Spandrels	8	2	16
Capitals	4	7	28
Voussoirs	3	3	9
		Total	169 Weeks

The 169 weeks involve the work of only the Étampes Master. Obviously, the assistants were carving the majority of archivolts, while the Master was finishing the superstructure.

The final question about Étampes concerns the date in which the portals were carved and assembled. Based on comparisons of the bases of the portals, ornament, capitals and their baldachins, and figure style (W.S.S., 1952, 27–31 and the above), it can be stated that Étampes predates Chartres. The Étampes Master was involved in the single campaign at Chartres, carving three jamb statues, seventeen inner-jamb statuettes, and eight capitals. Étampes would appear to be later than the Saint-Denis west portals, which were dedicated in 1140. In Part IV, I will try to prove that the Étampes Master is a specific Burgundian sculptor who knew Saint-Denis. Thus, it follows that the logical dating of the portal of Notre-Dame at Étampes is between 1140 and 1145 and more specifically 1140–1141 to 1143, with the beginning the Chartres West around 1143.

PART IV

ORIGINS OF THE CHARTRES SCULPTORS

INTRODUCTION

The 1952 publication evolved out of study carried out in the summer of 1939 and submitted as a dissertation in 1941 of the ornament of Saint-Denis and Chartres. Part V, now Part IV (42–54, Plates XXX–XXXVIII), stressed the possible sources of the ornamental style of the Île-de-France in the late 1130s at Saint-Denis and in the 1140s at Chartres. Languedoc, Western France, and Burgundy were the regions included, with emphasis focused on Burgundy. Denis Grivot and George Zarnecki (*Gislebertus, Sculptor of Autun*, 1961, 176–77 and fn. 10) wrote: "The belief that some of the elements in the sculpture of St. Denis and Chartres were of Burgundian origin has been somewhat compromised recently by a too emphatic insistence on their importance at the expense of the far more decisive influences of Languedoc and the West of France. Nevertheless, the connection does exist and it is undeniable that, even at Chartres, the elongation of the column-figures, and the spiral folds and ornamental bands across the thighs of a few figures on the Portail Royal, are derived from the Autun tympanum." Even though Grivot and Zarnecki credit me as "the exponent of this extreme view" (176, fn. 10), I will attempt to prove that Romanesque Burgundy is indeed the major source of Early Gothic sculpture in the Île-de-France, especially at Chartres.

WESTERN FRANCE

In Saintonge-Poitou, Angoumois, and Périgord (1952, 46–48 and Plates XXXII, XXXIII) there are literally hundreds of Romanesque churches, with an abundance of elaborately decorated portals, capitals, string-courses, and corbels, which show only slightly vague connections with the ornament of Saint-Denis and Chartres. The treatment of archivolts with single figures arranged radially, such as in the central portal of Notre-Dame-de-la-Couldre at Parthenay (Plate XXXIII, 1, 2), could be the origin of the archivolts of Saint-Denis and Chartres, although the date of Parthenay has not been established. Abbot Suger went to western France in 1137 to arrange and attend the marriage of Louis VII to Eleanor of Aquitaine and probably established the Early Gothic design of archivolts consisting of single figures on separate blocks.

Since there appears to be no stylistic connection between either ornamental or figured sytles between Western France and the Île-de-France, the western regions of modern France should not have been included.

The statement, "No progressive structural or spacial ideas (in Western French architecture) were evolved that were later encorporated in Gothic" (1952, 46) is blatantly incorrect. The domed churches, such as those at Angoulême, Cahors, and Fontevraud, the last only sixty-nine kilometers from Angers, inspired the design of the cathedral at Angers and the subsequent evolution of Angevin Gothic (see André Mussat, *Le style gothique de l'Ouest de la France (XIIe–XIIIe siècles*, 1963).

PROVENCE

Provençal Romanesque as a source for Early Gothic sculpture was omitted from the 1952 edition of my book on the grounds that no stylistic relationship between Saint-Gilles-du-Gard and Saint-Trophîme at Arles on the one hand, and Saint-Denis or Chartres, on the other hand, existed and that the Provençal sculpture seemed to be later in date than that of the Île-de-France. In my book *The Façade of Saint-Gilles-du-Gard, Its Influence on French Sculpture*, 1973, 127–59, I argued on the basis of the iconography, study of the crypt, dated epitaphs, and the relation to Provençal manuscripts and sculpture outside Provence that Saint-Gilles was begun in the 1140s and finished in the early 1150s and that the portal of Saint-Trophîme at Arles should be dated between the 1160s and the early 1170s. Robert Saint-Jean (*Languedoc roman, Le Languedoc Méditerranéen*, Zodiaque, 1975, 298–345) agreed with the dating of the Saint-Gilles. Ferguson O'Meara (*The Iconography of the Façade of Saint-Gilles-du-Gard*, 1977) linked the portals with the Second Crusade (1147). Finally, M. F. Hearn, (*Romanesque Sculpture, The Revival of Monumental Stone Sculpture in the Eleventh and Twelfth Centuries*, 1981, 191–92) stated that the dating of the Saint-Gilles sculpture seemed to have been settled by the independent studies listed above.

This dating of the portals of Saint-Gilles obviously negates any possibility of a Provençal influence on the formation of Early Gothic sculpture. However, there is one persisting fallacy of stylistic analysis that must be discussed, in spite of the fact that Provençal sculpture is later than the west portals of Saint-Denis and Chartres. Alan Priest ("The Masters of the West Façade of Chartres," *Art Studies,* Vol. 1, 1923, 28–44) believed that the "Little Master of Saint-Gilles," sculptor of some of the upper reliefs of the central portal of Saint-Gilles, was responsible for the two lintels of the right portal of Chartres and was an assistant of the Headmaster. The two lintels are the work of *two* assistants of the Headmaster, with the outside figures of the Presentation carved by the Angel Master, but there seems to be no real connection in style between the two monuments. Arthur Kingsley Porter (*Romanesque Sculpture of the Pilgrimage Roads,* Vol. 1, 1923, 284–88) elaborated on the conslusions of Priest, and Robert Branner (*Chartres Cathedral, Norton Critical Studies in Art History,* 1969, 149–68) reproduced Priest's article with illustrations.

LANGUEDOC, SAINT-ÉTIENNE OF TOULOUSE

Southwestern France has often been cited as one of the main sources of Early Gothic sculpture. In 1952, I attempted to prove that no stylistic relationship existed between the ornamental sculpture of Languedoc and the Île-de-France (42–46, Plates XXX, XXXI). At the same time, I argued that although the figures of Thomas and Andrew from the so-called portal of the chapter house of the Cathedral of Saint-Étienne in Toulouse bore some connections with both the lost columnar statues of Saint-Denis and the RP.R1 jambs at Chartres, these two figures, originally signed by Gilabertus, seemed to have more stylistic common denominators with jamb statues by the Headmaster and with sculpture on later portals. Dating the Saint-Étienne figures as late as the 1150s, which is probably incorrect in the light of the extensive, recent research, made moot the question of Languedoc influence on Early Gothic. There will be more discussion about the approximate date of the Saint-Étienne sculpture later.

Linda Seidel (*Romanesque Sculpture from the Cathedral of Saint-Étienne, Toulouse,* 1977, Ph.D. dissertation, Harvard University, 1964) proposed an entirely new theory, that the twelve Apostles, four in pairs and four single figures, articulated three bays of the barrel vault of the chapter house, not its portal (see Seidel, 1977, fig. 48). A summary of her thesis appeared in 1968 ("A Romantic Forgery: The Romanesque 'Portal' of Saint-Étienne in Toulouse," *Art Bulletin,* L, 33–42) and created dismay, since it reduced the possible impact of Languedoc on the formation of Early

Gothic portals. Basing her argument on careful studying of surviving plans of the cloister and on documents dealing with the destruction of the cloister and its attendant structures (1792–1812) and on descriptions of the sculpture by Alexandre Du Mège in 1823 and 1828, before he finally installed it as a portal in 1835, Seidel noted that a detail of the huge plan of Toulouse, drawn in 1750 by the engineer Saget (Seidel, 1977, fig. 8), reveals a structure opening off the east gallery of the cloister, which could have been barrel vaulted with the four single Apostles in the corners supporting the end transverse arches and the four pairs of Apostles holding up the two intermediate arches. Further, she found it curious that Du Mège made no mention of a portal until the installation of 1835; she explains this as part of the Romantic revival of the medieval heritage of France.

That twelve Apostles were rescued from the ruins of the cloister seems likely, but that they once comprised a portal seems doubtful. The Saget plan of the cathedral complex exhibits varying widths of walls but no thick, splayed wall for a portal in the chapter house. Richard Hamann (*Die Abteikirche von St. Gilles und lhre künstlerische Nachfolge,* 3 vols., 1955, 240–58), without knowledge of the 1656 plans of Saint-Guilhem-le-Désert, designed an elaborate portal to utilize the preserved fragments of sculpture in and from Saint-Guilhem. The 1656 plans reveal the fact that there is no location for Hamann's portal reconstruction but indicate that the sculpture was carved for the upper cloister (see Whitney S. Stoddard, *The Façade of Saint-Gilles-du-Gard, Its Influence on French Sculpture,* 1973, 307–24).

The major evidence for disassociating the Apostles from a portal can be found in the sculpture itself. How was the portal constructed? How were the Apostles tied into the matrix of the wall? Seidel pointed out that the edges of the blocks, outside the framing colonnettes, suggest they were isolated. Capitals and *tailloirs* are not interlocked over reentrant angles. All the above criticism would be answered by Seidel's conclusion that the Apostles were supports inside the chapter house and functioned just like the sculpture in the north and east vaulted galleries of the cloister of Saint-Trophîme of Arles.

Another possible location for the Saint-Étienne Apostles is on the piers of the cloister. A very large series of drawings of Toulouse was made by Grandvoinet between 1789 and 1808 (see Seidel, 1977, 12–13, fig. 11). The drawing of the *quartier* of Saint-Étienne shows the cloister with piers at the corners and in the middle of each gallery. The four double Apostles may have decorated the intermediate piers, while the four single Apostles, possibly in conjunction with carved reliefs, comprised the corner piers. If this theory is valid, the design of the cloister of Saint-Étienne would be dependent on the cloisters of Moissac and Santo Domingo de Silos in Spain and, at the same time, be prophetic of the more elaborate piers of the cloister of Saint-Trophîme at Arles, in which the figures are completely integrated with the arches of the barrel vaults. It is curious that the twelve Apostles, four pairs and four single figures, are the correct number for both chapter house and cloister. The late twelfth-century Camera Santa, at Orvieto, echoes the Saint-Étienne chapter house solution (see Seidel, 1977, fig. 72), while the possible theory of the Apostles animating a cloister would represent a phase in the development of cloister design in the Midi.

Linda Seidel's 1968 article was described as a "bombe," or bombshell, by Marcel Durliat (*Haut-Languedoc Roman,* Zodiaque, 1978, 197). In my opinion, Durliat did not refute Seidel's arguments against the Saint-Étienne portal or for the original emplacement of the Apostles inside the chapter house.

Lyne Lautard-Limouse in an article based on her thesis ("Gilabertus Sculpteur Roman Toulousan," *Archéologia,* No. 77, 1974, 40–49) stressed the formation of Gilabertus in Toulouse out of the second series of capitals of La Daurade, with influences from the Moissac porch and the cloister of Saint-Sernin. She disagreed with Seidel's reconstruction of the Apostles and capitals inside the chapter house of Saint-Étienne.

A simple scenario may have transpired in 1835, when the Apostles were first installed as a portal in the Musée des Augustins in Toulouse. As late as 1828, Du Mège reported that the sculpture was in a chapel off the cloister. Du Mège and others, acting within the framework of preserving the past as well as stressing the importance of Languedoc, were presented the problem of how to install the twelve Apostles. With the late La Durade chapter house portal and Early Gothic portals in mind, a portal, not a forgery, was conceived without any substantiating archaeological evidence.

No complete agreement among scholars exists on the date of the sculpture of the Saint-Étienne of Toulouse. Some critics date the Apostles as early as 1120 (Raymond Rey, *La sculpture roman Languedocienne,* 1930) and into the 1130s, but before Saint-Denis (c.1136 or 1137–1140), while others argue that the sculpture is contemporary with Saint-Denis or Chartres. Seidel places the sculpture at around 1125, on the basis of its position in the evolution of Languedoc sculpture and of its influence on the Atlantids of the chapter house of Durham Cathedral, a *terminus ante quem* of 1133–1140. Durliat (1978, 204–5) concluded that the Apostles were carved between 1135 and 1140, after the second series of capitals for the cloister of La Daurade. Durliat's conclusions will be born out by the analysis of style of the sculpture of Saint-Étienne of Toulouse.

Two sculptors with distinct styles were responsible for carving the Toulouse Apostles; two paired Apostles and two single ones were done by each artist. The Saint-James Master (Seidel, 1977, 107–9, 128–30) was firmly rooted in the Toulousan tradition, which commenced with the ambulatory reliefs of Saint-Sernin (1096) and evolved in the cloister reliefs and capitals of the Moissac cloister (1100), in the capitals of the First Series of La Daurade in Toulouse, in the Porte Miègeville of Saint-Sernin (ca. 1110), and finally in the portal of Moissac (see left-hand Apostle—Plate XXXI, 5). No stylistic connections seem to exist between the Saint James Master and any of the jamb figures of Saint-Denis and Chartres. Gilabertus, who signed the Apostles Thomas and Andrew (signatures now lost), projects an elaboration of costume and multiple loop-folds over thighs and knees, which was an innovation. The more minutely animated surfaces of the Apostles by Gilabertus grow out of the capitals of the second series of the cloister of La Daurade. It can be argued that Gilabertus indeed was responsible for many of the capitals of the La Daurade Second Series and certainly carved three capitals from the Saint-Étienne cloister: the Death of John the Baptist, the Wise and the Foolish Virgins, and the Legend of Saint Mary of Egypt (see Seidel, 1977, 115–20, figs. 85–91). Further, Seidel pointed out (1977, 150–55) that this new style of La Daurade Second Series and Saint-Étienne possessed strong Byzantine overtones, with drapery recalling Burgundian sculpture and with connections to the murals of Tavant. Tavant is probably later than Saint-Étienne. It is possible to conclude that some source outside Languedoc has made an impact on the Toulousan tradition. Yet it should not be assumed that Gilabertus' style is distinct from that of Languedoc, since the serrated, folded hems of the mantles of Thomas and Andrew have their counterpart in the Christ of the Moissac tympanum. It is equally valid to interpret the sculpture of Gilabertus as the result of an evolution within the Toulousan tradition.

If we assume for the moment that the Saint-Étienne Apostles and capitals are earlier than Saint-Denis (ca. 1137–1140) and Chartres (mid-1140s), is there any stylistic relationship between Gilabertus' sculpture and these two Early Gothic portals? When the six Apostles of Saint-Étienne by Gilabertus are compared with either the drawings of the jamb statues for Montfaucon or the engravings of the three portals of Saint-Denis (Plate X, 3 and figs. 1, 2), it is quite clear that any stylistic connections between the two monuments are very superficial. In spite of the fact that, with the exception of the four preserved heads from Saint-Denis, we are dealing with eighteenth-century drawings and engravings, all three Saint-Denis portals possess none of the complexity of surfaces of the Saint-Étienne Apostles, such as multiple folds and wide and elaborately decorated collars and hems. The left portal of Saint-Denis (fig. 1) has four cross-legged prophets, but no cascading mantles or arched folds over the figures, as seen over the right and left leg of Thomas and Andrew (Plate XXXI, 5). Further, the heads of Thomas and Andrew (Plate XXXI, 4) are totally different from the Baltimore head from Saint-Denis (Plate IX, 1, 2) with its greater projection and multiple planes. In the Saint-Denis central portal (fig. 2), two jambs with cascading folds over legs recall Gilabertus' Thomas and Andrew (Plate XXXI, 4, 5), yet the complexity of folds of the Saint-Étienne Apostles has no counterpart in the CP Saint-Denis figures. Heads of Thomas and Andrew and of the two paired Apostles by Gilabertus are entirely different from the two heads that originally were on the Saint-Denis central portal: the Baltimore head (Plate VIII) and the recently discovered head of a queen (fig. 3). When compared to the Saint-Denis right portal (Plate X, 2), the arrangement of drapery of the Toulousan figures is much more complex. The Gilabertus figures do not display the same amount of anatomical disjointedness in the arms and hands. It thus seems that the sculpture of Gilabertus has no influence on the formation of Early Gothic at Saint-Denis.

If compared with Chartres West, certain characteristics of Gilabertus' Apostles, such as their surface animation through multiple folds, are found in the CP jamb by the Headmaster (Plate XVII), yet the style of the carving of the surfaces and of the massive square heads of the Chartres figures is totally different. Drapery over the left legs of three of the Chartres jamb statues recalls Thomas and Andrew, yet the proportions of the figures and treatment of the folds have more connections with Burgundian Romanesque than with those of Saint-Étienne at Toulouse (see figs. 12–13). The RP.R1 and 2 Chartres jambs (Plate XVI, 2 and figs. 10a, 10b) are closer stylistically to the Toulouse Andrew and Thomas than are the Chartres CP jambs. Again, in spite of the double cascade of folds over legs of all four figures and the ornamented band across the thigh of one of the paired Apostles, the carving of drapery is more animated and complicated in the Toulousan Apostles. From the point of view of surfaces, Gilabertus' sculpture exhibits more stylistic common denominators with the Chartres CP than with the lost Saint-Denis jambs, yet it is questionable whether any connection exists between Saint-Étienne and either of these two Île-de-France portals.

Willibald Sauerländer, in an overview of early Gothic ("Sculpture on Early Gothic Churches: The State of Research and Open Questions," *Gesta*, IX / 2, 1970, 35, figs. 3–8), pointed out evidence of stylistic contacts between southwestern France and Chartres, specifically between Moissac and sculpture on the archivolts of the Chartres right portal. He compared the heads of Christ of the Moissac tympanum and of the so-called Aristotle and the heads of the Presentation on the Moissac porch with the Dialectic at Chartres. With more than a decade separating Moissac and

Chartres West, Sauerländer assumed an unidentified or lost intermediary link between the two monuments. Since the treatment of drapery of the Moissac Christ and smaller figures on the Moissac porch seem to continue the Languedoc tradition of flat, ironed folds, with animated, zigzag terminations, which is marked contrast to the rounded, plastic projection of the Chartres sculpture, it is questionable whether the ultimate source of Early Gothic is Languedoc. The head of the Moissac Christ does possess some similarities with the Baltimore head from the Saint-Denis left portal (Plate IX, 1, 2), but the multiple surface planes of cheeks, hair, and eyes are quite different in the Saint-Denis head. Again, the origin of the Early Gothic style does not appear to be in Languedoc.

The Infancy of Christ cycle, extending from the left pilaster capital through to the north tower, and the Passion cycle, extending from the CP.R to the south tower, have their basic sources in the West, in Languedoc, or Spain. Scholars have referred to the thematic connections between many of the Chartres scenes and the twenty-one cloister capitals of La Daurade of Toulouse, Second Series, now in the Musée des Augustins (see Heimann, "The Capital Frieze and Pilasters of the Portail Royal, Chartres," *Journal of the Warburg and Courtauld Institutes,* vol. 31, 1968, 75, fn. 12). Each face of many of these Toulousan capitals is framed by short columns supporting arches, which are often crowned with crenellated walls. In the case of the Last Supper capital, crenellated round towers strengthen the corners, yet this architectural frame is quite different from the elaborate baldachins above the Chartres capitals. From the point of view of style, these capitals from La Daurade relate to the Saint-Étienne capitals and Apostles by Gilabertus and exhibit no common denominators with the Chartres capitals, which were created by the Étampes Master and the Saint-Denis Master and their two assistants.

There are, however, two capitals that are stylistically unique to Chartres West. Carved by the same itinerant sculptor, these two depict the Flight into Egypt and part of the Massacre of the Innocents (LP.L1—fig. 80) and Peter cutting off Malchus' ear and the Betrayal (RP.L3—figs. 40, 41). The unusual rubbery anatomy, with limbs bending without aid of joints (see, especially, Herod in the Massacre and the soldier dragging Christ), wattled sleeves, and drilled hems, feet overlapping the torus molding, animation of surfaces by projecting ridge ribs, and undecorated, horizontally designed baldachins—all are characteristics that distinguish these two capitals from the eight by the Étampes Master, four by his assistant, six by the Saint-Denis Master, and two by his assistant.

Where did this interloper come from? Languedoc appears to be a possibility. If these two capitals are compared with the two from the cloister of Saint-Étienne of Toulouse by

80. Chartres, LP.L1 capital, Flight into Egypt and Herod and the Massacre of the Innocents

81. Toulouse, capital from Saint-Étienne (Musée des Augustins), Herod and Salome (Austin)

82. Toulouse, same capital as fig. 81, Presentation of head of John the Baptist (Austin)

Gilabertus (Seidel, 1977, 115–18, figs. 83–86, 88–90), certain common stylistic features emerge. The Toulouse capitals, depicting episodes in the Death of John the Baptist (figs. 81, 82) and the Wise and the Foolish Virgins, exhibit similar rubbery, bending anatomy. Raised ridge-folds and ringed or wattled sleeves animate the surface of capitals from both monuments, yet the complexity of drapery is more apparent in the Saint-Étienne capitals. Some of the heads of the Chartres capitals find counterparts in those of Herod and Salome in the Temptation episode and several in the Feast of Herod. In spite of the similarities between the Toulouse and Chartres capitals, the carving of the Chartres capitals is less subtle than in those by Gilabertus. It would appear, however, that the Itinerant sculptor of Chartres came from Languedoc. His two capitals seem to be the only stylistic connection between Languedoc and the Early Gothic sculpture of Chartres.

BURGUNDY

In contrast to monuments in Western France, Provence, and Languedoc, Burgundian churches of the 1130s and earlier contain ornamental sculpture similar in motif and style to ornament on Île-de-France buildings, especially Chartres West (see 48–49, Plate XXXIV). On the transept portals of Paray-le-Monial are four geometric and ornamental patterns (four-leaf clover, stepped meander, folded band or ribbon, and double-axe), which have their counterparts on thirteen of the fourteen surviving short columns that support the jambs on Chartres CP and the two adjoining splays (see Plate XIII, 3 and Plates XVII, XVIII). Surface treatment is similar on both monuments. Two of these motifs appear on the horizontal, flat plinths crowning the bases of the Saint-Denis portals (folded ribbon and double-axe—Plate III, 4, 5), yet at Saint-Denis all ornament on plinths was carved in very low relief. In spite of the fact that these patterns are common to the vocabulary of Romanesque art, the similarity in both motif and style between Paray-le-Monial and Chartres West seems to indicate Burgundy as a possible source for Early Gothic ornament.

Corinthian or composite capitals abound in Romanesque sculpture. Even though the majority are derived from a similar Roman format, great variety exists in the Romanesque transformations of antique models by sculptors of different regions of France. On the façade of Saint-Gilles-du Gard, three large capitals (LP.L and RP.L and RP.R) are Roman *spolia,* and five monolithic columns of different heights and design are also Roman. The remaining capitals on the portals, in the nave and on the fragment of the choir of Saint-Gilles, are Romanesque, but very close stylistically

to the antique models (see Stoddard, 1973, 118–21, figs. 3, 7, 166–69). In Languedoc, the Corinthian-type capitals are one step removed from the Roman. Although elements of the classical prototype, such as vestigal volutes and central rosettes, remain, the shape of the capitals and the flat surfaces of acanthus leaves and palmettes are unclassical (see the Moissac cloister, Plate XXX, 1, 2). A similar modification of Roman models is displayed in the capitals of Saint-Sernin of Toulouse (see Thomas Lyman, "Terminology, Typology, Taxonomy: An Approach to the Study of Architectural Sculpture of the Romanesque Period," *Gazette des Beaux-Arts,* LXXXVIII, 1976, 223–27 and "Raymond Gairard and Romanesque Building Campaigns at Saint-Sernin in Toulouse," *Journal of the Society of Architectural Historians,* XXXVII, 1978, 71–91).

In Burgundy, the impact of Roman architecture and decoration on Romanesque style is abundantly evident in the interiors of Cluny III, Paray-le-Monial, and Autun. Monuments such as the two city gates of Autun exerted a strong influence on the Burgundian master masons. A Roman Corinthian capital is preserved in the Musée Lapidaire at Autun (see Denis Grivot and George Zarnecki, *Gislebertus, Sculptor of Autun,* 1961, 23, fig. g). When this antique capital is compared with the Corinthian capital from the choir of Cluny III, it is difficult to determine whether the Cluny one is Roman *spolium* or Romanesque. In the Cluny capital, the continuous outward curve of the silhouette and the general flatness of leaves, as well as the stylistic parallels with the other seven Cluny capitals, prove that it is Romanesque (see Whitney S. Stoddard, "The Eight Capitals of the Cluny Hemicycle," *Gesta,* XX / 1, 1981, 51–58). Several capitals in the Vézelay narthex exhibit the evolution of the Corinthian capitals in Burgundy (Plate XXXIV, 6). All elements of the Roman format are preserved: three interlocking tiers of acanthus palmettes and tangent scrolls at the corners and under the central rosette. The proportions, however, have shifted to a narrower, more flaring profile when contrasted with either the Roman prototype or the Cluny capital. Like the tall pilasters, which articulate the nave piers of Cluny, Paray-le-Monial, and Autun, the proportion of the Vézelay capital is attenuated and unclassical. The predominance of classical sources for Burgundian ornament and the similar stylistic treatment whether in triforia, bases, portals, or choir screen can be found in the campaigns of 1120–1130 at Cluny III, Paray-le-Monial, and Vézelay, as clearly described and illustrated by C. Edson Armi and Elizabeth Bradford Smith ("The Choir Screen of Cluny III," *Art Bulletin,* LXVI, 4, 1984, 556–73).

It is capitals like this Vézelay example (W.S.S., p. 49, Plate XXII) or others in the Vézelay narthex that seem to have influenced those of the south tower of Chartres, which was under construction in 1145. The main stylistic differences between the sculpture inside the narthex of Saint-Denis (dedicated in 1140) and the Chartres north tower (begun in 1134) on one hand and those of the Chartres south tower on the other hand are so apparent that one must assume the presence of sculptors from outside the Île-de-France and, more specifically, it would seem, from Burgundy in the 1140s.

Corinthian-type capitals of Saulieu are also related to those in the Chartres south tower (see Plate XXXIV, 3). The sculpture of Saulieu cannot be dated around 1119, as previously assumed, but rather in the late 1130s. It was carved by at least three sculptors whose work can be identified at Autun.

Any discussion of manuscripts as possible sources of sculpture is questionable, since monks of the monastic establishment created the illuminations and lay masons carved the sculpture. Yet the role of the clergy in establishing the sculptural program should not be overlooked. We have already emphasized the fact that a Byzantine manuscript helped establish some of the scenes from the early life of the Virgin on the Chartres capital frieze. As discussed in 1952 (49–52, Plates XXXV, XXVI), many common denominators exist in motif and style between the Bible of Saint-Bénigne de Dijon, together with the Légendaire de Cîteaux and the plinths and colonnettes of Saint-Denis (Plates III–VI) and some of those on Chartres West. In spite of the fact that many of the designs in the folios of the Légendaire and the Dijon Bible can be found in manuscripts in other regions of Western Europe, it is the detailed treatment of vines and fillers set against a dark ground that suggests a relationship between these two related Burgundian manuscripts and the two Île-de-France monuments. Further, the illuminated initials of these two folios, with vines encircling and overlapping birds, have their sculptured counterpart in the fragment of a capital from the narthex gallery of Vézelay (Plate XXXIV, 5—now in Princeton). Finally, the origin of the statue-column in Cistercian initials should be mentioned, but only as the vaguest possibility (see Plate XXXVI, 3, 4). Abbot Suger made five trips to Rome between 1112 and 1129, probably passing through Burgundy, and attended a dedication at the Cluniac Abbey of La Charité-sur-Loire in 1107. He thus must have been very familiar with Burgundy.

VÉZELAY

In 1952 (52–53), the attempt to discover stylistic connections in the figural sculpture of Romanesque Burgundy and the Early Gothic Île-de-France resulted in extremely tentative conclusions. Francis Salet's detailed and profusely illustrated monograph of 1948 (*La Madeleine de Vézelay*)

greatly increased our knowledge of the architecture and sculpture of this extraordinary monument. In 1983, C. Edson Armi's two-volume study (*Masons and Sculptors in Romanesque Burgundy, The New Aesthetic of Cluny III*) was the first to coordinate the study of masonry, masons' marks, architecture, and sculpture and to describe a new chronology for Burgundian architecture and sculpture. In 1984, Lydwine Saulnier and Neil Stratford published the catalogue of the Musée Lapidaire (*La sculpture oubliée de Vézelay*). This publication is much more extensive than the usual catalogue, since it includes 140 plates of sculpture *in situ* at Vézelay and of comparative sculpture of other Romanesque monuments, as well as 291 figures of the sculpture in the new Musée Lapidaire, which opened at Vézelay in July 1977. The catalogue of 391 objects follows their provenance: the western façade, interior of the narthex, nave, and eastern sections of the church, monastic structures, and various unlocated fragments. In each of the six sections are essays on the provenance and the restorations, a stylistic study, and the detailed catalogue. For the past ten years, I have been studying sporadically the *in situ* sculpture of the western exterior portals, fragments from the façade housed in the narthex gallery until 1977, and related problems of the Vézelay sculpture.

VÉZELAY: HISTORY AND ARCHAEOLOGY

Following Salet (21–31), a bare outline of the history of Vézelay is as follows:

1096—decision by Abbot Artaud to replace the Carolingian Church.

1104, April 21—consecration of the Romanesque choir and transept (?).

1106—Abbot Artaud assassinated by townspeople of Vézelay.

1110–1120—Peter the Venerable at Vézelay.

1120, July 21 (Feast Day of Mary Magdalene)—fire destroyed the Carolingian nave, and many worshippers perished.

1132—dedication by Pope Calixtus II.

1146 (Easter Sunday)—Saint Bernard launched the Second Crusade.

Salet (148) integrated these facts with the study of architecture and sculpture and came up with the following building campaigns:

1096–1104—choir and transept (now replaced by the Gothic choir of 1185–1190, but vestiges of transept remain in the crossing).

83. Vézelay, north flank of western bay of nave and two eastern bays of narthex

84. Vézelay, interior of junction of nave wall (right)
and east face of narthex wall

85. Vézelay, narthex wall (left)
and west face of narthex wall

1125–1140 / 1145—narthex portals and nave (built from west to east).

c.1145—lower narthex and façade portals.

1150—gallery of narthex completed.

Saulnier and Stratford (19) follow generally Salet's chronology, but narrowed the span of dating as follows:

1120–c.1135—narthex portals and nave constructed west to east.

c.1135–1145—lower narthex and west façade.

1140–1150—capitals of upper narthex.

A study of the masonry along the flanks of the abbey reveals a continuity of masonry between nave and narthex that brings into question the construction of the narthex after completion of the nave. The north flank (fig. 83—the last bay of nave on left and the eastern two bays of narthex on right) exhibits similar-shaped blocks and almost the exact same number of courses (around thirty) between the bases and the sills of windows. If the restorations of the south flank are removed, the same continuous masonry is clearly evident from the nave into the two eastern bays of the narthex.

On the inside of the westernmost north aisle bay (fig. 84), the junction of narthex and nave exhibits the contemporaneity of the nave wall with its thirty courses, corresponding to the number of courses on the exterior, and the narthex wall of large ashlar blocks. Several of the courses of the narthex wall are dovetailed into the nave wall, including the crowning molding across the top of the portal and under the nave window. The narthex side of this portal (fig. 85) shows the same ashlar courses as the nave face (fig. 84), with the capital zone corresponding to the next to highest course below the spring of the archivolts on the north aisle face. Since the north wall of the narthex was rebuilt in 1843 (see Saulnier and Stratford, 71), it is difficult to interpret the juncture of the nave wall and the eastern narthex wall. On the other hand, the system of dovetailing the ashlar courses and abutting the north narthex wall against these blocks corresponds to the treatment in the north aisle with the original masonry (figs. 84, 85). Thus a study of masonry seems to indicate that the lower walls of the nave and narthex were erected simultaneously.

It is uncertain what part of the new Romanesque campaign of Abbot Artaud, begun in 1096, was consecrated in 1104. Following these eight years of building, one must not assume that the sixteen years before the disastrous fire of 1120, which consumed the Carolingian nave, were devoid of extensive construction. The murder of Abbot Artaud in 1106 may have interrupted building for a short time, but it is highly plausible to argue that the exterior walls of both the nave and narthex were constructed around and in front of the Carolingian nave before the 1120 fire. A generation later, Abbot Suger was confronted with the same practical problem—the safety of crowds of worshippers in a small Carolingian church. Suger constructed a new narthex (1140) and a new choir (1144) and began to construct the outer walls of the nave before his death in 1151. The Carolingian nave of Saint-Denis was finally replaced by the superb Rayonnant one in the middle years of the thirteenth century. At Vézelay, the fire of 1120 obviously necessitated the building of the present nave piers and vaults. Just when in the years between 1096 and 1120 the outer walls of the nave and narthex of Vézelay were constructed must remain uncertain, although Armi (89–90, 177–90) dated the lower exterior walls of the nave, the lower sections of the three narthex portals, including the capitals, in the 1096–1104 campaign on the basis of masons' marks, masonry molding, and stylistic relationships of these capitals to those from the chevet of Cluny III. It is certainly possible to state that the outer walls of both the nave and the narthex predate the fire of 1120.

The first campaign of the narthex was probably a lower porch of at least two bays in depth, as evidenced in the continuity of the masonry along the flanks of the abbey. Saulnier and Stratford (77–78 and Plate 42) compare this open porch with that of Perrecy-les-Forges. Two walled-up doorways on each side of the narthex gave access to the upper level of this porch from stairs in the aisles, which no longer exist (see figs. 84, 85). The change in design of the narthex was probably caused by the fire of 1120. Let us now turn to the sculpture of the outer, west portals and attempt to determine if indeed there is evidence for dating the façade around 1120 or earlier than c.1135–1145, as proposed by Saulnier and Stratford (5, 19, 33–37).

THE WEST FAÇADE OF VÉZELAY

In 1793, figures on the tympanum, lintel of the central portal, and capitals on the three portals were partially hacked off (see Salet, 1948, 32, and Archives des Monuments Historiques, Yonne, Vézelay, No. 1586, Dossier I (1824–1848). Largely because of pressure from Prosper Mérimée, Inspector of Historical Monuments, funds were voted in 1837 for the restoration of Vézelay, which was becoming a virtual ruin. On February 13, 1840, Viollet-le-Duc, at the age of twenty-six, was placed in charge of the restorations. Preserved in the Archives des Monuments Historiques are his detailed report, dated March 21, 1840, on the needed repairs and the bill for his drawings made between May 1840 and February 1842 (see figs. 86, 89). Since the condition of the vaults, roofs, and buttresses was so precarious, the restoration of the west facade was postponed until the 1850s, after Viollet-le-Duc had summarized the necessary repairs for each portal and their projected costs (November 4, 1850—*Archives Monuments Historiques, Yonne, Vézelay,* No. 1587, Dossier II, 1849–1870). Documents in the archives detail the cost of moving the damaged tympanum and lintel from the central portal to the cloister area south of the abbey in 1858. Although two letters of 1859 of Viollet-le-Duc are missing from the files, it can be assumed that by that year the new tympanum and lintel and thirteen new capitals, replacing those damaged, were completed. Only six original capitals are now *in situ* on the facade (LP.L2, 3; LP.R1, 2, 3; RP.R2), plus the abacus block over the trumeau; the majority of the damaged capitals are now in the Musée Lapidaire at Vézelay (Saulnier and Stratford, 27–37, Cat. 1–17, figs. 3–24).

The tympanum and lintel of the central portal, removed to south of the abbey in 1858, was drawn by Viollet-le-Duc in 1840 (fig. 86). Part of the wings of Matthew, the halo and two areas of drapery of Christ, and part of the wing of the angel supporting the lower right corner of the mandorla were accented by darker lines in the drawing and can be clearly seen today (figs. 87, 88a–d). The tympanum, 4.90 meters wide and carved originally in five blocks, rested on the lintel, which is in the garden and which is 6.31 meters wide. By contrast, the lintel of the central portal of the narthex is 7.57 meters wide, which proves that this tympanum and lintel were carved for the west facade of Vézelay.

The preserved sections of the tympanum (figs. 87, 88a–d) exhibit an unusual drapery style. Narrow, flat planes, shifting slightly inward at the bottom, are separated by a rounded, projecting ridge-fold, a more pointed ridge-fold, and by the top, undercut edge of the flat bands. Windblown terminations (fig. 88a, c) are animated by expanding, cascading pleats of rounded or edged ridge-folds with folded hems. The relief is relatively flat. Extensive drillwork, resembling metalwork, appears on the rim and cross of Christ's halo and a small section of the mandorla to the right of the halo (88b). The wing of Matthew is badly mutilated, but the wings of the angel supporting the mandorla (fig. 88d) display overlapping flat planes with rounded edges.

Saulnier and Stratford (1984, 33–34, 245–46, figs. 26–27) at first saw in the paired groups of ridge folds the signature of Gislebertus and the atelier of Autun and compared the tympanum with six fragments in the museum (Cat. 221–25, figs. 182–87), four of which will be discussed later. However, because of the deplorable condition of the tympanum and similar folds found in two capitals from the gallery of the narthex (Cat. 108—figs. 63–65 and Cat. 111—figs. 71–73 to be analyzed later), attributed by Salet to the Master of the Miracle of Tobias and dated 1140–

1150, the authors concluded that the tympanum was either carved by a sculptor from the Autun atelier or by the Tobias Master, who knew Autun indirectly. In my opinion, this tympanum is by Gislebertus himself and was carved around 1120, not between 1135 and 1140. I agree with the authors that the almost completely destroyed lintel, illustrated here only in Viollet-le-Duc's drawing (fig. 86), was carved by the same sculptor responsible for the tympanum.

When Viollet-le-Duc's drawing of the left and central portal of the façade (fig. 89) is compared with the recent photograph of the two portals (fig. 90), it is clear that in the left portal only the LP.L1 capital was replaced (see detail of the west face in fig. 89), while all the capitals of the central portal are nineteenth-century copies of the damaged ones now in the museum. Only the abacus above the central trumeau is original and supports the modern lintel and tympanum.

Ornamental capitals crown columns in the splays of each portal (fig. 90). The LP.R splay displays Jacob Wrestling with the Angel over the doorjamb and two Corinthian capitals (fig. 91). The complexity of their surfaces with extensive drillwork on stems and leaves is close stylistically to the decorative capitals in the lower narthex (see Salet, Plate 48). The shape of the facade capitals is squatter than those in the narthex, and the leaves project less. Most of the floral capitals in the nave are less complex, with simple concave leaves. However, several capitals in the western sections of the north aisle exhibit elaborate surfaces and extensive drillwork (Salet—Nave no.39, no.68, no.70). In general, it would appear that the ornamental sculpture on the facade and the lower narthex was carved by the same sculptor or sculptors. Saulnier and Stratford (36–37) stressed the strong connection between ornamental capitals of facade and lower narthex but stated, like Salet, a relationship between ornamental capitals in the eastern nave and narthex façade. The style of these façade and narthex capitals seems to me to be closer to the three capitals in the northwest corner of the nave.

The Struggle of Jacob and the Angel (LP.R1, doorjamb—fig. 92) portrays the two protagonists with interlocking arms and feet, in a subtle composition that accents the corner of the rectangular block. Thick necks support large heads with wide eyes and with hair covering most of the foreheads. Rounded, parallel ridge-folds animate chests, arms, and the mantle of the angel. The flaring folds with undulating hems between the legs recall details of the west tympanum (fig. 88c), although in the tympanum the convex folds are less rounded.

The same subject appears on the fourth, southern pier from the crossing (fig. 93). In the nave capital, the sculptural problem is quite different, since the feet of Jacob and the Angel must cling to the rounded base of the capital,

86. Vézelay, drawing of CP, façade tympanum and lintel
by Viollet-le-Duc (1840) (Arch. Photo, Paris)

87. Vézelay, CP, façade tympanum

88a. Vézelay, CP, façade tympanum,
detail of drapery over Christ's right arm

88b. Vézelay, CP, façade tympanum,
detail of halo of Christ

88c. Vézelay, CP, façade tympanum,
detail of drapery over Christ's left arm

88d. Vézelay, CP, façade tympanum,
detail of wings of angel (right of lower mandorla)

89. Vézelay, LP and CP of façade by Viollet-le-Duc (1840) (Arch. Photo, Paris)

90. Vézelay, LP and CP of façade

91. Vézelay, Façade, LP.R capitals: Jacob struggling with
the Angel, and two Corinthian-type capitals

92. Vézelay, façade. LP.R1, Jacob struggling with Angel

93. Vézelay, nave capital, Jacob struggling with Angel

and ornament and wings fill the rectangular, upper corners. In spite of similar emotional intensity in both capitals, there appear to be many stylistic differences, especially in the treatment of drapery. The undercutting of the surfaces is much less apparent in the nave capital. The façade capital has thick, rounded folds covering the majority of the surfaces, whereas the nave capital has these raised folds only on Jacob's right arm. Salet (157–58) attributed both these capitals to his "Master of the Deliverance of Peter," named after a capital depicting that subject on the easternmost north nave pier. Salet placed this sculptor at the end of the nave campaign, suggesting that he carved three capitals on eastern piers and five below the springing of the vaults. This Peter Master, according to Salet, then became the leading master in the lower narthex and sculpted three capitals and two on the façade, including Jacob and the Angel. In spite of some similarities, it seems to me that two different sculptors carved the same theme.

Another historiated capital from the right portal of the façade (RP.L1—S. and S. Cat. 10, 47–48) depicts Loth receiving two Angels. This fragment of the inner face (fig. 94) depicts a striding angel and foot, part of the mantle and wing of a second angel. The bodies are completely enveloped in multiple, curving, parallel ridge-folds that are exactly like the drapery on the upper torsos of Jacob and the angel on the left portal (fig. 92). Relatively large heads with practically no foreheads, and with wide eyes, thick necks, looping, closely packed ridge-folds, straight falling folds with folded hems are all characteristics found in the two façade capitals (fig. 92, 94), but not present in the nave capital (fig. 93). Salet attributed the Loth fragment to his Peter Master.

A capital in the narthex, Joseph and Potiphar's Wife (fig. 95), identified by Salet as by his Peter Master, is identical in style to the Loth capital (fig. 94), by the Façade Master. Rounded, projecting folds, evenly and closely spaced across the legs, chest, and arms like an all-over webbing, portray a distinct style. Eight other capitals in the lower narthex resemble the Façade Master's capitals in the narthex and on the façade (figs. 92, 94, 95), but they possess less quality. Salet attributed them to the "Artisan of the History of David," an assistant of his Peter Master. The strong stylistic relationships among all the lower narthex capitals and those on the west façade portals suggest that quite different sculptors, employing rounded ridge-folds, were responsible for the lower narthex capitals, both decorative and historiated. The connection between the lower narthex and west façade and nave seems tenuous at best.

Perhaps the reason for this divergence in style between the nave capitals on the one hand and the sculpture on and from the west façade and lower narthex on the other are the basic differences between the leading sculptors who dominated these two large projects. At least five sculptors were responsible for the nave capitals as described by Salet: the Tympanum Master (after the central portal of the narthex), the Assistant of the Tympanum Master, the Maker of Medallions, the Legend of Saint Eugénie, and the Master of the Deliverance of Peter. The artistic inspiration for all these capitals seems to be the two sculptors of the narthex portals. The Angel and Demon (narthex LP.L1—fig. 96), with thin figures surrounded by ornament and articulated by tightly clinging drapery of flat, overlapping folds, illustrates the basic style that is either continued in the nave capitals or transformed by the three sculptors not involved in the narthex portals (see fig. 93, nave capital). According to Armi (1983), the Avenas and Perrecy masters carved most of the sculpture of the narthex portals in three campaigns. Further, to oversimplify, Armi believes that the Perrecy Master began his career at Perrecy-les-Forges, continued at Vézelay (he sculpted capital LP.L1—fig. 96), carved some of the Cluny III chevet capitals, and returned to Vézelay to sculpt the tympanum and left-hand Apostles of the narthex central portal. From the point of view of the search for sources of the Early Gothic, the sculpture of nave and narthex portals of Vézelay manifest pure Burgundian Romanesque, as seen in Avenas, Perrecy, Cluny III, and other related monuments, and contains no stylistic relationships with the Île-de-France.

Sculpture of the lower narthex and façade of Vézelay is, however, a quite different style, dominated by raised, rounded ridge-folds and generally shorter figures with large heads. The leading sculptor of this campaign seems to have been the master of the central portal of the façade (figs. 87, 88), here identified as Gislebertus of Autun. More will be included later on the stylistic connection of the tympanum with fragments by Gislebertus in the Museum of Vézelay as well as with his sculpture at Autun. At least one assistant was responsible for capitals on the façade and in the lower narthex (figs. 92, 94, 95). A possible chronology for all the Vézelay sculpture will be proposed after the sections on the upper narthex and the sculpture by Gislebertus in the Museum at Vézelay are discussed.

THE VÉZELAY UPPER NARTHEX

Capitals of the upper narthex suffered extensively as a result of a fire in 1819 and the collapse of the central vault in 1843, after the restorations had commenced in the previous year. The decade of rebuilding witnessed the replacement of the vaults and the capitals of the freestanding piers and colonnade (Saulnier and Stratford, 71). When all this sculpture from the upper narthex, outer façade, and other parts of the abbey, removed from the fabric during the restorations or discovered during renovations, was stored

94. Vézelay, façade. RP.L1,
Loth and the Angels

95. Vézelay, lower narthex
Joseph and Potiphar's Wife (Austin)

96. Vézelay, narthex portal LP.L1,
Angel and Demon (Austin)

193

97. Vézelay, gallery of narthex,
Pharaoh and the Wise Women (left face)

97a. Vézelay, detail of fig. 97

98. Vézelay, gallery of narthex,
Pharaoh and the Wise Women (central face)

99. Vézelay, gallery of narthex,
Pharaoh and the Wise Women (right face)

100. Étampes, L2,
Annunciation
and Visitation

102. Vézelay,
gallery of narthex,
Three Angels

102a. Vézelay,
detail of 102.

103. Vézelay,
gallery of narthex,
Ascension
(right side)

101. Étampes,
Left jamb statues
(Austin)

in the upper narthex, along with more than one hundred plaster casts, it was difficult to study and photograph. The new installation of the Musée de Vézelay in July of 1977 and the superb catalogue of Saulnier and Stratford (1984) make it possible to analyze more thoroughly the Vézelay fragments and, more specifically for this study, the extraordinary capitals from the narthex gallery.

The capital, depicting the Pharaoh and the Wise Women (figs. 97–99), originally in the south gallery, second bay, fifth from the west, manifests many stylistic characteristics important to the search for the Early Gothic in Burgundy (see Saulnier and Stratford, 81, 95, Cat. 111, figs. 71–74). On the left face (figs. 97, 97a), two women with hands raised approach the enthroned Pharaoh (?) who is under an elaborate baldachin. The legs of the two attenuated women are articulated either by rounded, curving, projecting ridge-folds or by tangential, vertical ridge-folds. The cross-legged Pharaoh reposes on a throne with downward-looping folds decorating the mantle covering his chest. Both legs reveal projecting ridge-folds, while three wind-blown folds animate the hems of the undergarment over his ankles. His right, crossed leg is accentuated by parallel concave folds with a folded zigzag termination over the knee. Two antigravitation folds cover the edge of the throne. The treatment of drapery over the Pharaoh's left forearm and thigh is the most unusual stylistic feature (fig. 97a). Here, the plain rounded surfaces are animated by raised folds. On his thigh, two folds emerge from under the mantle, with a third creating a half oval over his hip. His left forearm is treated similarly, with an oval formed in the middle. Over these figures are two arches with exaggerated dentils that spring from an abacus of three moldings. Rounded towers of two stories, with one opening below, three and a conical roof, are set back above the spandrels and the outer corners of the capital, while triangular towers with three windows surmount the arches.

The badly damaged front face (fig. 98) portrays two women approaching a second enthroned figure. Although borders of pearls animate the hems of the mantle of the left-hand figure, the treatment of drapery resembles that of the women on the left face. The right face (fig. 99) contains two male figures and a second figure enthroned on the corner of the capital. Drillwork animates the concavities of the folds of the right-hand and enthroned figure. Cascading ridge-folds accent legs and protruding stomachs, as in figures on the left face. One curving bundle of ridge-folds covers the left leg of the middle figure.

When the Vézelay Pharaoh capital is compared with a capital of the Étampes portal, depicting the Annunciation and Visitation (L2—fig. 100), stylistic similarities are apparent in spite of the considerably smaller size of the Étampes capital (.665 meters, compared to approximately .32 meters).

All the figures at Étampes are articulated by projecting ridge-folds that curve upward or downward in a looped arrangement. Knees accented by raised circles of folds relate to the left hip of the Pharaoh, while the treatment of drapery over the arms of three of the Étampes figures is identical to that of the left arm of the Pharaoh. The rounded surfaces of the limbs of both the Vézelay and Étampes capitals are animated by uniform projecting folds. The baldachin over the Pharaoh capital appears to be the tentative model of the continuous one necessitated by the running capital-frieze of Étampes. If compared to the Étampes Nativity and Bathing of the Christ Child (L3—fig. 68), the same stylistic features are apparent. In some of the other capitals, such as the Adoration of Magi, in which each figure is framed by an arch, the flying folds, seen in muted form in the Pharaoh, are free to extend laterally (see Plate XXIII, 5). Thus, from the point of view of the capitals alone, it would appear that the Vézelay sculptor carved the left side of the capital-frieze of Étampes.

The south portal of Notre-Dame at Étampes was created by Louis VII to gain direct access to the church from the street connecting it to the royal, fortified château on the western outskirts of the town (see W.S.S. history of Étampes, 27–28, Plates XXXIII, XXXIV). Since the Étampes portal contained columnar jamb figures, it must be assumed that the Vézelay sculptor visited Paris and Saint-Denis. Since the role of the royalty was so important to Étampes, it is possible to suggest that Louis VII commissioned the single portal in answer to the elaborate consecration of portals and narthex of Saint-Denis in 1140 by Abbot Suger.

In light of the stylistic relationship between the Pharaoh capital of Vézelay and the frieze of Étampes, can these unusual characteristics also be found on the large-scaled sculpture of Étampes? As in the Vézelay capital, but within the limitations of the strict rectangularity and frontality of statue-columns, the Étampes jamb figures display the same emphasis on tubular anatomy animated by multiple ridge-folds (fig. 101 and Plates XXIII, XXIV), yet surfaces are more complex at Étampes. The projecting stomachs of the standing figures of the Pharaoh capital, with their circular folds, have their counterpart in four of the six Étampes statues. Parallel and closely spaced ridge-folds articulate the legs in two standing figures on the Pharaoh capital and four of the thighs of the Étampes jambs and the lower half of LP.L1 of Chartres (figs. 9, 9b), which is by the Étampes Master. Some details, such as the bottom hems of horizontal bands, vertical staffs held by hands, and bunches of vertical folds between legs are possibly derived from his study of the jamb statues of the Saint-Denis central portal (fig. 2). Once his transformed style was established in the different context of jamb-statues and running frieze, he finished the portal with at least two assistants (see fig. 69–78).

Upon completion of Étampes in the early 1140s, he was called to Chartres to collaborate with three other major sculptors on the Royal Portals.

A large fragment of a capital (fig. 102) depicting three angels (the north narthex gallery, third bay, southwesternmost capital) is also by the Pharaoh Master (see Saulnier and Stratford, 81, 96, Cat. 116, fig. 87). Drapery on the right leg of the central angel is related to that of the figure of the Pharaoh (figs. 97, 97a), while the unusual treatment of ridge-folds over the right-hand angel and the left elbow of the central one is evident on the left arm and thigh of the enthroned Pharaoh. The folded hems of cloaks, especially over shoulders, is identical on the left woman in the Pharaoh capital and on the right angel. Windblown drapery hems, with extra parallel ridge-folds at the hems over the ankles, appear in both capitals. Both the depth of relief and the carving of surfaces demonstrate that these two capitals were carved by the same sculptor.

A third capital (fig. 103), from the first north bay, fifth from the west, originally portrayed the Ascension, with the Christ and the kneeling Virgin on the angle and three Apostles under an arcade and approaching from the left and the right. Most of the Christ and the Virgin and the left-hand figures have been destroyed (see Saulnier and Stratford, 81, 94, Cat. 113, figs. 78–80). Square hands with fingers becoming hands without knuckles and ridge-folds over legs and arms resemble those characteristics in both the Pharaoh and three Angel capitals. Because of their beards, the Apostles' heads (fig. 103) appear more pointed when contrasted with the two womens' heads in the Pharaoh capital (fig. 97), yet treatment of the eyes and ears is similar. Surfaces of the Ascension capital are rougher and more crudely carved. The expressive power of this capital is also seen in the Angel capital (fig. 102). It would seem that the Ascension capital was an early work of either the Pharaoh Master or by his assistant.

Salet (160) attributed these three capitals and others to the Master of the Miracle of Tobias, after a capital in the upper narthex (his N. 37). On the other hand, Saulnier and Stratford (81–84), have three talented sculptors working in the gallery as follows: the Master of the Ascension (fig. 103), the most outstanding, carving the Three Angels (fig. 102) and two other capitals (Cat. 114, 112) and probably four more, which exist only in fragments (Cat. 228, 115, 235, 124); and the second sculptor is the Pharaoh Master (figs. 97–99), whom they associate with Salet's Master of the Miracle of Tobias (Salet, No. 37 and Saulnier and Stratford, Plates 50, 51). As already pointed out, the Pharaoh Master certainly carved the Three Angels. Also, the Ascension is very close to the style of these two capitals. The Tobias Master capital does exhibit certain characteristics, such as elongated figures and poses with parallel legs, which relate it to the Pharaoh capital, yet the grouping of parallel ridge-folds in twos and threes is closer to the Autun-like fragments at Vézelay, to be discussed later. As Saulnier and Stratford stated (84 and fn. 51), the Tobias Master followed the treatment of ornament of the façade and lower narthex, but his use of raised folds related him to the Autun sculpture at Vézelay and to Autun itself. They concluded that the west façade tympanum could have been the work of the Tobias Master just as well as of an Autunois sculptor, created just before the tribune capitals of the 1140s. Saulnier and Stratford's third sculptor (85–86) is the Master of the Resurrection of Lazarus (Cat. 121, figs. 93–96), whose style is totally foreign to Vézelay.

If the Pharaoh Master worked in the upper narthex at Vézelay in the 1140s, it would obviously be impossible for him to visit Saint-Denis soon after 1140 and create Étampes in the early 1140s. Before attempting to place the upper narthex sculpture in chronological campaigns, let us turn to the Autun-like sculpture in the Vézelay Museum.

AUTUNOIS SCULPTURE AT VÉZELAY: GISLEBERTUS

Four fragments in the Vézelay Museum (figs. 104–107) are closely related stylistically to both the outer façade tympanum of Vézelay (figs. 87–88d) and the sculpture at Autun by Gislebertus. Granted that the mutilated condition of the tympanum limits analysis, sufficient details do exist to allow significant comparisons. The drapery over the Christ's hands on the tympanum (figs. 88a, 88c) consists of rounded ridge-folds and convex edges in groups of three. This same system appears on two figures of the pedimentlike piece and in the fragments of lower legs and simple torso (figs. 104–107). Although the grouping of folds varies in number from three to five on the Autunois fragments, the predominant articulation of drapery on both tympanum and fragments is the projecting ridge-fold. The closest relationship is the single torso (fig. 106) and the tympanum. In the torso, the damaged flying fold resembles those on the tympanum (figs. 88a, 88c), although the relief is lower on the tympanum. Hems of mantles are not animated by geometric patterns in the only two preserved sections of drapery of the tympanum, as they are in the museum fragments, yet the halo and top of the mandorla of the Christ reveal elaborate drillwork of ovals and circles, ressembling metal work (fig. 88b). The parallel, vertical ridge-folds of the second figure from the right in the large fragment (fig. 104) has its simplified counterpart in the extreme left figure of the lintel of the façade central portal (see Saulnier and Stratford, fig. 30). Thus, there appears to be sufficient evidence to attribute the tympanum and fragments to the same sculptor.

197

104. Vézelay, Gislebertus, triangular fragment of a tomb (?)

105. Vézelay, Gislebertus, lower legs of two figures.

106. Vézelay, Gislebertus, torso of figures.

107. Vézelay, Gislebertus, upper torsos of two figures

There can be no doubt that these four fragments and the façade tympanum, all of which are of the highest quality, are the work of Gislebertus of Autun. This is confirmed by comparisons with three details of the tympanum of Autun, signed by Gislebertus (figs. 109–11). Drapery with bunches of ridge-folds in the Autun Christ, curving, falling parallel folds that terminate in serrated hems, and windblown folds at ankle level (see detail, fig. 110) are apparent on both the Autun tympanum and the Vézelay fragments. Every part of figure 104—aedicule with figure, door, tower, standing figure with skirt, female figure with parallel folds, and drapery of the other two figures—can be discovered in capitals by Gislebertus at Autun.

Grivot and Zarnecki (French edition, 1960, 152–53) argued that Gislebertus was at Vézelay between 1120 and 1125 and sculpted two of the fragments (figs. 104, 105). After fifteen years at Autun, he returned to Vézelay, where one of his best assistants carved the west tympanum. In the English edition (1961, 174), the authors postulated that Gislebertus was responsible for two of the fragments and probably the tympanum. They believed that the tympanum was carved soon after 1120 for the narthex central portal, but the present narthex portal was carved instead, with the Gislebertus tympanum finally erected on the west façade around 1140. As already pointed out, the narthex tympanum and lintel are considerably wider than the façade tympanum. Thus the Gislebertus tympanum and lintel were designed for and erected on the west façade.

Armi (1983, 109–13) proposed that Gislebertus came from Cluny around 1120, and he attributed to him two of the fragments (figs. 106, 107). He did not discuss the tympanum. Saulnier and Stratford (1984, 33–35) dated the west façade 1135–1145 and believed that the tympanum was either sculpted by the atelier of Gislebertus or the Master of the Miracles of Tobias, who worked in the narthex but who knew Autun indirectly. They believed that the fragments, just discussed, represented the style of Autun and dated from 1120–1130.

Where in the abbey were these Vézelay fragments by Gislebertus located? Salet (46–48) thought that they were parts of the side narthex portals for the lower porch campaign, but Saulnier and Stratford (172) pointed out that no space exists for portal sculpture below the doors in the narthex wall (see figs. 84, 85). These authors have discovered and catalogued other fragments that belong to this group (Cat. 224, 225, 242—figs. 185, 186, 187, 203; stolen pieces—fig. 185; Fogg Art Museum, Addendum IV, 1, 249, fig. 280); see also fragments in the Fogg Art Museum, in Walter Cahn and Linda Seidel, *Romanesque Sculpture in American Collections,* Vol. I, *New England Museums,* New York, 1979, 148–50, figs. 140, 142. As they pointed out in the catalogue (177–79), the majority of these pieces were discovered either in the demolition of the high altar or under the pavement of the first south chapel of the choir. Holes for the attachment on the flat back of figures 104 and 105 link these two fragments. Although no documentary proof exists, Saulnier and Stratford (173) suggest the fascinating possibility that these reliefs belong to a tomb, perhaps the Mausoleum of Mary Magdalene. Two reliefs (Saulnier and Stratford, Cat. 223, fig. 184) and a missing fragment (fig. 185) are scenes of people eating, perhaps Supper in the House of Simon. Since the majority of funds to construct Vézelay came from pilgrims and the focus of whose pilgrimage was the relics of Mary Magdalene, the creation of a tomb or monument housing the purported remains of the saint is decidedly plausible.

Gislebertus exerted a profound influence on Vézelay sculpture. Work on the west façade would seem to be divided between Gislebertus (central portal tympanum and lintel—figs. 87–88d) and his assistant, the Façade Master, with his extensive use of ridge-folds, who was the main sculptor of the lower narthex capitals (fig. 95). The intimate connection between façade sculpture, both figural and ornamental, suggests their contemporaniety. Capitals in the narthex gallery appear to depend stylistically on those on the façade and in the lower narthex, but a new personality, the Pharaoh-Étampes Master, makes his appearance from sculpture in the upper narthex (figs. 97–99, 102, 103).

Gislebertus' sculpture at Vézelay also exerted an influence on the central, narthex tympanum (fig. 108). Tubelike ridge-folds on the knee and hip of the Christ and as accents in other drapery folds appear for the first time in the last work of the Perrecy Master (see Armi, 90–98).

CONCLUSION

On the basis of study of masonry, sculptural style, and stylistic interrelationships in different areas of the abbey, the campaigns appear to have been as follows:

1. 1096–1104 (dedication)—new Romanesque choir and transept and nave and narthex exterior walls up to the sills, lower eastern narthex wall OR
2. 1104–1120 (fire)—nave and exterior walls and lower eastern narthex wall, including all capitals, side tympana, and lower parts of central portal.
3. 1120 (fire)—arrival of Gislebertus from Cluny either just before or after 1120.
4. 1120–1125—Gislebertus carves the central portal of the west façade and large tomb or mausoleum (?) and then goes to Autun in 1125.
5. 1120–1130—capitals of nave and narthex; façade by two different workshops. Sculptors of narthex portals

and nave dominated by Avenas and Perrecy masters, while lower narthex and façade was under the inspiration of Gislebertus.

6. 1130s—upper narthex capitals including the Pharaoh–Étampes Master.

Since Gislebertus seems to be the most important sculptor in our search for the origins of Early Gothic, let us turn to the sculpture of Saint-Lazare at Autun.

AUTUN AND GISLEBERTUS

In no other medieval monument is the entire sculptural program, including portrals and capitals, so completely dominated by a single artist as Autun. A summary of the formative years of Gislebertus is perhaps outside the scope of this study of the origins of Early Gothic, yet the more that is known about the entire career of this extraordinary sculptor, the clearer his probable leading role at Chartres West will be. All scholars agree that Gislebertus was a member of the Cluny *chantier* but disagree on details. Salet (152–55) says that Gislebertus was one of the assistants on the Cluny west portal, carving heads of Elders of the Apocalypse. According to him, Gislebertus, after his apprenticeship at Cluny, worked at Vézelay from 1120 to 1125, at Autun from 1125 to 1135, and then at Vézelay again, after 1140. Grivot and Zarnecki (French edition, 1960, 152–55; English edition, 1961, 174–75, ill. B21–32) agreed with Salet's conclusions and illustrated fragments of the Cluny west portal, details of Autun, and the tympanum and fragments of Vézelay.

Armi (105–13, esp. 109–10; figs. 129a–133b), relying on study of drapery as well as of heads, discovered the youthful Gislebertus in the Expulsion capital of Cluny (the original location is unknown) and in fragments from the west portal. He found the tentative use of isolated ridge-folds in loops on the Expulsion capital and their development with added borders of dots in the preserved fragments of the Cluny west portal (Armi, figs. 129a–131). According to Armi, Gislebertus, following the completion of the Cluny portal around 1120, went to Vézelay and was responsible for the fragments of two reliefs, now in the museum, in which the ridge-folds are multiplied and rhythmically grouped. It is these Vézelay fragments that Armi stressed as sources of Gislebertus' work at Autun, as seen in details of the Adoration of the Magi capital and on the Apostles in the signed, west tympanum (see Armi, figs. 134, 135).

I am inclined to agree with Armi's conclusions on the formation and evolution of Gislebertus, but I cannot help but wonder whether or not he was influenced by Cluniac painting: the frescoes of Berzé-le-Ville and the murals in the apse and refectory of Cluny, now lost. Sauerländer, without denying the connection between the sculpture of the Cluny portal and Autun, argued that Cluniac painting had a major impact on Gislebertus at Autun in style, composition, and emotional projection ("Gislebertus von Autun. Ein Beitrag zur Entstehung seines Künsterischen Stils," *Studien zur Geschichte der Europäischen Plastik,* 1965, 17–29). His comparisons of details of the Berzé-la-Ville and the Autun capitals and the lintel of Eve are revealing. Even though Gislebertus was a mason-sculptor, it is possible that he was affected by Cluniac murals, as multiple, parallel, painted lines were transformed into raised ridge-folds of relief sculpture. Since the number and complexity of rounded, projecting folds increases progressively in his sculpture from Cluny to Vézelay and culminates at Autun, the possible impact of Cluniac murals on Gislebertus' sculpture is most apparent in Autun.

At Autun after around 1125, Gislebertus was clearly in total charge of the entire sculptural program, including fifty capitals and the north transept and the west portals. Even when the surfaces of some capitals lack the sensitivity of the Master's carving and are obviously the work of assistants, the extraordinary subtle compositions confirm his dominant role.

Grivot and Zarnecki (French edition, 15–17; English edition, 17–19, 161–62) established the date of Gislebertus at Autun from around 1125 to 1135. The authors described the progress of Autun as follows: the start of church of Saint-Lazare south of the cathedral around 1120; the change in construction and sculpture of the second level of the chevet about 1125, with arrival of Gislebertus; the consecration on 28 December 1130 (there is no evidence of progress of construction); the charter of 1132 describing the road between the cathedral and the church, with mention of a portal, which could be only in the north-east transept; 1146, the porch is unfinished. The 1125 date corresponds to the collapse of the vaults of Cluny, and the authors are tempted to see a correlation between the changes in design of Autun, such as the reduction of clerestory windows from three to one, a change in chevet and other features, and Gislebertus' arrival from Vézelay.

Francis Salet ("La sculpture romane en Bourgogne à propos d'un livre recent," *Bulletin monumental,* 1961, 325–43), agreeing with Grivot and Zarnecki on the date of the start of Autun about 1120 and 1125 for the arrival of Gislebertus, pushed the date of the Last Judgment later, to 1140–1145. Most of his review was concerned with questioning the attribution to Gislebertus of capitals depicting the Incarnation.

The Christ in Majesty, on the second story of the chevet and damaged in the eighteenth century by the addition of a marble altar that I saw being removed in August 1939,

108. Vézelay, tympanum of central narthex portal (detail)

109. Autun, Gislebertus, Christ of west tympanum

110. Autun, Gislebertus,
detail of Christ

111. Autun, Gislebertus,
detail of tympanum (left)

portrays many stylistic characteristics related to fragments by Gislebertus at Vézelay (figs. 104–7 and Grivot and Zarnecki, 60, A5). Drapery folds over legs, ornamented hems, frontal feet, and decoration of the throne recall the Vézelay fragments. Gislebertus was certainly responsible for the preserved sculpture of the north transept portal, including the famous Eve from the lintel and four other fragments of the tympanum in the Musée Rolin at Autun, the archivolt angel in The Cloisters, New York, as well as *in situ* capitals. The enthroned Abraham with Lazarus, the L2 capital, is extremely close in arrangement and grouping of ridge-folds to the Christ in the pilaster capital of the chevet, as well as to all four fragments by Gislebertus in the Vézelay Museum.

The huge frontal Christ of the west tympanum is one of the greatest moments in all Romanesque art (figs. 109–11). Framed by a mandorla on the borders of which is written, "I alone dispose of all things and crown the just," on his right, and "Those who follow crime I judge and punish," on his left, and seated, or, rather leaning, against a throne, the Christ, by his physical size and relative scale to those acting out his words, must have been an intensely moving experience to worshippers in the twelfth century, as it is to us today. Human proportions are greatly elongated, and only the thin thighs, legs, and arms are articulated by the tightly wrapped, curving groups of delicate ridge-folds. The impression of the Christ is one of an enormous dematerialized figure flattened into the wall by a complicated, rhythmical net and exuding the power to save and to condemn, not by any expressive gestures but by his omnipotent, disembodied presence.

Under the feet of Christ, Gislebertus signed the tympanum "Gislebertus hoc fecit," and inscribed the molding between tympanum and lintel, "Thus shall rise again everyone who does not lead an impious life, and endless light of day shall shine for him," on the left, over the resurrected, and "Here let fear strike those whom earthly error binds, for their fate is shown by the horror of these figures," on the right over the condemned.

If details of this tympanum (figs. 110, 111) are carefully studied, it becomes apparent that the Autun Last Judgment is stylistically the quite logical descendant of the Christ in Majesty tympanum from the central portal of the Vézelay outer façade (figs. 87–88d). Although the Vézelay Christ appears to be framed by a double mandorla, the opened legs and outstretched arms are similar in both tympana. At Autun, the Christ's left leg, from knee to ankle, is animated by bunches of small ridge-folds alternating with flat planes, which is the same arrangement of folds in the preserved details of Gislebertus' tympanum at Vézelay. The upper, windblown drapery hem over his left ankle (fig. 110) also recalls the Vézelay tympanum, while the lower,

swooping fold is identical to that in the right figure of the fronton fragment at Vézelay (fig. 104). Hems of Christ's mantle and undergarment are decorated with wide geometric borders similar to those on the Vézelay fragment with two figures (fig. 105). The folded hem over his upper cloak has circles of dots across the left thigh that can be seen as motif on another fragment by Gislebertus at Vézelay (fig. 107). When contrasted with the Vézelay sculpture by Gislebertus, the number of groups of ridge-folds has increased and the relief of the drapery is lower, which further reduces the corporeality of the figure. The flat halo of the Autun Christ (figs. 109, 119) has the cross on a ground of concentric rings of circlets alternating with ridges and resembling a flabellum. The Autun halo is an elaboration of the one on the Giselbertus tympanum at Vézelay (fig. 88b). It thus appears that all the Vézelay sculpture attributed to Gislebertus was carved before he went to Autun, since details of drapery and ornamental borders and hems of his Vézelay pieces become more elaborate and more complicated in his sculpture at Autun.

The Adoration of the Magi capital from the east end of Autun (figs. 112–14) exhibits groups of two, three, or four ridge-folds, which loop downward and animate the legs of the left Magus and articulate the thighs and arms of the kneeling Magus. This system of folds is first seen in the preserved details of the monumental Christ of the outer façade tympanum of Vézelay by Gislebertus (figs. 87–88d). In the much smaller fragments from the Mausoleum of Mary Magdalene (?) by Gislebertus at Vézelay (figs. 104–107), the grouping of projecting folds is more elaborate than on the tympanum and identical to the surfaces of the Adoration of the Magi capital. When details of the Autun capital (figs. 112–14) and the later Autun tympanum (fig. 110) are compared, the treatment of groups of multiple ridge-folds is similar, although the great change in size of the tympanum necessitated a dramatic increase in the number of folds. In both capital and tympanum, silhouettes of figures are emphasized by folds that create a ridge that separate figures from the background (see, especially, the kneeling and standing Magi, figs. 113, 114, and the angels supporting the mandorla in the tympanum, figs. 110, 111. Thus the chronology of Gislebertus' work as illustrated appears to be as follows: the Vézelay façade tympanum, fragments of Mausoleum (?) at Vézelay, the Autun capital and the Autun west tympanum.

AUTUN AND CHARTRES

In an introductory course in art history, the Autun Last Judgment is often contrasted with the Chartres West central tympanum to point out basic differences between the

112. Autun, Adoration of Magi

113. Autun, Magus, detail of fig. 112

114. Autun, Magus, detail of fig. 112

115. Chartres, CP.L2 jamb (detail)

116. Chartres, CP.L1 jamb (detail)

117. Chartres, CP.L2 and 1 jamb (detail)

118. Corbeil, capital

Romanesque world and the new Early Gothic form. Having made this comparison (I confess to having done so many times), how can one then argue that they were both carved by a sculptor named Gislebertus? This important and difficult question must, if possible, be answered. Analysis of the Headmaster's sculpture at Chartres, the jamb statues, lintel, and tympanum of the central portal, and how his sculpture relates to Autun, to Saint-Denis, and to Étampes will, it is hoped, prove that Gislebertus of Autun and the Headmaster were the same sculptor.

Even though the eight preserved jamb figures of the Chartres central portal are frozen in attenuated, vertical poses to conform to the statue-column format and thus exhibit no animated movement like the Magi in the Autun Adoration capital or the secondary figures in the Autun tympanum, there are many stylistic characteristics that relate them to the work of Gislebertus at Autun. Details of the Chartres CP.L1.2 (figs. 115, 116, 117) reveal surfaces totally dominated by ridge-folds, like the Autun sculpture. At Autun, these ridge-folds are grouped in bundles of two or three, with the upper ridge projecting more than the others (see Magi—fig. 114, and tympanum detail—fig. 111). In the Chartres jambs, intervals between cascading folds are more varied, but every third or fourth ridge is more three dimensional (see, especially, fig. 115). A flangelike edge marks the silhouette of each jamb statue like those on the left side of the middle two Magi (fig. 114). Certainly the folds of the Chartres jambs are less linear and more rounded. Some interlocking of folds can be seen in CP.L1 (figs. 116, 117) as well as in the kneeling Magus of Autun (fig. 114). On the basis of treatment of drapery alone, it is plausible to argue that the same sculptor was responsible for both the Autun and the Chartres jamb statues. The rich surface complexity of the Chartres jambs has no counterpart in the Saint-Denis statues (figs. 1, 2), but appears to be a logical development from Autun.

As already stated, the Headmaster did not create any of the historiated capitals of Chartres. These were carved by the Étampes and Saint-Denis masters and their assistants. However, when the Headmaster was commissioned to sculpt the single portal of Notre-Dame at Corbeil (see Part V), he carved most of the portal, including the capitals. He modified the Chartres baldachins, but maintained the sylistic characteristics of the Chartres CP lintels for the capitals. In one capital at Corbeil, which depicts the enfeebled Isaac asking Esau for a serving of venison (fig. 118), the enthroned figures portray many features that recall the Virgin and Enoch and Elijah in the upper tier of the Autun Last Judgment (see Grivot and Zarnecki. p. 48, ill. M, N).

In spite of the fact that the figures of Christ in the tympana of Autun and Chartres appear different in style, close scrutiny reveals many simularities (figs. 119, 120). The flatness of the Autun Christ, created by the relatively low relief, the spread legs, and by the overall webbing of multiple, small ridge-folds, is in marked contrast to the Giotto-like bulk of the Chartres Christ—a spiritual, dematerialized presence as opposed to a spiritual, corporeal presence. Yet the upright position of heads against halos, the looping folds of the upper bodice, and the sweeping bundles of ridge-folds over their right legs exhibit a definite relationship.

The head of the Autun Christ, discovered in 1948 and replaced on the tympanum (fig. 119), contains several stylistic similarities common to the heads of Christ and the central portal jambs of Chartres. As illustrated by photographs of 1936 (Plate XX, 1, 3) and others taken recently (figs. 119–22), hair and beards in both Autun and Chartres consist of finely carved, parallel, and rounded ridges, which either undulate in depth to create a rippling effect, as in the Chartres Christ, CP. L 1, CP. R. 2, or are bunched and terminate in curls like the Autun Christ and Chartres CP. R. 1. In Autun and Chartres, hair is either pulled up and around the large ears or one curl overlaps their top or bottom.

As Edson Armi pointed out (1983, 114, fig. 139), the head of Christ of Autun (fig. 119) has unusual ears, with two separate concavities or conchas and with lobes replaced by the helixes (exterior roll of flesh), which turn back on themselves. Christ's right ear is a capital C becoming a capital G. Armi illustrated this unnatural treatment of ears by Gislebertus in the Cluny Expulsion capital and fragment from the west portal of Cluny as well as in the Autun Christ. Gislebertus thus created over a span of almost two decades ears that are completely different from those by Armi's Perrecy and Avenas masters, the major sculptors responsible for the Cluny capitals and Vézelay narthex portals (Armi, 103, figs. 121, 122).

The ears of Christ and the CP jambs at Chartres are close in style and format to those of the Autun Christ. Ears are given prominence by the parallel projections of the helixes and antihelixes and the reverse turn of the helix to replace the ear lobe, which can be seen in the Autun and Chartres Christs and in several of the jambs in a modified form (figs. 119–22). The structure of the eye is similar, yet the irises are much larger in the Autun head, while the mouths of both the Christ heads are turned down at the corners and the lips are slightly parted. In spite of all these stylistic connections, the tapering, more pointed frontal silhouette of the Autun head is markedly different from the rectangular shape of the Chartres head.

These heads from Autun and Chartres should be analyzed in their relation to those of Saint-Denis. It seems logical to assume that if Gislebertus is indeed the Chartres Headmaster, he certainly studied the revolutionary portals of the Abbey in the early 1140s. He was exposed to a new

119. Autun, Christ of tympanum (detail)

120. Chartres, Christ of CP, tympanum

121. Chartres, CP.L1, 2 heads

122. Chartres, CP.R1, 2, 3 heads

206

portal design with columnar jamb statues that integrate bases, jambs, capitals, and archivolts in a new unity. At Saint-Denis he also was possibly influenced by the articulation of legs by single loop-folds of varying intervals. Gislebertus may have reacted to the oval silhouettes of the heads from the Saint-Denis CP (Plate VIII, 1–4; fig. 3) or the wider ones from the LP. at Saint-Denis (Plate IX). Details of the Saint-Denis heads, such as ears, eyes, nostrils, and mouths, are relatively more naturalistic than those features in either Autun or Chartres.

Rough estimates of proportions of the Saint-Denis jamb figures, based on the Montfaucon engravings and drawings (figs. 1, 2 and Plate X, 2), reveal that they were roughly six heads high, with the LP jambs slightly taller, while the jambs at Étampes range from more than six to seven and one-half heads high. The Peter and Paul of Étampes, formerly flanking the portal and now inside the church, are eight heads high. Proportions of jambs by the Saint-Denis Master and Étampes Master remain much the same in their sculpture at Chartres, although the RP.R 2 has a small head that distorts its proportion, and the head of LP.L 1 does not belong to the body. The jamb statues of the central portal by the Headmaster become taller from the inner jamb (seven and one-half heads) to the outer jamb (eight and one-half). Thus the only jambs comparable to the CP Chartres statues are the Peter and Paul at Étampes. Proportions of figures at Autun vary greatly, depending on whether they are on the capital, the lintel or the tympanum. The first Apostle on Christ's right in the tympanum (fig. 111) is almost ten heads tall. Since Gislebertus was accustomed to employing every conceivable set of proportions according to the location on the architectural member being carved, it is not necessary to go as far afield as Byzantine mosaics at Cefalù and Palermo to explain the elongated proportions of the CP Chartres jamb (see Otto von Simson, *The Gothic Cathedral: The Origins of Gothic Architecture and the Medieval Concept of Order,* 1956, 151–52).

The jamb figures of the Headmaster have a different relationship to the column and to the design of each splay of the portals than we find at Saint-Denis, Étampes, and Chartres RP.R and LP.L. One jamb statue of Saint-Denis RP, destroyed before the drawings and engravings for Montfaucon (Plate X, 2 and fig. 11), exhibits two important pieces of evidence: 1. The top molding of the column proves that the columnar statue extended up to the capital; 2. The remains of drapery are attached to the front quarter of the column, and thus most of the figures, including the heads in the round, project out from the column. This figure-column relationship is also seen at Étampes and Chartres LP.L, which is by the Étampes Master, but in the latter, the heads are crowned by elaborate baldachins, with an

added section of columns, that separates the figures from the historiated capital-frieze, which did not exist at Saint-Denis. The Saint-Denis Master at Chartres (RP.R) followed the Étampes Master's format to balance the outside splays of the façade. The Headmaster's CP figures overlap more of the column than at Saint-Denis, Étampes, and the related statutes at Chartres. Heads, attached to flat halos, are essentially in high relief, not in the round as at Saint-Denis and Étampes. This greater overlapping of figure and column, together with the strict, elongated silhouettes of the statues, which repeat the verticality of the columns, with the moldings framing both the columns and the ornamented colonnettes, imparts a more powerful architectonic quality to his jamb figures than found at Saint-Denis and Étampes. Only small sections of columns prevent the heads from blurring the clarity of the capital-frieze. (These sections of columns were planned from the outset, since the height of the splays was established by the six figures of the doorjambs, which, on the central portal, were carved by the Étampes Master.)

The architectonic character of the Headmaster's figures is seen in the strict silhouette and attenuation. The triangular-shaped projection of the figures, with essential flat surfaces of forearms and hands holding symbols on a central, vertical axis, echoes the convexity of bases, abaci, and archivolts. His figures are thus both completely integrated to the shaft and to the entire portal (fig. 13a).

Is this subtle, sympathetic, and reinforcing connection between sculpture and architecture the natural evolution out of the first experiments with statue-columns at Saint-Denis and Étampes? The many stylistic differences between the sculpture of these earlier monuments and the central portal of Chartres precludes the possibility that the Headmaster came out of the Saint-Denis workshop. There is no doubt that the Headmaster knew both Saint-Denis and Étampes.

Since a high percentage of Romanesque sculpture, especially capitals and doorjambs, reveals figures or ornament reinforcing the architectural elements of which they are an integral part, it follows that the search for the Headmaster should lead to the monument and the specific sculptor who best integrates sculpture and architecture. Gislebertus is the strongest candidate. The design of the capitals of Autun, whether depicting the violent action of the Stoning of Stephen or the slow majestic movement of the Flight into Egypt, exhibits extraordinary variation in solving, with figures in different poses or with ornament, the architectonic nature of the two convex corners of the pilaster-shaped capitals. In the west tympanum and lintel, Gislebertus was presented with a different sculptural problem, namely, carving an enormous relief with innumerable sizes of figures and depth of carving to interject the last dramatic moment of salvation and condemnation. When the new idea of a statue-column was introduced to Gislebertus, he was well prepared to transform these early, tentative jambs into a more cohesive statement of total sculptural-architectural harmony.

At Autun, Gislebertus carved elaborate bands of ornament on collars and hems, but these borders blend into the overall surface texture of the drapery. In the Montfaucon drawings and engravings of Saint-Denis, the decorative hems stand out more, while in the central portal of Chartres they are present, but in a much more muted form.

Arrangement of the feet and their relationship to the ground or support are instructive when Autun, Saint-Denis, and Chartres West are compared. With the exception of the frontal Virgin and Child in the Flight into Egypt capital and the Christ and the enthroned figures in the top level of the west tympanum, Gislebertus usually carved feet parallel and in profile, resting on inclined planes. At Saint-Denis we see more variety in the stances of the jamb statues, which rest on marmousets. Cross-legged jambs have parallel feet, while the rest have slightly open stances. All the monumental jamb statues of Étampes reveal widely spaced feet resting on a narrow corbel of curving flanges (see Étampes Master at Chartres, fig. 9a). The frontal, unencumbered feet of the Christ in the Chartres central tympanum (fig. 120) resemble those of the Autun Christ (fig. 119), while the bare feet of the Apostles on the lintel are almost all frontal. In the case of the kings and queens of the Chartres CP, the feet are encased in slightly pointed slippers and stand with partially open stance on the cone-shaped corbels. The relationship of the feet to the steeply inclined planes recalls that in the Autun tympanum.

Several scholars have stressed the Burgundian–Île-de-France connection and, more specifically, the Gislebertus–Chartres West relationship. Bernhard Kerber (*Burgund und die Entwicklung der Französischen Kathedral, Skulptur im Zwölften Jahrhundert,* 1966, 24–25) pointed out the stylistic simularity between the lower torso of a female figure in the Vézelay Museum (now lost; see Saulnier and Stratford, fig. 185) and the righthand figure in the Birth of Christ capital at Autun, with vertical, parallel ridge-folds (Kerber, figs. 3, 4), and Chartres West. Sauerländer (1970, 34–35) refined Kerber's conclusions by pointing out that this Autun capital is closest stylistically more to archaic jambs, such as Chartres LP.L 1 (fig. 9b). It should be pointed out, however, that even though this lost Vézelay fragment is closer to the LP.L 1 jamb, the drapery of the latter has its origin in the second Wise Women in the Vézelay narthex capital by the Pharaoh-Étampes Master, who also carved the other two jambs on the same splay (fig. 97). Sauerländer added another comparison to Kerber's, namely the heads of the Eve from the Autun lintel and the queen from Chartres,

CP.R 3 (fig. 122 and his figs. 1, 2). Sauerländer (1970, 35) was intrigued, but puzzled, by this comparison and wrote as follows, "The meaning of the forms has been radically changed at Chartres, in the sense of severe axiality. One has the definite feeling that the affinity is undeniable, but that we lack the intermediary links of the chain of tradition. One can hardly imagine the sculptor of the Autun Eve going the next day to Chartres to create the Queens, . . . For the moment, I can only say: Chartres, in contrast to Saint-Denis, is unthinkable without Burgundy and especially without Autun. But there is a radical remodeling of the Burgundian forms, not to mention the entirely different iconography, figure types and costumes."

Edson Armi (1983, 111) argued that the drapery style of the late work of the Perrecy Master of the Vézelay narthex central portal and of Gislebertus in the west tympanum of Autun, in which every third or fourth ridge-fold projects more than the others, was carried further by the Headmaster of Chartres as he varied the size of the rounded ridges, the intervals between them, and the profiles of the differing projecting folds (Armi, figs. 134–36). He illustrated this development by a detail of the right hip of CP.L 2 (his fig. 136). Armi thus concluded that the Chartres Headmaster's style evolved out of Burgundy, and, most specifically, out of Autun.

Peter the Venerable was at Vézelay between 1110 and 1120, before he became Abbot of Cluny (1122–1156), and appears to be responsible for the iconographical program of portals and capitals. At Autun, no specific person has been linked to the sculptural program, but it was the clergy, not Gislebertus, who designed it. The emotional intensity and clear separation of good and bad, right and wrong, saved and damned in the Last Judgment are strong didactic statements that create a scary, pessimistic mood. Although Autun is separated from Chartres by a short span of time, the whole mood of Chartres West represents a totally new intellectual climate. None of the almost epileptic, dematerialized spirituality of Autun is visible at Chartres. Since the Chartres West program was not the product of sculptors such as the Étampes Master, the Saint-Denis Master, Gislebertus, and others, we must turn to its obvious origin, the School of Chartres.

In his book *The Sculptural Programs of Chartres Cathedral* (1959), Adolf Katzenellenbogen clearly illustrated how the program of Chartres West was created by the School of Chartres and how the underlying ideas of the program were linked with formal aspects of the portals. As I summarized in a review of this book (*Speculum*, October 1960, 613–17), Katzenellenbogen emphasized the new lucidity and explicitness of the tympana scenes representing the Incarnation, Ascension, and Second Coming of Christ. He further stressed the sacramental importance of the Incarnation (right portal) through the axial centrality of Christ in the manger (Nativity), Christ on the altar (Presentation), and the frontal Christ on the Virgin's lap in the tympanum. The *corpus verum,* his real flesh and the true substance of the Eucharist, which is symbolized by this arrangement, reflected the leading role of the School of Chartres in the fight against heretical movements, which culminated in the Second Lateran Council of 1139.

The tympanum of the right portal protrays the Christ Child enthroned as Godhead Incarnate but also as Wisdom Incarnate, since the surrounding archivolts contain the seven liberal arts. Basing their beliefs on the writing of Boethius and therefore indirectly on Plato, the School of Chartres utilized the liberal arts as intellectual vehicles for the understanding of theological doctrines. Thierry of Chartres, chancellor of the School of Chartres at the time of the carving of the Royal Portals, had compiled a handbook on the seven liberal arts and had stressed the importance of classical writings for the understanding of theological truths. The appearance of Priscian, Aristotle, Cicero, Euclid, Boethius, Ptolemy, and Pythagoras on the archivolts was ample evidence to establish the School of Chartres as the source of the sculptural program.

The author interpreted the large jamb statues as combining qualities of kingship and priesthood: *Regnum* and *Sacerdotium.* Louis VII was praised because "from the time he was anointed as king, he had followed the humility of David, the wisdom of Solomon and the patience of Job." Thus the monumental statues are Old Testament figures possessing qualities of kingship and reflecting the attitude of the French monarchy toward the investiture struggles in Germany. Suger emphasized the harmony of priesthood and kingship in the letter to the archbishop of Reims. The abbot of Saint-Denis certainly established the sculptural program of the abbey.

Finally, in the chapter on form and content, Katzenellenbogen explained the majestic frontality and lack of tension of the central west portal jamb statues by relating their figure style to treatises on the soul and the body. William of Conches, of the School of Chartres, had attacked the theory of the body as an appendage to the soul and had argued that the soul was more active from within man. The Chartres figures, with their controlled animation from within plus their variety of moods, reflect the protohumanism of the School of Chartres. A new sense of the power of reason dependent on Divine Wisdom manifests itself in the entire Royal Portals.

With these major differences in the intellectual climate of Autun in the 1130s and of Chartres in the mid–1140s in mind, it is certainly plausible to argue that Gislebertus of Autun was forced to alter his style to carry out the goals of the clergy. He had to employ the new statue-columns for the jambs that he had seen and studied at Saint-Denis and Étampes. At the same time, he retained many of his personal, stylistic characteristics. Since the clergy was faced with the problem of hiring a team of sculptors to bring this new, more humanistic program to a reality, they employed the Saint-Denis Master, the Étampes Master, and the famous Gislebertus, who was responsible for executing the entire program at Autun. Gislebertus and the "Headmaster" of Chartres are the same sculptor, with a productive career of approximately thirty-five years as follows: Before 1120 at Cluny, 1120–1125 at Vézelay, 1125–c.1140 at Autun, 1143–1146/7 at Chartres, and the very late 1140s or c.1150 at Corbeil.

PART V

TRENDS IN THE THIRD QUARTER OF THE TWELFTH CENTURY

INTRODUCTION

In 1952, four portals, Le Mans, Saint-Ayoul at Provins, Saint-Loup-de-Naud, and Senlis, were selected to illustrate the general evolution of portal design, of ornamental and figure style in the second half of the twelfth century (W.S.S., 32–41). Based on the interpretation of scholarship through the 1940s, these portals were tentatively dated as follows: Le Mans in the 1150s, before 1158, the dedication of the nave, and with 1158 serving as *terminus ante quem* for Chartres West; Saint-Ayoul at Provins after a fire of 1157; Saint-Loup-de-Naud after 1167; Senlis in the 1180s, before the dedication in 1191. Since 1952, extensive research on individual monuments in articles and monographs, together with books, such as Lapeyre's and Sauerländer's, on Gothic sculpture and the discovery of more twelfth-century sculpture, such as the cloister sculpture of Notre-Dame-en-Vaux at Châlons-sur-Marne and the fragments of the jamb of the Sante-Anne portal of Paris, have shown that the interrelationships of styles and regions give the portals of the second half of the century of much broader, richer, and more fascinating tapestry of sculptural forms.

The span of dating from the 1150s to the 1180s has been greatly narrowed in spite of the absence of any positive documentary evidence. Today, no one doubts the completion date of all the sculpture on the west portals of Saint-Denis for the dedication in 1140. I have argued that Étampes was carved in the early 1140s, closely followed by Chartres West in the mid 1140s (1143–1147), and *was all carved in one campaign*. With the general questioning of the significance of dates of dedications and consecrations, it is evident that the Senlis portal was completed around 1170 or, more probably earlier, not in the 1180s, before the dedication in 1191 (see Willibald Sauerländer, "Die Marienkrönungsportale von Senlis und Mantes," *Wallraf-Richartz-Jahrbuch,* Vol. 20, 1958, 151–62). This shortening of the span of time between Chartres West and Senlis (Mantes) to one generation makes it possible to pose and answer certain questions about the evolving careers of certain individual sculptors. In spite of the fact that probably over one-half of twelfth-century sculpture has been destroyed or is known only in drawings or engravings, it is perhaps possible, within the time-span of approximately twenty-five years, to find several sculptors who worked both at Chartres and on later monuments. Omitting discussion of the Itinerant Sculptor of Chartres, who carved two capitals, and the LP lower lintel Master *(spolium),* can we discover the work of any of the four major sculptors of Chartres West or their assistants in subsequent portals? We must assume, it would seem, that many sculptors lived longer than Masaccio (1401–1428)!

THE SOUTH PORTAL OF THE CATHEDRAL OF SAINT-JULIAN AT LE MANS

The major entrance from the town to the cathedral in Le Mans is the south portal under a porch in the fifth bay of the south aisle. As stated in 1952 (see W.S.S., 34–36, 39 and Plates XXV, 1; XXVI, 1; XXVII, 1; XXVIII, 1; XXIX, 1, 2), the sculpture of the jambs, tympanum, lintel, and capitals do not exhibit the same crisp quality and three-dimensional presence of work by the Chartres Headmaster. At the same time, there appear to be no stylistic connections between the Le Mans sculptors and the three other major sculptors of Chartres West or their assistants. Instead, the majority of the Le Mans monumental sculpture appears to replicate the central portal of Chartres by the Headmaster: R2 (fig. 124), a copy of Chartres CP.R4 (fig. 13a), with open hand like Chartres CP.L1; R4 and 5 (fig. 124), variants of Chartres CP.R2; the female jamb, R3, close to Chartres CP.L5. The left jambs of Le Mans (fig. 123), especially L3, 4, 5, display further decline in quality with the L3 female based on Chartres CP.L3, and L4 and 5, with sloping shoulders, tapering silhouettes, and looping bodices over stomachs resembling Chartres LP.R4 (fig. 15c) by the second Assistant of the Headmaster. Further, the drapery over the ankles of L2 of Le Mans recalls the carving of that area on LP.R2, the so-called Moses, also by the second Assistant of the Headmaster (see fig. 15a). Since all the jambs, tympanum, and lintel of Le Mans appear to be qualitatively inferior to Chartres and since this sculpture appears to be dependent stylistically on that of either the Headmaster or one of his assistants, it is tempting to argue

123. Le Mans, left jambs (Austin)

124. Le Mans, right jambs (Austin)

125. Saint-Loup-de-Naud, left jambs (Austin)

126. Saint-Loup-de-Naud, right jambs (Austin)

that the monumental sculpture of Le Mans was created by this assistant without the presence and supervision of the Headmaster.

In spite of the qualitative decline of the Le Mans jamb figures, lintel, and tympanum when contrasted with the Chartres central portal, a decline that is intensified by eroded surfaces and damaged heads, the archivolts of the Le Mans portal contain an inner archivolt of angles and outer three of historiated voussoirs. Their vitality and expressiveness are in marked contrast to the monumental sculpture of the portal. Stylistically, the archivolts are quite different from those at Chartres by the Angel Master and his assistant. Since the small-scale doorjambs and capital-frieze of Chartres were carved by the Étampes and Saint-Denis masters and their assistants, we are left with the Chartres double lintel of the right portal with which to compare the Le Mans archivolts. Since the lower lintel appears to be the work of the first Assistant of the Headmaster, the sculptor of RP.L2, 3, 4, and the upper lintel the work of the second Assistant of the Headmaster, the sculptor of LP.R2, 4, it follows that by the process of elimination these two assistants of the Headmaster are the only Chartres sculptors whom we can consider when analyzing the Le Mans archivolts. It is difficult to see any connection between the Chartres upper lintel (figs. 47–49) and the Le Mans archivolts, although there are certain vague relationships between the Chartres lower lintel and Le Mans. Detailed photographs of each voussoir and more research, both of which are beyond the scope of this revision, are essential. See also Lapeyre (*Des Façades occidentales de Saint-Denis et de Chartres aux portails de Laon,* 1960, 90–95, 281–85) and Sauerländer (*Gothic Sculpture in France, 1140–1270,* London, 1972, 46–47, 383, 386).

The date of 1158, which marks the dedication of the nave and, at the same time, serves as a *terminus ante quem* for Chartres West portals, does not necessarily prove that the portals were carved in the late 1150s. A more logical date for the Le Mans south portal would seem to be the late 1140s or at least a completion date of around 1150. The reconstruction of the Romanesque nave of Le Mans transpired between the fires of 1134 and 1137 and its dedication in 1158 (see André Mussat, *Le style gothique de l'ouest de la France (XIIᵉ–XIIIᵉ siècles),* Paris, 1963, 95–107). Since this campaign at Le Mans is contemporary with the west towers of Chartres, the north tower begun in 1134 and the south tower under construction in 1145, and since there are many common denominators between Le Mans and the Chartres towers in bases, ribs, vaults, and decoration, it follows that the portal, opening into the south aisle and strongly influenced by Chartres West, could have been created by 1150. (In 1952, I was wrong in arguing that the Le Mans porch was contemporary with the portal. It is later; see Mussat, 1963, 106.)

POSTSCRIPT: LE MANS

After this manuscript was in the hands of the publishers, an article appeared on Le Mans by Thomas E. Polk II ("The South Portal of the Cathedral at Le Mans: Its Place in the Development of Early Gothic Portal Composition," *Gesta,* Vol. XXIV/I, 1985, 47–60). The author's main concern involved the dating of Le Mans, possibly in the late 1130s, but certainly between Saint-Denis and Chartres on the basis of carefully study of the masonry of the porch and portal and analysis of the portal design of Saint-Denis, Le Mans, and Chartres. Because of the pinching of the outer embrasures, lack of alignment of the upper, central voussoirs with evidence of recutting, and because of the narrowing of some of the tympanum blocks, Polk argued that the portal was designed for a wider emplacement. This conclusion, which appears to be correct, does prove that nave, portal, and porch of portal are not contemporary, but does not help date Le Mans.

In his analysis of the portal design, Polk wrote (p. 56), "With respect to its composition, the Early Gothic portal of Le Mans stands between the Early Gothic portals of Saint-Denis, where the clear expression of tectonic relationships dominates, even taking into account the bad state of preservation, and Chartres, where that dominance of structural clarity diminishes in favor of visual homogeneity." The thick wall buttresses, with their responds, help create the tectonic character of the entire façade of Saint-Denis, and each isolated portal opens into three bays of the narthex, two supporting the towers and a wider central bay (Plate A). The composition and problem of Chartres West is entirely different. No massive buttresses were necessary to support towers, since the three portals were designed for a narthex of three bays in front of the nave of Fulbert's eleventh-century cathedral, with towers to the north and south. The three Chartres portals are more visually homogeneous than the Saint-Denis portals, but, as stated, the architecture-sculpture problem is totally different. At Le Mans, the single portal is set between buttresses and flat doorjambs and thus resembles Saint-Denis, yet the majority of portals after Chartres have flat doorjambs (Provins, Saint-Loup-de-Naud, Bourges).

The jamb figures of Le Mans are clearly based on those by the headmaster of Chartres and his assistants, with the strong possibility that these assistants, especially the author of the LP.R jambs of Chartres, were employed at Le Mans. If indeed Chartres West was finished by around 1147, the

Le Mans portal was completed in the late 1140s, but not before Chartres.

THE WEST PORTALS OF SAINT-AYOUL AT PROVINS

Since 1952, the study of Early Gothic sculpture in Champagne has been greatly enriched by the excavations of Léon Pressouyre at Notre-Dame-en-Vaux, at Châlons-sur-Marne and the discovery of capitals, columnar statues, and many fragments, now installed in a new museum. To the sculpture preserved on the façade of Saint-Ayoul at Provins (Plates XXV, 2; XXVI, 2; XXVII, 2; XVIII, 2) can now be added a statue column of David, discovered in excavations at Saint-Ayoul in 1953 and now in the Grange aux Dîmes in Provins (see Léon Pressouyre, "Réflexions sur la sculpture du XIIème Siècle en Champagne," *Gesta*, Vol. IX/2, 1970, fig. 14). The columnar statue of a queen in the Raymond Pitcairn Collection in Bryn Athyn, Pennsylvania, has been connected with the portal of Saint-Thibaut of Provins (see Jane Hayward and Walter Cahn, *Radiance and Reflection, Medieval Art from the Raymond Pitcairn Collection*, The Metropolitan Museum of Art, 1982, 98, fig. 31).

The west portals of Saint-Ayoul have deteriorated considerably in the last thirty years. As stated in 1952 (W.S.S., 33–37), the jamb statues of Saint-Ayoul appear to reflect sculpture by the Headmaster and the so-called Saint-Denis Master (L3 Provins and Chartres, RP.R3), in contrast to the Le Mans portal, where all the jambs relate only to the Headmaster and his two assistants. It would appear, however, that none of the Chartres sculptors worked in Saint-Ayoul. Lapeyre (*Des Façades occidentales de Saint-Denis et de Chartres aux Portails de Laon*, 1960, 187–93, figs. 129–34) believed that the four archivolts of the central portal were influenced by the central portal of Saint-Denis because of the presence of Paradise and Hell on the outer archivolt. Lapeyre is certainly correct in his observation that the costume and style of the Christ of the tympanum (fig. 134) is related to that of the Étampes Master. However, the Christ does not exhibit the crisp quality of the Étampes Master's work either at Étampes or at Chartres. Lapeyre dates the portals after the fire of 1157 and before 1167, his date for the portal of Saint-Loup-de-Naud. Sauerländer (1972, 28, 402–3) stresses the lack of quality of the jamb statues and dates the portal after 1157.

On the basis of careful study of the channeled moldings between the inner three jambs and the projecting arris between the third and fourth statue, Clark Maines (*The Western Portal of Saint-Loup-de-Naud*, 1979, 92–96; figs. 116–

25) believes that this portal was originally programmed for three jambs. Further, he argues that none of the statues were designed for their present location. For evidence, he cites the lack of alignment between shaft and capital (L1), the off-axis positioning of three jambs, the chiselling of the back of R3 to set it further back into the splay, and the fact that Peter and Paul statues are not flanking the portal. He thus concludes that the central portal, like the present side portals, originally had simple shafts and that the jamb statues were added.

Is the fire of 1157 a valid *terminus post quem* for the Saint-Ayoul portals? If one argues for a conservative, late flowering of early Gothic in Champagne, then a post–1157 date for the Saint-Ayoul sculpture is reasonable. However, fires tend to burn roofs, not façades, and Saint-Ayoul, like Le Mans, could be dated as early as 1150. The following discussion of Saint-Loup-de-Naud may help clarify the dating of the portals of Saint-Ayoul at Provins.

THE WEST PORTAL OF SAINT-LOUP-DE-NAUD

Clark Maines' monograph (1979) greatly augments our knowledge of this priory of Saint-Pierre-le-Vif in Sens. Although chapters on its history and architecture are included, the majority of the book concerns the portal—its physical and visual structure, iconography, and style. On the basis of careful study of literally hundreds of photographs of details, Maines argues that the portal, which has always been considered *the* most unified composition in Early Gothic sculpture, was, rather, an evolving program involving extensive use of *spolia* combined with sculpture specifically carved for the portal. According to Maines, the tympanum, lintel, jamb statues, and four voussoir blocks were created for another portal in Sens, perhaps for Saint-Pierre-le-Vif, while the trumeau of Saint Lupus, with its capital and the rest of the archivolts, were sculpted for their present emplacement (see Maines, 73–118).

Maines (117–19) presents two theories of a relative chronology for the west protal: 1. A portal contemporary with the porch and western bays of the nave was replaced by the present portal, which includes walls, bases, imposts, and capitals but undecorated columns instead of jamb statues. This intermediate portal was partially dismantled to include both spoliate sculpture (jamb statues, tympanum, lintel, and the four lower voussoirs blocks) and the sculpture carved for this portal (the trumeau and its capital and the remaining voussoirs). 2. The first portal was dismantled and redesigned to accommodate parts of two separate portals: the sculpture of the second and third campaigns described above.

As in the connection between the architecture of Saint-Loup-de-Naud and Sens cathedrals, Maines (21–71) finds strong stylistic relationships between the portal of Saint-Loup-de-Naud and sculpture *in situ* in the ambulatory of Sens, in the Palais Synodal and the Musée Municipal de Sens. Maines believes (230–33) that the same Sens atelier is responsible for all Saint-Loup-de-Naud portal sculpture in a short span of time. Similarities between Sens and Saint-Loup-de-Naud are certainly valid. Indeed, several capitals, of confronting griffins crowning the jambs and of details of the Visitation and Biblical figures on the archivolts (Plates XVIII, 3, 4 and XXIX, 4 and Maines, 244–45 and figs. 134–51), are so close to capitals on the dado of the ambulatory of Sens Cathedral and to a capital (?) from Saint-Pierre-le-Vif in the Musée Municipal that, in my opinion, the same sculptor or sculptors must have worked at both Sens and Saint-Loup-de-Naud. More connections will unquestionably be revealed when all the sculpture on or from Sens Cathedral has been studied in detail and the proposed excavations of Saint-Pierre-de-Vif have been implemented.

Can the strong connections between Saint-Loup-de-Naud and Sens help date the portal of Saint-Loup-de-Naud? Kenneth Severens ("The Early Campaign of Sens, 1140–1147," *Journal of the Society of Architectural Historians,* XXIX, May, 1970, 97–107) has proved conclusively that the Romanesque start of Sens Cathedral, which included the north chapel of John the Baptist, the peripheral wall and ambulatory of the chevet, and the south chapel (rebuilt 1295–1320), could not have been begun before 1140. He bases this conclusion on comparisons with architecture and sculpture in Burgundy and the Loire Valley. The transformation of this Romanesque chevet of groin-vaulted ambulatory and single columns around the hemicycle to the present Early Gothic ribbed-vaulted ambulatory with double columns was the result of the strong influence of the chevet of Saint-Denis (1140–1144). Capitals in the north chapel of the earlier Romanesque campaign as well as Atlas corbels for the diagonal ribbed vaults of the evolving Gothic campaign are very close stylistically to capitals and corbels in the choir of Saint-Denis (see Severens, 105, 106; figs. 6, 12, 13). Severens argues on the basis of these relationships that the change in plan at Sens, which involved raising the ambulatory windows and the conversion of groin vaults to ribbed vaults took place around 1145. Since the addossed siren capitals on the dado of the Sens ambulatory are extremely close in style to the capitals of the Saint-Loup-de-Naud portal, it is difficult to agree with the traditional dating of 1170–1175 proposed by Francis Salet ("Saint-Loup-de-Naud," *Bulletin monumental,* 1933, 166), followed by me (1952, 33–34 but modified to 1160s in W.S.S., 1966, 159) and Lapeyre (1960, 132). The Saint-Loup-de-Naud portal

cannot be dated on the basis of the gift of relics of Saint Lupus in 1161 or of the gifts of Count Henri-le-Libéral to Saint-Pierre-le-Vif of Sens and Saint-Loup-de-Naud in 1167. Sauerländer ("Sculpture on Early Gothic Churches: The State of Research," *Gesta,* IX/2, 1970, 40 and *Gothic Sculpture in France,* 1972, 394) argued for a date in the 1150s, or at least by 1160.

The Saint-Loup-de-Naud portal has also been linked with the sculpture of Notre-Dame-en-Vaux, at Châlons-sur-Marne, and the destroyed portal of Saint-Bénigne at Dijon. A Burgundian-Champagne-Île-de-France axis has been stressed (see Lapeyre, 1960, 126–38). Léon Pressouyre ("Réflexions sur la sculpture du XIIème siècle en Champagne," *Gesta,* IX/2, 1970, 16–31, figs. 12, 13) related the Louvre head (cat. no. 66), which he identified correctly as coming from the south portal of Notre-Dame-en-Vaux at Châlons and not from the cloister of Saint-Denis, with the head of Saint Bénigne (?) in the Musée Archéologique at Dijon. Pressouyre (20–21, figs. 12, 13) dates the Dijon head around 1160 and the Châlons portal to 1160–1170. Further, he finds stylistic relationships between statue columns from the cloister of Notre-Dame-en-Vaux at Châlons and archivolt figures of Saint-Loup-de-Naud, Magi before Herod (his figs. 15–17), and thus argues for the Saint-Loup-de-Naud style originating in Burgundy and the portal dating generally in the 1160s, or more probably after 1167, as part of a "retard champenois." This dating depends on the sequence of Dijon, Châlons, and Saint-Loup-de-Naud. Dating Dijon at about 1160 obviously pushes Saint-Loup-de-Naud late and does not take into account the stylistic relationships with sculpture of Sens (see Maines, 244–47), which would suggest a date of the 1150s and possibly early in that decade for Saint-Loup-de-Naud. The possible date of Saint-Bénigne de Dijon will be discussed in Appendix II.

In spite of certain stylistic relationships among Saint-Loup-de-Naud, Châlons, and Dijon, Maines and others have stressed the connections between Chartres West and Saint-Loup-de-Naud. This relationship is clouded by the fact that Sens seems to be the link between the two monuments and the source of the Saint-Loup sculpture. Undoubtedly, more Sens sculpture will be discovered if and when Saint-Pierre-le-Vif is excavated, but, in the meantime, it is possible to see direct stylistic relationships between Chartres West and Saint-Loup-de-Naud. The Senois sculptors of Saint-Loup-de-Naud obviously knew the west portals of Chartres, not just the Headmaster's sculpture but also the sculpture carved by other masters or their assistants. Since all of Chartres West, with the exception of the lower lintel of the left portal was carved, in my opinion, in one short campaign in the mid-1140s, following Saint-Denis (1140) and Étampes in the early 1140s, the multiplicity of styles at Chartres served as models for subsequent portals. Scholars have tended to see a general decline in quality at Saint-Loup-de-Naud-rather than to see positive differences. However, it is difficult to agree with the following suggestion of Maines (259): "One wonders whether the negative assessments of the column-figures at Saint-Loup would continue if they were proven to have been executed *before* the work at Chartres."

In pose and in general arrangement of drapery, several jamb statues of Saint-Loup-de-Naud (W.S.S., 37–38 and Plates XXV, 3; XXVI, 3; XXVIII, 3, 4 and figs. 125, 126) can be related to specific Chartres statues by the Headmaster. The body of Peter (R1—fig. 126) follows that of Chartres CP.L2 (Plate XVII, 1), while his head resembles that of CP.R1 (Plate XVII, 2). Saint-Loup-de-Naud R2 jamb is generally based on Chartres CP.R4, and R3 is a variant of Chartres CP.R2.

On the left embrasure (fig. 125), Paul (L1) has vague relationships in pose and gesture in Chartres CP.R2, yet his head and the treatment of the drapery over his right leg, which articulates his knee, reflects Chartres RP.R1 by the so-called Saint-Denis Master (see Plates XVI, 2 and XIX, 1 and fig. 10a). Sauerländer called our attention to the closeness of Paul's head to both the Chartres head and the so-called Dijon Saint Bénigne (1970, 40, figs. 12–14) and thereby questioned the late dating of Saint-Loup-de-Naud. The queen (L2) is indebted to Chartres CP.R3 by the Headmaster and to LP.L1 by the Étampes Master for its general arrangement of drapery, especially around the stomach, including the knotted, falling sash. The L3 jamb (fig. 125) is vaguely related to Chartres CP.L2.

In spite of dependence of the Saint-Loup jamb statues on Chartres West for general format, including gesture and arrangement of drapery, the squatter proportions, stricter rectangular silhouette, and generally decorative character of surfaces suggests that no Chartres sculptors were responsible for the Saint-Loup jambs, yet the sculptors must have known the Royal Portals. Instead of variations of the body contours inside the rectangularity of the outer edges of mantles of the Chartres jambs, which suggest some anatomical articulation, folds of the Saint-Loup jamb appear as a uniform surface overlay within the strict, rectangular blocks.

On the basis of careful study of Saint-Loup-de-Naud and of detailed photographs (1976 and 1977), I believe that two sculptors carved the jamb statues, one sculptor for each embrasure. Maines (254, fn. 16) argued that the queen (L2) was carved by the sculptor of the right-hand figures, but the carving of the heads, shoulders, and hems over the feet of the three left-hand figures looks similar, with differences caused only by the female dress. I agree with Maines that the Saint-Loup trumeau was carved by the sculptor of the right-hand jamb statues.

The capital, surmounting Saint-Loup on the trumeau (fig. 127), depicts the Miraculous Mass of Saint Loup, Archbishop of Sens in the seventh century, in which a precious stone fell into the chalice during Mass and subsequently worked miracles (Maines, 399–402). The architectural baldachin, articulating the event, recalls those of the capital-frieze at Chartres, while the relatively crude, squat figures with thick ridge-folds and large, oval heads with separated sections of hair over foreheads recalls capitals by the Assistant of the Saint-Denis Master at Chartres, especially the Washing of the Feet (RP.R1—fig. 128). It is possible that the same sculptor carved these two capitals.

The tympanum of Saint-Loup-de-Naud (fig. 129), in its construction of five blocks, in its general composition framed by undulating cloud border, in the poses of Christ and the symbols of the Evangelists, including the arrangement of the tails of the lion and ox of Mark and Luke, is so close to the Chartres tympanum (fig. 130) that it is impossible for the Saint-Loup sculptor not to have known Chartres. The Saint-Loup Christ exhibits more splayed legs and more elaborate, antigravity folds. The lion and ox are larger and flatter, with fewer surrounding voids. The angel of Matthew is a steam-rollered version of the Chartres figure, with pronounced V-folds between the legs, which recall both some of the archivolt figures of Chartres by the Angel Master (fig. 54) and statue columns from the cloister at Châlons. In spite of these connections, the greater bulkiness of the Saint-Loup figures and their more elaborately treated drapery suggest that they were not created by a Chartres sculptor. Rather, the Saint-Loup tympanum is very close stylistically to all the Saint-Loup jamb statues, but closest to the right-hand jambs (fig. 126). Emphasis on wide, geometrically decorated hems of mantles and complex terminations of folds over ankles tends to be closer to the right jamb than to the columnar figures on the left embrasure (fig. 125).

The Saint-Loup lintel (fig. 129), which Maines (85, 380–94) believes was cut down from a block containing the twelve Apostles to two blocks each, with four Apostles separated by the Virgin over the trumeau, portrays eight Apostles under individual arches, in contrast to the triple grouping at Chartres (fig. 130). The Chartres arches have simple floral fillers in their spandrels, while the Saint-Loup Apostles are crowned by elaborate crenellated baldachins that recall the Chartres capital-frieze and the Saint-Loup capital over the trumeau. The three left-hand Apostles of Saint-Loup seem to follow the fourth, fifth, and sixth Chartres Apostles, counting from the left. Again, as in the case of jamb statues and tympanum, the surface treatment of drapery is markedly different from that of the Chartres lintel by the Headmaster. Drapery and heads of the Saint-Loup lintel

128. Chartres, RP.R capitals, Christ washing feet of Apostles and Supper at Emmaus

129. Saint-Loup-de-Naud, tympanum and lintel (Austin)

130. Chartres, CP, tympanum and lintel (Austin)

seem relatively close to the jamb statues of the right embrasure.

A detailed discussion of the archivolts is beyond the scope of this revision. However, some general observations are in order. The four voussoir blocks on the bottom of the two outer archivolts, which depict the Annunciation and the Visitation on the left and the Magi before Herod on the right, and which Maines (234, figs. 47, 48, 61, 62 and Plate XXVIII, 3, 4) argued are *spolia,* seem to be related stylistically to the jambs, especially to the left statues. Animated, serrated hems over the ankles and on the folds of mantles recall those of the left jamb statues, while the heads of Herod and the Magi resemble the left no. 1 and no. 3 jamb heads, especially in profile. Maines (figs. 130–33) has related these heads to several on the Dijon Last Supper tympanum, while also finding stylistic parallels between the heads of the Visitation and heads on the capitals of the right embrasure at Saint-Loup and on capitals in the ambulatory of Sens Cathedral (Maines, figs. 139–49).

These four voussoir blocks are certainly more three-dimensional than the archivolts depicting scenes from the life of Saint Loup (Lapeyre, 1960, 288–90 and Maines, 430–76). There are no restrictions caused by location on the portal, such as in the jamb columns, lintel, and tympanum, so that sculptors are free to arrange scenes vertically on one archivolt or laterally across two archivolts. Along with the lower relief, there appears to be a concerted effort to fill each block with sculpture of drapery or objects related to the scene being depicted. In spite of the marked differences in subject when contrasted to the Annunciation, the Visitation, and the Magi before Herod and the diminution of the plasticity of these four blocks, the angels and scenes of the life of Saint Loup are stylistically related. The latter would seem to be an elaboration of the former, with the decorative character of the Christ of the tympanum intensified. Thus, in spite of the relationships of Saint-Loup with Chartres, Sens, and Dijon in spite of the fact that jamb statues, lintel, tympanum, and four voussoirs are considered *spolia,* there is a unity of style that points to a conclusion that all of Saint-Loup was carved by sculptors from one *chantier.*

THE WEST PORTAL OF SENLIS

Oversimplification is always dangerously misleading. In 1952 (34, 35, 38 and Plates XXV, 4, XXVI, 4 and XXVII, 4), I emphasized the paradoxical nature of the west portal of the Cathedral of Notre-Dame at Senlis, resulting from its dependence on the Saint-Denis façade for portal design and for some general formats of jamb figures, such as L4, John the Baptist, but combined with a new dynamic verisimilitude of natural appearances. The sculpture of Senlis was placed at the end of a linear development that started with Saint-Denis, continued with Chartres West and its progeny, and ended with a "baroque" explosion at Senlis. Clearly, this simplistic approach needs drastic alteration. However, there are connections between the portal design of Senlis and Saint-Denis West as originally constructed (see Plate A), such as the high, unadorned bases and colonnettes supporting the low lintel, but Senlis clearly breaks with the Chartrain tradition and manifests a new and much more complicated style with its direct source in the Valois portal of Saint-Denis and the strong influence of enamels, goldsmith work, and ivories from the Meuse Valley. Furthermore, dating the Senlis portal to the 1180s, before the dedication of the cathedral on January 16, 1191, has proved to be much too late, as several scholars have argued. The discovery of fragments of jamb statues of the Sainte-Anne portal of Notre-Dame in Paris and the revelation, as a result of recent cleaning, that a high percentage of the Valois portal of Saint-Denis is original, have placed the Senlis sculpture in a new, more vibrant context.

In 1958, Willibald Sauerländer ("Die Marienkrönungs-portale von Senlis und Mantes," *Wallraf-Richartz-Jahrbuch,* Vol. 20, 115–62) was the first to point out the influence of Mosan enamels and goldsmith work on the sculpture of Senlis, Mantes, and the Valois portal of Saint-Denis. However, he argued that the principal source of Senlis was the voussoir figures of the Porte Sainte-Anne of Paris (after 1163). He dated Senlis around 1170 on purely stylistic grounds. In 1972, Sauerländer (1972, 48–49, 407–8 and Plates 42–45) reiterated his conclusions concerning the impact of Mosan objects, such as the base of the Cross of Saint-Bertin in the Museum of Saint-Omer, on the archivolts of Senlis and the importance of the Paris archivolts as the major source for the Senlis sculpture.

In 1977, an important exhibition was held in Senlis that included capitals from the cathedral, plaster casts of five Senlis jamb statues made before their restoration, two casts of voussoirs of Paris and the two Louvre voussoirs from Paris, fragments of marmousets from the Valois portal of Saint-Denis, heads from the Senlis portal in the Musée du Haubergier in Senlis, as well as comparative sculpture from Saint-Germain-des-Prés, Mantes, and other monuments (see Diane Brouillette, *Senlis, un monument de sculpture gothique,* Le Sauvegarde de Senlis, No. 45–46, 1977). This exhibition offered a rare opportunity to compare the sculpture of Paris, the Valois portal of Saint-Denis, and the Senlis and Mantes portals.

In Diane Brouillette's Ph.D. dissertation for the University of California at Berkeley, "The Early Gothic Sculpture of Senlis Cathedral," 1981, the 507 uncaptioned illustrations are virtually invisible, which makes it impossible to follow her conclusions about the "four fairly well defined teams of sculptors responsible for the execution of the archivolt program" (313–49). Brouillette studied and photographed all the archivolts from scaffolding. Whereas Sauerländer dated the Senlis west portal about 1170 on stylistic grounds only, Brouillette was able to propose a date of 1170 at the latest, or preferably 1165–1170, based on the continuity of nave and façade masonry and on the fact that the choir was begun in the 1150s and work on the nave progressed in the 1160s. Her careful study of building campaigns illustrated connections between the ornamental capitals of nave and lower façade.

Brouillette's analysis of the portal design (121–25) includes relationships with the central portal of Saint-Denis, such as eight jamb statues, four archivolts, high bases, colonnettes supporting the low lintel, plus the dramatic changes of the oblique wall and cornice behind the jamb statues, which gives much greater projection to the columnar figures (Plate XXV, 4).

The jamb figures of Senlis (figs. 131, 132) were damaged in 1793 during the French Revolution, with the resulting loss of heads, hands, and symbols, and were restored between 1845 and 1847. However, in 1845, after the statues had been prepared to receive new additions, plaster casts of five of the jambs were made (L4, L2, L1, R1, R4). Prosper Mérimée protested the projected restorations, with the result that only heads were added and the rest of each figure was left in its post-revolution state. The crisp surfaces on the jamb statues, when compared to those of the Christ and the Virgin in the tympanum (figs. 131, 132, 133), suggest the possibility that the jambs were vigorously cleaned in 1845 and have thus lost their original patine.

According to Brouillette, the left four jambs were typological and refer to the Crucifixion of Christ and ultimate Redemption (167–230): L1, the Sacrifice of Isaac, L2, Moses raising the serpent of brass, L3, the Slaughter of the Paschal Lamb by Aaron, L4, John the Baptist (fig. 131); the right jamb statues are: R1, Simeon holding the Christ child, R2, Jeremiah holding the cross, R3, Isaiah holding the lance, the crown of thorns, and nails, R4, David (fig. 132). Brouillette (346–48) divides the eight jamb statues among four sculptors: L2, 3, 4 to one sculptor or team that was responsible for the tympanum and most of the voussoirs; L1, Abraham and Isaac, to a second sculptor, who also carved the lintel; R1 and R2, by two different sculptors, who carved only these two jamb statues. In my opinion, the four left-hand jambs were carved by one sculptor in spite of the great variety of poses and gestures. Drapery sweeping over hands and wrists, curving silhouettes, and hems of mantles are the same in the casts of 1845 (L4, L2, L1) and the restored statues. A small, bunched fold appears on the right side of both Moses and Abraham (fig. 131). Certainly R3 and 4,

Isaiah and David, are by the sculptor of the left statues, and I would attribute R2, Jeremiah, to this same sculptor (fig. 132). Thus it is only R1, Simeon and the Christ Child, that exhibits more complex folds over the legs and that can possibly be assigned to another sculptor.

The monumental figures with their dramatic twists and turns, which are in marked contrast to quiet, still Chartrain jamb statues, are held in check by their role as columnar statues, echoing on each embrasure the four staggered bases and supporting four capitals and four archivolts. No strict architectural role as column-sculpture inhibits the figures in the lintel, tympanum, and voussoirs, with the result that the relief sculpture is almost in perpetual motion in a deep space (fig. 133). The lintel depicts in the left half the Death and Burial of the Virgin and the Assumption and Crowning of her Soul, while the right half displays the bodily Assumption of the Virgin. The tympanum is the earliest Coronation of the Virgin in a portal, with Mary enthroned with her Son. Mary is seen as the Bride of Christ and, at the same time, is identified with the Church; so Christ, as bridegroom of the Church, sacrificed himself for the redemption of mankind.

In the tympanum (fig. 133), the Virgin and the Christ are seated on a throne with high rectangular backs, flanked by short colonnettes supporting a heart-shaped frame. On the sides, seated and standing angels, with busts of angels in oculi, complete the dramatic composition. Treatment of drapery with sinuously curving folds, which articulate arms and legs, recalls that of the jamb statues. Christ's head (Plate XXVII, 4) is so close stylistically to the head of a prophet in the Musée du Haubergier at Senlis (H: 0.34 meters— fig. 134) that the same sculptor must have carved both of them. Both heads have brows animated by three grooves, while bulging cheeks, clearly delineated eyes, moustaches, and beards are sculpted in the exact same manner. Brouillette (149–50) believes that this head possibly belonged originally to R1 or R2 jamb statues, yet the remains of Simeon's beard on the cast of R1 precludes that statue. If it were pulled from R2 in 1793, its similarity to heads in the tympanum and voussoirs would seem to indicate that it was carved by the major Senlis sculptor, who appears to have created at least seven of the jamb statues, the tympanum, and many of the voussoirs.

The small head of a youth from the Musée du Haubergier at Senlis (H: 0.15 meters—fig. 135), because of its small size and stylistic relationship to the two preserved angels in the occuli of the tympanum (fig. 133), came from the right-hand oculus, according to Brouillette (154). In spite of the very elaborately treated eyelids, I find it impossible to distinguish this head from those of the angels in the Asumption of the Virgin on the lintel and from the head of Isaac on jamb L1. They all possess the same oval shape,

131. Senlis, left jambs (Austin)

132. Senlis, right jambs (Austin)

133. Senlis, tympanum and lintel (Austin)

134. Senlis, head of a Prophet,
Musée du Haubergier (.34 meters high)

135. Senlis, head of youth,
Musée du Haubergier (.15 meters high)

similar hair, large ears, bulbous cheeks, and pouting mouth. I would argue that all the jambs, with the possible exception of R1 (Simeon), the entire lintel, and the tympanum were carved by the main Senlis Master.

On the basis of both careful study and detailed photography from scaffolding, Brouillette (247–349) divides the forty-four voussoirs of the archivolts among "four fairly well-defined teams of sculptors," with only three responsible for a considerable amount of sculpture. She stresses the uniformity of style of the majority of the voussoir figures and relates them to the jambs (L2, 3, 4 and R3, 4) and to the tympanum. It is impossible to interpret her conclusions without access to her detailed illustrations. But what does a team of sculptors mean? Perhaps a more logical approach is to interpret the voussoirs as having been carved by the main Senlis Master and several of his assistants. If the portal of Notre-Dame at Étampes, which is similar to Senlis in amount of sculpture, can be taken as a model of workshop practice, the major Étampes Master was responsible for all the jamb figures, flanking columnar statues, tympanum, lintel, angles in spandrels, half the capitals, and some of the voussoirs, with assistants involved in completing capitals and voussoirs. The breakdown of individual sculptors of Chartres West, a much larger program than at both Senlis and Étampes, involves four major sculptors and their assistants. The single portal of Corbeil, which will be discussed later, appears to be largely the work of one sculptor.

The ongoing cleaning and conservation of the Valois portal, set into the north transept of Saint-Denis in the thirteenth century, has revealed the fact that a majority of the sculpture is original and that the major sculptor was responsible for most of the sculpture at Senlis. The Valois portal has six kings as jamb statues, with the martydom of Saints Dionysius, Eleutherius, and Rusticus on the tympanum and the Martyrs before the Roman prefect, Scourging of the Martyrs, and their Last Communion on the lintel (see Sauerländer, 1972, Plates 48, 49).

The jamb statues were removed from the Valois portal in 1793 by Lenoir but remounted by Debret in the 1820s after crowns, noses, and plugs of stone were added to the heads and hands, and symbols were replaced. As in the case of Senlis, the jambs may have been overcleaned during this restoration. Brouillette (400–409) argues that four figures, R1, 2, 3, and L1, were carved by one sculptor, L3 by a second, and L2 by a third sculptor, and that L2 jamb is closest to Senlis sculpture such as L2, 3, 4, and the Christ of the tympanum. I agree that L2, because of its massiveness, is extremely close to most of the Senlis jambs, but it also seems similar to L1 and R1, 2, 3. It is only the frontal pose and stiff posture of L2 that are different, while treatment of drapery folds over chest, arms, and legs resembles

that of L1 and the three right-hand statues. L3 appears to be different and exhibits thick-looped folds over the left leg played against uncarved surfaces, characteristics probably derived from Mosan enamels. The presence of Mosan enamelists and goldsmiths at Saint-Denis in the 1140s and early 1150s is clearly documented by Abbot Suger himself. The influence of nonstone sculpture on stone carving seems to have occurred first in the Valois portal, which Brouillette (416–24) dates in the mid-1160s. The impact of Mosan art seems to have been intensified in the Senlis and Mantes portals.

It is hoped that the Valois portal will be published in the near future, and that Diane Brouillette's dissertation on Senlis will appear as a published book. With more study of Mantes, it should be possible to determine the work of the same individual sculptors in the three monuments. In the process of concentrating on the Valois portal of Saint-Denis, the Senlis west portal, and the two Mantes portals, the possible intrusion of sculptural forms from other portals should not be overlooked. The head of Moses and the head of a priest, which are from the central portal of Mantes and which are now preserved in the gallery of Mantes (Brouillette, 1977, figs. 42, 43), exhibit a stylistic relationship to two heads from Saint-Loup-de-Naud (R3 and L1—figs. 125, 126).

NOTRE-DAME OF CORBEIL

An attempt was made on previous pages to explore further the four portals, which were discussed in Part IV of the 1952 edition. Sculptors of the first three monuments certainly knew Chartres West, but the sculpture of Notre-Dame of Corbeil and the Sainte-Anne portal of Notre-Dame in Pairs seems to have been carved by specific sculptors who were involved in the single campaign of the Chartres Royal Portals.

Because of the many stylistic parallels between the sculpture from Corbeil and the jamb statues, lintel, and tympanum of the central portal of Chartres, it can be argued convincingly that the Chartres Headmaster was responsible for the majority of the sculpture from Corbeil and that Corbeil should be dated soon after the completion of Chartres West. As already stated, one Corbeil capital (fig. 118) is very close stylistically to the lintel of the central portal at Chartres (figs. 115–17) and reflects the enthroned Virgin and child and Enoch and Elijah in the Autun tympanum.

The portal of Notre-Dame of Corbeil was badly damaged in 1793 (see F. Salet, "Notre-Dame de Corbeil," *Bulletin monumental,* Vol. 100, 1941, 81–118). However, two jamb statues, of a king and queen, were saved and bought by Lenoir between 1803 and 1806 for his Musée des Mon-

136. Corbeil, Notre-Dame, right splays at Montgermont

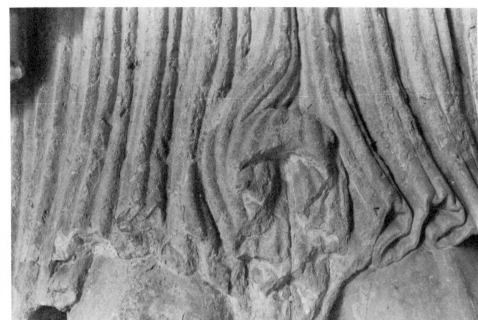

137. Corbeil, queen in the Louvre (2.28 meters)

138. Corbeil, detail of queen

139. Chartres, CP.R3, detail

140. Corbeil, king in the Louvre (2.38 meters)

141. Corbeil, detail of king

uments Français at Saint-Denis, exhibited in the north transept of Saint-Denis in 1817, overrestored by order of Viollet-le-Duc in 1860, and finally became part of the collection of the Louvre in 1916 (Marcel Aubert and Michèle Beaulieu, *Musée National du Louvre: Description raisonnée des sculptures du Moyen Age, de la Renaissance et des temps modernes,* I: *Moyen Age,* Paris, 1950, 70–72, figs. 79, 80). In 1823, the Count of Gontaud-Biron purchased for his château, Montgermont, near Ponthierry, a nave arcade, the right embrasure of the portal with four capitals, another capital of Cain and Abel, and fragments of the Corbeil tympanum. These elements were erected in the corner of a park (now a horse pasture) as a delightful but tragic ruin, tragic in the sense that they are exposed to the elements and are completely uncared for (Salet, 87–88).

The right splay, or embrasure, of the portal (fig. 136) seems to have been reconstructed correctly since the spiral colonnette, an integral part of the doorjamb, could be reconstituted only by following the spiral design from top to bottom. The breaks in the masonry of the inner jamb are carried across the entire splay in courses of dissimilar height. The three undecorated colonnettes in the reentrant angles between each jamb are part of the horizontal blocks, which serve as the matrix of the portal. Corbeil thus did not have the separate highly ornamented colonnettes between the columnar jamb statues, as at Chartres, yet the concave moldings flanking the colonnettes resembles Chartres West.

The Louvre jamb statues are 2.38 meters (the king) and 2.28 (the queen), while the splay from bases to capitals is 2.67 meters. This difference of .29 meters and .39 meters between the height of splay and of preserved jamb statues suggests that the portal design of Corbeil followed the central portal of Chartres, with small undecorated, columnar blocks separating the heads of the jamb statues from the historiated capitals. The narrower top course of the Corbeil splay seems to correspond to the differences between heights of splay and statues. The Louvre queen is slightly smaller than the shortest Chartres central portals (CP.R1—2.34 meters and CP.R2—2.32 meters), while the king is taller than these two but slightly shorter than the majority of the central portal jambs (see Appendix I for dimensions of the west portals of Chartres). In old photographs of the portal at Mongermont (see Salet, 103–4), undecorated drums appear on the jambs, but do not correspond in size to the horizontal courses of the masonry of the portal. They were probably added to the portal after its transfer from Corbeil.

In 1860, the two Corbeil jamb statues (figs. 137, 140) in the Louvre were heavily restored, as can be seen by comparing them to drawings for Lenoir before the fact (Salet, 107). Palmetted tops were added to the simple horizontal crowns, damaged noses replaced, moustache repaired, the king's beard elongated, and awkward hands and symbol added to the queen. Extensive patching with new inserts can be seen on the lower hems of the mantle of the queen and in smaller areas of the king's. On the basis of close study of the surfaces of these figures, it would seem that the restorer either recut all the surfaces or heavily employed a wire brush, which removed the original patine, in order to try and blend the patches and additions into the statues as a whole. Remnants of the original surfaces, however, can be seen in the areas of drapery over the ankles (fig. 137, 140).

The so-called Queen of Sheba (fig. 137) combines features of costume and arrangement of drapery from two jambs by the Headmaster of Chartres: CP.L3 and CP.R3 (figs. 12, 13a). The treatment of the bodice and the braided hair recalls CP.L3, while the knotted belt with falling tassles, swelling stomach (now covered by modern hands), and the outer sections of the mantle, extending to the ankles, are similar to CP.R3. With changes to the head, such as the addition of fleurons to the crown and the removal of the modern nose, the queen resembles the head of CP.L3. Both the Chartres and Corbeil statues possess the same strict, rectangular silhouette, although the shoulders of the Corbeil figure are slightly tapered. This Corbeil jamb has fewer vertical folds but more-decorated treatment of hems of mantle, and the braided hair is bound by ribbons.

A detail of Sheba (fig. 138) exhibits rounded ridge-folds, often in groups of three and with trefoil voids animating the hem. This drapery treatment resembles that of several Chartres jambs, such as CP.L2 and CP.R2 and 4 (figs. 12b, 13a and c). The grouping of the ridge-folds of the Corbeil jamb are also found on the Chartres female figure (CP.R3—figs. 139, 13a), while the central curved and raised fold seems to be a variant of the remaining bottom fold of CP.R3 (fig. 139). The greater complexity of this fold resembles generally the undulating hem of Chartres CP.R4 (fig. 13c).

The Louvre King Solomon (?) from Corbeil (fig. 140) is based on Chartres CP.R4 (Plate XVII, 2 and figs. 13a, 13c). The same arrangement of collar and folds over the chest and the mantle over his left arm, falling in a truncated mass, are exhibited in both jamb statues. Only his lowered right arm and the symbols are different. As in the statue of the queen, the drapery is simplified, with a smaller number of folds, especially over his right leg. Some of these differences could be the result of overzealous restoration. In spite of the unusual tonguelike fold (see detail, fig. 141), the general treatment of the hems is very close stylistically to Chartres CP.R4 (fig. 13c). If the modern top of the crown, the beard, and the nose are removed, the Corbeil head resembles those of both Chartres CP.R2 and 4 (Plate XIX, 3, 4).

Because of the extensive restorations including either recutting or extensive brushing of the surfaces, it is difficult

142. Corbeil, capitals (Montgermont)

145. Corbeil, right-hand section
of tympanum (Montgermont)

143. Corbeil, R2 capital, Isaac feels Jacob's covered
hands and Rebecca gives Jacob the Venison

144. Corbeil, R3 capital, Jacob brings Isaac
the Venison and obtains his blessing and Esau's
Venison is rejected by his Father

to prove that the Chartres Headmaster carved the two jambs from Corbeil, yet the many stylistic relationships certainly point to the conclusion that the same sculptor was employed at both Chartres and Corbeil.

The capitals of Corbeil (fig. 142), four on the right splay and one on the grounds at Montgermont, lost their heads in the Revolution, but escaped the restorers of the nineteenth century. Walter Cahn was the first scholar to identify the capitals of the right embrasure ("Observations on Corbeil," *Art Bulletin,* Vol. LV, 1973, 321–27). According to Cahn, these capitals of the right side of the portal (fig. 142) depict the old age of the patriarch Isaac and the establishment of his succession, based on Genesis (left to right): R1, the enfeebled Isaac asks Esau for a Serving of Venison, and Esau as Huntsman; R2, Isaac Feels Jacob's Covered Hands, and Rebecca gives Jacob the Venison; R3, Jacob Brings Isaac the Venison and Obtains his Blessing, and Esau's Venison is Rejected by his Father; R4, Jacob's Ladder, and Laban gives Jacob the Hands of Rachel and Leah.

The source of the format of these unusual capitals is certainly the Chartres West capital-frieze (figs. 32–44). The Corbeil "taillors" of curved acanthus (fig. 142) follow those of Chartres with the same ornamented palmettes and the same degree of relief, yet the central floral fillers at Corbeil are not arranged on a vertical axis, but rather on an alternating left-and-right axis. As at Chartres, the capitals are interlocked horizontally over the reentrant angles of the splay.

The architectural baldachins above the narrative scenes are simpler and occupy less of the total height of the capital when compared to the Chartres capitals. At Corbeil, the arcade above the figures, which articulates the figured compositions, is crowned by a horizontal molding and does not project up into the miniature architecture, as at Chartres. The architecture of the Corbeil capitals consists of alternating circular and rectangular structures, usually with domed, central buildings accenting the projecting corners, the middle of sides, and reentrant corners of the capitals (see R2, 3, and 4—fig. 142).

The baldachins of the twenty-two Chartres capitals vary considerably in design, often with two stories and with more pedimental structures. Since five different sculptors were responsible for the Chartres capital-frieze, one would expect considerable variety in the Chartres capitals, in contrast to the uniformity of those at Corbeil. The baldachins of the eight capitals by the Étampes Master are quite different from the four by his assistant (see, especially, capital CP.L 1, 3, 4, as contrasted to CP.L2 and the Annunciation, Visitation, and Nativity capitals by his assistant—figs. 32–35). Similar differences can be found in the six capitals by the Saint-Denis Master and the two by his assistant, while the baldachins of the two capitals by the Itinerant Sculptor are

different from all others. The Chartres Headmaster was not involved in the carving of the capital-frieze, but at Corbeil he seems to have created a simplified and quieter variant of the Chartres baldachins.

Unfortunately, all the heads of the five Corbeil capitals were destroyed during the Revolution, but the remaining figures reveal a refined drapery style with a great variety of pose and gesture, which is in marked contrast to the stiffer, more puppetlike figures by the Étampes Master, Saint-Denis Master, and their two assistants at Chartres. As in R2 and R3 (figs. 143, 144—Isaac Feeling Jacob's Covered Hands and Rebecca Giving Jacob the Venison; Jacob Brings Isaac the Venison and Esau's Venison is Rejected by his Father), treatment of drapery articulates gracefully the human forms whether standing or reclining, as Isaac in R3. Although the Apostles of the Chartres central portal lintel by the Headmaster (figs. 45, 46) are almost three times the size of the capitals and must conform to the triple arcades of the lintel, there are many stylistic similarities between the Apostles and the capitals from Corbeil. Anatomy is clearly expressed through the drapery on both portals, and the animated treatment of the hems over ankles and of the drapery falling from Isaac's bed is closely related to that of the Chartres lintel. Sauerländer ("Sculpture on Early Gothic Churches: The State of Research and Open Questions," *Gesta,* Vol. IX/2, 1970, 32–56, esp. 41 and figs. 15, 16) called attention to the relationship between the Chartres lintel and Corbeil capital of the Sacrifice of Cain and the Killing of Abel and calls Corbeil "a disturbing case of chronological inconsistency when the Corbeil sculpture is dated in the 1180's." Sauerländer (1972, Plate 30, 397–98) dates the Louvre jambs on the plates to 1140–1150 but in the text argues for the 1150s. On the basis of the capitals and their close relationship to the Chartres Headmaster, a date for the Corbeil portal in the late 1140s or certainly by 1150 seems plausible.

Fragments of the tympanum and archivolts of the Corbeil portal are gradually disintegrating in the park of Montgermont. This superstructure originally depicted the Last Judgment, with an enthroned Christ flanked by Saint John and the Virgin accompanied by angels. The Christ figure was destroyed but is known from an engraving after Jorand (see Salet, 111). Lapeyre reconstructed the superstructure (1960, 299–301, Diagram G). Arrangement and treatment of drapery appear to be a simplified variant of the Christ at Chartres (fig. 45). When compared with old photographs, the two side blocks have deteriorated considerably. The Virgin on the left block has disappeared, while the right one (fig. 145), which probably depicts Saint John and an angel, has lost a lot of its original surfaces.

The style of the right-hand block (fig. 145) has many parallels with the Corbeil capitals, especially R2, Isaac feeling Jacob's Covered Hands (fig. 143). The treatment of folds over the legs and of the hems of the mantle over the ankles of the angel is similar on the tympanum and capital. The damaged Saint John (?) on the left (fig. 145) resembles in proportion and drapery folds the exterior figures of Jacob and Esau on capital R3 (fig. 144).

Since the Corbeil portal appears to manifest both a stylistic consistency and a high degree of quality, it can be argued that it was carved basically by one sculptor. In the case of south portal of Notre-Dame at Étampes, which is a larger program than Corbeil, with carved spandrels and ten jamb statues framing the portal, it appears that the Étampes Master carved all the monumental sculpture and was aided by assistants in completing the archivolts. At Corbeil, the uniformity of style and high quality again points to the work of a single sculptor. Connections between the Corbeil sculpture and the Chartres West sculpture by the Headmaster argue for the conclusion that the Headmaster of Chartres was responsible for the Last Judgment portal of Corbeil.

A comprehensive and detailed study of Corbeil is outside the scope of this revision. Some action should be taken immediately to save the Corbeil sculpture at Montgermont. It should either be put under cover or, more logically, donated to the Louvre, where its splay could be reassembled with the jamb statues. This extraordinary Early Gothic sculpture would then be both properly preserved and enjoyed by the public.

SAINTE-ANNE PORTAL, NOTRE-DAME, PARIS

The cleaning of the entire façade of Notre-Dame in the late 1960s revealed, among many other discoveries, much more original sculpture on the archivolts of the Sainte-Anne Portal. In April 1977, the dramatic find in front of the Banque Française du Commerce extérieur (Hôtel Moreau) of forty-six fragments of the Sainte-Anne Portal, twenty-one huge High Gothic heads from the Gallery of the Kings, and sculpture from the later transept portals has greatly intensified the study of the sculpture of Paris and raised many questions about the chronology of Gothic sculpture, especially in the twelfth century. These sculptures, after being exhibited in Florence, New York, Cleveland, and the Soviet Union are now permanently installed in the Musée de Cluny in Paris (see Alain Erlande-Brandenburg, *Les sculptures de Notre-Dame de Paris au Musée de Cluny,* Paris, 1982). With this great increase in the amount of Early Gothic sculpture from and on the Porte Sainte-Anne, it is now possible at least to begin the process of identifying individual sculptors and, at the same time, of attempting to discover their work on other monuments.

Twelfth-century sculpture of the Sainte-Anne portal was mounted around 1210, with additions to make it fit into the High Gothic context of the façade as a whole. Thus, all of the Early Gothic sculpture is *spolia*. The lack of any iconographical unity suggests that the sculpture, intended for more than one portal, was combined to complete the right, Sainte-Anne Portal. The tympanum (fig. 146) depicts the Virgin and Christ Child enthroned, flanked by angels with censers and three figures. The discrepancy between the twelfth-century, slightly pointed tympanum and the larger, sharply pointed archivolts was reconciled by the insertion of a floral border and angels at the apex. Of the lintels, only the upper one is of the twelfth century and depicts, from left to right, the Annunciation, the Visitation, the Nativity, the Annunciation to the Shepherds, Scribe and Pharisee, and Herod and the three Magi. This lintel was lengthened in the early thirteenth century by a compressed Presentation of the Virgin on the left and half of the horses of the Magi on the right.

Lapeyre (1960, 147–53) summarized the literature on the Sainte-Anne portal. Concentrating on the tympanum, Lapeyre disagreed with Wilhelm Vöge (*Die Aufänge des monumentalen Stiles in Mittelalter,* Strassburg, 1894, 135–65), who had argued that the same artist created the tympana of Chartres (RP) and Paris, and instead followed the conclusion of Émile Mâle (*Art et artistes du Moyen Âge,* 1947, 190) that Paris was carved by a disciple of the Chartres Master. He also cited Marcel Aubert (*La sculpture française au debut de l'époque gothique,* 1946, 52), who saw two different personalities carving the Paris and Chartres tympana and who gave the Paris upper lintel to artists other than those responsible for the tympanum and voussoirs. Lapeyre followed Aubert's dating of the portal—1165–1175.

The most extensive article on the Sainte-Anne portal, following its cleaning, is by Jacques Thirion ("Les plus anciennes sculptures de Notre-Dame de Paris," *Comptes-rendus de l'Académie des inscriptions et belles-lettres,* 1970, 85–112). Aided by scaffolding and extensive photography, Thirion stressed the disparate character of the portal, with the Nativity and Visit of the Magi to Herod on the upper lintel, implying that the tympanum should be the Adoration of the Magi, as in Bourges, Laon, and the Chartres north transept (86–89). Further, he pointed out the fact that the original twelfth-century lintel is slightly wider than the tympanum. Decisions to widen and heighten the portal were made as the sculpture was being mounted, so that additions were made to both the upper, twelfth-century lintel and the lower, early-thirteenth-century lintel. The shift to a more pointed arch for the portal made obsolete the original keystones of the archivolts, which are now in the Louvre.

Thirion (92–97) opposed the interpretation of all previous scholars that the king and bishop on the tympanum are Louis VII and Bishop Maurice de Sully and argued correctly that King Childebert, the first benefactor of Paris, and Bishop Saint Germain are depicted. This identification was based on a charter of 528, in which Childebert gave the first donation to Paris to thank the bishop for healing him.

In terms of style, Thirion (97–109) stressed both the disparity of points of view and the varying degrees of quality, with only the tympanum exhibiting an influence from Chartres and thus appearing to be later in date. He attributed the upper lintel to two artists, continuing a more Romanesque graphic style: the right, larger section, the Nativity through the Magi before Herod, and the left, the Annunciation and the Visitation. He agreed with James Rorimer that the head of David from the jamb statue, now in New York, was carved by the same sculptor responsible for the right side of the lintel (see James Rorimer, "A Twelfth-Century Head of King David from Notre-Dame," *The Metropolitan Museum of Art Bulletin,* 1940, 17–19). The voussoirs of Kings, Prophets, and Elders of the Apocalypse, according to Thirion, represent a different style than that of the lintel, and with their crossed legs and animated treatment of drapery are closer to Saint-Denis than to Chartres.

In analyzing the torso of Saint Peter (fig. 107), discovered in 1839, Thirion stated that this fragment bore no relationship to Chartres, Le Mans, or Saint-Loup-de-Naud, but rather to mural painting and manuscripts. Finally he made a distinction between the archaic character of the lintel, the torso of Peter and the head of David, and the more advanced angels of the archivolts, tympanum, and trumeau of Saint Marcellus.

Since both the date of 1163 for the beginning of the cathedral and the presence of Bishop Maurice de Sully on the tympanum have been questioned, Thirion (109–12) dated the sculpture between 1150, for the oldest sculpture, and 1165, for the latest, instead of the traditional dating of 1165–1175. To justify his early dating of the Sainte-Anne portal sculpture, Thirion hypothesized that either work on Notre-Dame began before Maurice de Sully became bishop or that the sculpture was created for the old cathedral. He tended to favor the second.

Sauerländer (1972, 404–6), dating the Sainte-Anne sculpture shortly after 1160, contended that the Paris tympanum was in the style of "the Chartres archivolt master," but its decorative character precluded the conclusion that the two tympana were created by the same sculptor. Basing his arguments on the Montfacon engraving, the torso of Peter, and the head of David, Sauerländer saw no stylistic connection between the Paris jamb statues and those of Chartres West. He did, however, find traces of Saint-Denis,

such as compact bodies and large heads in the archivolts of Paris, stemming from the doorjamb of the central portal and the statue-columns of the right portal of Saint-Denis. The two Paris keystones, in the Louvre since 1894, were, according to Sauerländer (Plate 41), carved for another portal, which would have included the Christ in Majesty, discovered by Viollet-le-Duc but now lost, and the Elders of the Apocalypse, now *in situ* on the Sainte-Anne portal.

The intriguing story of the discovery in April 1977 of 364 pieces of sculpture from Notre-Dame in Paris in the courtyard of the Hôtel Moreau, which included thirty fragments of the jamb statues of the Porte Sainte-Anne, five pieces of their supporting consoles, and nine unidentified pieces, is described and illustrated in a handsome book (François Giscard D'Estaing, Michel Fleury, Alain Erlande-Brandenburg, *Les rois retrouvés, Notre-Dame de Paris,* 1977). Using the Montfaucon engraving of the Sainte-Anne portal (fig. 149), Erlande-Bradenburg reassembled fragments of the eight jamb statues in the Musée de Cluny, following their gift to the state. Erlande-Brandenburg (24–29) distinguished two hands: one responsible for Peter, Paul, Saint Marcel and David, and influenced by metal work; and a second, the sculptor of kings no. 2 and no. 8. He dated the Sainte-Anne jambs about 1150, between Saint-Denis and Chartres and probably carved for the old Cathedral, and stressed their stylistic isolation with no antecedents and no progeny.

Michel Fleury recounted the discovery of 1977 and described the process of locating the fragments on the Montfaucon engraving of the eight jamb statues ("Les sculptures de Notre-Dame de Paris découvertes en 1977 et 1978," *Cahiers de la Rotonde,* I, 1978, 39–56). He dated the Sainte-Anne sculpture around 1150. Finally, Alain Erlande-Brandenburg's detailed catalogue (*Les sculptures de Notre-Dame de Paris au Musée de Cluny,* 1982) and the thoughtful installation of the remains of the eight jamb statues and the trumeau of the Sainte-Anne portal facilitates further study. Erlande-Brandenburg placed the Porte Sainte-Anne between Saint-Denis (1140) and Chartres, which he dates between 1145 and 1155, and, at the same time, saw the jamb statues as somewhat related to Chartres RP.R in date. He followed Thirion in concluding that the disparate parts of the Porte Sante-Anne belong to an unfinished campaign to refurbish the old cathedral with more than one portal.

The tympanum of the Sainte-Anne Portal (figs. 146, 147) has the following nineteenth-century restorations: the crook of the bishop's crozier, the Christ Child's right hand, and the Virgin's sceptre. If the tympana of Paris and Chartres are compared (figs. 47, 50, 146, 147), it is evident that the same sculptor created both, as Vöge had argued. In spite of the loss of the enframing baldachin at Chartres, the pose, gestures, and arrangement of drapery of the central blocks

146. Paris, Notre-Dame,
Sainte-Anne portal,
tympanum and upper lintel

147. Paris, Notre-Dame,
Virgin and Christ enthroned

148. Chartres, RP
Virgin and Christ enthroned

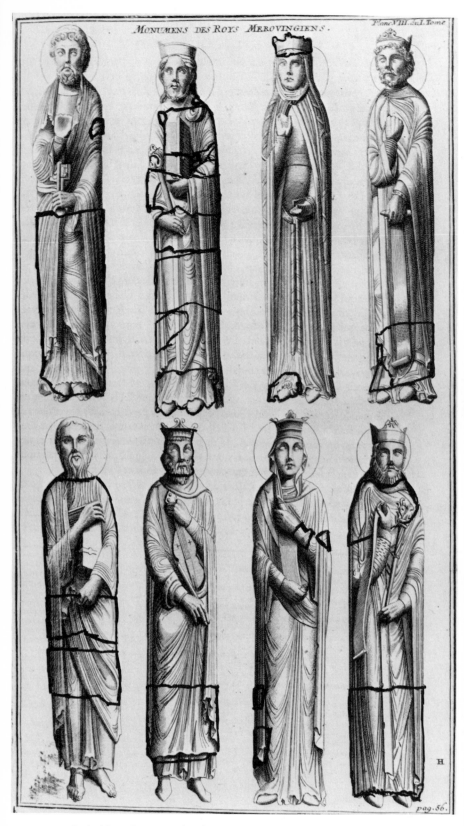

149. Paris, Notre-Dame, jambs of Sainte-Anne portal (Montfaucon);
drawing on engraving after Erlande-Brandenburg

150. Paris, Notre-Dame, Torso of Saint Peter (Musée de Cluny)
(RP.L1 and upper left-hand jamb in fig. 149)

151. Paris, Notre-Dame, Fragment of RP.L2 jamb
(Musée de Cluny) (second from left fig. 149)

152. Chartres, RP.R1

153. Chartres, RP.R2

154. Paris, Notre-Dame, Detail of Paul, RP.R1
(Musée de Cluny) (Lower left, fig. 149)

155. Paris, Notre-Dame, Fragment of David, RP.R2
(Musée de Cluny) (second from left, fig. 149)

233

of both portals are almost identical. Drapery folds over the chest, legs, and ankles of the Virgins and over the legs of the Christ Child are so similar that it is impossible to conclude that two different sculptors were involved. In the Paris tympanum, the sculptor has increased the number of folds over the Virgin's legs and has changed the folds of the hems of Her undergarment. Decorative features of the Chartres figures are intensified in the Paris Virgin and Child. We attributed the Chartres RP tympanum to the Angel Master, who also carved the LP tympanum and many of the voussoirs in all three portals. The RP tympanum appears to be his earliest work at Chartres, followed by the LP tympanum, with the lower archivolts of the CP comprising his latest sculpture. It is in the latter, the lower archivolts of the CP (figs. 55, 56), that the increase in surface animation by a greater complexity of folds is clearly revealed. Thus, the Paris Virgin and Child appears to follow almost exactly the format of the Chartres tympanum, but in surface details it continues the more mannered, decorative quality of the sculptor's latest work at Chartres. The subtle difference between the two Virgins and Childs can be explained by the evolution of the Angel Master at Chartres. Since, in my opinion, all the sculpture of Chartres West was *in situ* in the mid-1140s, the carving of the tympanum, now on the Porte Sainte-Anne, took place around 1150, as Fleury, Thirion, and Erlande-Brandenburg believed.

Flanking angels swinging censers complete the composition of the Chartres tympanum, while the inclusion of bishop, king, and clerk in Paris force the angels into a vertical pose. However, the organization of folds in the right-hand angel is similar, with the exception of the increase in number and complexity of folds. The left-hand angel of Paris is somewhat different from the angel of Chartres, especially in the elaborate treatment of its left leg, with oval folds for knees and shins and pointed folds over the ankle. This surface animation with curving ridge-folds seems to relate to some of the fragments of the jamb statues of the Sainte-Anne portal and to the jambs of Chartres RP.R. Figures of the king (Dagobert), the bishop (Saint Germain), and the recording cleric were certainly carved by the same sculptor. The five blocks that make up the Paris tympanum present a more complicated program, but appear to be the creation of the Chartres Master of the Angels after he had finished his work on the lower archivolts of the Chartres central portal.

On the basis of comparisons between fragments, discovered in 1977, and the Montfaucon engraving of the Sainte-Anne Portal (fig. 149), thirty pieces have been identified as belonging to the eight jamb statues (see Erlande-Brandenburg, 1982, 14–27). When the torso of Saint Peter, discovered in 1839, and the head of David, in The Metropolitan Museum of Art, New York, are added, it is now possible

to study the style of most of the jambs as handsomely installed in their proper order in the Musée de Cluny.

The Montfaucon engraving of 1725 depicts the eight jamb statues (fig. 149): top row, left to right: Peter (RP.L1), Old Testament King (RP.L2), Old Testament Queen (RP,L3), Old Testament King (RP.L4); bottom row, left to right: Paul (RP.R1), David (RP.R2), Old Testament Queen (RP.R3), Old Testament King (RP.R4). Since drapery folds in the preserved torsos and fragments are close to their representation in the engraving, it is possible to use cautiously the engravings of each figure in their entirety to compare them with jamb statues of other monuments. The top row of left-hand statues exhibits several characteristics that recall Chartres RP.R jambs (figs. 149, 10). The proportions of figures, heads to bodies, are similar, while the awkward articulation of wrists and forearms, with the resulting jerky gestures, appears in both monuments. In contrast to the top row jambs, those on the bottom row display fluid poses, with parallel arms and more complex treatment of drapery.

The torso of Peter (fig. 150) and the bottom fragment of RP.L2 (fig. 151) exhibit stylistic similarities with Chartres RP.R1 and 2 jambs (figs. 152, 153). The left upper leg of Peter is animated by curving, rounded ridge-folds that frame pointed voids. The rounded loop folds over and between the legs of Paris (RP.L2, fig. 151) have their stylistic counterparts in Chartres RP.R2 (fig. 153). Although the bottom hems of both the Paris and Chartres figures have been severely damaged, the way the undergarment flares outward over the frontally placed feet is similar. Clearly the Paris figure is carved from a more finely grained limestone.

Is it possible to conclude that the so-called Saint-Denis Master at Chartres carved these two Paris jamb statues? As in the comparison of the tympana of Chartres and Paris, it is necessary to include in the discussion both the later sculpture on the doorjambs, on pilasters, and on the capitals by the Saint-Denis Master at Chartres and to assume that the evolution of an individual sculptor can occur over time. Drapery of the Chartres jambs (RP.R1, 2—figs. 152, 153) is starker and less fluid than that of the Paris figures (figs. 150, 151). However, when doorjambs (RP.R) and pilasters are studied (figs. 18–23), the smaller size and lack of restriction of the column permits greater fluidity of drapery. The narrative cycle of the Chartres capitals, the latest work by the Saint-Denis Master (figs. 40–42, 44) exhibits even more movement in drapery folds, although it is greatly reduced in complexity because of the small size of the figures. Thus, it would appear to be quite possible that the Chartres Saint-Denis Master also carved Paris RP.L1, 2. The queen (RP.L3) is related in general format and costume to Chartres RP.R3. However, the fragment of her right foot and drapery is much more undercut than the corresponding area in the Chartres jamb.

Details of Paul (RP.R1—fig. 154) and David (RP.R2—fig. 155) suggest that the right-hand Paris jamb figures were carved by a different sculptor. Deep, drilled folds and high ridge-folds accent Paul's left arm and chest, while these folds in alternation animate David's right knee. Much greater variation of surfaces, apparent in all four right-hand jambs and taken together with a uniform parallel placement of arms and a lack of disjointed, anatomical treatment of the wrists, points to an attribution of these four Paris jambs to a different sculptor whose work did not appear on Chartres West. Moreover, the head of David in The Metropolitan Museum of Art strongly resembles the heads of the upper lintel of the Sainte-Anne portal (fig. 146), but has no stylistic relationship to the heads of Chartres RP.R jamb (fig. 10). The closeness in style of the heads of David and of the lintel as well as the general complicated and animated surfaces of figures of the lintel and the right-hand jamb strongly suggest that the same sculptor or his assistant carved both lintel and jamb. One cannot help but wonder whether or not the right-hand jambs and upper lintel are slightly later in date than are the tympanum and left-hand jambs.

A detailed study of the archivolts *in situ* on the Sainte-Anne portal and the two keystones in the Louvre (see Sauerländer, 1972, Plate 41) is beyond the scope of this revision. Careful scrutiny from scaffolding and macrophotography are necessary to distinguish nineteenth-century restorations. In general, the Angels, Prophets, and the Elders of the Apocalypse on the archivolts and the two voussoirs in the Louvre have more stylistic common denominators with left-hand jambs (Peter and RP.L2, 3, 4—figs. 149, 150) and Chartres RP.R jambs than with the Paris tympanum, sculpted by the Chartres Master of the Angels, or with the right-hand jambs, carved by the third sculptor.

The date of around 1150 seems plausible if it is assumed, correctly, I believe, that all of Chartres West was completed in the mid-1140s. A recent article by William Clark and Robert Mark ("The First Flying Buttresses: A New Reconstruction of the Nave of Notre-Dame de Paris," *Art Bulletin,* Vol. LXVI, 1, 1984, 47–65) argues that the choir of Notre-Dame was begun between 1150 and 1155. According to them, this dating is based on the similarities of capitals in the Paris choir to those in the choirs of Saint-Germain-des-Prés and Saint-Denis. Thus the Sainte-Anne portal sculpture could have been carved for either the new or the old cathedral.

Several premises should be considered in summarizing the development of Early Gothic sculpture in the middle and third-quarter of the twelfth century. First, the dedication of the façade, narthex, and west portals of Saint-Denis in 1140 and the choir of Saint-Denis in 1144 unleashed an unprecendented building and sculptural activity in the Île-de-France and in surrounding regions. Second, more often than not, work on sculptural programs began when new building campaigns were inaugurated. Third, since many monuments were destroyed with the resulting loss of possible links between early and later portals, the search for individual, evolving sculptors is more difficult.

On the basis of the first two premises, it is possible to suggest earlier dating for the south portal of Le Mans, Corbeil, and the Sainte-Anne portal of Paris—all around 1150. The right jamb statues of Le Mans could have been carved by an assistant of the Headmaster of Chartres, while the Chartres Headmaster seems to have been responsible for most of the Corbeil portal. In the case of Paris, the Master of the Angels of Chartres was responsible for the tympanum of the Sainte-Anne portal. There is also stylistic evidence in Chartres West to argue that the Saint-Denis Master went from Chartres to Paris and created the left jambs, now in the Musée de Cluny.

More detailed study of the portals of Le Mans, Provins, Corbeil, Paris, the Valois portal of Sainte-Denis, Senlis, and Mantes is necessary in order to establish more completely the personal styles of the sculptors involved and to locate these individuals as they evolved over time in a sequence of monuments.

APPENDIX I

MEASUREMENTS OF
WEST PORTALS OF CHARTRES

(Detailed Drawings of Each Splay of the Royal Portals
Were Made in the Summer of 1939)

LEFT PORTAL, LEFT (Plate XVI, 1)

JAMB FIGURES (all measurements refer to height in meters)

LP.L 1   2.20 meters
    .53 canopy
    .16 top piece
LP.L 2   2.15 meters
    .47 canopy
    .19 top piece
LP.L 3   2.52 including canopy
    .35 top piece

ORNAMENTAL COLONNETTES (bottom to top)

LP.L 1   1.78, 1.52, .24 meters
LP.L 2   1.73, 1.03, .78 meters

LEFT PORTAL, RIGHT (Plate XVIII, 1)

JAMB FIGURES

LP.R 2   2.19 meters
    .65 canopy
LP.R 4   2.25 meters
    .63 meters

ORNAMENTAL COLONNETTES (bottom to top)

LP.R 1   1.75, 1.46, .41 meters
LP.R 2   2.58, .79, .20 meters
LP.R 3   1.57, 2 modern blocks

CENTRAL PORTAL, LEFT (Plate XVII, 1)

JAMB FIGURES

CP.L 1   2.47 meters
    .15 top piece of column
CP.L 2   2.55 meters
    .16 top block
CP.L 3   2.56 meters
    .15 top block

CP.L 5   2.57 meters
    .15 top block

COLONNETTES

CP.L 1   1.70, 1.34, .55 meters
CP.L 2   1.63, 1.44, .53 meters
CP.L 3   1.63, 1.21, .76 meters
CP.L 4   2.21, 1.21, .18 meters

CENTRAL PORTAL, RIGHT (Plate XVII, 2)

JAMB FIGURES

CP.R 1   2.34 meters
    .35 top
CP.R 2   2.32 meters
    .31 top block
CP.R 3   2.53 meters
    .31 top block
CP.R 4   2.52 meters
    .30 top piece

COLONNETTES

CP.R 1   2.28, 1.31 meters
CP.R 2   2.30, 1.27 meters
CP.R 3   2.40, 1.19 meters
CP.R 4   2.27, 1.30 meters

RIGHT PORTAL, LEFT (Plate XVIII, 2)

JAMB FIGURES

RP.L 2   2.33 meters
    .54 block including canopy
RP.L 3   2.24 meters
    .60 block including canopy
RP.L 4   2.43 meters
    .65 upper block

COLONNETTES

RP.L 2   1.30, 2.26 meters
RP.L 3   1.65, 1.11 meters

RIGHT PORTAL, RIGHT (Plate XVI, 2)

JAMB FIGURES

RP.L 1   2.59 including canopy
          .40 top block

RP.L 2   2.30 not including canopy
          .59 top block including canopy

RP.R 3   2.13 jamb statue meters
          .63 block including canopy
          .14 top block

COLONNETTES

RP.R 1   3 modern blocks, top block .90 meters
RP. 2   1.58, 1.07, .90

BASES ACROSS FAÇADE (see Plates XI, XIII, 3, and XXI, 3, 4)

Lowest block capped by scotia molding: .29 meters
Upper block extending up to bottom of decorated columns and colonnettes: .63 meters (these dimensions are uniform on all six splays).

WIDTH OF PORTALS

At lowest step: 16.45 meters
Width at level of geometric ovals of bases, which is actual width of the three portals between the responds of the north and south towers: 15.92 meters
Width of openings of portals: LP—1.94 meters; CP—3.00 meters; RP—1.85 meters.

APPENDIX II

DIJON, SAINT-BÉNIGNE

(W.S.S. and Ruth Pasquine)

Sculpture of the Benedictine Abbey of Saint-Bénigne in Dijon has often been included in discussions of the origins of Early Gothic. Some scholars have argued that Dijon grew out of Saint-Denis and then influenced Chartres West, especially the central portal by the Headmaster, while others have perceived the Dijon sculpture as emerging from Île-de-France monuments. First, the tympanum of the Last Supper and the head of Saint Bénigne (?) will be analyzed and then compared with both Saint-Denis and Chartres West (figs. 156–59). Then, the opinions of scholars on the chronological relationship of Dijon and Early Gothic will be summarized.

The tympanum of the Last Supper, originally on one of the side, west portals of Saint-Bénigne and now in the Musée Archéologique de Dijon, shows Christ, the swooning John, six Apostles seated or standing, two smaller Apostles seated at corners, and the kneeling Judas in front of the table (figs. 156–58). Figures are thin, with sticklike legs revealed through tightly stretched drapery. Collars and hems of bodices and mantles are decorated with wide bands of geometric ornaments, while folds of drapery over chests and some legs consist of slightly raised, curving ridges. Groups of vertical folds, usually in bunches of four, fill the areas between the legs (fig. 157). Feet are flat, with long toes of almost equal length and clearly marked toenails. Squarish heads reveal cheeks and eyebrows formed by uninterrupted curving planes, while hair and beards consist of evenly spaced, parallel ridges. Eyes are accented by narrow, rounded upper and lower eyelids, converging at the corners, and by bulging eyeballs (see Christ—fig. 158).

The head of Saint Bénigne (?), probably from the trumeau of the central portal and now in the Musée Archéologique of Dijon (fig. 159), would appear to be by the same sculptor responsible for the Last Supper. Planes of cheek, eyebrows, and forehead, delineation of eyes, pursed, downward-turning lips, and hair and beard of evenly spaced ridges can be seen in the heads of the Last Supper tympanum and in Saint Bénigne. The majority of characteristics appear un-Burgundian in a Vézelay-Autun sense.

By comparisons of Dijon with Saint-Denis and Chartres West, it is possible to establish the chronological relationships of these three monuments. The Saint Bénigne and the heads of the Last Supper (figs. 158, 159) have no connection with the two preserved heads of the Saint-Denis central portal (Plate VIII and fig. 3). In the Saint-Denis heads, shifting planes of foreheads and cheeks, which create edges, are totally different from the continuously rounded surfaces of the Dijon heads. Beards and hair are more coarsely chiseled in the Dijon sculpture. The treatment of the eyes, with flat lids and drilled irises, has no counterpart at Dijon, where bulging eyes are within rounded eyelids that converge to a point against the noses. Similar differences, but to a lesser degree, can be seen in the comparison of Dijon heads and the two Saint-Denis heads of the left portal by a different sculptor (Plate IX). The eyelids of the two heads are still flat, but the shape of the eye is closer to that of the Dijon heads. Hair and beard are more crisply carved and more rhythmically arranged in the Saint-Denis heads.

The thin sticklike legs of the Apostles (figs. 156, 157), with bunches of raised folds between the legs, have no counterparts in the Saint-Denis jamb figures as copied for Montfaucon (Plate X, 2 and figs. 1, 2). Further, the preserved sculpture on the Saint-Denis central portal (figs. 4–6) has no stylistic connection with the Dijon Last Supper.

Saint-Denis sculpture, which invites comparison with Dijon, is the Crosby Relief of Twelve Apostles (Plate X) and the king from the cloister in The Metropolitan Museum of Art (Sumner McKnight Crosby, Jane Hayward, Charles T. Little, William S. Wixom, *The Royal Abbey of Saint-Denis in the Time of Abbot Suger* (1125–1151), 1981, 45–46). Both of these can be dated around 1150, or a decade later than the Saint-Denis portals. The Apostle relief, as already stated, is based upon the poses and arrangement of drapery of the RP jamb statues of Saint-Denis (see Plate X). When compared to the Dijon Last Supper, the Saint-Denis figures are squatter and portray more variety in drapery. In spite of the recutting of some of the surfaces of the king from the Saint-Denis cloister, some vague connections with Dijon can be seen. Multiple vertical folds appear in both, yet the grouping of four folds in a flat bunch in the Dijon relief is entirely different. However, the Saint-Denis king is much closer stylistically to some of the Headmaster's jamb statues on the central portal, especially CP.R 3 (Plate XII and fig. 13a). Chartres West was carved in the mid–1140s and seems to have influenced the sculptor responsible for the Saint-Denis cloister column-figure.

Even though there is a general feeling of similarity between the Dijon Last Supper and some of the sculpture of Chartres West, close comparisons suggest that the Dijon sculpture had little to do specifically with the Royal Portals. Details of the Chartres jamb statues (figs. 9–15c) portray the work of five sculptors: the Headmaster (CP), his two assistants (LP.R and RP.L), the Étampes Master (LP.L), and the Saint-Denis Master (RP.R). Jambs by the Headmaster (figs. 12–13c) are the closest, yet the Chartres jambs display a variety of drapery folds that is in marked contrast to the somewhat mechanical treatment on the Dijon Last Supper. The rich texture of drapery on the Apostles of the Chartres central portal lintel by the Headmaster is totally absent from the Dijon relief. When compared with double lintel of the right portal by the Headmaster's two assistants (figs. 47–49), the same differences are apparent, with the folds appearing repetitious on the Dijon relief. None of the heads of the Chartres jamb statues or lintels reveal eyes animated by narrow, rounded eyelids and hair in crude, parallel ridges (Plate XIX). Thus the stylistic connection between the Île-de-France and Dijon appears to be tenuous at best, with vague similarities with Saint-Denis of around 1150 and Chartres West of the mid–1140s.

Scholars have been arguing for many years over the priority, or lack of priority, of Dijon over Île-de-France monuments. A summary of the conclusions follows.

Pierre Quarré started the fairly recent debate in 1957 ("La sculpture des anciens portails de Saint-Bénigne de Dijon," *Gazette des Beaux-Arts,* 177–94) by stating that the tympanum of the Last Supper was carved between the fire of 1137 and the dedication of March 31, 1147.

156. Dijon, Saint-Bénigne,
Last Supper tympanum
(Musée Archéologique)

157. Dijon, Saint-Bénigne,
detail of fig. 156

158. Dijon, Saint-Bénigne,
head of Christ detail of fig. 156

159. Dijon, Saint-Bénigne,
head of Saint Bénigne (?) from
trumeau (Musée Archéologique)

He based his conclusion on the inscriptions located across the lower border of the Last Supper and the *Maiestas Domini* tympana; the latter was carved for the connecting link between the church and cloister. Both inscriptions mention the important role of Petrus in rebuilding Saint-Bénigne after 1137. These inscriptions, which were added later, honor either Pierre de Genève (abbot from 1129 to 1142) or Pierre de Beaune (abbot from 1142 to 1145), but they do not necessarily date the tympana. The *Maiestas Domini* is clearly by a totally different sculptor (Sauerländer, 1972, Plate 22). Besides the Dom Plancher engraving of the central portal before its destruction in 1794 (Sauerländer, 1972, 390, ill. 8), there exists the head of Saint Bénigne from the trumeau, a fragment of Peter (?) from a jamb statue, and the splays without their statue columns. The portal as a whole as depicted by Plancher seem close in style and composition to the largely destroyed portal of Saint-Germain-des-Prés in Paris, which can be dated no earlier than 1150. Since the Last Supper tympanum and Saint Bénigne head were carved by the same sculptor, the contention that the Dijon sculpture predates Chartres West is questionable.

André Lapeyre (*Des Facades occidentales de Saint-Denis et de Chartres aux Portails de Laon,* 1960, 101–8, 286) related the Dijon sculpture to the south portal of Le Mans on the basis of iconography and treatment of the archivolts. He thus implied that Dijon was later than Chartres West. In 1959, Louis Grodecki, having read Lapeyre in manuscript, disagreed with him on his analysis of Dijon and agreed with Quarré ("La 'première sculpture Gothique.' Wilhelm Vöge et l'état actuel des problèmes," *Bulletin monument,* CXVII, 265–89, esp. 280–81). He argued that Dijon was the intermediary monument between Saint-Denis and Chartres and dated Dijon as early as 1142. Pierre Quarré also reacted negatively to Lapeyre's conclusions on Dijon ("Sur l'art des portails à statues-colonnes," *Annales de Bourgogne,* XXXV, 1963, 256–58).

Bernhard Kerber (1966, 41–46) considered the Dijon central portal and Last Supper to date from 1147. Kerber compared the Dijon Saint Bénigne (fig. 159) with the Baltimore head from Saint-Denis (Plate IX, 1, 2) and also argued that a fragment of Peter's head from the Dijon central portal was carved by the same sculptor responsible for the Chartres LP.L 1 head (Kerber, Plates 8, 9). As already stated, any stylistic connection between the Dijon head and all the preserved Saint-Denis heads is questionable, while the Chartres head does not belong to the jamb figure and, since the 1981 cleaning of the Chartres left portal, appears to be of a different type of stone than the body. Kerber then compared the Dijon heads and tympanum with the sculpture from the Saint-Denis cloister: The Metropolitan columnar figure and the Louvre Head (no. 66). Basing his argument on the Montfaucon engraving of Saint-Denis figure and on the Louvre head, which is now assigned to Notre-Dame-en-Vaux, at Châlons-sur-Marne, Kerber reasoned that the Saint-Denis cloister was the intermediary link between Dijon and the Headmaster at Chartres West and that the Chartres Headmaster's style grew out of the Saint-Denis cloister (45–46). Since Chartres West was carved in one campaign of five years or less in the mid-1140s and the Saint-Denis cloister belongs to around 1150, it would appear that the Chartres Headmaster and his two assistants influenced the Saint-Denis cloister figure. The Louvre head, connected with Châlons-sur-Marne by Léon Pressouyre, is indeed very close stylistically to the head of Saint Bénigne, which suggests a dating of around 1150 for the Dijon portal.

Wilhelm Schlink (*Zwischen Cluny und Clairvaux. Die Kathedrale von Langres und die burgundische Architektur des 12. Jahrhunderts,* 1970, 120–37) opposed Kerber and dated the Dijon central portal 1155–1160. He saw a relationship between the Dijon heads and the Chartres LP lower lintel (fig. 52) and believed that Chartres influenced Dijon. Schlink saw strong connections in format between the Dijon central portal and the south portal of Notre-Dame-en-Vaux, at Châlons-sur-Marne, and stylistic similarities between the Dijon heads and Louvre Head no. 66, which he attributed to Châlons-sur-Marne (his fig. 121). To buttress his late dating of Dijon, Schlink compared fragments of capitals from Dijon with a capital from Saint-Germain-des-Prés and the head of Christ in the archivolt from Paris in the Louvre (his Plates 117, 119, 120).

Sauerländer (1972, 389–91, Ill. 8, Plates 22, 23) interpreted the style of the Dijon sculpture as un-Burgundian, with close connections to Chartres West, to the Saint-Denis cloister figure in The Metropolitan, and to the Crosby relief. On the basis of the design of the Dijon portal and architectural details, he dated the sculpture around 1160.

Quarré, Grodecki, and Kerber argued for the priority of Dijon, while Lapeyre, Schlink, and Sauerländer interpreted Dijon as later in date, reflecting influences from Saint-Denis and Chartres. On the basis of analysis of Dijon and comparisons with the Île-de-France, I believe that Dijon had no influence on Saint-Denis or Chartres but rather, like other Burgundian monuments that will be discussed next, exhibits the general spread of Early Gothic to Burgundy.

APPENDIX III

CHARTRES WEST TO BURGUNDY—
LA CHARITÉ-SUR-LOIRE

The tympanum, lintel, and jambs of the Chartres West central portal by the Headmaster and the figures of the Chartres LP.R and RP.L splays and double lintel of RP by his two identified assistants are the major source of inspiration for portals with columnar statues in Burgundy, Berry, and other regions outside the Île-de-France. Although Hermann Giesau argued that the transept portals of the Cathedral of Bourges in Berry could be dated 1140–1150 or earlier and predated Chartres West (W.S.S., 52–54, especially fn. 75; Plate XXXVII, 4), it is impossible to agree with this notion that Chartres West grew out of Bourges. The south and north portals are Early Gothic *spolia* added to the High Gothic cathedral in the 1220s. Poses, costumes, and arrangements of folds of jamb-statues of both portals and tympanum of south portal are derived from specific sculpture by the Chartres Headmaster or his assistants, while these jambs are surrounded by a profusion of ornaments that are related to late Burgundian portals such as Saint-Lazare, at Avallon (Plate XXXVII, 3). At Avallon, the single preserved jamb-statue out of the original seven is a hybrid of Chartrain body and late Burgundian head. The two Bourges portals have been dated around 1172 by Robert Branner (1962, 132–36) and about 1160 by Sauerländer (1972, 399–400, Plates 34–39). In light of the closeness to Chartres West central portal sculpture, a date in the 1150s seems more plausible.

Bourges, Avallon, and Dijon thus seem to represent the extension in Berry and Burgundy of the Chartrain style in the late 1140s and 1150s in various degrees of assimilation, but none of these portals was carved by Chartres sculptors, in contrast to some portals such as at Le Mans (?) and Corbeil and the Sainte-Anne portal in Paris, where specific Chartres sculptors were involved.

Since some scholars state that the lintels of La Charité-sur-Loire influenced the Chartres RP double lintels, a brief discussion of the La Charité sculpture is in order (figs. 160, 161). La Charité-sur-Loire, a Cluniac Priory, has two of its five western portals preserved: one *in situ* on the north tower and the second in the south transept, where it was moved in 1835. André Lapeyre (1960, 112–17, figs. 71, 72) described the debate of critics over the priority of La Charité or Chartres and concluded that La Charité, like Avallon and Bourges, follows Chartres. In 1967, Jean Vallery-Radot outlined the building campaigns of La Charité and argued that the north tower of the façade was finished around 1135 ("L'ancienne prieurale Notre-Dame à la Charité-sur-Loire. L'architecture," *Congrès Archéologique de France,* 125, 43–85). In the same publication, Marie-Louise Thérel ("Les portails de la Charité-sur-Loire. Étude iconographique," 86–103) dated the portals around 1135 on the basis of iconographical references to Peter the Venerable of Cluny. Around 1132, Peter the Venerable introduced the Transfiguration into the liturgical calendar of Cluny. This scene is depicted on the inner tympanum at La Charité. The damaged outer tympanum portrays kneeling monks in the lower corners, flanking a floral Paradise, two angels to the left of the Christ enthroned, and the Virgin Mary approaching the Christ with her hands overlapping the mandorla. Thérel interpreted this tympanum as the first depiction of the bodily Assumption of the Virgin in which the Virgin is welcomed by her Son in a celestial Jerusalem. This scene clearly prophesizes the Coronation of the Virgin of Senlis. Again, Peter the Venerable's letters, between 1132 and 1135, revealed his belief in the corporeal assumption of the Virgin. Thus, according to the author, this linkage of the portals and Peter the Venerable proved that the portals were carved around 1135. Sauerländer (1970, 388, Plate 21) dated the illustrations of the two lintels between 1140 and 1155, but in the text argued that La Charité was earlier than Chartres, with the earliest possible date of 1140.

The two tympana seem to have been carved by the same sculptor (see A. K. Porter, *The Romanesque Sculpture of the Pilgrimage Road* 1923, Vol. II, Plates 115–17, 120). This sculptor appears to be quite eclectic, with slender figures carved in relatively low relief and with hems of sleeves, mantles, and undergarments accented by flattened, serrated folds. This treatment of drapery is reminiscent of Languedoc, as Thérel and other scholars have pointed out. However, stomachs and knee areas are accented by curving ridge-folds, which are reminiscent of Burgundian rather than Languedocien sculpture. Oval heads with prominent, rounded ears, naturalistic mouths and noses, and eyes with large drilled irises have no counterpart in the sculpture of Vézelay or Autun.

In the case of the La Charité lintel on the west façade (fig. 160) and the Chartres RP lower lintel (figs. 47–49), there are so many similarities, such as identical subjects and composition of scenes, that these two lintels could not have been created in isolation. The Chartres Annunciation, Visitation, and Nativity (figs. 47, 48) have thinner, quieter figures with multiple folds as opposed to the stockier, more active figures in more voluminous costumes of thick loop-folds at La Charité (fig. 160). The composition of the Nativity and the design of the mensa and bed are so alike that the sculptor of La Charité must have seen Chartres, or the Chartres sculptor seen the La Charité portal. The Chartres lower lintel was carved by an assistant of the Headmaster, who was also responsible for the RP.L jamb statues, and represents a narrative version of the Headmaster's style. Since one can reasonably, but not conclusively, assume that the sculpture on the splays of the three Chartres portals, including the columnar statues, doorjambs, and capital-frieze, were carved before the tympana, lintels, and archivolts, the Headmaster was probably carving the Apostles of the CP lintel (fig. 46) at around the same time as his two assistants were completing the double lintel of the RP Stylistically in terms of treatment of drapery and of the heads, the lower lintel of the RP is closer to the CP. lintel than to La Charité. Since the Chartres lintel is an integral part of the collaboration effort of Chartres West, it seems unacceptable to argue that La Charité influenced Chartres and more logical to reason that a La Charité sculptor visited Chartres in the mid-1140s and then carved the La Charité lintel sometime soon thereafter.

The lintel in the south transept of La Charité, depicting the Adoration of the Magi in a large panel and the presentation in the Temple in a smaller section (fig. 161), is totally at variance in style when contrasted with the Presentation lintel of Chartres, with its central Christ

160. La Charité-sur-Loire, Annunciation, Visitation and Nativity of west portal

161. La Charité-sur-Loire, Presentation in Temple, detail of lintel
of west portal, now in south transept

243

standing on a sacrificial altar (see, for interpretation, Katzenellenbogen, 1959, 7–21). Again, the handling of drapery and the treatment of heads is markedly different in the two lintels (figs. 48, 161). At Chartres, the Headmaster's style in small scale is projected by his second assistant, the sculptor of the LP.R jambs. (The single figures on the right and left blocks of the RP upper lintel at Chartres were carved by the Master of the Angels.) As in the case of the lower lintel, the drapery and heads of the upper lintel are closer to the CP lintel by the Headmaster than to the La Charité lintel. Thus for the same reasons as discussed above, La Charité is influenced by Chartres. The specific centrality of Christ standing on the altar, directly above the Christ Child in the lower lintel and below the Christ in the lap of His Mother in the tympanum, has a special meaning at Chartres, whereas the program at La Charité was totally different.

If these two La Charité lintels are compared (figs. 160, 161), there appear many similarities, such as the treatment of heads, feet and their position on the ground, and general treatment of drapery, which makes it plausible to argue that the same sculptor was responsible for both lintels. Some of the heads of the Transfiguration tympanum, especially the right two, resemble those in the Presentation scene on the lintel,

yet it appears as though one sculptor carved the two tympana and one carved the lintels.

Dating sculpture such as the portals of La Charité-sur-Loire around 1135 on the basis of events transpiring in Cluny (1130–1135) does not follow, since new theological ideas do not necessarily become transferred to stone immediately. Perhaps incidental to this discussion but not without interest is the fact that because of the change in emplacement of the Chartres portals, the Chartres RP upper lintel has two and one-half shepherds in the Annunciation, while the La Charité lintel has two, which is unusual.

If Chartres West is interpreted as a collaborative effort being carried out by four major sculptors and their assistants in the middle years of the 1140s, with the entire iconographical program dictated by the School of Chartres, it is questionable whether La Charité is an essentially needed inspiration for Chartres, when both style and iconography were conceived and evolved at Chartres. Thus La Charité-sur-Loire, like Saint-Bénigne de Dijon, Saint-Lazare of Avallon, and the transept portals of Bourges Cathedral, seems to represent the spread of ideas from Chartres West, not its origins.

SELECTED BIBLIOGRAPHY
SINCE 1952

GENERAL BOOKS AND ARTICLES

Cahn, Walter, and Seidel, Linda, *Romanesque Sculpture in American Collections*, Vol. I, *New England Museums*, New York, Franklin and Co., 1979.

Grodecki, Louis, "La 'Première Sculpture Gothique.' Wilhelm Vöge et l'état actuel des problèmes," *Bulletin monumental*, CXVII, 1959, 265–289.

Hearn, M. F., *Romanesque Sculpture, The Revival of Monumental Stone Sculpture in the Eleventh and Twelfth Centuries*, Cornell University Press, Ithaca, N.Y., 1981.

Lapeyre, André, *Des Façades Occidentales de Saint-Denis et de Chartres aux Portails de Laon*, Mâcon, 1960.

Sauerländer, Willibald, "Sculpture on Early Gothic Churches: The State of Research and Open Questions," *Gesta*, IX / 2, 1970, 32–48.

————, *Gothic Sculpture in France 1140–1270*, New York, 1972.

Scher, Stephen K., et al., *The Renaissance of the Twelfth Century*, Providence, Museum of Art, Rhode Island School of Design, 1969.

Simson, Otto von, *The Gothic Cathedral: The Origins of Gothic Architecture and the Medieval Concept of Order*, London and New York, 1956; rev. ed., New York, 1962.

PART I

THE WEST PORTALS OF SAINT-DENIS

Aubert, Marcel, and Beaulieu, Michèle, *Musée National du Louvre: Description raisonnée des sculptures du Moyen Âge, de la Renaissance et des temps modernes, I: Moyen Âge*, Paris, 1950.

Crosby, Sumner McKnight, *L'Abbaye royale de Saint-Denis*, Paris, 1953.

————, "An International Workshop in the Twelfth Century," *Journal of World History*, X, 1, 1966, 19–30.

————, "The West Portals of Saint-Denis and the Saint-Denis Style," *Gesta*, IX / 2, 1970, 1–11.

————, *The Apostle Bas-Relief at Saint-Denis*, New Haven and London, 1972.

————, and Blum, Pamela Z., "Le Portail central de la façade occidentale de Saint-Denis," *Bulletin monumental*, 131, 1973, 209–66.

Crosby, Sumner McKnight; Hayward, Jane; Little, Charles T.; Wixom, William D., *The Royal Abbey of Saint-Denis in the Time of Abbot Suger* (1125–1151), 1981, catalogue of exhibition at The Cloisters, The Metropolitan Museum of Art, with complete bibliography of Saint-Denis.

Gerson, Paula, *The West Façade of St.-Denis: An Iconographic Study*, Ph.D. dissertation, Columbia University, 1970, microfilm.

————, "The Lintels of the West Façade of Saint-Denis," *Journal of the Society of Architectural Historians*, XXXIV, 3, 1975, 189–97.

Ostoia, Vera K., "A Statue from Saint-Denis," *Bulletin of The Metropolitan Museum of Art*, XIII, 10, June 1955, 298–304.

Panofsky, Erwin, ed. and trans., *Abbot Suger on the Abbey Church of St. Denis and its Art Treasures*, 2nd ed., Gerda Panofsky-Soergel, ed., Princeton, 1979.

Pressouyre, Léon, "Une Tête de reine du portail central de Saint-Denis," *Gesta*, XV, 1976, 151–60.

PART II

THE ROYAL PORTALS OF CHARTRES CATHEDRAL

Branner, Robert, ed., *Chartres Cathedral*, Norton Critical Studies in Art History, New York, 1969.

Chadefaux, Marie-Claude, "La portail royale de Chartres," *Gazette des Beaux Arts*, LXXVI, 1960, 273ff.

Chevallier, Marie-Anne, and Pressouyre, Léon, "Fragments récemment retrouvées du Portail Royal," *Revue de l'Art*, 57, 1982, 67–72.

Crozet, René, "À propos des chapiteaux de la façade occidentale de Chartres," *Cahiers de civilisation médiévale*, XIV, 1971, 159–65.

Fels, Étienne, "Die Grabung an der Fassade der Kathedrale von Chartres," *Kunstchronik*, Vol. 8, 1955, 149–51.

Grodecki, Louis, *Chartres*, New York: Harcourt, Brace, 1963.

Heimann, Adelheid, "The Capital Frieze and Pilasters of the Portail Royal, Chartres," *Journal of the Warburg and Courtauld Institutes*, Vol. 31, 1968, 73–102.

James, John, *The Contractors of Chartres*, 2 Vols., Dooralong, N.S.W., Australia, 1981.

Katzenellenbogen, Adolf, *The Sculptural Programs of Chartres Cathedral*, Baltimore: The John Hopkins University Press, 1959. Paperback Edition, W. W. Norton (N233), 1964.

Kidson, Peter, *Sculpture at Chartres*, London, 1958.

Lapeyre, André, *Des Façades occidentales de Saint-Denis et de Chartres aux portails de Laon*, Mâcon, 1960, esp. 19–28.

Meulen, Jan van der, "Sculpture and Its Architectural Context at Chartres around 1200," *The Year 1200: A Symposium*, The Metropolitan Museum of Art, 1975, 509–60, esp. 512 and fn. 23, 530–31.

————, and Hohmeyer, Jürgen, *Chartres, Biographie der Kathedrale*, Köln: DuMont Buchverlag, 1984.

Meulen, Jan van der, with Price, Nancy, *The West Portals of Chartres Cathedral*, Vol. I, *The Iconology of the Creation*, Washington, D.C., University Press of America, 1981.

Sauerländer, Willibald, "Zu den Westportalen von Chartres," *Kunstchronik*, Vol. 9, 1956, 155–57.

————, *Gothic Sculpture in France, 1140–1270*, London, 1972, 383–86.

Simson, Otto von, *The Gothic Cathedral: Origins of Gothic Architecture and the Medieval Concept of Order*, New York, 1956.

Villette, Jean, "Le portail royal de Chartres a-t-il été modifié depuis sa construction?" *Bulletin des Sociétés Archéologiques d'Eure-et-Loir*, Vol. 115, 1971, 255–64.

SELECTED BIBLIOGRAPHY

PART III

THE SOUTH PORTAL
OF NOTRE-DAME AT ÉTAMPES

ÉTAMPES

Grodecki, 1959, 265–89, esp. 278–79.

Lapeyre, 1960, 53–60.

Sauerländer, 1972, 398.

Baratte-Bévillard, Sophie, "La sculpture monumentale de la Madeleine de Châteaudun," *Bulletin Archéologique du Comité des traveaux historiques et scientifiques*, 1972, 105–25.

Grosset, Charles, "Les sculptures du portail sud de Notre-Dame d'Étampes à propos du livre récent," *Cahiers de civilisation médiévale*, VII, 1964, 53–61.

Maines, Clark, "Le Portail Ouest de St.-Pierre-au-Parvis, Soissons (Aisne): Reconstitution Iconographique," *Revue archéologique de Picardie*, No. 4, 1982, 178–98.

PART IV

ORIGINS OF THE CHARTRES SCULPTORS

PROVENCE

Hamann, Richard, *Die Abteikirche von St. Gilles und ihre künstlerische Nachfolge*, 3 Vols., Berlin, 1955.

O'Meara, Carra Ferguson, *The Iconography of the Façade of Saint-Gilles-du-Gard*, Garland, 1977.

Saint-Jean, Robert, *Languedoc roman, Le Languedoc Méditerranéen*, Zodiaque, 1975, Saint-Gilles, 298–345.

Stoddard, Whitney S., *The Façade of Saint-Gilles-du-Gard. Its Influence on French Sculpture*, Wesleyan University Press, Middletown, Conn., 1973.

LANGUEDOC

Durliat, Marcel, *Haut-Languedoc Roman*, Zodiaque, 1978.

Lautard-Limouse, Lyne, "Gilabertus, Sculpteur Roman Toulousan," *Archéologia*, 77, 1974, 40–49.

Lyman, Thomas W. "Terminology, Typology, Taxonomy: An Approach to the Study of Architectural Sculpture of the Romanesque Period," *Gazette des Beaux-Arts*, LXXXVIII (1976), 223–27.

———, "Raymond Gairard and Romanesque Building Campaigns at Saint-Sernin in Toulouse," *Journal of the Society of Architectural Historians*, XXXVII, 1978, 71–91.

Mesplée, P., *Toulouse, Musée des Augustins: Les sculptures romanes*, Paris, 1961.

Seidel, Linda, "A Romantic Forgery: The Romanesque 'Portal' of Saint-Étienne in Toulouse," *Art Bulletin*, L, 1968, 33–42.

———, *Romanesque Sculpture from the Cathedral of Saint-Étienne, Toulouse*, Garland, 1977, Ph.D. dissertation, Harvard University, 1964.

BURGUNDY

Archives des Monuments Historiques, Yonne, Vézelay, No. 1586, Dossier I (1824–1848); No. 1587, Dossier II (1849–1870).

Armi, C. Edson, *Masons and Sculptors in Romanesque Burgundy. The New Aesthetic of Cluny III*, 2 Vols., Pennsylvania State University Press, 1983.

Armi, C. Edson, and Smith, Elizabeth Bradford, "The Choir Screen of Cluny III," *Art Bulletin*, Vol. LXVI, 4, 1984, 556–73.

Conant, Kenneth J., *Cluny: Les Eglises de la Maison du Chef d'Ordre*, Mâcon, 1968.

Grivot, Denis, and Zarnecki, George, *Gislebertus, sculpteur d'Autun*, Paris, Trianon, 1960.

———, *Gislebertus, Sculptor of Autun*, New York, Orion Press, 1961.

Kerber, Bernhard, *Burgund und die Entwicklung der französischen Kathedralskulptur im Zwölften Jahrhundert*, Recklinghausen, 1966.

Salet, Francis, *La Madeleine de Vézelay*, Melun, 1948.

———, "La sculpture romane en Bourgogne à propos d'un livre recent," *Bulletin monumental*, 1961, 325–43.

Sauerländer, Willibald, "Gislebertus von Autun. Ein Beitrag zur Entstehung seines kunsterischen stils," *Studien zur Geschichte der Europäischen Plastik*, 1965, 17–29.

Saulnier, Lydwine, and Stratford, Neil, *La sculpture oubliée de Vézelay*, Paris, Arts et Métiers Graphiques, 1984.

Schlink, Wilhelm, *Zwischen Cluny und Clairvaux. Die Kathedrale von Langres und die burgundische Architektur des 12. Jahrhunderts*, Berlin, 1970.

Stoddard, Whitney S., with Kelly, Franklin, "The Eight Capitals of the Cluny Hemicycle," *Gesta*, XX / 1, 1981, 51–58.

PART V

TRENDS IN THIRD QUARTER OF
THE TWELFTH CENTURY

LE MANS

Lapeyre, 1960, 90–100 (figs. 55–64), 281–85.

Sauerländer, 1972, 46–47, 383, 386 (Plates 16–18).

Mussat, André, *Le Style Gothique de l'Ouest de la France (XIIᵉ–XIIIᵉ siècles)*, Paris, 1963, 104–7.

Polk, Thomas E. II, "The South Portal of the Cathedral of Le Mans: Its Place in the Development of Early Gothic Portal Composition." *GESTA*, Vol. XXIV / 1, 1985, 47–60.

PROVINS, SAINT-AYOUL

Lapeyre, 1960, 187–93, figs. 129–34.

Sauerländer, 1972, 402–3, ill. 22.

Maines, Clark, *The Western Portal of Saint-Loup-de-Naud*, Garland, 1979, 92–96, figs. 116–25.

Hayward, Jane, and Cahn, Walter, *Radiance and Reflection, Medieval Art from the Raymond Pitcairn Collection*, The Metropolitan Museum of Art, 1982, 98–99, fig. 31.

Pressouyre, Léon, "Réflexions sur la Sculpture du XIIème siècle en Champagne," *Gesta*, Vol IX / 2, 1970, 16–31.

SAINT-LOUP-de-NAUD

Lapeyre, 1960, 132–38, figs. 133–37, 288–90.

Sauerländer, 1972, 393–94, Pl. 24, 25.

Maines, Clark, *The Western Portal of Saint-Loup-de-Naud*, Garland, 1979.

Pressouyre, Léon, "Réflexions sur la sculpture du XIIème siècle en Champagne," *Gesta* IX / 2, 1970, 16–31.

Salet, Francis, "Saint-Loup-de-Naud," *Bulletin monumental*, 1933, 129–69.

SELECTED BIBLIOGRAPHY

Sauerländer, Willibald, "Sculpture on Early Gothic Churches: The State of Research," *Gesta,* IX / 2, 1970, 32–48, esp. 40.

Severens, Kenneth, "The Early Campaign of Sens, 1140–1147," *Journal of the Society of Architectural Historians,* XXIX, May 1970, 97–107.

SENLIS

Lapeyre, 1960, 239–42.

Sauerländer, 1972, 406–8, Plates 42–45.

Brouillette, Diane, *Senlis un monument de la sculpture Gothique,* La Sauvegarde de Senlis, No. 45–46, 1977.

———, *The Early Gothic Sculpture of Senlis Cathedral,* Ph.D. Dissertation, University of California, Berkeley, 1981, University Microfilms International, Ann Arbor, Michigan, 1983.

Sauerländer, Willibald, "Die Marienkrönungsportale von Senlis und Mantes," *Wallraf-Richartz-Jahrbuch,* Vol. 20, 1958, 115–62.

CORBEIL

Lapeyre, 1960, 256–63, figs. 197–202; 299–301.

Sauerländer, 1972, 397–98, see 17, Plate 30.

Cahn, Walter, "Observations on Corbeil," *Art Bulletin,* Vol. LV, 1973, 321–27.

Salet, Francis, "Notre-Dame de Corbeil," *Bulletin monumental,* Vol. 100, 1941, 81–118.

Sauerländer, Willibald, "Sculpture on Early Gothic Churches: The State of Research and Open Questions," *Gesta,* Vol. IX / 2, 1970, 32–56, esp. 41 and figs. 15, 16.

PARIS, SAINTE-ANNE PORTAL

Lapeyre, 1960, 147–53, figs. 96–99 and bibliography.

Sauerländer, 1972, 404–6, Plates 40, 41.

Clark, William, and Mark, Robert, "The First Flying Buttresses: A New Reconstruction of the Nave of Notre-Dame de Paris," *Art Bulletin,* Vol. LXVI, 1, 1984, 47–65.

d'Estaing, François Giscard; Fleury, Michel; and Erlande-Brandenburg, Alain, *Les rois retrouvés, Notre-Dame de Paris,* Paris, 1977.

Erlande-Brandenburg, Alain, *Les sculptures de Notre-Dame de Paris au Musée de Cluny,* Paris, 1982.

Fleury, Michel, "Les sculptures de Notre-Dame de Paris découvertes en 1977 et 1978," *Cahiers de la Rotonde,* I, 1978, 39–56.

Rorimer, James, "A Twelfth-Century Head of King David from Notre-Dame," *The Metropolitan Museum of Art Bulletin,* 1940, 17–19.

Thirion, Jacques, "Les plus anciennes sculptures de Notre-Dame de Paris," *Comptes-rendus de l'Académie des inscriptions et belles-lettres,* 1970, 85–112.

APPENDIX II
DIJON, SAINT-BÉNIGNE

Grodecki, 1959, 280–81.

Kerber, 1966, 41–46.

Lapeyre, 1960, 101–8, 286.

Sauerländer, 1972, 389–91, ill. 8, Plates 22, 23.

Schlink, 1970, 120–37.

Quarré, Pierre, "La sculpture des anciens portails de Saint-Bénigne de Dijon," *Gazette des Beaux-Arts,* L, 1957, 177–94.

———, "Sur l'art des portails à statues-colonnes," *Annales de Bourgogne,* XXXV, 1963, 256–58.

APPENDIX III
LA CHARITÉ-sur-LOIRE

Lapeyre, 1960, 112–17, figs. 71, 72 and bibliography.

Sauerländer, 1972, 388.

Thérel, Marie-Louise, "Les portails de la Charité-sur-Loire. Étude iconographique," *Congrès archéologique de France,* 125, 1967, 86–103.

Vallery-Radot, Jean, "L'ancienne prieurale Notre-Dame à la Charité-sur-Loire. L'Architecture," *Congrès archéologique de France,* 125, 1967, 43–85.

ADDENDUM

The following publications appeared too late to be discussed in the text:

Clark, William W. "The Early Capitals of Notre-Dame de Paris," *Tribute to Lotte Brand Philip,* New York, Abaris Books, 1985, 34–43.

Gerson, Paula Lieber, ed., *Abbot Suger and Saint-Denis. A Symposium,* The Metropolitan Museum of Art, 1986. Note especially the following: Paula L. Gerson, "Suger as Iconographer: The Central Portal of the West Facade of Saint-Denis," 183–198; Pamela Z. Blum, "The Lateral Portals of the West Facade of the Abbey Church of Saint-Denis: Archaeological and Iconographic Considerations, 119–229; Léon Pressouyre, "Did Suger Build the Cloister of Saint-Denis?," 229–245.

Gesta, The International Center of Medieval Art, Vol. XXV / 1, 1986. Note; John James "An Examination of Some Anomalies in the Ascension and Incarnation Portals of Chartres Cathedral," 101–9; William W. Clark and Franklin M. Ludden, "Notes on the Archivolts of the Sainte-Anne Portal of Notre-Dame de Paris," 109–18; Walter Cahn, "The 'Tympanum' of Saint-Pierre at Étampes: A new Reconstruction," 119–25.

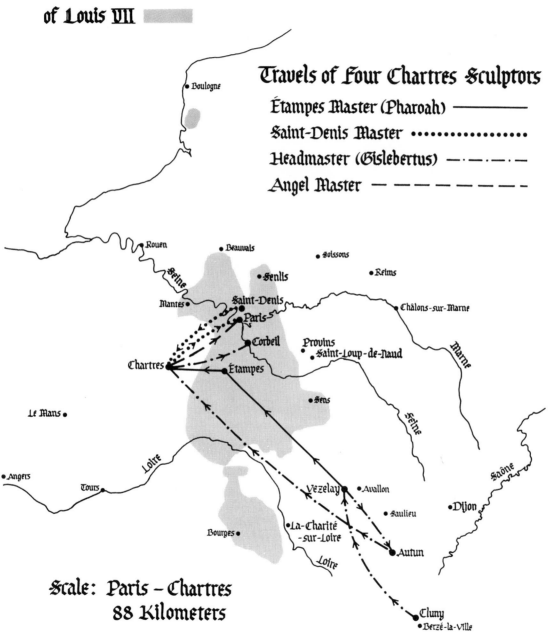

Map of France – 1150's

**Under Direct Control
of Louis VII** ▨

Travels of Four Chartres Sculptors

Étampes Master (Pharoah) ————
Saint-Denis Master ••••••••••••••
Headmaster (Gislebertus) —·—·—·—
Angel Master — — — — — —

Boulogne

Rouen
Beauvais
Soissons
Seine
Senlis
Reims
Mantes
Saint-Denis
Châlons-sur-Marne
Paris
Corbeil
Provins
Saint-Loup-de-Naud
Marne
Chartres
Étampes
Sens
Seine
Le Mans
Loire
Saône
Angers
Tours
Vézelay
Avallon
Dijon
Saulieu
La-Charité
-sur-Loire
Bourges
Autun
Loire
Cluny
Berzé-la-Ville

Scale: Paris – Chartres
88 Kilometers

INDEX: 1952 and 1986

MAJOR MONUMENTS

INDEX

MONUMENTS DISCUSSED BUT NOT IN GREAT DETAIL

AUTHORS

PERSONS AND EVENTS

MUSEUMS

INDEX